THE
OTHER MOHAN

THE
OTHER MOHAN
IN
BRITAIN'S INDIAN OCEAN EMPIRE

Amrita Shah

FOURTH ESTATE · *New Delhi*

First published in India by Fourth Estate 2024
An imprint of HarperCollins *Publishers*
4th Floor, Tower A, Building No. 10, DLF Cyber City,
DLF Phase II, Gurugram, Haryana – 122002
www.harpercollins.co.in

2 4 6 8 10 9 7 5 3 1

Copyright © Amrita Shah 2024

P-ISBN: 978-93-6213-961-0
E-ISBN: 978-93-6213-564-3

The views and opinions expressed in this book are the author's own and the facts are as reported by her, and the publishers are not in any way liable for the same.

Amrita Shah asserts the moral right
to be identified as the author of this work.

The maps of Southern Africa and the Western Indian Ocean coastline featured in the book are provided for general information purpose only. The author and the publisher make no warranties, expressed or implied, regarding the accuracy or completeness of the maps for any particular purpose. While every effort has been made to ensure accuracy, the maps and the international boundaries might not be drawn up to scale. The author and the publisher do not represent the official or legal boundaries of the region and disclaim all liability for errors, omissions, or inaccuracies. The maps should not be used for navigation or any other purpose requiring precise spatial data.

For sale in the Indian subcontinent only

All rights reserved. No part of this publication may be reproduced, stored in a retrieval system, or transmitted, in any form or by any means, electronic, mechanical, photocopying, recording or otherwise, without the prior permission of the publishers.

Typeset in 11.5/15.2 Adobe Garamond Pro at
HarperCollins *Publishers* India

Printed and bound at
Replika Press Pvt. Ltd.

This book is produced from independently certified FSC® paper to ensure responsible forest management.

For Mammaji

The detailed notes pertaining to this book are available on the HarperCollins website. Scan this QR code to access the same.

Contents

Prelude ... xi

Part One: *Leaving Home*

1. Perfumed Ocean ... 3
2. The Merchants ... 10
3. Hatmen ... 19
4. Cotton Mania ... 31
5. Urbs Prima Indis ... 44

Part Two: *The Trail*

6. Table Mountain ... 57
7. Cecil Rhodes ... 64
8. Gandhi Square ... 75
9. First Lady ... 84

Part Three: *Mauritius*

10. Île Maurice ... 105
11. Hits and Misses ... 124

12. Port Louis	140
13. Love Island	147

Part Four: *Natal*

14. Arriving	157
15. The First Trader	164
16. The Lawyer Gandhi	171
17. Storm Gathering	180
18. Seeking Fairness	189
19. Indian CBD	196

Part Five: *Settling*

20. Indian Quarter	211
21. The Sea, a Town	227
22. The Interpreters	234
23. The Examination	241

Part Six: *Cape Town*

24. Moving	251
25. Mohanlal in Cape Town	260
26. Taking Umbrage	268

Part Seven: *Satyagraha*

27. After the War	281
28. The Asiatic Menace	289
29. Resisting Degradation	299

30. Forward Ye	304
31. Educated Protesters	310
32. Hind Swaraj	320

Part Eight: *Pretoria*

33. Archive, Pretoria	329
34. Twist	342
35. The Unravelling	354

Part Nine: *The Sea*

36. View from Mumbai	365
37. Mohan at Home	370
38. Sea Tales	372
Acknowledgements	377
Notes	381
Index	383

Prelude

As the British and the Boers buried the hatchet in the aftermath of the bitter Anglo-Boer War (1899–1902), paving the way for a white-dominated Union of South Africa, jails in the Transvaal filled up with Indians. Led by their leader, the charismatic Mohandas Karamchand Gandhi, the Indians opposed a new law that required them to register their fingerprints and to produce the certificate of registration upon demand, likening them to criminals. Indians who were normally law-abiding practised a novel form of peaceful resistance by breaking sundry laws to court arrest; respectable shopkeepers hawked without a licence in the streets and businessmen of good standing cocked a snook at registration officials. The unrelenting authorities insisted on retaining the offending law and moved to restrict the entry of Indians into the colony altogether by introducing a tough test of fluency in a European language under the Transvaal Immigration Restriction Act.

The Indians kept up the pressure. As the end of winter approached in 1908, a group of fresh campaigners boarded the Johannesburg Mail from Durban. In the throng of harried travellers, these clean-shaven, brown-skinned resisters in their Western-style suits stood out, their stiff bearing advertising how well they knew their standing as the proud professional elite of the migrant community. They were teachers, accountants and interpreters, all sufficiently versed in English to pass the enhanced language test under the immigration law.

The plan was for them to lawfully enter the Transvaal and, having done so, abstain from registering within the prescribed period, forcing the border authorities to arrest or deport them. While they waited for their grace period to run out, they were to travel around various parts of the Transvaal collecting identity papers volunteered by local Indians for burning in an ultimate and flamboyant display of protest at a mass meeting in Johannesburg.

Among those men was my great-grandfather Mohanlal Parmanandas Killavala.

I was told about the 1908 expedition by the educated group of resisters and of Mohanlal's participation in it by Enuga Reddy, a former diplomat and New York-based collector of scholarly materials and memorabilia related to Gandhi. It is not every day that one hears of an ancestor having played a role in the making of history and I was indescribably overwhelmed when I read Enuga Reddy's email in October 2012 conveying this intelligence. I imagined, with a skin-tingling rush of pride, a band of crusaders on the train chugging through the moonlit midlands. But I was also overwhelmed, probably more so by the fact that the information I had received from Enuga Reddy about the event, accompanied by a few lines about Mohanlal that he had culled from Gandhi's South Africa-based newspaper *Indian Opinion*, was my first clue regarding a mystery that had long preoccupied me.

The mystery revolved around a journey undertaken by my great-grandfather who, I was told, had travelled to South Africa as a young man. This was not a common occurrence at the turn of the twentieth century, which is presumably when he travelled, because voyaging abroad was expensive and also because Hindus belonging to the so-called respectable castes were forbidden by a taboo from crossing the 'black waters' of the ocean. That Mohanlal did not let such considerations stop him suggested a strong motive; that he had gone on his journey, upending a well-settled life in Bombay, abandoning parents and a young bride, indicated an even greater imperative. He returned a few years later to his home in Bombay and had six children with the wife who had patiently awaited his return, and died eventually at a ripe old age in India. And yet—and this to me was a mystery—nobody appeared to know when he went or returned, why he went away or what he did overseas.

The uncanny lack of information surrounding Mohanlal's journey was accompanied by an even more mystifying absence of what I would call atmosphere—tokens and stories that cling to an event, thickening it with mood and detail. I never saw nor heard of any letters, preserved tickets or photographs, not even a stray knick-knack in a showcase that might have provided a glimpse into his travels. More strangely, I heard no anecdotes related to his journey: no stories of mishaps, fearful encounters, exotic customs, schemes gone wrong or spectacularly right, the kind of eyebrow-raising travellers' tales customarily passed down through generations, becoming part of family lore and mythology. Mohanlal's journey seemed to exist in a vacuum-sealed airtight box. Or at least that is how it appeared to me and for that reason I found it enigmatic.

The absence of particulars did not diminish the sheer excitement, though, that I felt as a child about having an ancestor who had travelled so far. The fantasy of a wide ocean and a ship carrying away my young great-grandfather sent me into raptures. Surely, I thought, with an ancestor so adventurous, I too was bound to take flight someday. I do not know if anybody else in my family was as enraptured as I was, and my engrossment says something about how I felt at the time about the cul de sac-ness of my small existence.

My parents and I lived in a northwestern Bombay suburb called Santacruz, a mile from the seashore, originally inhabited by a group of Christian converts from the former Portuguese enclave of Bassein. When my parents moved here in the early 1960s, it was shedding the vestiges of its bucolic past. Bungalows with tamarind and jamun trees in the backyards were giving way to angular buildings. Mossy waterbodies were being drained and sandbagged, with snakes occasionally appearing on the road and causing a minor commotion. Hawkers and wandering entertainers surged through the streets, their cries merging with the sizzle of mustard seeds and gurgling transistor feed.

It was like any other developing suburban neighbourhood in Bombay, except for one feature, which was that it was on the flight path of not one but two airports. The city airport repurposed from an old British World War II airfield was a couple of kilometres east of our apartment building. At a similar distance to the north was the Juhu aerodrome, a field of yellow grass where aspiring pilots trained on the Piper Cubs of the Bombay Flying Club. One early September morning in 1972, a pilot flying in from Tokyo landed a DC-8 in the hay field of the Juhu aerodrome. My father and I went to take a look and saw it spreadeagled like a clumsy white bird on the grass, its startled snout pointing to the cars whizzing past on the road. The red logo of Japan Airlines, 'JAL', on the tail made me feel good, thinking that the Japs weren't all that smart after all.

Aeroplanes screamed through our days and nights. When India acquired its first jumbo jet, my friends and I prophesized that all the crockery would fall off from our shelves, so violent would be its tremble. Nothing like that happened, of course. But living with the reminder of relentless comings and goings filled me with a deep, keening wanderlust. Often, I climbed into a life-sized model of an aeroplane in our neighbourhood park, to sit on one of the red clay seats, unmindful of the odour of urine and clandestine couplings,

Prelude

and pretended that I was on my way somewhere, scooping imaginary meals with a plastic spoon.

I was lonely, I suppose, and the reason for my loneliness was not a lack of friends or loved ones, but a feeling of always being out of place. In the neighbourhood, I ran with a barefoot army of children exploring every remaining backyard with its last fluttering jamun tree and checking out the new buildings with their concrete playgrounds and water tanks, starting a wild game of seven tiles or kho-kho any time the mood took us and returning home with scabbed knees and scratched elbows. But I only half-belonged at home, for come weekday mornings and my playmates would walk to the nearest Gujarati or Marathi vernacular medium school, older kids clutching their younger brothers' and sisters' hands, while I would take a school bus to a hilly, seaside suburb a few kilometres from home.

My school had Gothic windows and red gable roofs. In the semi-circular driveway, nuns in their white habits waited for students to arrive before the bell announced the start of assembly. As we neared our destination, my mouth would be dry from anxious anticipation. What infraction would I be pulled up over today? A frayed tie? Forgotten homework? An unsigned remark? A climbing hem? All day long the pale dread stayed with me, suffusing the bright sky over the hockey field, hanging about the gleaming corridors, murmuring in the needle room where we learnt to embroider handkerchiefs and tea cosies, and tinkling from the piano in ballet class. It was there all the time, the dread that sooner or later I would put a foot wrong. Had my grandmother felt it too? My maternal grandmother, Damayanti, had briefly attended a reputed Convent school in the city much like mine, a fact that deeply influenced my own mother's choice of a school for me. How did it happen, though, that my grandmother went to an elite girls' school at a time when women of her social class barely received any schooling at all? It did not occur to me then, but it must have had something to do with her father, Mohanlal, and his travels.

Between the city airport and Santacruz is the eastern suburb of Vile Parle. A highway barrels through it, at the side of which is a thriving market in marble slabs. In the early twentieth century, when it was a sleepy village of peepul trees and temples, Mohanlal scouted in Vile Parle for land. He had returned from his travels and turned out to be a canny prospector, identifying prime property, developing it and selling it for a tidy profit, sometimes renting out plots in the interim to tenants with whom he was a typically stern landlord, according to one of his grandsons.

For himself and his family, Mohanlal built a house 'entirely of wood', as an aunt recalls. He was a stereotypically conservative Indian patriarch in many ways, but the picture that emerges from my conversations with many family members is of a solitary figure given to certain idiosyncrasies. For instance, instead of the spicy fare served in traditional Gujarati households, Mohanlal liked to have porridge and English biscuits for breakfast and often used a fork instead of his fingers at meals. Some mornings he ambled over to the train station, nicked a newspaper from a vendor and rode the train downtown and back, returning the paper to the vendor and walking home.

I wanted to know what Mohanlal looked like. I was told that he usually wore a Western suit with a tall, flat-top black cap commonly worn by gentlemen of his caste, and carried a cane and perhaps a cigarette tin, since he smoked. I asked to see a photograph and frayed photo albums were brought out; yellowing photos were released from plastic packets where they had lain untouched for years and small black-and-white snapshots were shaken out of books where they had served as bookmarks and been forgotten. Eventually a single photograph came to light, not a very good one, half in shadow, of a seated sharp-featured old man with staring eyes. I was disappointed and someone observing my reaction said, 'If you want to know what Mohanlal dada looked like as a young man, think of his sons, he looked just like them!'

I closed my eyes and saw young Mohanlal: 5 feet 7 inches, small watchful eyes, thin lips and a sprightly, restless energy that added a ruddy sheen to his sultry complexion and gave off a pushy eagerness, which could be both arresting and annoying. I could see young Mohanlal forcing his way in the world and demanding to be heard, not often succeeding but yet persevering.

There were other clues in the older Mohanlal to his younger self. The oldest surviving member of his household told me that he, like his brothers, was a matriculate. In Mohanlal's papers, which I accessed in the course of my research, I found claims to a wider education and also a stint as a British government servant which one of his grandsons believes he would have been very proud of ('to do anything for the government was an honour'). The older Mohanlal was known to boast about his proficiency in 'thirty languages'. I found it hard to believe this claim. What were these thirty languages and where had he picked them up? I asked various family members who repeated the claim and found no answers, leading me to believe that it was possibly exaggerated. All I could say with certainty was that he was fluent in English and at least two vernacular languages, Gujarati and Hindi, which he taught to fair-skinned Westerners working for multinationals in Bombay. One of his granddaughters told me he was extremely enamoured of white people. The fact that he gave private tuitions when he had an income from speculation suggested that he enjoyed the company of his students and also perhaps the opportunity to speak English, a language he admired and which he periodically burst into, quoting fine aphorisms to his grandchildren and goading them in Gujarati: 'English bhan (Learn English)!'

I gather from these cues that Mohanlal was, at heart, an educationist and linguist, and his South African odyssey may well have been connected with a search for opportunities in this field. There were, at the turn of the twentieth century, approximately 150,000 Indians living in South Africa. They came from every part of India, propelled by the mineral discoveries of the late nineteenth century, but the main communities were of indentured agricultural workers from eastern India, and Muslim traders and retailers from Gujarat in western India. Gujarati, Hindi, Tamil, Telugu and Oriya were some languages commonly spoken by Indians in South Africa and people who could translate them into English and vice-versa were few. In May 1893, Mohandas Karamchand Gandhi had travelled to South Africa as a lawyer to provide his services on a legal case to a Memon trader from his hometown Porbandar in Gujarat, and part of his job was to translate the Gujarati correspondence that formed the main testimony in the case and to communicate between his client and the English lawyers.

Gandhi had lurked at the back of my mind all the while that I contemplated Mohanlal's journey; and how could he not? The father of the Indian nation, revered by millions, had been formed by the two decades that he spent in South Africa. 'You gave us Gandhi, we gave you the Mahatma,' Nelson Mandela is believed to have once said, partly in jest, but most scholars of Gandhi believe it to be true—that in South Africa, which he entered as a twenty-three-year-old and left permanently at the age of forty-four, Gandhi evolved as a political activist, social experimenter and spiritual leader. Though his fame derived from his leadership of the Indian freedom struggle, his personality and mission were shaped by his experiences in South Africa. The significance of this phase in his life has drawn his many biographers to South Africa; conversely, what is known of the history of the Indian diaspora there has also been narrated largely through the prism of Gandhi and his struggle against racial discrimination.

Prelude

One day, my aunt Manjula surprised me by saying, 'Mohanlal dada was with Gandhiji in South Africa.' I looked at her, startled, for I had never heard anything of this sort before. Her expression was beatific. Manjula is my mother's eldest sister, the one closest in age to my grandmother and the one most likely to know of something related to our ancestor's journey. She was a pious woman, preoccupied with prayers and rituals, and I wondered if wishful thinking might have played a role here, investing her with a wish for a family connection with a saintly leader where there was none. So, I asked my uncle, her brother Vinod, a corporate and altogether more worldly man, if he knew anything of this and right away, he said: 'Yes, it is true, Mohanlal dada was with Gandhiji!' I was flabbergasted. For so many years I had been seeking information about Mohanlal's journey and suddenly out of the blue I was presented with information, that too of a rather dramatic nature.

What did they mean by saying Mohanlal was 'with' Gandhiji? Conventionally, one would assume that the former was an acolyte and a supporter, probably a co-campaigner. I looked around and found that among Killavalas of a later generation were respected social workers and ardent followers of Gandhi. A letter I come across from Gandhi to Mohanlal's son Ramchandra in November 1945 suggests that the latter may have participated in the Quit India Movement.[1] But in Mohanlal I could find no sign of the qualities associated with Gandhi, such as simplicity, a revolutionary spirit or a bursting national pride. Quite the opposite, in fact, appeared to be the case. Mohanlal in his fine suit, feasting on English biscuits in his wooden house and playing the forceful landlord, did not seem to be a person likely to be an agitator against racial injustice. But given the contradictory ways of humans, I could hardly discount the possibility.

Gandhi himself had been an admirer of the English and aped aspects of their lifestyle and manners in the early years of his adult life. He also professed love for the English language and many of his closest friends in South Africa were white. The more I thought about it, the more I realized that at least at the superficial level, my great-grandfather and Gandhi had much in common. They were both Hindu Gujarati vanias of whom there could not have been more than a handful in South Africa at the time. As a London-trained barrister, Gandhi's grandeur was unmatched in the migrant community, but Mohanlal could lay claim to belonging to the same professional class by virtue of his education and his profession. A decade separated the two men but by coincidence both had been named 'Mohan' after the dark-skinned god Krishna, one of the most complex deities in the Hindu pantheon.

Of the many forms in which Krishna manifested himself (romantic lover, architect of the opulent city of Dwarka and counsellor of duty over ambivalence in the Bhagavad Gita), the form worshipped by Gujarati vanias was the mischievous child god, Shrinathji. In popular mythology the child god is a charming prankster. His namesake, Gandhi, is described by his sister as being 'mercurial' and 'full of curiosity' as a child, scattering utensils of worship and trying to make friends with dogs by twisting their ears. Erik Erikson in his 1969 Pulitzer prize-winning book, *Gandhi's Truth*,[2] writes that young Mohan's teasing of people and animals in childhood became, in a more subtle form, a lifelong trait.

Perhaps it was the infectiousness of this playful spirit that led me to consider the coincidence of two Mohans in the same space and at the same time as a narrative device. From a researcher's point of view, the possibility of a connection between the two had opened up a gold mine of material to me. Trying to track an ordinary person with no primary data in the form of letters or travel documents, no exact information about destination or dates and no anecdotes to follow up on would have been like looking for the proverbial needle in a haystack. But with Gandhi in the picture, my chances were miraculously improved. Somewhere in the hundreds of books, films and documentaries on Gandhi or in his own copious writings, speeches, and correspondence or in detailed accounts of his activities and meetings I hoped I might find a mention of my insignificant great-grandfather, which could serve at least as a starting point if nothing else for further research into Mohanlal's journey.

But I also began to think of the dramatic and investigative possibilities of the concurrence. My need to look into my great-grandfather's journey was born of a personal and subjective need, but fate had placed him in the shadow of an extraordinary man (about whom Einstein famously said: 'Generations to come will scarce believe that such a one as this walked the earth in flesh and blood.') It had also placed him at a historical juncture, an epic confrontation between Gandhi, India's future emancipator, and the mighty British Empire. The story had been told countless times and almost always through the Gandhian framework of a moving and liberatory struggle. More than half a century after Carlyle's dictum 'History is but the biography of great men' had been successfully challenged by a range of fresh historical perspectives and approaches, perhaps my exploration of the journey of an ordinary man, not quite your run-of-the-mill person but an everyman in relation to the heroic figure nevertheless, might yield something of historical and wider interest.

These were the thoughts running through my mind in the year 2012 when I received word that a small overseas travel grant attached to a fellowship I had successfully applied for two years before was due. I had to avail of it by the beginning of 2013 at the latest, otherwise it would lapse. The grant was customarily used by fellows to present their work in suitable fora outside India. But I was only just nearing the end of the book I had been working on and was not quite prepared with a presentation. Also, most people in the United Kingdom or the United States where I might have gone would have been on holiday and the prospect of speaking to stragglers wandering into a lecture room to escape the bleak winter streets was too dismal to contemplate.

It occurred to me then that it would not be winter in the southern hemisphere and suddenly it dawned on me that I was looking at an unexpected and rare opportunity—for there is virtually no research assistance for Indian writers and independent scholars—to take an exploratory trip to South Africa to see if I could discover anything about Mohanlal. I enquired with the fellowship's trustees if I could use the grant for research. The book for which I had been given the fellowship was about the city of Ahmedabad where Gandhi had set up his first settlement in India after returning from South Africa (via London) in 1915. Since I had to find a connection between the supported work and my intended research, I proposed an interest in visiting sites associated with Gandhi, including his ashrams in South Africa, a project that dovetailed with my game plan to search for traces of my great-grandfather.

The trustees agreed. In the little time I had to prepare, I hurriedly wrote to a few eminent Gandhi scholars, asking them if they had come across my great-grandfather's name in the course of their research. My friend Venu Madhav Govindu, who was writing a biography of the Gandhian economist J.C. Kumarappa, introduced me to Enuga Reddy. I sent him a mail. Meanwhile, I had begun to look into Mohanlal's family history. I did not know till then that the Killavalas, an eminent and well-regarded family in Mumbai's northwestern suburbs, were originally from Surat, about 200 kilometres north of Mumbai. A dusty industrial city, Surat had been the grand port of the Moghul Empire. I had known that, of course, but what I had not adequately registered was the scale of the port's pre-eminence on the Indian Ocean trading circuit. I looked at maps, at thin black lines signifying trading routes converging on the Gujarati port, the dizzy profusion of the lines also offering a glimpse of the big bazaar that was the Indian Ocean, and I was entranced.

Enuga Reddy responded to my email with the ringing assertion: 'Your (great) grandfather was a Satyagrahi!' and pointed me to the 1908 campaign of the educated group which I looked up in the *Collected Works of Mahatma Gandhi*. Enuga Reddy had also sent me a paragraph culled from Gandhi's South African newspaper, *Indian Opinion*[3]:

> KILLAVALA (KILLIWALA), Mohanlal Parmandas
> Interpreter and teacher in Natal. Formerly a government servant in India. He had a passport issued to him in Mauritius in His Majesty's name entitling him to proceed to and travel anywhere in British South Africa.

From Enuga Reddy's input, I derived a rough time frame for Mohanlal's presence in South Africa. My speculation that he was an 'interpreter and teacher' was confirmed. I learnt that Mohanlal had travelled via Mauritius, which was a popular destination for Indians, contrary to the understanding in my family that he had gone directly to South Africa. This was more than I had expected to find so quickly. My quixotic project suddenly took on a more realistic aspect. I was on my way.

To where?

My tickets pronounced names of cities of departure and destination: Mumbai, Durban, Cape Town. But my mind was now also on the ocean that lay between them and on a time before these cities existed. I was going to places where people of different races had violently clashed. And I was going over an ocean, the Indian Ocean which, for centuries, had ferried people of different races wherever they wanted to go. And there, on its blue waters, I will begin my story.

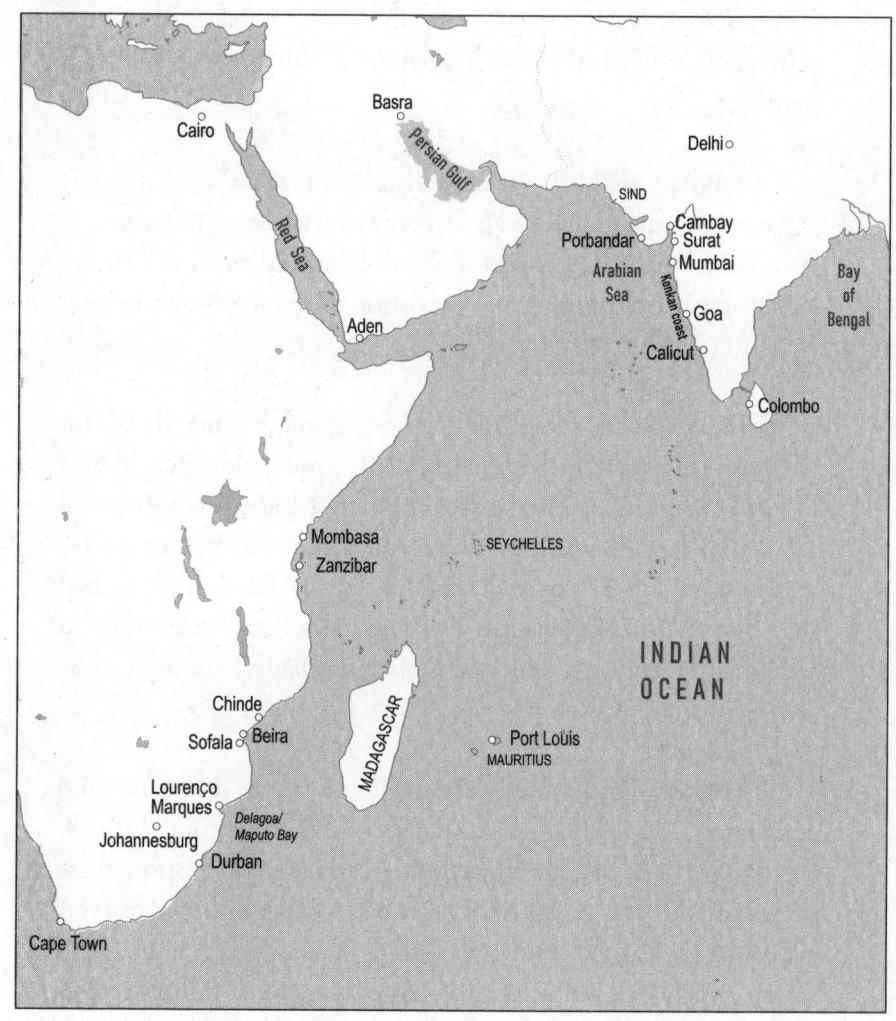

Western Indian Ocean circa 1900

PART ONE

LEAVING HOME

1
Perfumed Ocean

The mosque lies at the edge of the Tapi River in Kholvad, a village 20 kilometres outside Surat. Called the Kinara or 'border' Mosque, it is jammed in on two sides by houses tilting on hilly ground and narrow potholed lanes just wide enough to let a couple of big-bellied buffaloes or motorcycles go by at a time. It looms unexpectedly at the end of a dusty cul-de-sac, a white tabernacle on a rocky path to the river, a pause, an interregnum between land and water. I descend rough-hewn, uneven steps into light from the river, blazing and rippling over the threshold. The Tapi tugs the mosque as if it were a barge, a chalky, bulky wooden whale, drawn in a halting, swaying motion downstream. The mosque resists. The river waits, blue, flat, unhurried in its inexorable progression towards the Arabian Sea and the vast expanse of the Indian Ocean beyond.

An invisible cord runs between mosque and ocean, an umbilical memory of origins. The Indian Ocean, the world's third-largest body of water, extending from the southeastern tip of Africa to southwest Australia, has the oldest history of human traffic. Hoary accounts tell of people borne on rafts of animal skin and dugout canoes, and long-distance sailors following the lengthy, broken coastline. By the first century CE the pattern of the monsoon winds was understood:

the southwestern monsoon beginning in March on the East African coast reaches Malabar in late May-early June and the northeastern monsoon beginning in late October and lasting until February or March blows the opposite way; if timed well, a boat could rely on a friendly push clear across the ocean. The understanding launched the era of dirāt al-matlaq or journeys on routes that were 'out of sight of land between two known ports'[1] and turned the vast ocean into a highway for people, cultures, languages and religions. On its blue waters, Hinduism surged east from India. In the holds of ships, between bales of cargo, Buddhist monks transcribed arcane texts. And Islam, founded in Hejaz by Mohammad in the early seventh century CE, spread and established itself as the dominant faith of the region, making its way to the mud-and-wattle dwellings of the Swahili coast and as far east as Guangzhou in South China.

One August morning in the year 1490, a bagla[2] appeared in the wide blue sea at the entrance to the Gulf of Aden. Infinitesimal, insect-like, it left a sharp trail and a faint pair of arcs in the twinkling expanse. The wide sea reared and splashed wildly at the shore, prepared to toss the fragile object against its outcrops and foaming reefs. But the bagla was stronger than it looked. It had a resilient lateen sail woven from the leaves of the muql tree and its wooden planks, sewn together with coconut fibre cord and greased with shark and castor oil, enabled it to slip easily past reefs and lie on sandy banks, creaking and sighing with the ocean's ebb and flow.

On board, a Muslim sailor, a khalasi, shaded his eyes against the glare of the ascending sun. The humid air was suffused with a woody fragrance from smouldering incense sticks by which time was measured at sea. The Al-Bahr-Al-Hindi, 70 million square kilometres wide, stretched endlessly all around. The sailor's pale grey-green eyes were fixed on a rugged mountain top pitched against a clear blue sky. The impossible coast backed by bleak desert and escarpment was his birthplace, a harsh terrain that drove its men away as soon as they came of age. It had driven him away too when he was a stripling, a mere boy, to a career at sea. And now he gazed at his native land, registering the coast but imagining the valley that lay beyond, the desert and the mountains, green, fertile and bountiful, of which he had heard. Wheat, millet and coffee grew there amidst date-palm trees and coconut groves.³

'What are you thinking about, brother?'

The man who enquired was a recent friend who had come aboard with a new crew at Massawa; the khalasi liked his trusting, guileless ways and answered with a sweeping gesture, indicating the broad glittering sea and the distant mountain, 'I am thinking of my home and wondering what it would be like to leave all this and to settle on land.'

'*You?* You would leave the sea? After all this time!' The younger man was incredulous. 'And the land? It is not an easy life there, you know!'

The khalasi was familiar with his friend's sad story: debts left by a deceased father, abusive creditors, long trips on dhows for little money … a battle lost before it was begun.

'It was just a thought,' the khalasi said with a laugh to lighten the mood. 'Can a fish walk?'

'Yayayayaya … yaaaa-hh!' A legless beggar's caterwaul hung in the air pregnant with the aroma of ripe bananas and clove in the crowded marketplace of Cambay, the primary port of the top half of the angled line of the western Indian coast known as Gujarat. Considered to have become the greatest economic power of the Indian Ocean by the end of the fifteenth century, Gujarat derived its significance from many factors, not least its importance as a leading contributor to the supply of cotton cloth from India, a commodity so much in demand that it was as good as currency on the ocean. Blessed with a 1,600-kilometre-long shoreline, rivers, valleys rich in black soil and industrious weavers, Gujarat was a breeding ground for entrepreneurship. Its vanias went everywhere and settled in distant places, such as the east coast of Africa and along the Red Sea. When a religious taboo banned travel across the 'black waters' of the ocean, Hindu vanias withdrew from sailing, continuing to trade but leaving the journeying to Gujarati Muslims, giving rise to the well-known aphorism: '*Vohra no safar ne vania ni kasar* (the journey of the Muslim and the toil of the Hindu merchant)'.

The khalasi and his companion spent the night in the yard of an Armenian merchant after helping him with the unloading of a consignment of indigo cakes and the next morning, they went down to the harbour and joined a fleet headed south up to the mouth of the Tapi river, where they negotiated a passage on a boat loaded with grain, heading upstream. In the long days at sea, floating past sunlit minarets and high city walls, strolling through Basra with the stench of the polluted Tigris in their nostrils, they had plotted and conspired. And when the moment came, they had loped across the long beach at Cambay, observing the dhows become the size of tadpoles and their familiar bagla with its distinctive pattern of hibiscus petals on the prow merge with the rest.

The plan was to go to Rander, a port town on the river, of which they had heard much. The townsmen there, called Navayats or newcomers by the locals, were strong, fair-skinned Arabs from Kufa, owners of fine ships that sailed the eastern part of the Al-Bahr-Al-Hindi from where they brought back tall porcelain vases displayed in windows by the owners' beautiful, unveiled wives. But when the riverboat stopped at Rander, the men from the bagla did not have the will to move, exhausted by weeks of sailing and open seas and entranced by the buzz of dragonflies. They rested and presently found themselves at a mossy overhang where flies and yellow butterflies danced amidst tall weeds and the loamy earth opened its dark heart. With a wordless signal, they disembarked, clambered up the banks and disappeared into the tall grass.

The children of the khalasi inherited their fathers' grey-green eyes and their mothers' cinnamon skin. They did not smell of the sea but of the wet earth, the threshing shed and above all, of the river, which did not clasp them like a seaweedy second skin, but sprayed them with a mystique of mossy roots and sunlight. It had taken the khalasi time to adjust to his new life, retraining his muscles and his hands for unaccustomed tasks and learning to endure the monotony of his days, broken only by occasional trips upstream to sell potatoes or listen to a visiting Sufi preacher in the neighbouring village. Sometimes he dreamed of distant ports, of Mogadishu and the Maldives, and saw the faces of townspeople come out in sumbuqs with covered platters of food or green coconuts to welcome arriving sailors. Sometimes he told his grandchildren stories of the sea, tales of fabulous sea excursions led by the Chinese imperial eunuch Zheng He for the Ming emperor, describing the appearance through a spectral mist of those fabled fleets of treasure ships, each 400 feet long and accompanied by horse transports, supply ships, troop carriers, warships and water tankers; pale-faced men in their thousands, striding the decks of ghostly ships with massive rudders and giant billowing sails of red silk, and signalling to each other with lights and wild drumbeats.

Gradually the dreams and stories lost their hold over him. Memories of the sea weakened. Family, friends and neighbours bound him to terra firma. Over the years, others had come by sea and over land and joined him, former sailors and soldiers left behind by Muslim invaders. They had married good women and so many locals had converted to Islam that their expanding community was spread out on both sides of the riverbank and beyond, in villages with names like Kholvad, Kathor, Barbodhan and Lajpur. And in the Kinara Mosque which they had built, they sent their prayers up to the skies.

◆

Let me intervene here, for this is a work of non-fiction, and clarify that the khalasi is not a real person but a composite figure I have generated from historical records and villagers' tales. Someone— or many—like him did exist and built the Kinara Mosque, which is one among countless mosques on the western Indian seaboard, constructed by migrants arriving from the Arabic coast in the medieval age, a manifestation of the relentless oscillation that characterized life around the Indian Ocean. Muslim communities were scattered all along the coast[4] and the reason I have focused on this small, undistinguished settlement on the banks of the Tapi is because of its relevance to the story that I am about to tell. We will come to it by the by. Till then, let us leave the khalasi and his nascent community proliferating on the quiet riverbank and move on to other things.

Over the next few pages is a pastiche of historical events, not a fulsome history but a selection of circumstances that have a direct bearing on the ancestral journey I am about to retrace. As the collage suggests, unrelated events jostling against each other randomly or by design create the possibilities for individual stories to play out. I am setting the backdrop, so to speak, for Mohanlal's adventure.

We begin our montage with the arrival of Vasco da Gama in India in the summer of 1498, the first European to arrive in India by sea. Since the traditional routes by which European merchants accessed spices, silks and other luxuries from the east came to be blocked by political turbulence on land and the stranglehold of the Ottoman Turks and the Venetians over commercial access to the Mediterranean Sea, sailors from new nations on the Atlantic shores of Europe had been seeking oceanic routes to the east, a phenomenon beginning in the fifteenth century that has come to be known as the Age of Discovery.

The most enthusiastic players, the Portuguese, were motivated as much by the lure of spices as an urge for religious dominance.

They believed that there were Christians outside Europe (including a legendary red-robed king called Prester John, living in Africa and said to be richer and more powerful than any other man in the world) who would help them outflank the Islamic world. Vasco da Gama did not find these friendly Christians. Known to be 'violent of temper, and quick to react to perceived insults',[5] he got into skirmishes with native dwellers on the African coast and received help in the form of a Gujarati pilot from the kindly ruler of Malindi who guided him across the ocean. In his landmark 1776 work *The Wealth of Nations*, Adam Smith clubbed da Gama's crossing of the Indian Ocean with Columbus's discovery of America in 1492 as 'the greatest and most important events recorded in the history of mankind'.[6] His accomplishment stoked Portuguese ambitions, leading them to seek ascendancy in the Indian Ocean by attacking ports and building fortresses along the littoral. Their plans fizzled out, but by the end of the sixteenth century they had paved the way for other Western powers—the Dutch, the French and the English—to make their way to the east.

While these developments were taking shape, some alterations had taken place on the Indian coast. An excessive build-up of silt had eased the great port of Cambay in Gujarat out of the oceanic trading circuit. The nearby port of Rander, the town of Navayats and beautiful unveiled women, was also decommissioned after an attack by the Portuguese captain Antonio da Silveira in 1530 who left it utterly destroyed, smoke hanging over its treetops and spires for weeks like a fine mist.[7] The new port of significance, Surat, also the hometown of my great-grandfather Mohanlal's forefathers, was a few kilometres downstream from Rander, located on the southern bank of the Tapi at the point where the river began an upward curve, a clumsy water scrawl of an upside-down 'U'.

2

The Merchants

The fortified town was 25 kilometres inland. Ships were anchored in the deep waters off the village of Suvali, with visitors being ferried upstream on boats and then carried ashore through waist-deep water on the backs of porters and delivered into the probing hands of notoriously corrupt customs officials. After this unceremonious welcome, one imagines a visitor looking around him disconsolately, thinking the town did not have much to offer. A 35-by-15-yard burnt-brick fort built in the mid-sixteenth century by a Gujarat sultan to secure it against Portuguese invasions, the customs house, a mint, an open ground or maidan and a market. Could this damp, gloomy habitation be the greatest market of its time in the Indian Ocean and 'indeed maybe in the whole world',[1] as one historian claimed?

It was. The Moghuls, who had taken Gujarat from its provincial rulers in 1572, had opened up a vast hinterland for trade to the new port. Large caravans of ox and camel carts headed to Surat from centres near and far, bringing indigo, spices and precious cloth. From neighbouring Dholka, Navsari and Gandevi weavers sent duttee, a coarse cotton cloth useful for making sails, and varieties of Gujarati calico called bafta, the finest of which came from Broach.

Ahmedabad and Cambay sent a range of calicos and cuttanies, a cotton-wool mix useful for quilts, painted cloth and patolas, a silk cloth much in demand in the Malay Archipelago. A cheaper type of coloured calico also popular in East Asia, called birames, came from Burhanpur in central north India.[2]

The contemporaneous rise of two other great Muslim empires, the Ottomans and the Safavids in the western Indian Ocean, also boosted Surat's significance. Tycoons such as the Sunni Bohra merchant Mulla Abdul Ghafur, who maintained fleets of trading ships and had homes in other parts of the ocean littoral, had garden estates the size of boroughs in the town. A number of trading houses from western Europe had also set up factories or trading houses in Surat, the most prominent of which was the English East India Company, a monopolistic trading body incorporated by royal charter in London on 31 December 1600. Intending at first to challenge the Dutch foothold in the spice-rich islands of Southeast Asia, the Company had made the discovery that the spice trade there relied heavily on 'the cloths of Cambay' and so it came to Surat, defeating the Portuguese who resisted its entry in a small skirmish off the coast. The Vereenigde Oost-Indische Compagnie or the Dutch East India Company also came to Surat, as did the French who went on to form the Compagnie des Indes at L'Orient in Brittany in 1664.

The port bustled with activity. Javanese square-rigged ships bobbed alongside thin-hulled dhows with lateen sails. Malabari paraus floated beside skittish Sri Lankan praus. Long convoys of caravels called in on their way from Goa, where the Portuguese had established their headquarters, to their fortified settlement in Diu on the Gujarati coast. Country boats came loaded with rice from southern Indian ports. Tiered Bengali juncos brought cloth, pepper and cardamom picked up in Malabar. Ponderous Gujarati naus loaded with pilgrims for Mecca and textiles headed to the Red Sea and to Muscat, Gombroon, Basra and Kung in the Persian Gulf. Local ghurabs, dingris, haoris and batilas darted about in between, making short runs on the coast. From western ports ships brought ivory, aloe, myrrh, dates, almonds, slaves, pearls, rosewater and madder. From the east came tin, camphor, healing plants, Chinese lacquer, porcelain, copper and vermilion. European companies exchanged Persian horses for cloth, which they took beyond the Indian Ocean to West Africa to purchase slaves, to colonies in the Atlantic and to Europe where fashionable ladies revelled in the brightness and tenacity of Indian dyes. By the end of the seventeenth century, European companies were importing as many as two million pieces a year, binding up the world in taffeta; satins; soft muslins; striped, checked and printed cottons; chintzes; calicoes; bafta; and Guinea cloth from India.

Opportunism brewed in the medieval port town. And how could it not when its dank liminal space was a theatre of a million uncertainties and negotiations? Prodigious quantities of wealth and commodities collected from around the mighty ocean spilled daily across the soggy threshold of this port city tucked away in a bend off the long western coast. Spanish rials; Mexican, Peruvian and Lion dollars; German crowns; European ducats; and bars of silver and gold flowed in. The foremost merchant in town, a Jain banker and commodities' trader called Virji Vora, who wore a small powder mark on his forehead and a stiff modest turban, had an asset base recorded in French Company records at 8 million francs, making him one of the world's richest men. His fortune was amassed by cornering supplies and juggling prices: in 1668 he and a fellow merchant had 'stored upp some thousands of maunds' of vermilion and quicksilver 'sufficient to supplye the whole countrey for many years'.[3]

Virji Vora, Mulla Abdul Ghafur and anyone indulging in trade or commerce, regardless of religion or caste, were called vanias. But vania also referred to those who belonged to the Hindu vania caste who formed the backbone of this port city, its bourgeois heart. A lot has been said of caste vanias. They were a 'plodding commercial race'[4] for whom 'the market was their veritable temple and the account book ... their scripture.'[5] They were abstemious by habit, and wary of exposing their wealth for fear of attracting the covetous gaze of Moghul officials. They were classic middlemen, timid by nature and preferring compromise at all times to confrontation.

In the seventeenth century there were 30,000 caste vanias in Surat, less than a sixth of the city's 200,000-strong population. Among them were Mohanlal's forebears, the Killavalas, then known as the Sankalias before they changed their name for reasons I will come to. They lived 500 metres from the fort, in the neighbourhood of Nanavat, a name that literally translates as 'dealing with money'.

In those times when work was circumscribed by caste, vanias had a limited number of occupational options. Poorer vanias swarmed Suvali, ambushing new arrivals with offers of deals. John Fryer, surgeon to the English Factory, in his scoffing account described them as plentiful as 'sand-flies' and brazen, crowding 'in their service, interposing between you and all civil respect, as if you had no other business but to be gulled'.[6] They were choksis (assayers of gold and silver) and parekhs (examiners of coins) at the mint. They were observed in street corners cutting deals on commodities with silent gestures or clasped fingers under a handkerchief. And they could be found squatting on plump muslin-covered gaddas in the commercial precinct of Balaji Chakla, attending to a motley clientele of farmers, widows and other small depositors and loan-seeking merchants, administrators and army men, recording naam (debit) and jama (credit) in long notebooks bound in red cloth.[7]

The proliferation of European companies opened new opportunities for the resourceful vania. Vanias or 'Banyans' as the Europeans called them were essential to the smooth functioning of European houses; they worked as modis (stewards) supervising the weighers, packers and porters looking after the loading and unloading of ships, customs clearance and the organizing of pack animals for caravans into the interior of the country.[8] Some of these vanias were influential men in their own right and company officials relied on their contacts and know-how. Jadu, a broker and linguist, was probably the first local agent hired by the English Company when King James's ambassador, Thomas Roe, was wooing Moghul Emperor Jehangir for a firman to set up a factory in Surat. Later historical accounts mention a Surti bafta dealer, Somji Chitta, and Chota Thakur (chief house broker and linguist) and the Parakhs; Tapidas, who was paid an annual allowance of 500 mahmudis in 1634, his sons Bhimji and Kalyan, and his brother Tulsidas, a cashier earning as much as a junior English staffer.[9]

I do not know what my ancestors, the Sankalias, did for a living, whether they scuffed the sand at Suvali, whether they weighed and assessed coins in the mint, if they had a shop in Balaji Chakla or if they worked for an influential merchant or a European company. Somehow, they thrived in a seaport of abundant wealth and a permanent aura of transience. Surat, like many port cities in the ocean which existed for trade alone, was a chimera, appearing and disappearing through the year. In the off season the castle and its environs wore a deserted look, the silence broken only by the knocking on wood of houses being repaired and by the heaving, clinking and shouting from the riverbank where a great deal of activity was underway. Boats were overhauled and refitted with hollows dug in the mud to set them upright and stakes fixed to secure them. Sailors on shore competed with labourers to make a few pice each day, fetching and carrying loads, digging and sweeping rubbish all over town.[10] In September the masts of the first ships arriving from the Red Sea appeared on the horizon and the commercial intelligence they brought rippled from the port to the market and sent looms humming in the villages. And still more ships arrived. By November, every room in town was occupied and the bursting markets thronged with Arabs, Persians, Turks, Armenians, Englishmen and Hollanders.

By March, kafilas from upcountry arrived and unloaded their cargo on the maidan, a large expanse of grass near the fort. Fabrics, indigo and other goods packed and ready awaited inspection and official seals of approval. In the season, traders rushed about frantically amidst hundreds of pitched tents seeking majurs to carry their bales to barges. Sailors carried small sacks of putchuk, a fragrant root used for making incense sticks in China, printed cloth or copper, which they were allowed to trade privately to supplement their wages. Pots gurgled on stoves, tempers flared. As a ship prepared to depart, pandemonium broke out and the threat of sudden fires and sword clashes permeated the brittle air.[11]

Wild-haired, raggedy-clothed fakirs, lured from the shadowy tombs where they slept by the onset of the season, hung about busy bazaars attempting to blackmail passers-by. One vowed to hang by his heels till he collected enough wealth to build a mosque. Another fettered himself in an iron chain two yards long, each link 'thicker than a man's thumb'. Some ran amuck, thrusting themselves into the way of passing carriages and stopping well-dressed Christians to ask: 'Why He suffers him to go afoot and in rags, and this caffir to vaunt it thus.'[12]

In a fluctuating, temperamental town, the English East India Company chose to anchor its factory in a house of 'stone and excellent Timber ... very strong, for that each Floor is half a Yard thick at least, of the best plastered Cement, which is very weighty'.[13] The house had galleries, rooms for conferring, tanks, a hamam for washing, an open place for meals and a small chapel. Below stairs was a continual hurly-burly of banyans, 'packers and warehouse-keepers, together with merchants bringing and receiving musters (samples), make a mere Billingsgate'.[14] The lifestyle of the company president was said to resemble a Moghul Emperor or his representatives, such as the Surat governor. He dined off silver plates with trumpets ushering each course of the 'choicest viands' and moved about town on the shoulders of attendants in a palkhi emblazoned with the royal escutcheon, his council following in large coaches, drawn by stately oxen. Other European companies were equally profligate. The Dutch, like the English, built splendid tombs for their deceased presidents and indulged in drunken revelry while word about the French Company was that it was 'better stored with Monsieurs than with cash, they live well, borrow money, and make a show'.[15]

This was Surat, pride of the Moghuls, in the seventeenth century, at the height of its glory. Over the next hundred years, both the port and its rulers would be rendered insignificant in a series of dramatic shifts that put the country in foreign hands. The baffling particulars of how the English East India Company came to control India are not relevant to our story and a brief version will suffice. In 1707 the last great Moghul Emperor Aurangzeb died, leaving a power vacuum in which various regional powers asserted themselves. Surat, for instance, was repeatedly attacked by the Marathas, a rising guerrilla force in the Deccan. The European companies were no longer restricted to western India but had extended their presence along the Indian coast, setting up fortified bases close to textile manufacturing regions in Calcutta and Madras. The outbreak of the Seven Years' War in 1756 pitted Great Britain against France, hostilities intensifying over the American Revolutionary War and the Napoleonic wars. The global contestation between the two powers spilled over to India in the course of the long, uncertain eighteenth century, the early encounters taking place in the east and the south. Reckless, greedy officers of the companies fought each other with regional Indian powers as proxies or signed protection treaties, making vassals of local rulers across the land. The English East India Company emerged a winner, mopping up revenues countrywide and leading a local fighting force of 200,000 men. The Company took the Surat Fort in 1759 and the whole city in 1800.

The commercial class played a critical role in boosting the English East India Company's prospects. The Company was backed wholeheartedly in Bengal by prominent bankers, the Jagat Seths. In Surat, a section of vanias supported by Trawadi Arjunji Nathji, a Nagar Brahmin silk trader who supplied funds for the English East India Company's military manoeuvres through his extensive banking network, campaigned for it to assume control of the port city. By then, Surat had declined. Political instability in the Indian Ocean region had led to a waning of trade. Ships left the once-glorious port for Persia and Arabia with half their previous loads. The jagat nakas or custom houses on the Tapi were deserted and officials were twiddling their thumbs. To add to the port's woes, the Maratha attacks had triggered a state of lawlessness in which bands of thugs roamed the highways stalling the movement of goods and bullion and attacking traders. A foreign company with its private military force, its commercial processes and access to global funds, might have seemed like a saviour from anarchy. Though individual self-interest also played a role for many, vanias were allied to the Company and Trawadi Arjunji Nathji, as Lakshmi Subramanian points out in a profile of the banker-merchant, was an influential and reliable ally of the Company.[16]

I wonder if the Sankalias were part of the group that campaigned for the English East India Company. In Nanavat, their neighbours were the Parakhs, a family with a long history of employment in the Company. Trawadi Arjunji Nathji had his office in a street running parallel to Nanavat. The possibility that the Sankalias supported Company rule is suggested by the fact that Mohanlal's great-grandfather Gangadas was employed by the Company after it took charge of Surat in 1800. This is the only piece of early family lore I find and it claims that Gangadas was employed at the Surat Fort where the Company had moved its police and revenue departments. His designation was 'Chief Officer', though what this position implied or what the scope of his duties was is not known. How important the job was as a means of self-identification, however, can be seen from the fact that the family name changed at this point. Among vanias, the name 'Killewala' had a provenance as a 'handler of the keys' in a sahukar or moneylender's operation,[17] but an elderly Surat-based relative is emphatic that the name was a by-product of the job: 'There were many Sankalias in town and people identified Gangadas as "the killa wala" meaning the one who worked at the Fort and the name stuck.'

3

Hatmen[1]

The slate-grey ramparts of the Surat Fort, framed by the watery blue of the Tapi, have the crumbly appearance of a gnawed biscuit. Inside, some sort of repair work appears to be underway, for there is a scattering of rubble and scaffolding tied with bits of green matting. The first brick structure was reinforced with stone and large brick slabs, four watchtowers and a daunting 60-foot-high wall. Now, a door, heavy and elephant-high with iron spikes running across it, is the only evidence of the fort's former impregnability. In 1540 (Islamic year 947 H), a Persian poet Mulla Muhammad of Astrabad, better known by his nom-de-plume 'Razai', wrote eulogistically: '*This Castle will stand like a block on/ the breast and the life of the Firangis.*' The 'firangis' he was referring to were the Portuguese who made every effort, first by sending armed vessels on the river and, when these failed, by means of bribes to the local governor, to scuttle the building of the castle. They failed in their efforts to stop the fort from coming up, but two hundred years later, it did fall to another set of firangis.

I pick my way through ant hills and wooden shards, some collected under the drooping leaves of a lime tree. A black plastic water tank sits amidst loose soil and rubble. Behind it is a long colonial-style building with a pitched roof and shattered window frames and doors which, in their regular recurrence, suggest rooms of a consistent shape and size and make me wonder if this might be where the English East India Company housed its administrative offices. Did Mohanlal's forefather and my ancestor Gangadas work in this building? How would it have felt to adapt to the ways of the 'hatmen', as the English were called by the locals? One imagines it would have been a sea change from the feudal, easy-going ways of previous administrations, but one cannot say for sure, for the English history books do not comment at any length on this period. This is partly because Surat, after it had served its purpose as an entry point, was of no particular importance to the East India Company.

The grand port of the Moghuls had had its day. The East India Company's attention had long been focused on developing an archipelago of seven islands, 240-odd kilometres south of Surat, which it had acquired from King Charles II who had procured it as dowry from his bride, Portuguese Princess Catherine of Braganza, in 1661. Bombaim, as the Portuguese called it, renamed 'Bombay' by the British, was a breeding ground for illnesses like cholera, which caused a Company chaplain to dub it a 'parish graveyard'. But the archipelago had many advantages, such as a natural harbour, and was conveniently located between the teak-rich forests of Gujarat and the Malabar. The East India Company made it a base for a naval force called the Bombay Marine and persuaded Lowji Nasserwanjee Wadia, a reputed Parsi carpenter from Surat, and a team of Parsi carpenters, to move there and build a dry dock and boats.

In 1810, the 74-gun HMS *Minden*, the first ship of the line to be built for the Royal Navy outside England, made of teak and comparable 'for beauty of construction and strength of frame … with any man-o-war that has come out of the most celebrated Dockyards of Great Britain',[2] sailed out of Bombay. From England, their Lordships of the Admiralty sent the architect, Jamsetjee

Bomanjee Wadia of Surat's Lowji family, a letter of appreciation and a piece of plate, a moment commemorated in a painting hanging at the Maritime Museum in Greenwich: Wadia robed and turbaned in white, holding callipers and a drawing of the *Minden*, the half-built ship visible through a window. At the turn of the nineteenth century, Bombay's naval facilities and the Indian forces were deployed to extend Britain's influence in the oceanic region with strategic bases established in Ceylon, Malacca and the Moluccas in 1795, the Cape in the same year and again in 1806, Egypt in 1801, Mauritius in 1810 and Java in 1811.

Other Indians were sent overseas in the service of the growing British Empire as well. New revenue systems and taxes, accompanied by natural disasters, caused widespread destitution particularly in the regions stretching from north to south straddling the country's eastern belt: the United Provinces, Bihar and its neighbouring hilly region, Bengal, and districts that form parts of modern Odisha, Andhra Pradesh and Tamil Nadu. Impoverished peasants from these regions came to the attention of contractors looking for able-bodied recruits to sign up as indentured labourers.

Britain had abolished slavery in most British colonies by 1834 and needed cheap labour to work in plantations in their dominions. Indenture was a form of semi-bondage in which Indian workers were contracted to overseas employers for a predetermined period, usually five years, with remuneration and paid expenses. Indentured workers could return home at the end of their terms, stay on in the colonies by renewing their indentures, or become free migrants. Depots came up in the Company port towns of Calcutta, Madras and Bombay. Most people who signed up were illiterate and had no clear idea what they were enrolling for. Some thought they were being taken to the Company ghar on the coast and were stunned to find themselves on a boat heading for an unknown destination.

The experiment was launched with the export of 24,000 'coolies' to Mauritius between 1834 and 1839; the colony would receive a total of 450,000 or so. Transportation to the West Indies started a few years later and by 1872, 80,000 Indians had been sent to British Guiana, 44,000 to Trinidad, 16,000 to Jamaica and 6,000 to other West Indian islands. A few thousands went to Fiji. From 1860 onwards, thousands of Indian indentured workers were also sent to Natal in South Africa.[3]

Before we throw ourselves across the seas, let us linger on the Indian west coast a little longer. Surat might have been of no importance to the British, but it was home to Mohanlal's family, even after their move to Bombay, so let us stay and watch what happens there.

An air of abandonment swept through the old town, blowing over the gloomy old fort, the bleak mint, shuffling past homes, ponds, burial grounds and barrelling towards the ghats of Fulpada at the opposite bend of the Tapi where Hindus cremated their dead among ash-smeared sanyasis who inhabited the riverbanks. In their magnificent garden estates, scions of once-powerful merchants wasted away in a narcotic haze. Sandbanks criss-crossed the estuary and loomed below Surat town. A stench of excrement arose from a line of slum tenements stretched along the banks of the choking river.

In this sad and desolate town, circa 1845, an oil lamp flickered in the pre-dawn darkness in a house in Gopalpura. The pale light shone upon a young Nagar Brahmin boy, Narmad, rocking back and forth, muttering in Sanskrit. Close by sat his father, Lalshankar Dave, a pen in his hand, which he dipped occasionally into an inkwell to construct elegant blocks of text in Gujarati on sheets of paper spread out around him. There was no movement in the houses around them and for a long time, both remained absorbed in their separate tasks. After a while, the boy got up, stretched himself and, without disturbing his father, silently collected his books and left the house, shutting the door gently behind him.

The pinnate leaves of tamarind trees formed a canopy on his path. Trees of enormous girth appeared to hide infinite dangers, cunning thieves, for example, or ghosts. The boy was not afraid of thieves as he was of ghosts. Eight years ago, a fire had spread through the city and raged for three days. Many pregnant women had died in the conflagration and it was widely believed that their spirits roamed the streets, waylaying young men. The boy shivered from cold and fear. A Kalkadevi temple appeared in his path. He entered it and looked around furtively to check if he was being observed before he slapped himself hard and muttered a fervent entreaty to the deity: 'I am guilty, Mother, forgive me.' Then, after another furtive glance he left, walking at a brisker pace to reach his tutor's house for a lesson on the Vedas.

While Narmad was absorbed in his study of Sanskrit and Hindu religious texts, a few Englishmen were rewriting his future. In 1813 while renewing its charter, the British Parliament had directed the East India Company to take an initiative in educating Indians. The directive had sparked off a discussion on the kind of education most suited to India. Some British administrators felt that a new education system should be based on classical Indian learning, but others argued for what came to be known as the Anglicist view, which was most forcefully argued by Thomas Babington Macaulay, president of the General Committee of Public Instruction. In his celebrated 1935 Minute, which was to become a template for the colonized world, Macaulay said: 'We must at present do our best to form a class who may be interpreters between us and the millions whom we govern; a class of persons, Indian in blood and colour, but English in tastes, in opinions, in morals, and in intellect.'[4]

As a new education system emerged, Lalshankar Dave, who was a lahiya or a writer copying texts for circulation, was offered a job in Bombay, preparing printer's copies for the English East India Company's education department. By the early nineteenth century, buffeted by the port's decline and sensing opportunities in the new city, one-third of Surat's population had moved to Bombay. It is possible that the Killavalas were among them, though they kept their home in Surat. Narmad grew up as many in Surat were learning to do, making a life in two cities. He and his mother visited Lalshankar several times a year. They walked most of the way, accompanied by a vast convoy of people trekking the same route. In his descriptions of those journeys, Narmad recalls tramping over hills and through swamps and fields, feeling the satiny-soft tenderness of white sekta petals underfoot, reaching for low-hanging mangoes, wading through shallow ponds, observing the ethereal shapes of trees at dusk and the unfamiliar taste of ghee-khichdi cooked by strangers in rest houses where they stopped for the night.

Over two hundred years the Company had wrought a miracle in Bombay. On a collection of swampy islands ringed by fish bones and samphire leaves, a printing press, a mint, courts of justice and forts had come up. Islets joined by causeways enabled British residents to move from the increasingly fortified town to bungalows, elegant single-storey structures with pitched roofs and verandas in the suburbs. A promise of religious tolerance and tax breaks offered by its late governor, Gerald Aungier, had attracted a stream of migrants, among them a Baghdad-born Jewish businessman, David Sassoon.

Bombay emerged as a hub of Britain's eastern empire. It also became a base for a thriving clandestine trade to China of opium purchased in India. Victorian England's addiction to Chinese tea cost precious English bullion, just as the import of Indian cloth used to do. Britain had leveraged its commanding position to snuff out India's vibrant and age-old textile-manufacturing industry, making it a market instead for its own machine-produced cloth. In the course of a hundred years, from importing 11 million yards of hand-woven Indian cloth in 1750, Britain exported 1,358 million yards of machine-made cloth to India.[5]

The clandestine trade in opium offered a similar solution in China. The Company dared not sell opium under the nose of the Chinese authorities. But it could sell it in India to country traders and India-based British free merchants who would ship it to China and arrange for its sale in China in exchange for tea (or a claim on tea). The tea would then be sold to the Company in exchange for a bill that the Company's headquarters in London would redeem in sterling. In this roundabout way, Indian receipts made their way back to Britain.

The East India Company, though, was no longer the force it used to be. The Charter Act of 1813 stripped the Company of its monopoly over Indian trade, and in 1833 the Act ended its commercial activities, leaving it a purely administrative body. The dwindling monopoly of the English East India Company was a clarion call to enterprising young Europeans, a new breed of entrepreneurs who, operating through commercial partnerships called managing agencies, quickly acquired a 'limpet-like grip on the local pattern of trade' from Burma (where they were teak-wallahs) to ivory-rich East Africa, with India as 'the pivot, the indispensable engine-room'.[6] A few Indians were also swept up by the tide, most notably Jamsetjee Jeejeebhoy, the son of indigent weavers in Olpad, 20-odd kilometres north of Surat. His parents' early demise left him in the care of relatives who were small-time traders in Bombay. His chance meeting with William Jardine, a surgeon for the East India Company and future founder of the successful firm Jardine, Matheson & Co., in 1805 through a hijacking and a storm off the coast of Point de Galle, is the stuff of legend. Hirji and Maneckji Jivanji, brothers from Navsari, 30 kilometres south of Surat, also profited from the snowballing trade in new commodities and opium and expanded into lending, their easy access to cash earning them the sobriquet 'Readymoney'.

Jamsetjee, the Readymoneys and the Lowji-Wadias who built the Bombay dockyards belonged to the Parsi community. The Parsis were Zoroastrians who had fled religious persecution in Persia and settled in western India between the eighth and tenth centuries. They and their descendants were an enterprising and fair-skinned people who bonded easily with the colonial regime. Jamsetjee Jeejeebhoy, the first Indian to become a baronet, had a peacock and palm trees on his coat of arms and a palatial mansion in Bombay, which was featured in an 1858 edition of *The Illustrated London News*. British travel writer Maria Graham wrote about the Lowji-Wadias that they 'speak and write English so well that if I did not see their dark faces and foreign dress, or read their unusual names at the end of a letter, I should never guess they were not Englishmen'.[7]

In their growing prominence, the Parsis, like the Bengali baniyas in Calcutta and Tamil dubashes in Madras, reflected the need of the English for local collaborators and intermediaries who understood the requirements of the new commercial environment accompanying the onset of Company rule spreading swiftly from the colonial cities to the rest of the country, even to Surat where old, time-tested ways of trade were rendered redundant by new forms of contracts and municipal regulations requiring copious paperwork, for which literacy and a knowledge of English was essential.

In the Bombay Presidency, covering much of Gujarat and Maharashtra, Lieutenant-Governor Mountstuart Elphinstone, an astute Scottish administrator who was keen to employ Indians in his administration, started the Bombay Native School and School Book Society to open primary schools all over western India. The local elite, which supported the society, also opened an institution of higher learning, Elphinstone College, named after the sagacious governor in Bombay, and collected Rs 229,636 by public subscription to fund teaching professorships in the English language and the arts, science and literature of Europe.

Thousands of children enrolled in the new schools and as they came of age, they were recruited by the education department to develop educational materials for succeeding generations, often by applying Western forms or concerns to the local context. A list of the department's commissions for 1866 reveals a wide range of projects: Kursandas Mulji's *Englandma Pravas* (Travels in England) was a 'spirited and sensible book' likely to 'produce a good influence among the Gujarati people'. *Chronological Tables* in English by Cowasjee Sorabjee Patel was 'a learned work of reference, suitable to be used in offices where dates given according to different Oriental systems have to be reduced to the Christian era'. Nandshankar Tuljashankar Mehta wrote *Karan Ghelo,* a historical novel, the first Gujarati novel in fact. Lakshman Moreshwar Shastri Halbe wrote *Ratna Prabha,* a novel in Marathi advocating widow remarriage.[8]

An evangelical fervour underlay the modern education project. Alexander Kinloch Forbes, who started the Gujarat Vernacular Society, described himself as being moved by a 'religious obligation … to lift up the language of the province from its present ignoble condition and encourage the more gifted fancies among those to whom it is vernacular …'.[9] Macaulay spoke about 'a great people sunk in the lowest depths of slavery and superstition'.[10] The suggestion that Indian society was flawed, regressive and in need of cultural and spiritual regeneration made a deep impression upon the recipients of new education. Bright, fiery, fashionable men started societies to discuss the real and imagined imperfections of Indian society and cranked out periodicals with articles on science (the shape of the earth, comets, vaccination) and self-improvement (praising values of loyalty against evils of anger, lethargy and superstition) in new proliferating printing presses.

The call for sudhar (reform) spread like wildfire from Bombay to other parts of western India. Two schoolteachers went from Bombay to Surat where the Irish Presbyterian Mission School, Gujarat's first government English school, was established in 1842. Backed by Henry Green, the school's 'agnostic' and 'rationalist'[11] headmaster, they started a humanist society called the Manav Dharma Sabha, which challenged what it perceived as obsolete traditions, shaking up the old, settled society of the port town with its flamboyant experiments such as inviting practitioners of occult arts to a test in the market square.

In this seething cauldron of change, copying, adaptation, experimentation and translation, Narmad moved between Surat and Bombay. His fervid childhood anxieties and religious learning were overlaid with new influences as he entered the Irish Presbyterian Mission School and Elphinstone College. The assiduity with which he had studied Sanskrit and the Vedas he now applied to new subjects, looking up the meaning of words and practising spoken English with friends during school recess. An inspector from the Company's education department visiting his school was blown away by his fluid rendition of a passage from John Dryden's translation of Virgil's *Aeneid*:

> Not fiery coursers, in a chariot race
> Invade the field with half so swift a pace;
> Not the fierce driver with more fury lends
> The sounding lash, and, ere the stroke descends,
> Low to the wheels his pliant body bends ...

The most popular Gujarati poet of the mid-nineteenth century was Dalpatram, who read out his best-known poem, 'Hunnar Khan ni Chadai (The Invasion of King Industry)', for the first time at the Andrews Library in Surat in 1851:

> Mussalmans and Hindus, people of my country!
> Make the trade route your rope-snake, the ship your churn…
> 'King' Industry rules, your wealth is gone
> To foreign hands …
> Learn new skills, bring industry and new machines.[12]

The poet who advocated an embrace of modernity was unexpectedly eclipsed by a youngster who was the very embodiment of modernity itself. Narmad's rise was meteor-like, his eclectic aspects coming together to produce innovative works: new styles of poetry, the first autobiography in Gujarati and a Gujarati lexicon. His unusual gifts were not suited to the ordinary business of making a living.

He made desultory attempts at employment (procuring an official certificate from the Oriental Translator to the Government enabling him 'to teach Guzerathee' to an officer of a Bombay-based regiment and getting a job as a schoolteacher in Rander) but preferred to while away his days in an intoxicated haze, chasing women or throwing himself into social reform. His fellow reformists were a Nagar Brahmin and a classmate from the IP Mission School, Mahipatram Ruparam, who challenged the Hindu taboo against foreign travel by visiting Europe in 1860 on an invitation from the education department, and Karsandas Mulji, a Kapol vania from Bombay who edited a reformist publication called *Satyaprakash* (Light of Truth). Young, reckless, charismatic and gifted, this trio of warriors fought against religious fanaticism and orthodoxy, blazing a trail of controversy and debate in Gujarat's ritualistic custom-bound Hindu society. Narmad, the most iconoclastic of them all, even committing the forbidden act of marrying a widow with reckless disdain for the consequences (including on his pre-existing marriage).

In an oil painting made when he was twenty-seven, Narmad is thin with bony shoulders, a narrow face and prominent ears. Dressed in a traditional flowing kurta and a distinctive turban, a flat disc with a flap over the forehead, he leans an elbow on a round table with a European-style flowered cloth. A finger at his forehead suggests that he is lost in thought, but his expression and stance are clearly geared for action. He seems high-strung and impatient.

The portrait would have been made when Narmad was in the middle of an extremely high-profile and contentious campaign led by Karsandas Mulji against the alleged misdeeds of the priests of a powerful Hindu sect. A libel suit pitted the reformers against Hindu traditionalists. Crowds surrounded the Bombay Supreme Court where the case was heard between January and March 1862. There were well-known public faces on both sides. Karsandas and Narmad won the case, a major triumph in their eyes and for the rationalists' lobby. And the judgement was reproduced bit by bit for months following the outcome on the pages of *The Times of India*.[13]

4

Cotton Mania

An alabaster-white neoclassical building rises incongruously on a dusty back street passing by the high walls of the dockyards in Mumbai. The white mansion with its Grecian portico and eight Doric-styled pillars was once the Bombay Town Hall. In 1858, India was brought directly under Crown rule and a proclamation read out on its sweeping steps expressed Queen Victoria's will 'that so far as may be, our subjects, of whatever race or creed, be freely and impartially admitted to offices in our service, the duties of which they may be qualified, by their education, ability and integrity, duly to discharge'.[1]

In the mid-nineteenth century, the town hall occupied a mid-point between the English-dominated fortified area close to Apollo Gate in the south and the densely populated native town. Much of the land around it was an open space called the Bombay Green or Cotton Green, an unencumbered ground where merchandise, mostly cotton, lay piled up on its way to the docks, where it would be loaded onto ships headed to China, since Lancashire mills preferred to source their cotton from America. The country's first passenger train, a set of fourteen carriages hauled by three steam locomotives, made an introductory run between Bombay's Bori

Bunder station and the outlying district of Thane on 16 April 1853. Great big viaducts came up in the countryside, extending the reach of the railways to cotton-growing regions in the Deccan. By 1863 a railway line also snaked northwards past Surat and reached the fertile Gujarati hinterland.

Post and telegraph services connected Bombay to other colonial centres. Calcutta was the base from which the East India Company controlled its sprawling possessions, but Bombay's importance as a commercial city was on the rise. In 1720, the East India Company had opened a modern bank in Bombay with a share capital of Rs 1 lakh to gather money for its activities and to attract commercial men to the city. Heavy borrowings to inflate the Company's war chest made it a short-lived venture and after that for many years traditional indigenous bankers prevailed. The Company looked to them and to agency houses such as Forbes & Co. and Bruce Fawcett & Co. to bankroll its surging military expenditure, but by the mid-nineteenth century, a number of modern banks, including the Bank of Western India, the Commercial Bank of India and the Chartered Mercantile Bank of India, London and China, had opened shop.

A prominent addition was a new Bank of Bombay with a seal of an elephant and a palm tree, established in April 1840 and oversubscribed, partly by the government, which put up a substantial portion of the Rs 52.5 lakh capital base. With a board of nine members, six elected and three government representatives, it received deposits, kept cash accounts, discounted bills, drafts and other investments and issued bank notes that were accepted by the Treasury. By 1861, when free banking was brought to an end by the Paper Currency Act, a crore worth of rupee notes was in circulation, including the Bank of Bombay's large rectangles with two British administrators posing like Roman senators on either side.

The bank was housed in an ornate building of yellow stone, which is claimed variously to have been in the vicinity of the town hall or at Rampart Row to the south. A photograph of important men in finance at the time shows a group of them, mostly Caucasian, some whiskered, many thin and not particularly robust in appearance. A couple of Indians are also present, dressed in suits with their hair slicked back and in turbans. A few Indian guards in elaborate ethnic uniforms bookend the gathering.[2]

In 1851, some Indians who were probably not a part of this elite group formed an informal organization called the Native Share and Stock Brokers Association by contributing a rupee each and started meeting under a spreading banyan tree in the Bombay Green to dabble in cotton and opium futures. Among them was a thin, moustachioed twenty-year-old with a quick mind and a good memory, Premchand Roychand. Premchand's father, an Oswal Jain timber trader, had moved the family from Surat to Bombay, probably to supply the dockyards with timber, and sent his son to Elphinstone College. It is likely that Roychand, an ambitious man by some accounts, had envisaged a future for his son as a commission agent to traders and exporters. Premchand was more inclined towards speculation and instead became an assistant to a broker, Ratanchand Lala, building up a modest fortune of about a lakh rupees by 1858.

Rumblings were beginning to be felt at this time of an approaching civil war in distant America. Shrewd businessmen in Bombay assumed that it would have an impact on the demand for cotton from India. In its 1860–61 report, the Bombay Chamber of Commerce reported: 'Recent events in America have invested the Indian cotton question with unusual interest in Lancashire.'[3] Leading cotton merchants at the time, including Jamsetjee Jeejeebhoy's son, Rustomji, and Goculdas Tejpal, followed the news closely. Publications like *Home News* and *Overland Mail* arriving twice a month by the mail boat from England contained information on the Liverpool cotton market and merchants employed ingenuous methods of outpacing each other for early access to the news, including giving bribes to men on board and sending fast boats to meet mail ships at sea.

Premchand thrust himself into the approaching cotton boom. He established agencies in various cotton-growing districts in Gujarat. He also leveraged his close links with Europeans in the city's thirty-odd firms and half a dozen large banks, both to obtain information on the market overseas and to advise his clients, the largest of the Bombay firms, Ritchie Stuart & Co., on conditions at the Indian suppliers' end. In April 1861, war broke out and as observers in India expected, the blockading of Confederate ports disrupted cotton supplies to Europe. England looked at India to meet the shortfall, ordering a million bales, more than twice the size of the tonnage departing annually from the Bombay port. The price of Indian cotton rose from around 4 pence a pound in the Liverpool market to between 20 and 24 pence.[4] The British government aggressively encouraged the substitution of American cotton with Indian supplies.

Moneylenders and bankers descended on farms, waving rupee notes at tillers for seeds and urging them to move to commercial farming. The governor of the Bombay Presidency announced that 'every piece of land within reach of the sea wall will be laid down this season with nothing but cotton'.[5] The demand was so great that people with 'hardly a hundred rupees in their pockets' tried to get hold of cotton any way they could, even, it is said with some exaggeration, tearing up mattresses and delivering the stuffing to speculators. Huts with wooden ladders stood on the Bombay Green with small traders conducting negotiations mounted atop sacks, their feet swinging in mid-air. Around them, bales mounted like the Alps, fluff sailing through the air like thickly falling snowflakes.

Fortunes were made overnight and Premchand, quick as always to anticipate the future, proposed a scheme where people could be persuaded to invest their new-found wealth. His idea was to expand Bombay's land by reclaiming the quantities of it that still lay submerged beneath creeks, shallows and low tides. He approached the Bombay Bank or the Presidency Chartered Bank of Bombay, as it was officially called, and charmed the whiskered men in their suits with his Elphinstone-trained turn of phrase and talk of wresting precious real estate from the sea.

Not everybody was convinced. Cowasjee Jehangir, a Parsi director in the Presidency Chartered Bank, objected to Premchand's demand for easy terms of credit. Cowasjee Jehangir belonged to the well-known Readymoney family. Born into ancestral wealth made from the opium trade, he had evolved into a modern Indian, embracing progressive British values of loyalty and civic duty. He was a notable public figure and philanthropist, funding a number of public buildings, including water fountains for thirsty wayfarers. One of his public fountains in Bombay was built in memory of 'Henry of the Municipal Council when he fell down of his buggy of a stormy night at this particular spot'. Fierce-eyed, with an unkempt moustache and sideburns and a tall turban, Cowasjee Jehangir took issue with Premchand's flashy hard sell and, when he failed to be heard, he resigned.

The juggernaut moved on. The bank gave Premchand the money. He started or inspired a rage of new companies pursuing a whole gamut of activities—land reclamation, trading, cotton cleaning, pressing and spinning, hotels, shipping and the manufacture of bricks and tiles. The *Bombay Gazetteer* records that in December 1864, there were thirty-one banks, sixteen financial associations, eight land companies, sixteen press companies and ten shipping companies.[6] The number of insurance companies had doubled over a decade (from ten in 1855 to twenty) and sixty-two joint-stock companies had sprung up where none had existed before. Shares in dodgy companies were sold at highly inflated prices. Banks prospered. The speculative mania was led by Premchand, thin, solemn-faced with a tikka on his forehead and 'worshipped ... not only by his own fraternity but by the vulgar mass who flocked like geese in the Share Market and willingly chose to be entirely guided by him'.[7] Nobody was in a mood to heed an alarm raised by the press: 'There is a gambling saturnalia going on!', it warned in 1865. 'This must end in a fearful smash, and we warn the Bombay public to beware!'[8]

The crash it warned of came with the ending of the American Civil War in 1865 and the tapering demand for cotton. On the Liverpool market, the price of cotton fell from 20 to 10 pence. The bubble broke and panic spread in Bombay as people tried to offload shares in worthless companies. By mid-May, one by one, the city's wealthy businessmen went bankrupt. The swollen, giddy money market contracted and overdue bills piled up at the Bank of Bombay. A commission was set up to inquire into the bank's failure. Dinsha E. Vachcha, in his book *A Financial Chapter in the History of Bombay City*, writes: 'Lakhs were given away on personal security ... These again were permitted to be renewed to an indefinite extent at any rate till the mischief was done irretrievably.'[9] Premchand was allowed by other shareholders and directors 'to withdraw vast amounts of money from the Bank to finance his multitudinous schemes—directly and indirectly Rs 1.38 crore ... a colossal and unheard-of advance' and also, half of the Bank of Bombay's total capital.

As the doomsayers had predicted, thousands of shareholders were wiped out and many households in Bombay teetered on the verge of ruin. The saga of the cotton boom with its magical possibilities and eventual collapse became a morality tale in the consciousness of urban India. But the phenomenon also had ramifications for people outside of cities. The alternating phenomena of enrichment and impoverishment spread like wildfire through the rural districts of western India.

One area where they percolated was the villages around the Tapi where I last left my imaginary khalasi and his neighbours, on the riverbank, praying in the Kinara Mosque in the early sixteenth century. Their descendants were Sunni Bohras, a Muslim sect of trader-agriculturists which included, on the one hand, a leading Surat-based trader like Mulla Abdul Ghafur and on the other, the indigent farmer community on the riverbank. An article in a community publication describes them in the late 1800s as 'toiling tillers, with calloused hands, and sunburnt skins, illiterate and ignorant ... a colony of poor, struggling peasants ... like hundreds of others of its kind and size throughout British India'.[10]

One imagines that much had happened to the khalasi's grand progeny over three hundred years. The spread of famine, drying out crops and spreading hunger. Disease, chronic, wasting fevers depleting bodies, hastening death. Political shifts, rulers passing the baton from one to another and extracting profits in the form of new, onerous taxes. Yet through all these vicissitudes, they continued to live their simple lives, fishing in a clear lake and cultivating their plots of land, growing, among other things, brinjals, which the Census office reported were 'soft and full of agreeable taste'.[11]

And then came the cotton mania, hitting the bucolic community like a tornado. The 'rural Bohras are not in so good a condition,' the 1877 *Gazetteer* reported. 'Many of them contracted expensive habits during the prosperous times of the American war, and have fallen into debt.'[12]

The situation created by the cotton boom seems unprecedented, for this time life did not continue as before, with the farmers surmounting adversities with stoic resignation. Something shifted permanently. What brought about the shift? What made the villagers seek to completely alter their way of life? One cannot say for sure, but what is known is that in the nineteenth century, a certain Ismail Ibrahim Turawa from Surat and a Haji Eesop Boatawala from Rander had gone to a little island called Mauritius, adrift miles off the African coast, and become successful businessmen there. Presumably they sent home news of the proliferation of Indian indentured workers on the island, of thousands of Indians needing to be fed, clothed and supplied with items of daily use. In 1877 Queen Victoria, declared Qaisar-i-Hind or Empress of India in the grand style of the Moghuls, reiterated the sentiments of her 1858 proclamation binding the Crown to 'the natives of our Indian territories by the same obligations of duty which bind us to all our other subjects'. By then indentured workers were in South Africa, the land where diamonds and gold had been discovered. A new geography of empire beckoned, or so it seems from the community's account which claims: 'To this humble and obscure community came tales of the discovery of Gold in a far-off land, at the bottom of the continent of Africa, in a country called the South African Republic which we know as the Transvaal.'[13]

Some enterprising villager must have worked it out: the price of tickets, the timing of ships from the Bombay port and a way to get to the city. Assorted unconnected elements came together—dismal economic prospects, a feeling of belonging to an empire, spare cash from the cotton mania, profits jingling in threadbare pockets. A long-abandoned memory of the sea and distant lands was triggered. Something stirred the depths, bringing to surface an impulse, old and long-forgotten. 'Attracted by the lure of adventure and wealth, and the chance of making a new life in an unknown land,' continues the author of the community account, 'a number of energetic and adventurous young men set sail braving the open sea'.[14]

An inherited rhythm of the ocean, an awakened restlessness hit the progeny of the khalasi and once loosened, these tremors surged through the medieval villages and were impossible to hold back.

Young men sliced up kerosene tins and hammered and nailed them to make trunks. They threw their meagre belongings into them. And they left. Like waves nudging each other, swelling into a tide, moving, irresistible, they went. From villages with lilting names: Kholvad, Kathor, Barbodhan, Lajpur, Navsari, from all around the Tapi. Some went to Mauritius, some to Natal or the Transvaal. One after another they flung themselves into an unknown future starting with a 'treacherous sea voyage'. They were 'passenger Indians', the term that would emerge to describe migrants who travelled outside of official arrangements between Indian and overseas governments, who left voluntarily, at their own expense. 'Illiterate and ignorant' youths, from a 'humble and obscure community' left by the thousands starting in the mid-nineteenth century to establish new communities in faraway lands, just as their ancestors had done many lifetimes ago.

Surat is a three-hour train ride out of Mumbai. On my way to a more distant town, I have often caught a glimpse through the window of its neon hotel signs haloed by dust and exhaust fumes, a dispiriting sight, which aligns with its reputation as a dynamic small-scale manufacturing centre. Thousands of migrant workers from other parts of the country live and work in its dingy workshops, many of them for the diamond-processing industry of which Surat is a hub: over half of all diamonds hewed out of mines in Australia, the Democratic Republic of Congo, Botswana, Russia and South Africa in a given year are cut and polished here, doubling their value in the world market.

I walk around the old city in Surat and find it hard to tell that this was once a great port or the place where the British established their first significant foothold on Indian soil. Across the road from the fort is a library built in 1850 by a pearl dealer, Rao Bahadur Naginchand Jhaveri. Somewhere close by, amidst a snarl of two-wheelers and smoke, is a Moghul-era building housing the Surat Municipal Corporation and an 80-foot clock tower donated by a Parsi philanthropist. Of the erstwhile English Company's factory there is no sign; there has not been for a while, for Henry George Briggs, looking for it while writing his *Cities of Gujarashtra* in 1847, claimed it had disintegrated into a 'noble pile'.

An air of slow decrepitude hangs over the old markets where I come across fruit stalls, heaps of plastic boxes, cheap clothes leaning against a sagging wall and a cage of parrots dangling on a small dirty porch. Lanes and public squares, misshaped by clumsy efforts to meet the requirements of new traffic, lead to residential spaces where mossy art deco façades are interspersed with small temples, bejewelled deities glimmering in their dark recesses. I pass parked two-wheelers, a drainpipe with a shredded kite and a board with a newly painted sign for 'Happyy Men's Tailors' above a bright, tube-lit basement.

The Lakhpati Hospital extension is a two-storeyed block of concrete punctuated by windows with horizontal grilles. A banner hanging on a gate at ground level offers a toll-free number for a dengue or malaria test. Another has a slogan above an image of a finger pressing a button: 'Your Vote is the Life of Democracy'. Two closed white jeeps with a red stripe on the sides and an ambulance light on the roof are parked outside the entrance. Clothes dry on a balcony. A street sign says Muglisara, Ward 13. This was where the Killavala house stood before the municipal corporation requisitioned the plot for a hospital extension. It was a large house, one, maybe two, storeys high, and straddling the space between two lanes. My ancestor Gangadas who worked at the fort had a son, Nandkor, and a daughter, Alka. Nandkor had two sons, Rangildas and Parmanandas. Parmanandas was married to Gangaben and they had three sons, Dahyalal, Chhaganlal and the youngest, my great-grandfather, Mohanlal.

Nobody can tell me when the Killavalas moved to Bombay, but it was probably in the early part of the nineteenth century, long before Mohanlal's birth which, according to documents I discover in the course of my research, was in Bombay in or around the year 1880. Tarunika, who grew up in the house next door to them in Surat and married Mohanlal's nephew, claims that they retained strong links to their hometown long after they moved, visiting several times a year including over long summers and at festivals.

Nanavat was still a neighbourhood of genteel vanias then, though its celebrities were no longer bankers and nagarsheths but cotton, sugar and pearl merchants, piece-goods dealers and men like Maganlal Prabhalal Desai, a teacher much admired for his fluency in English, and Tansukhlal 'Master', author of a well-known mathematics textbook. The necessity of a modern education for jobs had rapidly increased with the introduction of standardized weights and measures and the beginning of the post and railways motivating wealthy Surtis to fund schools and colleges.

Gujarati society was shaken up by Narmad and his fellow reformers but continued with its old ways, unwilling to surrender its long-preserved social norms without a fight. In other ways, change was visible, for Surat's elite had learnt to embrace new values such as loyalty and citizenship with guidance from the British. In his study of Surat's public culture, Douglas Haynes draws a vivid picture of Moghul style durbars and celebrations organized by the civic authorities in which the elite sat 'silently in their positions of privilege, with a solemnity befitting the occasion and their personal status, perhaps shaking the collector's hand at the event's end'.[14] They accepted awards for community service from the administration with extreme deference. As a recipient of a Rao Bahadurship said in 1894:

... the benign British government, which has been graciously pleased in recognition of my humble services to confer on me the distinction ... I shall not be so ungrateful as to believe or to let it be understood that I could have performed one-tenth of the work that fell to my lot had I not received support and encouragement from my immediate superiors and the appreciation and commendation of Government from time to time.[15]

As a child, visiting his ancestral town from Bombay, my great-grandfather Mohanlal would have witnessed a people in love with Empire. He would have seen crowds throng railway stations to welcome visiting governors and viceroys, and banners proclaiming 'Long Live Emperor Edward VII' and 'God Save the King'. He might have been in Surat in 1900 when Nawab Mir Muzaffar Hussein Khan organized an event to mark a British gain in the Anglo-Boer War in South Africa. City notables attended and gave speeches, each of which, the *Gujarat Mitra* newspaper reported, 'breathed a spirit of intense loyalty to the crown of Her Gracious Majesty.'

At Shahpore, the Parsi General Hospital sits fatly on the road, its peeling yellow walls resembling a lemon sponge cake. Men sporting the traditional Parsi cap work at a long table in the Parsi Panchayat office across the road, managing the affairs of Surat's large Parsi population. Mohanlal would have heard of Rustomjee Jiwanji Ghorkhodu, who went as a seventeen-year-old in 1878 to Natal to work in an aerated-water company and became a leading businessman, known as Parsi Rustomjee. On his frequent arrivals and departures, Mohanlal would also have seen the Turawa Mosque opposite the railway station and noted that it was built by a businessman who made his fortune in Mauritius. It is likely that he also knew of the other Mauritius businessman, Haji Eesop Boatawala, who funded a scholarship for students.

The exodus from the villages around Surat had entered public consciousness. Magazines tailored subscriptions for overseas readers and the term 'Natal' entered the Gujarati vocabulary as a generic term for a foreign place. Mohanlal would have known of the traffic of Sunni Bohra Muslims headed overseas. And, as a modern young man, he would certainly have followed with interest the fervid discussion sparked off by Karsandas Mulji's essay 'Deshatan' on the necessity of permitting foreign travel for Gujarati Hindus.

He would have heard of a few high-caste Hindus of his generation venturing abroad. Chimanlal Chabildas Chinai, a dealer in precious metals, a Hindu from the Dasha Porwad vania community, had gone to work as a clerk for an Indian in South Africa in the late 1800s.[16] And then there was an advocate, London-trained no less, called Mohandas Karamchand Gandhi, who had gone to South Africa and was complaining about the unfair treatment of Indians by the British in their overseas colony.

Mohanlal might have read Gandhi's petitions, reproduced in leading newspapers like *The Times of India*. He may even have heard him speak in perfect English, like an English lawyer, in fact, and dressed like one too, on a visit to Bombay in 1901. And perhaps he knew that the dynamic young lawyer was encouraging young educated men to travel to South Africa to avail of opportunities and be of service to the Indian community.

Perhaps all these played on his mind.

5

Urbs Prima Indis

Bombay's native town had come up north of the fortified city. It was carved out of the swamp, and names of neighbourhoods indicated their recent pastoral state: Umarkhadi (fig tree creek), Pydhoni (foot-wash creek), Girgaum (hill village) and Khetwadi (place of fields). Amidst paddy fields and ponds, houses with long sloping roofs were transplanted from the Marathi-speaking hinterland, interspersed with the more ornate wooden façades of Gujarati houses. For a long time after the British acquired the islands from the Portuguese, this nascent habitation was a place of comings and goings, of trials and adaptation. In Narmad's autobiography, he writes about living alongside other transients from Surat while visiting his father. It was in this milieu that they heard about the great fire of 1837. Someone came running to break the news that 'all Surat has burnt down'.[1] The men were away at work, but women and children huddled and discussed the calamity in hushed whispers.

A great white mosque, a cotton exchange and a huge covered textile market marked the beginning of native town. The old Indian Ocean trade had revived and spread out after Surat's decline to smaller ports like Mandvi, Porbandar and Dwarka on the Gujarat coast and to Bombay, which grew every day in importance, particularly after the opening of the Suez Canal in 1869 that cut travel time to Europe by half. Indians had adapted to their changed circumstances and developed new commodities. Pearls bred in fisheries in the Arabian Sea by Bhatia and Khoja businessmen in Muscat and Bahrain went to Bombay en route to Europe, where they were in high demand after the Paris Exposition of 1878.[2] Textiles, spices, ropes, sugar, alum, chemical and herbal substances, ghee, tobacco, iron and lead also went overseas from Bombay while dates, coconuts, ivory, cloves and nutmeg travelled into the hinterland. In between were wholesale bazaars and warehouses (known in Anglo-Indian parlance as 'godowns'). There, according to the city's biographer, Gillian Tindall, the 'real life of Bombay' was lived, where 'samples of raw cotton or opium or silk or ivory or inlay-work were passed from hand to hand, on wharves—and, most of all, in the yards of the shipbuilders, from which vessels of Malabar teak went out all over the world'.[3]

A hero in this commercial world was Premchand Roychand. The man who had sunk a million hopes with reckless speculation had salvaged his reputation after the great fall. He had made good on his debts and earned respect for his philanthropic work, which was mainly in the field of education. His nemesis, Sir Cowasjee Jehangir, was also interested in education. In 1864, Cowasjee Jehangir had donated a sum of Rs 100,000 to build a permanent structure to house the University of Bombay, relocating it from the town hall. Premchand had followed up with a donation that was twice as large. And then, almost as a casual afterthought, he added another Rs 200,000 for the 'erection of a Tower to contain a large clock and a set of joy bells'.[4]

On the last Friday of February 1880, the who's who of Bombay gathered at the university buildings on the Esplanade for the inauguration of the new university library. The bony, fiercely whiskered governor and chancellor, Sir Richard Temple, Indian philanthropists in their high turbans, grave-faced scholars and civil servants in suits. Hindus rubbed shoulders with Europeans and Parsis and many women were present as well, resplendent in satins and silk. The sea murmured its presence 200 hundred metres away, past a long line of palm trees and an open maidan. Guests milled about enjoying the mild winter air and illuminations mounted at a cost of Rs 4,000, exclaiming as a sudden strong wind sent dhotis and saris flapping and butty-wallas racing to relight lamps. The invitation described the event as a 'conversazione',[5] suggesting that the august gathering had a responsibility to participate in a ritual that sought to match the city's burgeoning prosperity with the refinement of culture.

Around the university, magnificent stone buildings rose up against the clear darkening sky. In Venetian Gothic and Indo-Saracenic styles, ornamented with gable roofs, cusped window arches and domed corner towers, they housed the High Court, the Secretariat, the Central Telegraph Office and the Municipal Corporation. A kilometre away, the headquarters of the Great Indian Peninsular Railway, a monumental Gothic-revival style structure replicating London's St. Pancras station, was taking shape. Profits from the cotton mania had enabled the former governor, Sir Bartle Frere, to embark on a city-building spree that made Bombay the grandest city of the empire, a close replica of London and deserving of the title Urbs Prima Indis, the primary city in India.

On that windy evening in 1880, Bombay's clever and beautiful people basked in the munificence of their city fathers. They cast their admiring gaze skywards, relishing the glow on stained-glass windows prepared in the studio of Messrs Heaton, Butler & Bayne of London and felt pride at the soaring quality of the tower above them, of a height 'sufficient to make the largest and tallest buildings around look very pigmy structures'.[6] On the columns they saw the corbelled heads of Homer and Shakespeare and in niches cut into the pillars, Porbandar stone figures of various types of local men: 'the mild Hindu, the shrewd Kutchi ... a sleek high-caste Brahmin, a Maratha, a Kathiawari ...'⁷ The library building and tower and the convocation hall completed earlier had been designed by the acclaimed architect Sir Gilbert Scott who had never been to India, and his vision (more suited to a 'western college chapel' as the historian G.W. Forrest pointed out), was 'as exotic as the system of education which we have introduced into the land'.⁸

In the 1840s, the colonial administration planned new docks to deal with expanded trade and the traffic of coastal steamers that started in 1866. A map of the city in the 1880s shows a heavily reclaimed eastern foreshore north of the esplanade sprinkled with wet docks. A railway station came up at Ballard Pier. Like the Great Western Hotel recommended in *Murray's Guide* for its 'large, airy rooms', hotels and boarding houses sprang up opposite the dock walls. About 3 kilometres west, between the emerging labour area and the docks, was the red-light area of Kamathipura. Further north were the new suburbs of the white and native elite. Somewhere west of Prince's Dock, at its northern edge, was a neighbourhood that came to be known as Sandhurst Road after William Mansfield, 1ˢᵗ Viscount Sandhurst, governor of Bombay between 1895 and 1900. I do not know what it was called before then, but it was where the Killavalas had their Bombay home.

Memories have faded and nobody can tell me what Mohanlal's father Parmanandas did for a living and when he died. I assume, though, that according to the custom of the time the household was a multi-generational one with elders, parents, unmarried daughters, sons—both married and single—and their families living under one roof. One of Mohanlal's brothers was a registrar in the Old Customs

House in Ballard Pier. Known then as the Fort Custom House, this was an old two-storeyed building next to the town hall. It housed the Imperial Opium Department, the Office of the Collector of Customs and the Commissioner of Customs, Salt, Appeal and Abkari, a King's warehouse for storing gold seized by the Customs Department and the Coast Guard service.

They appear to have been a family of modest but comfortable means. In a travel document I come across, Mohanlal claimed: 'I have immovable property at Surat - India. I have accounts in the Natal Government Savings Bank, Bank of Bombay and Government Savings Bank Bombay.' He also referred to a deposit in the Goolam Baba Spinning and Weaving Co. Ltd., Bombay. This was one of the many mechanized mills that had sprung up in western India in the mid-nineteenth century and it was a common practice for the Gujarati middle class to park its savings as small investments in these mills.

A late nineteenth-century photograph shows Sandhurst Road to be a wide road with a round temple in the centre and buildings on either side. According to its chroniclers, in the 1870s, British metropolitanism was imported into Bombay complete with water pipes, gas pipes, paving authorities, sewage disposal authorities, tramlines, parks and apartment blocks. I notice that modern buildings are interspersed with galleried wooden tenements and a tram runs through the centre. This was probably where my great grandfather was born.

Let me picture him, say at age ten, small, dark-eyed, curious. The lanes around Sandhurst Road led into the heart of native town. Whole lanes of printing presses going clank-clank-clank, shops with wide awnings and counting houses where mehtas or clerks pored over account books and the Bhat Bazaar where rice market wholesalers sat in shops divided horizontally by wooden partitions.[9] Young Mohanlal absorbing the sights and sounds of native town, genuflecting as he passed temples on his way to school, stopping to sip water trickling from a stone-faced cow at a fountain, the water splashing cool on his warm skin. At night in the family home in a high-galleried tenement he heard the groan of dredgers wresting land from the sea and the rumble of trains on their way to distant places.

Native town was where the Killavalas lived, but it seems to me that as a genteel family, belonging to the upper echelons of a caste-based social hierarchy, they had placed their future aspirations not on the old vania ways of dhandho or business but on modern education and service. The matriculate examination, which the Killavala children had passed, tested for proficiency in English, Indian languages, mathematics and general knowledge and was a reasonably good level of education by the norms of the time. The examination was conducted by the University of Bombay in big open halls with students sitting singly in long rows of chairs.

According to the same travel document, Mohanlal had chosen to acquire a professional qualification after matriculation, passing the 'London Accountants' Examination' in Bombay. He married early, as was the custom in his time. His bride was sallow skinned, sharp-featured and small-built. He was well-qualified and a foreseeable future for him lay south of native town, in the evolving banking centre in the Fort where a magnificent, new three-tiered fountain sculpted from Portland stone played amidst flat-faced stone buildings housing half a dozen international banks and a few nationalist banks appealing to an Indian clientele.

Bombay had become one of the most important financial centres in the east, rivalling Hong Kong, Tokyo and Shanghai and in 1875, a stock exchange, a European version of the trading group under the banyan tree, the first in India, had opened in Dalal Street in the Fort area. Mohanlal could have earned the princely sum of Rs 300 a month as an assistant accountant. So why did he choose a path that was so unpredictable, so laden with risk, so different from the safe path that conceivably lay before him?

When I look at sepia-toned pictures of old Bombay and read its history, I am struck by two contradictory sensations. One emanates from a perception of contrast, of how ant-like the humans dressed in their native fashions appear against the backdrop of massive, magnificent colonial buildings. Another is a feeling of chutzpah emanating from those same ant-like figures. Bombay provided the space for resourceful and enterprising Indians like Jamsetjee Jeejeebhoy and Premchand Roychand to thrive. A native who felt diminished by colonial rule would not be stopped from throwing a punch on his own behalf in this maverick city that was markedly different from other colonial cities in its liberal attitudes and its easy, thriving cosmopolitanism, a legacy perhaps of Aungier's promise of openness and religious tolerance.

In 1903, proof of the absolute limitlessness of possibility emerged in the shape of the Taj Mahal Palace, a new hotel built by the sea. The story goes that an Indian, a wealthy Parsi called Jamsetji Nusserwanji Tata, was refused entry into Watson's Hotel, then the finest hotel in town. Humiliated by its 'Europeans Only' policy, Tata swore to avenge the insult by building a classy hotel that would be open to all. The establishment he planned was swankier than anything Bombay had ever seen, the most fabulous hotel built on Indian soil. It would have air-conditioned rooms, its own electric laundry, Turkish baths, a post office, chemist and a resident doctor. And then there was the look, a confection of domes and arched balconies in yellow basalt mixing Florentine, Oriental and Moorish styles. Right there on the seafront, by the old harbour which for many years had provided visitors with their first glimpse of the city, there stood a palace-like fantasy given form to by a local brown man.

Did Mohanlal feel torn by the contradictory pull of diminution and possibility? Did it fuel a discontentment with a life that by ordinary standards was promising? He was a respectable member of his social class. He was part of a reputable family. He had a wife and could look forward to children. But perhaps Mohanlal was not like other people. Perhaps in his safe cocoon he heard another strain, like this one, an ode written by A.C. Benson, a schoolmaster turned don for the coronation of King Edward VII in 1902, which, accompanied by Elgar's brilliantly rousing music, was the transcendent anthem of Empire:

> *Land of Hope and Glory, Mother of the Free,*
> *How shall we extol thee, who are born of thee?*
> *Wider still and wider, shall thy bounds be set;*
> *God who made thee mighty, make thee mightier yet.*[10]

Perhaps Mohanlal, unlike his peers who were content in a web of family and caste affiliations, thought of himself more as a proud subject of a great empire, one that at the turn of the twentieth century was spread over one-fourth of the globe, 31 million square kilometres out of a habitable total of 155 million and comprising Australia, New Zealand, South Africa, Canada, India, Ceylon, Aden, Mauritius, the Seychelles, Gibraltar, Malta, Cyprus, Nigeria, the Gold Coast, the Gambia, Sierra Leone, the Anglo-Egyptian Sudan, British Somaliland, the East Africa Protectorate (Kenya), Uganda, Nyasaland, Rhodesia, Bechuanaland, Basutoland, Swaziland, Hong Kong, Malaya, Burma, Singapore, and parts of Borneo, Fiji, the Gilbert and Ellice Islands, the Solomons, Jamaica, Trinidad, British Guiana, British Honduras, the Leewards and Windwards, the Bahamas and Bermuda.

Deep sea cables linked London with Bombay, Melbourne and Wellington. A standard postal rate of 1 penny or 2 cents was proposed and accepted between all parts of the empire. Telegraphs, submarine cables and steamships, which Macaulay thought were among the greatest civilizing forces, had provided a new logic to the concept of overseas dominion. Writes Jan Morris in *Pax Britannica*: 'Suddenly the world seemed smaller, more manageable, and the notion of a political unity scattered across all the seas, and through all the continents, seemed to make new sense.'[11] And if the colonizers believed that the vast, variegated world had shrunk under their benevolent gaze, could Indians not also have shared their perception?

The world was shrinking. A new religion called theosophy, founded in the United States, was becoming popular among the Bombay cognoscenti. In the pages of newspapers, in the *Bombay Gazette* in July 1904, squeezed between reports on the christening ceremony of the Viceroy Lord Curzon's daughter and the Russo-Japanese War and advertisements for Ithaca clocks, ices, cakes and sweets from Mongini Bros., I find announcements of imminent departures: French mail steamers leaving for Marseilles and Australia and a German East Africa line to Africa on 1 July; four days later, the 1,200-ton SS *Dwarka* leaving for 'Kurrachee direct' and another steamer of similar tonnage heading for the Seychelles, Mombasa, Zanzibar, Beira and Delagoa Bay. In the first decade of the 1900s, more than 12,000 free or non-indentured migrants left Bombay for East Africa and 30,000 'non-labour' immigrants landed in Malaya.[12] And Mohanlal left for South Africa. Or so goes the family legend. Nobody knows when he went, or why or even what he did there.

The fare for a ticket from Bombay to Durban at the time was Rs 90 for a deck passage without food,[13] a considerable sum which suggests some preparation, kept hidden it seems from the family because his niece, recalling what she has heard, believes that Mohanlal's decision to leave was sudden and caused a great deal of consternation. I imagine family elders remonstrating with him and anxiously discussing the potential repercussions from the *nath* or the caste brethren. Then there was Mohanlal's wife, probably a young girl in her teens at the time, sobbing and fearful about what the absence would mean and whether he would ever return.

Undaunted by the kerfuffle and probably believing that he would be forgiven, as Indian families always forgave wayward sons, Mohanlal persisted. And presumably he was sent off with a flurry of rituals, taking a horse buggy from home and heading for Ballard Pier from where the steamers left. I assume he was accompanied by his brothers or a friend or two. There they go, the young Gujarati vania men, vending their way through the crowded pier. There are passengers everywhere. Men in dhotis and jackets dangle long black umbrellas from their wrists and collars and women in the traditional nine-yard Maharashtrian sari with gajras in their hair patiently wait for a boat to their village. There are porters accompanying white sahibs and memsahibs fanning themselves.

Mohanlal and his companions make their way through the crush, avoiding the insistent call of hawkers. Mohanlal leans his elbows on the ship rails. Whistle and bells ring out, the ship hoots and with a jerk, it begins to move. He sees his farewell party waving. He waves back. The figures become smaller and blurry. For a few minutes his view is obscured by large parked steamers and when he catches sight of the harbour again, it has merged with its environment and all he sees is a flank of land. The hubbub in his ears and heart ceases till there is only the throb of the engine underfoot. Seagulls float above. He turns around and looks out at the wide blue open.

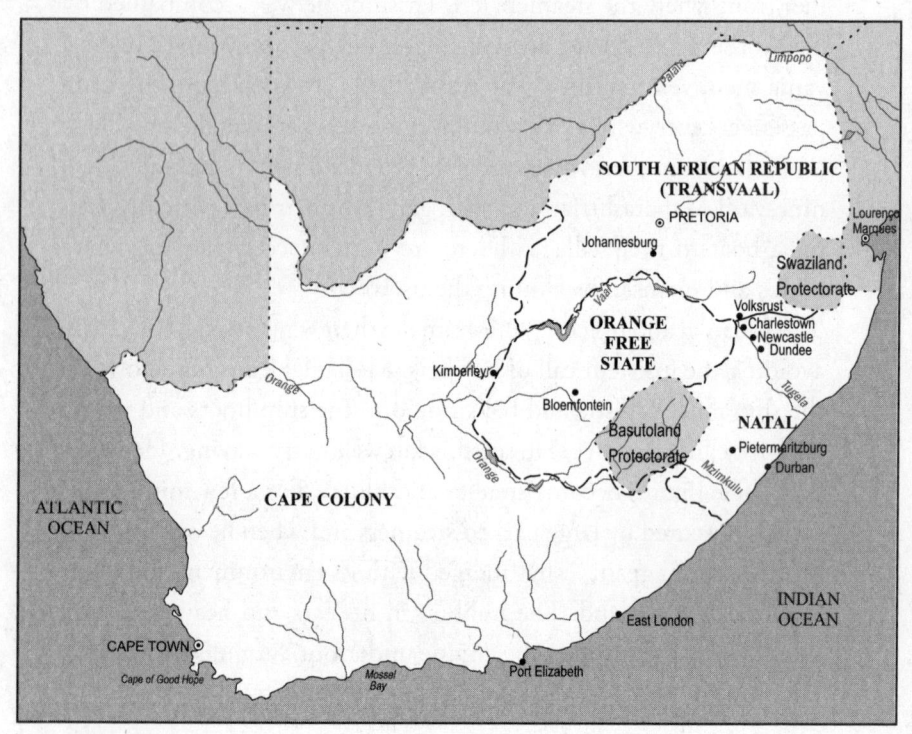

Southern Africa at the turn of the twentieth century

PART TWO

THE TRAIL

6

Table Mountain

From the top of Table Mountain, the sea appears deceptively calm. Ant-sized hikers move up the slope. Every few minutes, a cable car arrives at the summit, releasing a fresh burst of tourists—a chattering mass brandishing tripods and flashing cell phones, excited to explore one of the world's great natural wonders. I share their excitement, the surreal feeling of entering a picture frame and the moment of surprise at encountering the real thing. I am unprepared for its materiality, its width, for instance, customarily flattened out in postcards, the dips and curves on its pictorially level surface and the revelation of the two thousand-plus species of flora blossoming on its craggy sides. And then there is the cableway, a marvel of technology upgraded three times since its installation in 1929. The latest version, a Rotair cableway, was installed by a Swiss company in 1997, the car ascending up to a point over 1,000 metres above sea level in a matter of minutes, suspended on strong double cables, the cliff sides flashing past the windows of the capsule fitted with a rotating floor.

I wander alongside the aimless tourists. Everywhere the grey sea confronts us, still and deep. Many incorrectly believe that this is the southernmost point of the African continent; the tip is not here but

160-odd kilometres to the east. There the sharp cold Atlantic meets the warm eager waters of the Indian Ocean. Directly below us, long rocky strips of land protrude into the water. I lean forward into the gusting wind. Early Europeans were oblivious to the existence of the Indian Ocean and thought of their seas as an enclosed space;[1] later, the Cape was thought to be insurmountable. But in 1488 Bartolomeu Dias broke through the barrier. Sailing from Lisbon, following the limestone markers planted along the coast by his fellow sailors, the Portuguese explorer braved rocks, raging winds and mammoth 30-metre-high rogue waves to travel further east than his predecessors. He, rather than da Gama, could have been the first Westerner to cross the Indian Ocean. But his crew was tired and impatient to be home and Dias agreed to turn back from Mossel Bay. As he returned, Dias noted the challenging Cape, which he had conquered not once but twice now and conferred upon it the name 'Cabo das Tormentas' (Cape of Storms).

Some tourist guides say that Bartolomeu Dias's ghost lurks on those rocks. What does he seek, I wonder. When Dias returned home from his landmark achievement, the Portuguese King John II decided to rename the Cape, rejecting Dias's gloomy choice in favour of the more upbeat 'Cabo da Boa Esperança' (Cape of Good Hope). I remember being confused by the two names as a child and not being able to work out that they referred to the same place. I wonder if it was also a precocious recognition of the schizophrenic nature of the phenomenon. The crossing of the Cape by Dias might have been a cause for elation and hope for the Western world, but for a sizeable section of the world's population living beyond it, the discovery was an intimation of tormentas.

Africans call Table Mountain 'Hoerikwaggo' (Mountain in the Sea), and it does seem to rise in all its smouldering glory right out of the ocean, a smoky iceberg visible for miles around. Rocks painted by Bushmen thousands of years ago show images of the eland and the twirly-horned kudu, figures dancing at harvest, and a twilight world of shamans and spirits. Nomadic people moved through the searing African landscape and lions ranged the slopes of Table Mountain. Europeans, with their sights set firmly on the spice-rich islands of Indonesia and the trading centres of India, sailed by this idyllic wilderness without stopping. Only the Dutch East India Company used it as a way station for its ships, which were supplied with vegetables and wine by a few migrants who had settled there, a motley mix of Dutch, Germans and French Huguenots assisted by Indian and Malay slaves working lands usurped from the local Khoikhoi. A hundred and fifty years later, the sleepy way station came to the attention of the British. Concerned that the Cape, strategically positioned between Europe and Asia, would fall into French hands, the naval power ousted the Dutch and made it a British colony in 1814.

Almost 3,500 British men and women landed up at the Cape in the early months of 1820, turning the open beach of Algoa Bay into a tent city. Since the sixteenth century, influential Englishmen such as Walter Raleigh and his half-brother Humphrey Gilbert had been arguing for colonies as a solution to Britain's problems of overpopulation and shrinking economic opportunities. Richard Hakluyt wrote *Discourse of Western Planting* in 1584, the first manifesto of English imperialism overseas. The idea, however, was not well received until the turn of the nineteenth century when a sudden snowballing of the British population forced an urgent rethink. Government officials, philanthropists and church parishes came together to facilitate the transportation of British settlers to Canada, New Zealand and Australia. Some colonies were retained as penitentiaries for convicts to ease the lack of space in English prisons. India, with its scorching heat, was thought to be unsuitable for white settlers but the Cape, with its temperate weather conditions, was considered ideal.

Thomas Pringle, a poet and one of the 'Eighteen-Twenty Settlers', described the arrivals as:

> respectable tradesmen and jolly farmers, with every appearance of substance and snug English comfort about them ... watermen, fishermen, and sailors from the Thames and the English seaports, with the reckless and weather-beaten look usual in persons of their professions ... pale-visaged artisans and operative manufacturers from London and the large towns, of whom ... a proportion were squalid in their aspect, slovenly in their attire, and discourteous in their demeanour ... parties of pauper agricultural labourers sent out by the aid of their parishes, healthier perhaps than the class just mentioned, but not apparently happier in mind.[2]

British arrivals spread fear among descendants of the original European settlers who lived on the rural outskirts of Cape Town. The 'Boers' as they were called were sober, highly religious, fiercely independent, slave-owning farmers. Convinced that the British with their liberal ideas about slave emancipation would adversely affect their freedom, they piled their meagre belongings onto ox wagons and took off into the interior, a journey over hundreds of miles that would later be commemorated as De Grote Trek ('the Great Trek').

The proliferating white settlers were brought into bitter conflict with the Khoikhoi and other natives of the land among whom were the reclusive Bushmen who still lingered in the dry scrub of the Western Cape and the formidable Bantu Africans of the Xhosa tribe. The latter were a tall, strong people, deep brown or black-skinned, wearing girdles of ox tails and copper anklets, and carrying spears of hammered iron. They thrived in the savannahs, following game herd and cattle pasture in the dry uplands of thorn-scrub and sparse trees where there were no lakes or navigable rivers and only rare patches of forest. During the eighteenth century, Bantu tribes drifted southwards and organized themselves into regiments (impis) carrying short stabbing spears (assegais) under the leadership of Shaka, king of the Amazulu.

The story goes that Shaka gifted the bay of Natal, about a thousand kilometres east of the Cape, to a group of British traders. The latter made repeated efforts to win recognition from the British authorities for its small camp but failed until a local commando of Boers besieged the little British garrison and threatened to set up its own base on the coast. Most of the Boers who trekked from the Cape had settled in the Highveld across the Orange River to the north, in an area which came to be known as the Orange Free State, and to the west in the grasslands around the Vaal River, which came to be known as the Zuid-Afrikaansche Republiek or, more commonly, the Transvaal. A few Boers, however, had trickled into the coastal hills below the escarpment of the Drakensberg and formed the Republic of Natalia with its capital at Pietermaritzburg. Their attempt to move seawards alarmed the British government in Cape Town, which dispatched a small force and chased them away. A few stayed behind, but the Republic of Natalia dwindled and disintegrated. The British claimed Durban and annexed Natal in 1843, making it first a dependency of the Cape and then a separate colony in 1856 with a partly elected legislative council. In 1887, they expanded their hold over neighbouring Zululand.

The eastern portion of the Great Escarpment, the Drakensberg, enclosed the central Southern African plateau. The highest peaks, banked by thick clouds, were over 3,000 metres high and gave way to the velvet-green plateaux of the midlands, gently descending to the coast with its surf-laced waters. Natal's slopes, watered by the Tugela and the Mzimkulu rivers, were extremely fertile. The British takeover brought a stream of entrepreneurs from the Cape Colony who tried to grow cotton along the Mdhloti river, north of

Durban. The attempt failed and much of their land was acquired by a heavyset, florid, smooth-talking Irish developer called Joseph Charles Byrne. Byrne's advertisements for 'new Natal and its wooded hills and grassy plains, its swarming game and its benign climate' and his offer of a 20-acre freehold plot and steerage for the six-week voyage at a cost of £10 attracted 2,500 English and Scottish emigrants who arrived on twenty ships between 1849 and 1851.[3]

A part of the former Crown lands was also acquired by William Jonah Irons, a Wesleyan Methodist and proponent of the Christian Emigration and Colonisation Society. Inspired by a lofty vision, he founded a town on a hill overlooking a marsh 30 kilometres north of Durban, like his own city, St. Albans outside London, and named it Verulam, as in 'Verulamium', the name of the pre-Roman and Romano-British town which preceded St. Albans.[4] In this way, in an African landscape teeming with wildlife, elephants, lions, leopards and pythons and scattered with grasslands and native kraals, a European-style town emerged.

The new settlers experimented unsuccessfully with tobacco, coffee and arrowroot. In 1849, a local farmer successfully planted sugarcane with the help of four Indian workers from Mauritius. Sugarcane was labour-intensive, but the settlers were unwilling to do the farming themselves and believed the native African population to be unsuited to daily farm work. They considered other options for sourcing labour, such as bringing over destitute English orphans, freed slaves from America, Chinese workers and so on. The decision eventually swung in favour of indentured workers from India, 'coolies' as they were called, and the first batch of 340 Indians, men, women and children, arrived in Natal in mid-November 1860, on a ship called the *Truro*.

The event was covered by the man who was to become Natal's first elected prime minister, John Robinson, then a reporter working for his father's newspaper, the *Natal Mercury*. Robinson wrote about swarthy hordes ... pouring out of the boat's hold, laughing, jabbering and staring about them with a very well-satisfied expression of self-complacency on their faces ... A queer comical, foreign-looking, very Oriental-like crowd. The men with their huge Muslim turbans, bare scraggy shin bones, and coloured garments; the women with their flashing eyes, long dishevelled pitchy hair, with their half-covered, well-formed figures, and their keen, inquisitive glances; the children with their meagre, intelligent, cute and humorous countenances mounted on bodies of inconceivable fragility, were all evidently ... of a different race and kind to any we have yet seen.[5]

7

Cecil Rhodes

In 1870, a seventeen-year-old boy from Hertfordshire came to Natal, hoping that its milder climes would provide relief from his chronic asthma. Cecil Rhodes, the fifth son of an Anglican clergyman, had an older brother who was already in Natal growing cotton, but when he arrived, he found his sibling had left for the scrubland bordering the Cape where a rich deposit of diamonds had been discovered. Soon after, Rhodes too made his way to the semi-arid wilderness at the confluence of the Orange and Vaal rivers.

A few years prior to his arrival, a Boer farmer had found a child playing with a sparkling pebble, the first of the accidental discoveries that sparked off a rush. Boers were not interested in mining and found the business of speculation antithetical to their puritanical ideals. But prospectors turned up from England, Germany and France, and in October 1871 the British took over the diamond fields and named the territory in which they were located 'Kimberley', after the British colonial secretary, Lord Kimberley. Rhodes used the £2,000 he had been gifted by an aunt, and his brother's claims, to begin work. 'I found a 17 ⅝ carats on Saturday, it was very slightly off, and I hope to get £100 for it … Yesterday I found a 3 ½ perfect stone, but glassy, which I sold for £30. I find on average 30 carats a week,'[1] he wrote in a letter to his mother in his early days.

The names of Boer farms—De Beers, Dutoitspan and Bulfontein—circulated in newspapers, but the main site of exploration was the Colesberg Kopje, a small hill 30 feet high and spread over 180 by 220 square yards on flat, level country. Diggers swarmed over it like ants, whittling away till the mound became a crater. Deeper and deeper they dug. The partitions between pits, separately mined, collapsed. Often a cart loaded with excavated mud tipped over, taking mules and driver with it. Photographs reveal an upside-down vision of a hellish metropolis strung with filaments of rope and insect-like figures gouging out a vast, cavernous pit in the scrubland.

Around the 'Big Hole' a tent city emerged. In a scorching, dust-blown landscape, a rudimentary township with boarding houses and street names took shape. Bushmen, Korana, Griqua, Matabele, Batembu and other tribesmen swarmed the makeshift city. Africans were not allowed to mine for themselves but they came to work at the digs to earn money to pay colonial taxes or to buy weapons on behalf of their tribes. Workers earned a little and left and were replaced by others, a constant stream of cheap labour.

Life was hard in the remote spot with no source of fresh produce or drinking water at hand and bare essentials in short supply. Like Africans, it appears likely that Indians were not permitted to buy claims, but they arrived to supply ancillary services. In the 1880s there were 700 to 1,000 Indians in the diamond fields. The first to get there were ex-indentured or 'free' Indians, including, possibly, the men brought from Mauritius to teach local farmers how to grow sugarcane; others were passenger Indians who came from India. Amidst open-trench latrines and rotting carcasses of pack animals, they sold wine and worked as cooks and cleaners at eating houses for native Africans or 'kaffirs', as they were disparagingly called. An Indian, Sam Vincot, offered hot showers for 2 shillings and cold for 1 shilling and 6 pence at the Lanyon baths on New Main Street. Sammy Pillay (Sam/Sammy was a shortened form of the common Tamilian suffix 'swamy') supplied fruit to big mining companies from his building in Jones Street and a Naidoo family from Mauritius set up a workshop to cut diamonds.[2]

Rhodes, the clergyman's son and adolescent adventurer, prospered beyond his wildest expectations. In a place where an obsessive greed for diamonds led to high incidences of illness, death, murder and suicide, the young man kept his wits about him, digging for diamonds but also exploiting other opportunities, such as a requirement for machinery. He had a good head for business and could get along with different kinds of people. He reached out for support to the Rothschilds, the wealthy banking family which had bankrolled Britain's purchase of shares in the Suez Canal in 1875. With their backing, he came to control 90 per cent of the world's production of diamonds through his company De Beers Consolidated Mines Limited.

The unearthing of a gleaming blue seam in the wilderness around the Cape confirmed myths about the continent's abundant mineral wealth. The year 1885 saw the publication of H. Rider Haggard's *King Solomon's Mines*, a runaway bestseller about a group of adventurers trekking into the dangerously mysterious African interior in a quest for fabled treasure. And miraculously, around this time, gold was indeed detected in southern Africa.

The find was made in the Transvaal, in a barren stretch of the Highveld, 1,800 metres above sea level. The site, prone to erupting with fires in the dry winter and dribbling streams after rainfall, was christened the Witwatersrand (the ridge of white waters) by Boer farmers.[3] News of the find, potentially the largest deposit anywhere in the world, travelled quickly and sparked off a gold fever more frenzied than any previous gold rush in California, Alaska, Australia or Siberia. The Witwatersrand became the 'Rand' and a tent town, which would spawn the city of Johannesburg, sprang up on it. Sam Kemp, a mine overseer, described the sudden appearance of global fortune hunters, adventurers, seasoned speculators, itinerants and rogues in the summer of 1886 as 'the wildest, toughest human stampede the world has ever seen':

> Rich man, poor man, beggar-man, thief ... raced across the veld to Witwatersrand ... On horseback, afoot, in buckboards, and by stage the mob travelled. Plodding oxen were lashed mercilessly; human bodies were driven just as fiercely ... Every horse obtainable was purchased or stolen; stages were crowded to the boot, heavy-wheeled transports drawn by oxen were chartered. These, however, proved too slow, and during that dash I saw many men pile from the wagons and hurry on afoot. I saw, too, a human team in action. An old paralytic in Pretoria, unable to buy horses for the trip, hired two native blacks and hitched them to a buck-board. Out across the veld they went, trotting at a heartbreaking speed.[4]

Free Indians also headed there from Natal and word spread back home to India. The *Golden Jubilee Number* of the Madressa Anjuman Islamia of Kholvad describes how news of Transvaal's newly discovered gold fields spread excitement in the villages around the Tapi. Peasants who had never been further than the nearest town booked themselves passages on the *Congella*, the *Reichstag*, the *Umtata* and other steamers run by British and German shipping companies and set out on the open sea.

The widespread hysteria generated by the gold finds gave no indication of the hardships that lay ahead. The deposits lay deep underground and the process of extracting them was difficult, as vividly explained by the Chamber of Mines:

> Imagine a solid mass of rock tilted ... like a fat 1,200 page dictionary lying at an angle. The gold bearing reef would be thinner than a single page, and the amounts of gold contained therein would hardly cover a couple of commas in the entire book. It is the miner's job to bring out that single page—but his job is made harder because the 'page' has been twisted and torn by nature's forces, and pieces of it may have been thrust between other leaves of the book.[5]

Today, on the M1, a few kilometres from downtown Johannesburg, in a barren landscape marked by mine dumps and long pyramids of shimmering dust, an amusement park called Gold Reef City offers trips into a disused mine shaft at Crown Mines, which yielded a staggering 1.4 million kilogrammes of gold over ninety years until it closed in the 1970s. I don a helmet and take the elevator to Level 5 of Shaft 14. Lights offer a patchy glimpse of uneven walls and low ceilings hollowed from the innards of the earth. Rail tracks move into tunnels, which are only partially visible before they head into the darkness in a maze where one could so easily get lost. It is silent now, except for the soft footsteps of a small batch of tourists, but back in the day these gloomy passageways would have been lit by candlelight and the air would be rife with the sound of chipping and the occasional ear-shattering noise of drills.

As previously noted, the Boers were not enthusiastic about the windfall in their terrain. Paul Kruger, the deeply devout president of the Transvaal, frequently described in British accounts as uncouth, greasy-haired and reeking of tobacco, feared the dissension, misfortune and unexpected plagues which he believed would follow the discovery of gold. 'Pray to God as I am doing,' he said in 1885, 'that the curse connected with its coming may not overshadow our dear land ... for I tell you today that every ounce of gold taken from the bowels of our soil will yet have to be weighed up with rivers of tears.'[6]

Kruger, however, allowed prospectors, a large number of whom were British, to build mines. Those who laboured in the mines were mainly native African, though in later years mineworkers would be imported from China. Indians were mostly employed in ancillary jobs around the mines, though some might have worked in them as well. In the gift shop, I come across a postcard of a vintage photograph titled: 'FIRST INDIAN GOLD MINERS VILLAGE DEEP G.M. JOHANNESBURG SOUTH AFRICA, 1905'. The sepia-toned picture shows half a dozen workers—two of them turbaned, two Africans and two of indeterminate nationality—standing around a walrus-moustachioed white man in a waistcoat and a sola topee, in a tin-and-wood shack with pieces of drilling and digging equipment artfully arranged in the foreground.

◆

In 1873, Rhodes enrolled for a bachelor's degree at Oxford, the breeding ground of Britain's future politicians and policymakers. Heady jingoism was in the air. The philosopher John Ruskin, as Slade Professor of Fine Art at Oxford, had delivered his influential talks urging the need for England to form colonies 'as fast and as far as she is able, formed of her most energetic and worthiest men; seizing any piece of fruitful waste ground she can set her foot on, and there teaching her colonists that their chief virtue is … fidelity to their country'.[7] Music halls would soon resound with anti-Russian ditties and Queen Victoria would be declared Empress of India in 1877.

All these motley events coincided with Rhodes' own strong belief that the British race was 'the first race in the world and that the more of the world we inhabit the better it is for the human race'.[8]

Aware that his weak lungs and heart (he had suffered his first heart attack at twenty), could give way at any time, the idealist, who was also astonishingly rich and self-made for a man his age, composed a series of political wills. One, written in September 1877 at the age of twenty-four, set out a grandiose vision for

> the extension of British rule throughout the world ... the colonization by British subjects of all lands ... and especially the occupation by British settlers of the entire Continent of Africa, the Holy Land, the Valley of Euphrates, the Islands of Cyprus and Candia, the whole of South America, the islands of the Pacific ... the whole of the Malay archipelago, the seaboard of China and Japan, the ultimate recovery of the United States of America.[9]

His precocity was not misplaced; the time and circumstances were aligned to make someone with his overvaulting ambition and peculiar gifts not the least of which was a mystique created by his ease with tribal chiefs, a love of the rough wagon trail and striking looks—a rangy physique, a cleft chin and piercing blue eyes—inordinately successful.

In November 1884, diplomats from thirteen European states and the US gathered at the German Chancellery in Berlin for a meeting that would come to be associated with the phrase 'a Scramble for Africa'. Thirty-odd men in fine suits collected in the rococo mansion on Wilhelmstrasse. The curtains were drawn, lamps blazed and a large map of Africa hung on the wall; or so at least were the impressions of the artist who sketched this particular scene. Africa was deemed ripe for colonization. The aim of the dignitaries seated at the table was to agree on how to divide the spoils. Among the decisions taken at this Berlin Conference was supporting chartered companies with armies and funds, a green flag for buccaneering entrepreneurs like Rhodes. He became prime minister of the Cape Colony and used his chartered British South Africa Company to add 753,700 square kilometres of African territory to the British Empire. But he was not satisfied with these territorial acquisitions, setting himself another target: the extension of British control from the 'Cape to Cairo'. This goal, however—which he shared with influential figures such as former Colonial Secretary Lord Carnarvon—faced an obstacle awkwardly close to home: the Boers.

Towards the end of the twentieth century, Britain's imperial aspirations in the region were firmly impeded by the Boers who continued to control the Orange Free State and the gold-rich Transvaal, refusing Britain's offer of a Confederation and asserting their independence in various ways, including commissioning a railway line from Johannesburg to Portuguese-held Delagoa Bay to reduce the Transvaal's dependence on British ports. Acute tensions erupted in a war between Britain and the Transvaal and the Orange Free State in 1899. The British and the Boers had faced off previously in 1880-81 but this was the confrontation that came to be known as the defining Anglo-Boer War. Britian had the upper hand. It had the world's most modern army: a professional fighting force of 450,000 troops in khaki (the first time this form of camouflage was used in battle), state-of-the-art hardware (field telegraphs, automatic weapons and machine guns) and officers schooled in military strategy. But the expected easy victory proved elusive. The Boers put up a tough fight, using guerrilla tactics that drove the British to desperate measures, setting villages ablaze and locking up women and children in disease-ridden camps. After three years, the British finally prevailed and forced the Boers to submit. Rhodes did not live to savour a British victory, though, dying painfully of asphyxia in March 1902, a few months before the Treaty of Vereeniging was signed, ending the Anglo-Boer War.

◆

The first time I see the Union Buildings in South Africa's administrative capital, Pretoria, I wonder if it is a mirage. A vast, endless spread of clipped green (an English garden or a period film set?) materializing at the edge of a dreary street. And, rising from it, even more unrealistically, what looks like an English castle but somehow appears even more mammoth, looming over a steep hill. I am reminded of what Jan Morris wrote in *Pax Britannica*: 'There was something almost unreal to the scale of Rhodes ... it was shiftiness in the grand manner, as though he dealt in millions always—millions of pounds, millions of square miles, millions of people.'[10]

My apprehension of a Rhodesian personality emanating from the building is not groundless: it turns out that the Union Buildings were designed by Rhodes's protégé Herbert Baker in 1910; around the same time, incidentally, when he collaborated with Edwin Lutyens in designing a monumental red sandstone complex to house the imperial government in New Delhi. Baker came to South Africa in 1892 after completing his architectural apprenticeship in London and was sent by Rhodes on a tour of the classical sites of the Mediterranean. In planning the complex of government buildings, Baker drew on his exposure to the symmetries of Renaissance classicism and his memory of Rhodes himself. His design of a monumental colonnade puts one in mind of a well-known illustration depicting Rhodes as a lumbering Colossus, feet planted at either end of the African continent. Baker further maintained that his projecting porticoes and balconies were inspired by Rhodes's habit of taking his guests out on his porch in Cape Town to look at Table Mountain. Baker imagined that the balconies would draw ministers out of their offices to 'lift their eyes up to the surrounding hills and the vanishing distances and splendours of the high veld, from which they may gather inspiration and visions of greatness'.[11]

A closer inspection of the buildings, of their Cape Dutch detailing, suggests that they had a more complex message. If, on the one hand, they were a celebration of British triumph after one of the ugliest wars in contemporary history, they were also symbolic of a subsequent reconciliation between the two antagonists, the British and the Boers. In 1907, the Transvaal and the Orange Free State were granted self-government and in 1910, Britain amalgamated its four colonies into a Union of South Africa. A significant plank that enabled the two sides to resolve their other differences was an agreement on a white-dominated racial hierarchy. As Lord Alfred Milner, British high commissioner in South Africa, crudely put it in a private letter: 'You have only to sacrifice "the nigger" absolutely and the game is easy.'[12] Africans were excluded from negotiations, leading to the founding of the Union of South Africa, and denied political rights under its proposed Constitution.

Racial discrimination affected other people of colour, including Indians. At the turn of the twentieth century a number of laws were enacted, limiting Indians' rights of entry, free movement and commerce. This was in keeping with a similar trend in British colonies elsewhere where efforts were underway to control the proliferation and economic advance of the Indian. In South Africa, however, these efforts met with a firm and flamboyant form of resistance, due mainly to the presence of a remarkable individual, Mohandas Karamchand Gandhi.

Gandhi came to South Africa with a barrister's degree from London in the last decade of the nineteenth century. A self-professed colonist and admirer of British liberalism, he was dismayed by the racially discriminatory laws enacted against Indians and organized a resistance movement within the migrant community. In South Africa, he evolved a method of non-violent protest called Satyagraha, which hinged on the idea that the voluntary acceptance of punishment for resisting unjust laws could expose an oppressor to the error of his ways. His nascent campaign became the seed of a full-blown movement against the British Empire in India and an inspiration for struggles against colonialism and racism the world over. The fecund environs of South Africa, foreign to both Cecil Rhodes and Gandhi at the turn of the twentieth century, became the breeding ground for the most potent symbol of colonialism, as well as its greatest antithesis.

8
Gandhi Square

A bronze Gandhi stands on a 5-foot plinth in Johannesburg's Central Business District. He holds a book, a legal robe flapping at his ankles as if he is hurrying somewhere. The location, a desolate downtown neighbourhood redeveloped by a property developer in collaboration with local authorities in 2002 at a cost of 2 million rand, is now a buzzing commercial hub and the site of a bus terminal. A continuous stream of people passes by, shoppers and commuters, some dragging small suitcases on wheels, and office staff heading to and from immense stalactites of steel and glass, including what is said to be Africa's tallest building, the Carlton Centre. Red-and-white signage for 'Liquor City' marks one edge of the square from which roads lead off on either side lined with office buildings, fish-and-chip shops and signs for Western Union Money Transfer.

A hundred-odd years ago, the real flesh-and-blood Gandhi would have been whipping through these streets himself. His erstwhile legal office and the law courts where he practised would have been close by. And it was in the busy streets of downtown Johannesburg that he and his fellow campaigners protested discriminatory laws. Mohandas Karamchand Gandhi, lawyer and resister. In his book *Satyagraha in South Africa*, which he wrote many years later after his return to India, he recalled a particular moment at the time of his first arrest in January 1908 when his two roles, as a professional working within the British justice system and a protestor, collided as they were bound to. He had deliberately flouted the Black Act and been taken into custody. The arrest, which he had assiduously courted, should have filled him with jubilation. Instead, as he writes, he was assailed by embarrassment and doubt.

> In the Court there were hundreds of Indians as well as brother members of the Bar in front of me. On the sentence being pronounced I was at once removed in custody and was then quite alone. The policeman asked me to sit on a bench kept there for prisoners, shut the door on me and went away. I was somewhat agitated and fell into deep thought. Home, the Courts, where I practiced, the public meeting—all these passed away like a dream, and I was now a prisoner. What would happen in two months? Would have to serve the full term? If the people courted imprisonment in large numbers, as they had promised, there would be no question of serving the full sentences. But if they failed to fill the prisons, two months would be as tedious as an age. These thoughts passed through my mind in less than one hundredth of the time that it has taken me to dictate them. And they filled me with shame. How vain I was! I, who had asked the people to consider the prisons as His Majesty's hotels, the suffering consequent upon disobeying the Black Act as perfect bliss, and the sacrifice of one's all and of life itself in resisting it as supreme enjoyment! where had all this knowledge vanished today? This second train of thought acted upon me as a bracing tonic, and I began to laugh at my own folly.[1]

As it turned out, about 150 Indians joined Gandhi in jail and were housed together, which made the first experience of prison convivial and tolerable. His later incarcerations would not be as pleasant. He was arrested repeatedly, spending a total of 249 days in various South African prisons, during which time he was subjected to hard labour, physical attacks by inmates and other privations.

The Old Fort Prison where Gandhi and his associates were held and which was later used to confine several anti-apartheid activists such as Robert Sobukwe, the founder of the Pan Africanist Congress, and former African National Congress President Albert Luthuli, is a former Boer-era fort on a ridge overlooking Johannesburg. Ascending the steep incline within a rectangle of forbidding ramparts, I can feel the dull weight of war and racial oppression. Prison Number Four, built to house black prisoners, has blotchy walls and an uneven tiled floor. Black-and-white photographs of prominent civil rights campaigners stare out at the visitor, asking the poignant question in bold black letters: 'Who is a Criminal?'

On another wall, Gandhi's evocative words are displayed: 'I have a call I must answer. I must deliver my message to my people. This humiliation has sunk too deep in me to remain without an outlet. I, at least must act up to the light that has dawned on me.'

Four kilometres to the southwest is the Hamidia Mosque, where Indians had gathered to burn their passes and permits on 16 August 1908. I referred to the event in the opening paragraphs of this book because, according to the information sent to me by Enuga Reddy, Mohanlal and his companions who had travelled with him from Durban were likely to have been present at the event and at a similar one a week later. The public burning of identification documents by Indians was one of the dramatic highlights of Richard Attenborough's 1982 Oscar-winning film, *Gandhi*. In 1960, anti-apartheid leaders Nelson Mandela and Duma Nokwe also burnt their passes in solidarity with victims of the Sharpeville Massacre. The burning at the Hamidia Mosque has become etched in public consciousness as an iconic moment in the history of anti-colonialism.

As I had planned, I have been visiting memorials to Gandhi. There are quite a few in Johannesburg. Museum Africa in Newtown has a photographic display of places associated with him, such as the law courts and the vegetarian restaurants he frequented in the city. A rondavel-style house in the suburb of Orchards, which Gandhi shared for a few months with his architect-friend Hermann Kallenbach, has been recreated by a French tourism company with Gandhi's spartan lifestyle translated into a chic aesthetic using floor pillows and sunlight on bare white walls.

While moving from one site to another I am transported to the past, witnessing Gandhi as a young man in his milieu. I see photographs of the streets he walked, the people he consorted with and the houses he lived in. I become familiar with small, little-known anecdotes from his life in South Africa, such as the fact that a caretaker would not let him ride the elevator at Victory House on Harrison Street because of his colour and that he delivered lectures on religion at the Masonic Temple. I see the table he worked at (or one resembling it) displayed at the Fort Prison, a small wooden one with two drawers on either side accompanied by an armless wooden chair. His wife and his secretary become people to me, not just names in a book. I am immeasurably moved by snatches of his speech flashed on walls and screens and by his process of self-realization, reflected in his changing appearance: at the time of his last great campaign in South Africa in 1913, a march of Indian labourers, Gandhi had a shaven head and the plain garb of a peasant.

I am concerned, though, that I have not come across any fresh leads on my great-grandfather. I had hoped to find something at Gandhi's communes in South Africa but Tolstoy Farm, which he set up outside Johannesburg in 1910, has become a brick factory. I hear also that the Phoenix Settlement outside Durban where he printed his newspaper, *Indian Opinion*, was damaged by rioters in 1985; visiting it later, I find only trees and abandoned buildings there. A chance meeting puts me in touch with a niece of Thambi Naidoo, who was Gandhi's most prominent supporter and co-campaigner in the Transvaal, and she shows me her small collection of books and photographs.

I begin to sense that I am not likely to get far with an approach focused on Gandhi alone. I need to broaden my search. I look for books on South Africa's migrant communities where I see photographs of young Indians wrestling with sugarcane stalks and turbaned Indian servers at the Clarendon moving with choreographed ease. I read about passenger Indians in small interior towns: a Parsi with a licensed billiards table in Waterval Boven and an unidentified Indian running a cinema in Vrededorp. A family announces its new-found prosperity in silk saris, gold jewellery, waistcoat, fob chain and frills. A dust-streaked Indian miner relaxes with his African mates at a bar in Kimberley. A tall, rake-thin hawker in trousers too short for his long legs and a small, flat cap stops to stare. I suspect that back home in India, his shoulders may have slumped and his gaze cast down; each figure would have been lost among many, unnoticed, unsurprising. In these photographs, a house or a picket fence in the backdrop and small sartorial touches suitable to the climate lend a touch of the exotic. But what sets the migrants apart from the mass of their countrymen, still at home, is less tangible. Perhaps it is a sense of having taken charge of their destinies, a satisfaction of having seized opportunity, taken the wheel, for better or for worse, which leads to an intensification of individuality. Or perhaps it is just me, stopping long enough to pay attention and finding myself riveted.

Fascinated though I am, I am beginning to feel like a dilettante, perusing historical material for pleasure rather than for any professional purpose. It has been five days since I arrived in the country. The next day I am to leave Johannesburg for Durban, reputedly home to the largest community of Indian expatriates anywhere in the world. I plan to stay there a fortnight and have collected names of people to meet—a couple of historians, a sociologist, writers and Gandhi's granddaughter who is also a former parliamentarian. I expect these will lead to more meetings. I hope to travel to Cape Town too and meet with another of Gandhi's descendants, who is also a historian writing about Indian immigrants. But the difficulties and limitations of my enterprise have become startlingly clear to me. My hope of finding out about Mohanlal through a possible Gandhi connection has become a hit-and-miss business.

Other avenues offer little hope. Records for arrivals and departures of indentured workers, maintained by the Protector of Indian Immigrants office, are easily accessible, but the same is not the case for passenger Indians like Mohanlal. I am told that logbooks for arrivals are missing or are in bad shape. Newspaper and government archives are potential sources of information, but trawling through the records would take years and I have no guarantee that there is anything to be found.

It is still too early to lose hope, I tell myself. But the dawn of another glorious Jozi morning with birds twittering in a luminous peach-gold sky does nothing to alleviate my despondency. The sight of fellow guests at my modest bed and breakfast, business-suited InfoTech professionals and mid-level corporate executives in the city for a day attacking bread rolls and eggs in the dining room, only deepens my feeling of purposelessness. I have a meeting later with a historian at the University of Witwatersrand. I had hit upon her dissertation with its promising title, 'Turbans and Top Hats: Indian Interpreters in the Colony of Natal, 1880-1910', by chance while searching the internet for information about Indians in South Africa. Mohanlal was not mentioned in it, not even in the official lists of government interpreters, but I am keen on talking to the author, Prinisha Badassy, who has invited me for a chat over lunch.

Cars whoosh through downtown Johannesburg, flinging bits of music into the air. Glassy towers loom overhead. I want to slow down to an amble, take in my surroundings, look at second-hand books and records stacked on the pavements. But I am stopped by fear, which reminders of the high local crime rate, such as frequent glimpses of barbed wire and ubiquitous warnings of menacing dogs, do nothing to alleviate. The University of Witwatersrand in the heavily built-up central neighbourhood of Braamfontein too is secured like a high-risk military complex with barred gates, card-reading machines and a posse of guards.

I provide the necessary information at the gate and the bars clang open, momentarily engulfing me in a sea of hoodies, backpacks and books. Pushing against the robotic tide, each member deaf from the tendrils dripping from its ears, which threatens to carry me up a flight of wide stairs, I break free and look around for directions. I am at the edge of a sprawling campus dotted with old and new buildings arranged around gardens blissful in the summer light. The Department of History is in a labyrinth of silent corridors around a corner. The door to Badassy's office is ajar. I catch a glimpse of a woman who looks to be in her early thirties, with glossy brown waist-length hair, sitting in the gloom, staring at a computer screen. I knock tentatively. She beckons me in without looking up. I stare at the back of her head and wonder what to do with myself. I am about to cross the room and lower myself into a chair when she speaks.

'Hey, I ran a search for your great-grandfather!'

She has still not turned around, but her tone is warm, as if we have been friends for a while and not strangers meeting for the first time. My awkwardness and surprise at the absence of a preamble instantly dissipate. I am touched that someone should take the trouble of running a search on my behalf and intensely curious at the same time. I drop my bag in the chair and move towards her.

'... there are a lot of entries!'

I peer over her shoulder, abandoning all attempts at formality. Her computer screen shows the home page of the National Archives and Records Service. I recognize it because I have tried and failed to figure out its search system. Badassy's fingers fly expertly over the keyboard.

'I tried to search with various spellings—"Killawala", "Killavala", even "Killovala"; sometimes they get the names wrong,' she says. 'But look!'

A page opens up:

DEPOT KAB

SOURCE IRC - Regional Representative, Department of Home Affairs, Cape Town, Asian Series (1905 –)

TYPE LEER

VOLUME_NO 1/1/66

SYSTEM 01

REFERENCE 1626A

PART 1

'This is in the Cape Town Archives Repository.'

The words make no sense to me, but I gather that the reference number is for a file at the archives in Cape Town.

She taps again: 'There is a file in the National Archives Repository in Pretoria ...'

My heart sinks. It is too late to go to Pretoria, which is an hour's train ride from Johannesburg.

'Most of the files are in the National Archives Repository in Pietermaritzburg,' Badassy says. 'It is close to Durban; you are going to Durban?'

'Yes, tomorrow ...' I say, relieved by the possibility that the material in Pietermaritzburg might make up for my inability to access the Pretoria archive. I am still baffled by the turn of events. 'Why are there entries on Mohanlal in the archives?'

Badassy shrugs. 'Many reasons ... he might have written to the authorities about something, or it might be an application for a licence or ... anything. You never know what will turn up.'

'I see ...' I am still partly in disbelief.

'I also ran a search on *Indian Opinion* and found a few mentions.'

I take a look. There are five mentions and the dates suggest that they are more extensive than what Enuga Reddy sent me. Badassy jots down names of places where I can view the files on microfilm. 'Wait,' she says, 'I will print it all out.'

I hear a printer wheezing in a corner, inking blank sheets with reference numbers and names and addresses of archives, and it slowly sinks into my consciousness that my great-grandfather has left me a paper trail!

9

First Lady

The first call is a gentle splash in the pink-lit dawn, a soft, diffident 'Haa!' As the sky brightens and unseen things set the grass aquiver, a pair calls out together, harshly, like chalk sliding with a squeak on a blackboard. 'Haa!' 'Haa!' The breeze lifts, setting the leaves in motion, and falls. And then it starts: 'Haa, haa, haa, de-da!' 'Haa, haa, haa, de-da!' 'Haa, haa, haa, de-da!' 'Haa, haa, haa, de-da!' Grenades exploding. 'Haa, haa, haa, de-da!' 'Haa, haa, haa, de-da!' 'Haa, haa, haa, de-da!' 'Haa, haa, haa, de-da!' I shut my ears and bury my head. The grating call of the ubiquitous Hadeda, a bird South Africans seem to hate and love in equal measure, is a cross to bear every morning.

It is a lovely balmy day in Durban. Insects buzz around pink and blue flowers. The sea splashes the shore where the fluted white roof of the Moses Mabhida Stadium stands like a giant origami flower plonked next to the ocean. A long curving beach heads north to hillsides bright with waving yellow sugarcane stalks, bearing names of old plantations where thousands of Indian indentured workers once toiled: Tongaat, Mount Edgecombe and La Mercy. My bed and breakfast is called the D'Urban Elephant, the name being reminiscent of a time when elephants lumbered about the

Berea, a hill that hangs over the busy Durban harbour and the city centre. The Biblical name was conferred on the hill by Allen Francis Gardiner, a British naval officer-turned-missionary who founded a Christian mission in Port Natal after being rejected by the natives of Zululand; the experience reminded him of Saint Paul who found refuge in Berea in Macedonia after being spurned in Greek Thessalonica. The neighbourhood was developed as an alternative to the increasingly crowded downtown area and the *Natal Mercury* described the wooded plots as being 'just the thing for people who prefer a country residence, a nice view and ideal habitation'.

The D'Urban Elephant is a rambling Edwardian property with an upstairs where the hosts live, and airy guest rooms with high ceilings below, equipped with a large kitchen and a lounge filled with an eclectic collection of novels and books on South African history. The multilevel garden has a saltwater pool and the house, filled with paintings, African fabrics and bric-a-brac, has a warm, welcoming and faintly bohemian air about it. It is a revolving carousel of visitors, many of whom are researchers drawn by the warmth of the hosts, Howard, a lawyer, and his wife, Marleen, a former history teacher.

On my first morning in Durban, Marleen drives a fellow guest, an American researcher and me to the Killie Campbell Africana Library in Essenwood. The mansion housing the library was owned by Sir Marshall Campbell, a leading sugar baron and entrepreneur who came to Natal with his parents as a two-year-old on J.C. Byrne's emigration scheme. The elegant white Cape Dutch-style building is right out of *Gone with the Wind*. There should be heiresses in hooped skirts melting on the porch, except that Sir Marshall's daughter Dr Margaret Roach 'Killie' Campbell was more seriously inclined than Scarlett O'Hara and her sisters and spent her energies building a prominent Africana collection instead. I spend the morning trawling through newspaper files. For lunch, we get a pie from a gas station nearby, my standard recourse in the weeks to come, and eat in the split-level garden planted with indigenous shrubs collected by Dr Campbell, a tropical paradise of aromatic boughs and emerald-green, rubbery, thick-leaved trees.

Two kilometres up the steep road from the D'Urban Elephant is the University of KwaZulu-Natal. I walk up sometimes to meet Goolam Vahed and Kalpana Hiralal, historians and leading experts on passenger Indians, and also to hitch a ride on a shuttle along with students kitted out in the usual way (hoodie-backpack-earplugs) to UKZN's other campus in Westville to refer to books on Indian migrants at the Gandhi-Luthuli Documentation Centre. Finding transport is a necessary preoccupation because, averse as I am to driving on unfamiliar roads, I have to rely on public transport, which is extremely limited. The most important commute I have to make, to the archives in Pietermaritzburg, an hour's drive away, is a logistical nightmare. Marleen looks around for someone travelling that way; Goolam spreads the word among his colleagues. Meanwhile, I do some research and find a bus service called Eldo Travels, which offers a reasonably priced ticket for the short leg, Durban–Pietermaritzburg, on its long-distance coach service.

It is a mini adventure. Howard drops me off at the bus station on his way to work. I stroll past the operators' cabins: Greyhound, Transliner, Megabus, strung out in a straight line. At Eldo Travels, a girl with bored eyes and frizzy hair in a yellow-and-black uniform sells me a ticket for 50 rand. The Durban Bus Terminal is dusty and has a few passengers waiting around desultorily on benches, a mute beggar shuffling around them. Through an opening in the wall, an Indian family serves tepid coffee and bunny chow, an iconic Durban dish of a curry-filled bread loaf, apparently an apartheid-era invention for labourers who were not allowed to sit at a restaurant. On the other side of the wall, in the docking area, where the ungainly double-decker buses are parked, a little carpet is rolled out before a makeshift counter and passengers, mostly African and Indian, in make-up, gaudy clothes and dyed hair, are lined up.

For many days I travel in this manner, gliding past gentle green slopes and cow-dotted fields on what feels like a comfortably cushioned pogo stick. Then Will, an imperial historian from the UK, also a guest at the D'Urban Elephant, expresses an interest in visiting the archives in Pietermaritzburg. We ride out on the Eldo, occupying the top front seat, much to the annoyance of covetous passengers headed all the way to Johannesburg. Passing the market on our way back to the bus terminal in Pietermaritzburg in the evening, we spot a kombi about to head out to Durban and impulsively jump in. I have been warned against taking the kombi, a shared taxi with fixed fares, on grounds of danger. The small white van we find ourselves in is packed with smiling working-class mamas, doe-eyed children and muscled men in short-sleeved T-shirts. It gets us home in no time and we never go back to the bus.

It soon becomes clear to me that as an outsider on a tight researcher's budget, rather than a tourist's lavish purse, I am an anomaly in the highly stratified society I am attempting to navigate. Post-apartheid South Africa is a minefield of conflicting aspirations. Lingering effects of racial, class and geographical inequality are everywhere, not least in the ever-present, menacing spectre of street crime. Naively exploring back alleys or blundering into places where I would not be expected, I experience a sense of desolation and bristling tension. I feel no safer in the wide tree-lined roads of gracious upscale neighbourhoods; their armed guards and security booths, instead of reassuring me, make me fearful. Another concern is the potentially distracting attraction of the contemporary, which I try to minimize by avoiding newspapers and letting the language of the archives build a time warp.

In this anachronistic state I slip into another kind of watchfulness.

At a dinner party given by friends of a friend in India, at their home in the leafy, tony suburb of Killarney in Johannesburg, I engage in small talk and study the faces of the Indian guests. A bureaucrat, a doctor and a few others whose professions I cannot recall. I examine their features, their bone structure and the timbre of their voices. One of them puts me in touch with a cousin who has worked on a family tree. He is a tall, friendly lawyer whom I catch up with over coffee in the financial district, Sandton. While he talks, I observe his hands and the way he holds the cup.

In Chatsworth, one of the designated Indian areas in Durban under apartheid, three kaftan-clad sisters tell me about an ash-coloured blemish, which they say afflicts all the women in their family in middle age. In a house next to theirs an elderly woman in a large sitting room, sparsely furnished and dominated by a huge portrait of Satya Sai Baba, offers me a cup of tea and I accept, glad for the opportunity to assess her tea-making style. On the bus to Pietermaritzburg, I recognize descendants of passenger Indians by their features and style of dressing: the men in kurta-pyjamas, the women in headscarves. At malls, in coffee shops and in casinos, I observe young Indians in their trendy clothes. Misguided though it may be, my obsessive people-watching or Indian-watching has a purpose.

To explain it, I have to reveal an aspect of Mohanlal's journey I have not yet touched upon.

When I described Mohanlal's departure from Bombay, I mentioned that he had a wife, a young bride he left behind. Eventually he returned, they were reunited and had a long life as husband and wife, producing six children, two girls and four boys. But on his travels something happened, something that families were bound to worry about when a young man went away to a distant land: Mohanlal met a woman. The details are meagre. She was the daughter of a house where Mohanlal lived as a tenant during his travels. Whether they were married or not was unclear, but a baby was born in Durban, a girl. And that girl was my grandmother, Damayanti.

To look at, my grandmother was a conventional Indian matron. She was dark, small-built and wore pale muslin saris in the traditional Gujarati style, often covering her head. My cousins and I teasingly call her the Queen, after her contemporary Queen Elizabeth II, because of her smattering of Convent-school English. But she was regal in her own way with a natural authority that made people do her bidding without question and even fear her. I did too, a little, but I also thought that she must be incredibly sad because as I knew, her mother had died when she was a child and she had been brought up by that ogre of children's fairy tales—a stepmother. I knew too that her father, the wandering Mohanlal, had had other children. I had met them, her stepbrothers and sisters.

My earliest memory of the Killavalas is of a large, boisterous group of people descending on us at a family event. Men, women and children, vivid in diamonds and silks, surrounding our family party with loud cries, exclamations and hugs. I was a child then and bewildered by these strangers whom I was invited to address by intimate honorifics. Maamas and maasis who I did not know at all and who were nothing like us. We, with our low voices and constrained movements, and they, with their flamboyance and expansiveness; what did they have that we did not? I would not then have known the meaning of the word 'entitlement', but I felt the lack of it, and had no idea why.

When Damayanti was about four, Mohanlal decided to return to India and took both mother and daughter with him. One does not know if letters had been exchanged in the years of absence and what they conveyed. Doubtless, Mohanlal would have been welcomed back home with tears and joy. There would have been feasting and thanks given at the local temple. But the arrival of three, not one, would have triggered a complicated set of emotions all around. For the wife, having grown into a young woman as she awaited her husband's return, to find herself supplanted. For my great-grandmother, lost and friendless in Bombay, and surrounded by people who might not have been kindly disposed towards her. There she stands in my fancy, on a veranda in Bombay, watching a tram clatter through the street, tasting the salty breath of the sea and feeling alone, desperately alone.

Things did not work out, or at least so it seemed, because in a while—one does not know how long, a year or two perhaps—my great-grandmother was on a ship headed home by herself. I am perplexed by the fact that she was sent alone on a ship to South Africa and I assume there might have been a chaperone or a family on board to look after her. It is also odd that she left her daughter, then merely six, with the father, which raises the possibility that the parting was temporary. Or, of course, it could be that my great-grandmother was so deeply unhappy that she just left. One cannot say. One only knows that she never made it home. On the sea, afloat on the vast blue ocean, away from Mohanlal and her daughter and not yet in sight of her childhood home, she took seriously ill. And somewhere en route, under an open sky, she breathed her last. Without the facts it is hard to know where to look for any logs of her death. My uncle Yogesh, the younger of my mother's two brothers, maintains that there was a letter of condolence that had come to Bombay from my great-grandmother's brother, but which has since been lost. All he recalls of it is a smudged signature that looked like: 'Murli Murari'.

I had a great-grandmother about whom nothing is known, not even her name. In a society where everyone knows everything about everybody and where everyone's place is defined by caste and lineage, a mystery such as this casts a long shadow. I remember an afternoon at my grandmother's house when, after what sounded like a heated altercation between the grown-ups, I caught my mother muttering to herself as she tidied her hair in the mirror.

'And we don't even know who she *was*!'

'Who was?' I asked, startling her.

She narrowed her eyes, considering whether to tell me: '*Your* great-grandmother!'

When I first heard about my anonymous great-grandmother and the story was revealed in small instalments over the years, I felt as if a backdrop I had taken for granted had been suddenly pulled away, revealing a vague hollowness. The certainties that had framed my inconsequential but clear existence on earth had been yanked away, leaving me disoriented. I was suddenly unsure about who I was and where I came from. At that moment, I wanted to know everything about this mysterious woman. Who was she, where did she come from? What did she look like?

A phantom ancestor is a powerful absence and I found that unlike Mohanlal's travels, which seemed to fascinate me alone, my enigmatic great-grandmother had a firm place in the consciousness of most of my family members. The unknown presents myriad possibilities. A cousin felt instantly 'at home' on a holiday in Africa. Another cousin once followed a family around at an airport, convinced that it was an unmet branch of ours. For me the thought of her, without whom my tan-limbed, moody maternal kin and I would not have been, lying nameless in the waters, haunted me.

I move through South Africa absurdly convinced that I will spot something—a feature, a gesture, an inflexion, a proclivity—that will produce a flash of recognition. And interestingly nobody makes light of my preoccupation. Many South African Indians, descended from indentured migrants, have searched for their roots in India, and my search in the other direction evokes empathy and helpfulness rather than disdain.

I have with me a handful of hypotheses about her ethnic identity. My uncle Vinod believes that she was 'a Brahmin lady'. An aunt claims that my grandmother herself told her that her mother's forefathers were from Sind, west of Gujarat. It did not occur to me to look for physical clues. My mother and her sisters have a soft brown complexion, many shades lighter than my grandmother's, and silky hair with a hint of auburn, which leads my cousin Smita to place my mysterious great-grandmother's origins a little east and north of Sind, in the desert region of northwest Gujarat. All these theories rest on the possibility that our anonymous ancestor was part of a migrant community from the subcontinent. This is not necessarily true, for as my mother said, the truth is 'we don't know who she *was*.'

Nevertheless, I decide to check each hypothesis, beginning with Sind, and write to Claude Markovits, an authority on merchant networks and Sindhi traders in particular at the Centre for Indian and South Asian Studies in Paris. I also write to Rita Kothari, India-based author of a book on Sindhis. I ask them if they know of Sindhi communities in South Africa and if the name 'Murari' rings a bell.

Markovits writes back:

Dear Amrita Shah,
Thanks for your message. The presence of Sindworkies in South Africa is mentioned by Gandhi in *Satyagraha in South Africa*. He estimates there were 200 of them in the 1890s. They were all over: Durban, Johannesburg, Capetown, Port Elizabeth. There was a very successful firm (Tikamdas Bros?), which was based in Port Elizabeth. Old commercial directories are a good source. Best of luck in your search.

Rita Kothari's response is:

'Murari does not evoke Sindhiness to me ... but with diasporic populations you never know.'

◆

A thin, tremulous whine from bagpipes fills my small white hotel room. It surges up from the street, loud and so close I can feel the floor reverberate. Two seconds later I hear it again, on my tinny television set, but it is overlaid by a low thunderous drum roll from below—dum-dum-dum-da-*dum* ... dum-dum-dum-da-*dum*! Now the drum roll is on the telly and the bagpipes below. I have arrived in Cape Town on the morning of the most important day on the calendar of South Africa's legislative capital—the State of the Nation Address of the President of South Africa, an annual event in which the president reports on the status of the nation to the resumption of a joint sitting of Parliament. Having booked my ticket much in advance, I had no idea of the significance of the date until I find myself in the midst of a crush at the airport and then the hotel lobby, overflowing with legislators dressed in radiant colours and tribal finery, a change for me from the stereotypical white garb of Indian politicians.

Quite inadvertently I have picked a hotel a stone's throw from the neoclassical-style Parliament building, a prime spot for anyone wishing to be in on the action, but a terribly bad idea for my purposes. I have arrived on a Thursday morning, intending to stay three days with a plan to relocate to the other side of the peninsular strip the next day. There is a reference number for a single set of documents at the Western Cape Provincial Archives and Records Service and since this particular archive does not allow photography, I have written ahead and requested a photocopy. The archives are on Roeland Street, a short walk from my hotel, and I imagine I have arranged things rather efficiently, but I had not bargained for the fact that the roads around the Parliament complex will be shut down by early afternoon for the State of the Nation Address. I have a short window within which to get the job done at the archives and return to the hotel.

The Cape Archives Repository is housed in a stately wide building backed by the craggy face of Table Mountain. I deposit my bag in the locker room, feeling a chilly bleakness about me, which I comprehend when I find out later that the site is a former prison. A lanky young man at the counter asks me to fill up a request form and return for a photocopy after a fortnight. I tell him I will be back in my country, thousands of miles away, by then. He shakes his head firmly. I stand there helplessly, recalling stories from friends about the stalling tactics of bribe-seeking clerks in India. As I wonder what I should do, I suddenly recall the mail I had sent earlier and the name of the supervisor that I had picked out from the internet. I take a chance and mention the name. The man relents slightly, enough to make a telephone call to an upstairs office, and fortunately (miraculously!) immediate permission is granted. I smile at the grim young man, apologizing silently for suspecting his motives, and leave with my precious takings safely stowed in my backpack.

I have spent more time than I anticipated and have to race back through streets emptied of ordinary people. Uniformed men belonging to various arms of the police and security forces are gathered at every intersection and I have to urge my way past them. I reach the hotel just as the National Ceremonial Guard Band makes its jangling entry on my street. My TV shows people gathered on the steps of Parliament House, men in black suits, women in pastel hats. Newspapers have been full of allegations of corruption against President Jacob Zuma, and the forthcoming parliamentary session is likely to be a fiery one. But this is a pleasant interlude, an occasion for smiles and civilities, warm greetings and laughter, a celebration of the personal underlying the political. My South African friend

Ruth tells me that there is always speculation about which of his many wives Zuma will bring to the State of the Nation Address, but inevitably it will be his first wife. 'Always,' she says, 'for important ceremonies, he gives her that respect.'

My backpack is on the floor and the copy of my documents—loose sheets faintly warm and smelling of copier's ink—is on the bed. Mohanlal visited Cape Town, travelling by ship from Durban, in March 1908. He filled in a 'Declaration by Passenger' form as per the Immigration Act of the Colony of the Cape of Good Hope and an application for a permit to enter the Cape Colony. Mohanlal was accompanied by a two-year-old baby and a 'wife'. My great-grandmother was eighteen or nineteen years old in 1908 and her name, penned on the form scribbled over with clerical notes, is 'Foolkore'.[1]

The word 'ful' or 'phool' and its variations mean 'flower' in a host of Indian languages. 'Fulkori' in Bengali means 'new flower', the term 'kaur' or 'kuwar' and its phonetic equivalent 'kor' is a common suffix with feudal associations in northern and western India. There is also a possibility that Foolkore was not my great-grandmother's original name but one given to her by her husband after marriage, a common practice at the time. If it is her birth name and a clue to her origins, then it lays open much of the subcontinent; if it is a given name at marriage then it reveals nothing more about her origins.

City maps and property records are stored for tax evaluation at the rates office in the Durban City Hall building. The impressive neo-baroque structure, framed by palm trees and a soft blue sky and now under the Ethekwini Municipality, also houses the Natural Science Museum, and the lobby with its grandly sweeping staircase has a stout model rhino on a chequerboard floor. The air conditioners are on full blast at the rates office, presumably to preserve old documents. A dainty woman, a shawl draped around her delicate shoulders, tottering around on stilettos, proves surprisingly adept at operating the heavy wheel that works the storage facility and teeters towards me bearing oversized volumes bound in blue cloth and embossed in gold.

I go through the maps. They are large and delicate and have to be carefully unfolded. I open them one by one, turning them this way and that. They do not tell me anything I can use. Nor do the property records. I give up and look for other kinds of data. Almanacs and business directories are generally useful, but they are scattered across various libraries in the city and I spend time tracking down volumes for the first decade of the 1900s. The publications contain a rich store of miscellanea, weather conditions, government rules, commercial activity, advertisements for businesses and goods and, most importantly for me, residential addresses, just a house number and a street in most cases and a three-digit telephone number. I test the various hypotheses articulated by my relatives, first, the one that claims my great-grandmother was of a migrant Sindhi family and that her maiden surname might have been 'Murari'.

Sindhis are an enterprising people spread all over the world, prominently in Southeast Asia. The 'Sindworkies' Markovits mentions were traders of curios and silk, Hindus by religion who also venerated the Sikh spiritual leader Guru Nanak. The only Sindhi name I find listed in the almanacs is Poohoomull of Poohoomull Bros., a famous firm of Sindworkies. By this time I have seen letters from Mohanlal filed in the archives with his address in Durban. The two do not tally.

I also do not find a 'Murli' or a 'Murari' listed anywhere, though there are several names that sound close: 'Moodally', 'Mudali' and 'Moodley', all a corruption of the Tamilian name 'Mudaliar' from

South India, which makes me wonder if my great-grandmother was a South Indian; the daughter of an ex-indentured worker who had moved downtown perhaps?

Even as I look for clues to my great-grandmother's family, a question niggles at the back of my mind. Various clues suggest that Mohanlal left South Africa at the end of the first decade of the 1900s. I do not know how long my great-grandmother, Foolkore, stayed with him in Bombay, but it is clear that the earliest date on which she could have embarked on a ship back to South Africa would have been after 1910. Anyone contemplating such a journey would be aware that South African authorities had been tightening immigration laws over the years and had not only closed entry to new Indian immigrants, but also made it extremely difficult for old residents to enter without offering various documents as proof. In 1910, the colonial authorities de-recognized traditional Indian marriages, turning many women of passenger origin into 'prohibited immigrants'. Hundreds of such cases were brought before the Natal Supreme Court and some women were deported to India. Single women were virtually barred on the suspicion that they were prostitutes. One does not know if Foolkore was accompanied by a relative or a friend, but she was travelling without her husband and would certainly have been deported. Records of the time show thousands of people being stopped at the harbour, including a well-known Natal-based Hindu preacher and his family, travelling home after a visit to India.[2] Ships' captains were tasked with checking passengers' documents before accepting them on board and were liable to be punished for ferrying 'prohibited' immigrants. Under these circumstances, it is hard to make sense of Foolkore's last and fatal voyage.

◆

I am in a bright drawing room in somebody's house somewhere in Durban. I do not know where, since I have not come on my own but have been brought here by a woman who sits on an adjacent sofa talking to a large elderly gentleman with a booming voice. He is the owner of the house, but I have not caught his name in the quick introductions. I recall him saying he is a former journalist, or an occasional one—something like that—but it seems he may also be involved in other activities. Right now, for instance, the conversation on that other sofa is about a beauty contest he recently organized or judged.

If I am inattentive, like a child accompanying a parent on a visit, it is because this is how I feel sometimes when I am with Loshni. An attractive businesswoman in her early forties, Loshni heads the local chapter of the Global Organization of People of Indian Origin. The president of the organization, whom I met through a Delhi-based journalist covering the Indian diaspora, wrote to her introducing me. Initially she viewed me as a professional obligation, but the element of the personal in my mission and the fact that I am alone in an unfamiliar place strikes another chord and she ends up treating me with a brisk maternalism. She arrives periodically to fetch me from my bed and breakfast and take me to places where she thinks I might find something useful and meet people who she thinks might contribute to my research. I am touched by her thoughtfulness amidst her many responsibilities and grateful for the introductions. But her often-cryptic explanations as to where we are headed and her habit of introducing me as 'This is Amrita, she is searching for her granny' make me feel somewhat childlike in her bustling company.

So I sit quietly while they talk, trusting that the purpose of the meeting and the value of this person as an interviewee will gradually become clear. I play with my necklace, a new acquisition from the bead market in Warwick. Pauline, a fellow guest at the D'Urban

Elephant, her colleague Lingani and I had been to the market the day before. Pauline is a Canadian, a financial consultant who visits the city periodically to assist an NGO working with various underprivileged groups, including street hawkers.

I found my necklace nestling in a sea of beads, thousands of strands in every imaginable colour, blood-red, ochre, coral, turquoise ... and amidst the flashy hues this odd one, greyish-brown, a sparrow among peacocks. It wasn't even made of beads but of seeds picked up from a riverbank. I pointed and one of the turbaned African women plucked it from the pile and plopped it in my palm. And then Lingani, whose name she said means 'What are you waiting for?', dragged us away from the iridescent mounds of jewellery and led us past the hanging feathers and animal parts of the medicinal market to the top of a staircase from where we could observe the market spread out below, in the dust and the sun, with a mural of the Zulu goddess of fertility, Nomkhubulwane, watching over it, arms spread wide as fish, plants, animals and cities lapped at her skirts.

In the basement herb market, the hawkers were all women and their wares were football-sized spheres of white and red lime from Ndwedwe, north of Durban, waiting to be picked up by sangomas or traditional healers. 'Tobacco leaves, burn, grind, make snuff.' A bent woman circled with her arm while rubbing her fingers before bringing them to her nose. The gesture of scattering was for ancestors to partake. Next to her was a huge pile of dried twigs from Lusikisiki in the Eastern Cape Province, thin sticks with tiny soft flowers called impepho, lit like incense in African homes to communicate with one's forefathers. I bought some of it. In the evening, I borrowed a matchbox and went to the sit-out adjoining my room, which I rarely used, preferring the lively public veranda. I watched the twigs catch the flame and emit a thin white vapour. I thought of my great-grandmother and the great gulf of time and water that separated us and I told her that I had come all this way to find her.

◆

The gentleman, whose name is Farouk Khan, I discover, has turned to me and I tell him my story. I have become used to repeating it often, taking care to add any new finding, because one never knows what will be of particular importance to each individual expert. I tell him of my great-grandfather heading out from Bombay. I tell him about the passport from Mauritius and about my great-grandmother and two-year-old grandmother mentioned in the form in Cape Town.

Mr Khan listens with half-closed eyes. We have moved to another part of his enormous sitting room where there are numerous books, many of them hardbound and of a rather specialist nature, which leads me to presume that he has a serious interest in history and the Indian migrant community. He does not say anything about my story, though occasionally he reaches out and picks a book and looks up something. After a while we say our goodbyes and Loshni drops me off at the 1860 Heritage Centre, a repository of materials on the South African Indian community, on Derby Street in Greyville.

A couple of hours later I am working my way through a pile of grainy photographs. I am the only person in the reading room apart from the supervisor. The muggy afternoon and the chemical smell of old photographs is making me drowsy. A sharp ring from my phone startles me to wakefulness. I look at my phone in bafflement. Nobody calls me on my South Africa number; communication is mostly by email or text.

'Hello?'

'AMRITA!' I have no trouble identifying the caller. The booming voice belongs to the gentleman I have just come away from meeting.

I wince, feeling the sound bounce off the walls of the hushed room.

'Amrita! *Your great-grandmother was not travelling to South Africa! She was going home to visit her family … in Mauritius!*'

Mauritius!

Click, click, click!

One word and a hundred light bulbs come alive in my head. Of course! Everything is suddenly clear. The form I sourced in the archives in Cape Town tells me that my grandmother was approximately two years old in March 1908 which, when I connect it to the date that Mohanlal has provided in the same voluminous form for his arrival in South Africa, makes it clear that Foolkore was expecting for some months prior to their arrival in Durban. The paragraph sent by Enuga Reddy states that Mohanlal came to South Africa via Mauritius. It is so clear. How did I not see it? The dates fit. Mauritius did not have rules prohibiting the entry of Indians that South Africa did. It may be that Foolkore did not leave Bombay in a state of loneliness and depression, abandoning her husband and child. She may have been yearning to visit her family whom she had not seen for many years. It makes perfect sense. Mohanlal did not meet Foolkore in South Africa, he met her in Mauritius.

PART THREE

MAURITIUS

10
Île Maurice

Among the world's smallest countries, the Republic of Mauritius lies in the Indian Ocean, 900 kilometres east of Madagascar. Two thousand square kilometres in size, no larger than the cities of Delhi or Seoul, it lies surrounded by miles and miles of blue water. Too small and remote to make more than an occasional demand on the world's attention, it has, however, an enduring place in public memory as the land of the dodo, the famous short-winged bird whose extinction has become something of a parable reflecting our current ecological crisis.

A thousand-odd years ago, Mauritius was a primaeval jungle, innocent of human footfall. An increase in long-distance voyaging after the tenth century put it in the path of venturesome seamen, Arab and Portuguese sailors who took refuge there from rough weather. In 1598, sailors in a Dutch convoy, marooned on the island by a storm, thought it might make a convenient site to supply Dutch East India Company ships on their way to the Indonesian islands and tried to establish a station in the wilderness. But the enormity of the challenge proved overwhelming and the Dutch abandoned Mauritius in 1710, preferring the easier option of the Cape in Africa. Before they left, they stripped its forests of ebony and some of its fauna. The celebrated dodo, once secure enough in its environs to surrender flight and evolve into a walking bird, was wiped out by unprecedented competition for food from predatory rats and pigs that came off Dutch ships.

The teardrop-shaped island was left alone once again. But not for long. Competition was brewing between the French and the British in India and Mauritius, conveniently located on the ocean route, offered strategic possibilities that were hard to ignore. The French took control of Mauritius, named after Dutch Prince Maurice of Nassau, and renamed it Isle de France. They used it to station armed forces that could be urgently recruited for military manoeuvres against the English East India Company and turned it into a naval dockyard for building and repairing warships, like the British had done with Bombay.

During the Napoleonic wars, Mauritius proved useful as a site for launching covert attacks on British ships. Corsairs or privateers, abetted by the island's wealthy French traders and backed by Lettres des Courses, which sanctioned such attacks in wartime, assaulted and plundered British merchant vessels travelling between India and Europe and loaded with cargo and soldiers. Annoyed by the recurring attacks and in view of Mauritius's strategic importance, Britain landed a few thousand troops, including Indian soldiers, in Mauritius in December 1810 and easily overpowered the small French force stationed there.

The British occupation of Mauritius scotched Napoleon's ambitious scheme to dominate Asia in the bud. The victors then proceeded to make use of the strategically located island in some of the ways the previous occupants had. They made it a base for their own reserve garrisons, drawing on them for various emergencies such as quashing the Indian Mutiny in 1857 and for the Zulu and Anglo-Boer Wars in the following decades. Before the advent of wireless communication, they also used the island for laying transoceanic cables. In the words of British historian Ashley Jackson, Mauritius became an essential 'everyday rivet' in Britain's naval machinery and the colony's Latin motto—granted in 1905 along with its coat of arms—proudly proclaimed the island to be 'the Star and Key of the Indian Ocean'.[1]

Steamships plied between Bombay and Port Louis. The opening of the Suez Canal in 1869 diminished the importance of Mauritius as a stop for Europe-bound traffic from India. But with the British government providing subsidies to encourage mail communication between London and its colonial spots and to urgently transport soldiers when required, ships continued to ply as frequently as before. European shipbuilders, working to meet the needs of slave traders and dealers in perishables grown in the colonies, had improved steamships considerably. The new ships were larger, hardier with the addition of steel and powered by boilers, turbines, propellers and double- and triple-expansion engines that abolished the need for frequent coal supply halts, allowing them to scuttle across distances faster than before.

Mohanlal's journey from Bombay to Mauritius would have taken two weeks with a stop at Colombo. He would have possessed a ticket with a printed serial number, his name written by hand and a signature from an employee of the shipping company. A third-class ticket would have cost him Rs 50 or so. I assume, of course, that the luxuries of first-class travel, the snug comforts of a cabin, dancing, tennis and drinks in plush salons with pictures of famous sea captains on the walls, were out of his reach. My great-grandfather probably travelled deck amidst hundreds of co-travellers with hardly any space to put down his luggage or rest undisturbed.

These, I imagine, were not privations for a young man embarking on his first sea voyage and setting out into the world. In his memoir *Growing: Seven Years in Ceylon*, Leonard Woolf described his departure for the colonies as his 'second birth'.

The umbilical cord by which I had been attached to my family, to St Paul's, to Cambridge and Trinity was cut when, leaning over the ship's taffrail, I watched through the dirty, dripping murk and fog of the river my mother and sister waving goodbye and felt the ship begin slowly to move down the Thames to the sea.

The prospect of foreign shores, unlike the 'subdued, flat, accepted reality' of life at home, felt like 'one were acting in a play or living in a dream'.[2]

I wish I could replicate Mohanlal's slow journey across the ocean. Days upon days of being rocked by a rolling sea, salt lingering on the tongue, the feeling of being unmoored from family, tradition and land and to watch the stars come out amidst a multitude of sleeping figures all bound for some great adventure. A British administrator wrote this vivid description of travelling on a Gulf steamer:

> … men lying, sitting, squatting, singing, chattering, cooking, eating, sleeping; and all in the midst of a piled labyrinth of quilts, and carpets, and boxes, of sailcloths and ropes, of sheep, and birds in cages, and fowls in coops, of trays, Band samovars, and cooking-pots, of greasy donkey-engines and clanking chains …[3]

Another colonial traveller in the early 1900s was struck by the extraordinary 'Britishness', the availability of 'Kodak films, Whisky, Picture Postcards and other British delights'[4] amidst the exotic sights and sounds of the African coast.

But I am travelling in 2015, the age of cheap air fares. And a late-night flight from Mumbai on an August night deposits me in the early morning hours in Mahe. Three planes stand on the tarmac and the transit lounge is bursting with an exceedingly motley collection of passengers. Items of hand baggage are sprawled everywhere, emanating an air of irate lassitude, indicating the martyrdom of a long wait. I saunter through the duty free, past the familiar collection of perfumes and chocolates, racks of yellow sundresses and pod-shaped bottles of Coco d'Amour and ascend the stairs to an empty lounge on the first floor where I watch white yachts bobbing on a turquoise-blue sea of the Seychelles, their sides gleaming in the pale dawn light. By noon I am at the Sir Seewoosagur Ramgoolam International Airport in Plaine Magnien, Mauritius.

Ever since I planned my itinerary, I am abashed to admit, I have dreaded this moment of arrival, this landing on a speck in the middle of the ocean, an earth form so tiny that it shows up as a pinhead even after I repeatedly punch the magnification key on my keypad. Exiting the airport, I find my feet instinctively curling, as if by doing so I can hold on to a ground that might suddenly slip off its moorings and float, adrift in the immense ocean. I realize this is silly and that I do not walk pigeon-toed at home in a city that was also an archipelago. Perhaps in Mumbai it is the proximity of the mainland, the vast, reassuring subcontinent, that makes me feel anchored. Or perhaps it is not size alone but the awareness that the little rock I stand on now was once fluid, liquid lava.

Mauritius, along with Réunion and Rodrigues, comprises the Mascarene Islands, named after the sixteenth-century Portuguese explorer Dom Pedro Mascarenhas. Born of massive underwater eruptions occurring over ten million years, the islands display the physical signs of cataclysmic natural processes. Mauritius, when seen from the air, is a volcanic mountain with a collapsed centre. Thin, chipped, steep walls surround the basin or caldera, which also has a central plateau and plains composed of solidified lavas poured out by smaller, later eruptions, the cracks in which are filled with streams and rivers. White sandy beaches ring the island, its lagoons protected from the open sea by the world's third-largest coral reef.

The unusual landscape knocks the unease right out of me. Basalt heaps rising 300–800 metres, a tribe of leviathans, gigantic flying elephant gods. There is no end to them. You pass one and another one looms up. You turn your head and another one comes into view. Omnipresent and omniscient, they evoke in me an urgent need to genuflect, to ask for their blessings, to apologize for disturbing their silence. On and on they go, brightened by the lush stretches of green in between and then again solemnly grey. Ours is the only car for a while on the smooth road cutting through open fields and hills. The person at the wheel is Manish (name changed), the owner of the guest house I have booked myself into. He is of Indian descent, from Bihar, well-built with thick, powerful shoulders and blunt features that remind me of villainous sidekicks in Bollywood movies of the 1970s, hoodlums whose main job was to leer menacingly from the sidelines of whatever action was occurring in the frame. His appearance is deceptive, for far from being threatening, I find Manish ill at ease and glancing at me from time to time as if he is trying to place me and not succeeding. Suddenly he says, 'Indians are very good, very good!'

I realize that by 'Indians' he means me and others currently residing in India. I nod, unsure yet about what our language of communication should be. I speak in English and he responds in Hindi, but a Hindi so stilted that it is hard for me to match him. He has already assured me that in his guest house I will get any Indian dish I could wish for. I tell him I am happy to eat the local food. No, no, his wife can make anything … I let it go. He tells me about one of his recent guests, a software engineer from Bangalore, a 'very nice man' who came once for work and returned for a holiday with his family. 'I took them everywhere, to Ganga Talao, Chamarel, the waterfall,' Manish exults before coming to the point of this story. 'I can take you also. Full day. When you want to go? Tomorrow? Tomorrow is Sunday, I am free.'

'Not now Manish,' I say. 'Maybe some other time.'

'Okay, okay.' He seems disappointed. 'You tell me. Tomorrow will be good but okay, you tell me.'

We drive on through thin traffic. Some generic Western pop has been gurgling on the car stereo without my noticing it. But Manish suddenly reaches for the dashboard and makes an adjustment. 'We are Hindis,' he says, 'we should not be listening to this.'

A Hindi song comes on, a duet about aching hearts and rainy skies. It sounds familiar yet strange, counterfeit Bollywood, with copycat lyrics and poor singers, and it seems to affect Manish deeply.

'Listen to the words!' he says, turning up the volume and singing along gruffly.

❖

Indians have been in Mauritius since the eighteenth century. They came with Bertrand-François Mahé de La Bourdonnais, a celebrated captain in the French East India Company who became the governor of Isle de France in 1734 and who is widely credited with initiating the development of the island. His name and likeness are everywhere in contemporary Mauritius, most prominently in Port Louis, where his statue stands at the quayside end of Place d'Armes, a broad forehead and pointed chin rising from wide, sloping shoulders, his tall, stout figure in ruffles and a long open coat revealing a shapely extended leg, all gloriously framed by an avenue of royal palms.

To lure Frenchmen to the island, Mahé de La Bourdonnais offered inducements of land and slaves. The slaves were drawn mostly from Mozambique and Madagascar, but also among them were a number of Bengali women from India who were imported to serve as domestic workers and concubines, on account of their 'gentleness, good manners and cleanliness but also for their hair and features, which were similar to those of Europeans, differing only in colour, ranging from a light tan to very dark'.[5] The governor also brought lascars, rugged Muslim seafarers from coastal India, to build a shipyard and repair centre at a site on the northwest blessed with a friendly southeastern wind. In the cove overlooked by an arc of hills dominated by the thumb-like protuberance known as 'Le Pouce', a town named Port Louis after Louis XV emerged, dotted with thick-walled stone churches and public buildings constructed by Indian temple masons from French territories in South India.

By the time the British arrived, descendants of the original Indian migrants had made a place for themselves in alien surroundings. The lascars had established their own neighbourhood, known alternatively as Camp Malabar or Camp des Lascars in Port Louis, and led a riotous annual procession through the city for Muharram or 'Yamse' as they called it. Heirs of Bengali slaves and stone masons were spread out through the colony and some of them had climbed out of their servile status and become owners of estates. About forty traders who had moved from French enclaves in India, such as Pondicherry, had set up thriving businesses.

More Indians came to the island, known again as 'Mauritius' after the handover to the British. Some Indian soldiers who came to fight the French, for instance, chose to stay on and make a home there. Then there were convicts whose crime was political in nature, mostly sepoys guilty of military offences, who were brought to Mauritius by its new governor, Robert Farquhar, to build roads and fortifications in the new colony. Business entrepreneurs came from British colonies. The most prominent one was Ratanji Bickaji, who came in 1810 or thereabouts. A Parsi from Bombay, Bickaji seems to have been an inordinately enterprising man with a finger in every pie. He was a representative of the Imam of Muscat and various Bombay firms, which included 'Frith & Co.' (possibly Francis Frith, a grocer, printer and photographer in the Middle East) and 'Jujabbey' (most likely a misspelling of Jejeebhoy, the owner of

Bombay's Jubilee Textile Mill) and 'Dadebhoy' (Dadabhoy) & Sons. He paid bills of transaction, equipped bricks and schooners, lent money (there is a record of 500 piastres given to a Mr Collier in 1815[6]) and arranged for the scavenging of Port Louis, for which he had a tender in 1835.

Vellivahel Anassamy of the mercantile Chettiar Hindu community, who was probably from a French-occupied part of India since he could speak French and doubled as an interpreter, came to Mauritius as a storekeeper with the British navy and went on to buy the Bon Espoir estate, once owned by Mahé de La Bourdonnais. It was his son, Inonmondy, and their neighbour, a Britisher, E. Arbuthnot, who first hit upon the idea of importing Indians to labour for plantation owners and for Bickaji, who needed workers to meet his scavenging contract. Arbuthnot's brother was an indigo planter in India and used workers from the hills as labour.[7]

The need for a scheme of this or a similar nature arose in the context of abolition. The British had left the French administrative and judicial systems intact in Mauritius and permitted the widespread everyday use of French Creole while English became the language of administration. But they discontinued commercial activities on the island, turning a thriving port and shipbuilding centre into a vast plantation: the area under sugarcane cultivation increased five-fold to over 20,000 hectares and sugar factories multiplied from a mere 10 in 1798 to 157 in 1823. The Franco-Mauritian elite, facing no threat to their privileges, raised no objection to the new orientation, but the 1833 British law abolishing slavery and threatening their own right to keep slaves, filled them with alarm.

Under Mahé de La Bourdonnais, the ratio of slave to master was ten to one and as many as 110,000 slaves, arriving between 1767 and 1810, made Mauritius the British Empire's most productive sugar colony. Estate owners protested the abolition act and their consequent loss of a free labour force. A Franco-Mauritian lawyer, politician and slave-owner, Adrien d'Épinay made representations to the British government in London in 1831 and 1833 on behalf of sugar planters and negotiated a compensation for farmers for the loss of their slaves. Following the enactment of the British Slave Compensation Act 1837, Adrien d'Épinay and his wife successfully lodged claims against the release of their 455 slaves and received £15,192.[8] A total sum of £2.1 million was awarded as compensation. Plantation owners replaced their lost slaves with 25,000 bonded workers from India in 1834. In 1837, the colonial government of India passed an ordinance, setting in motion a formal system of indenture which, over the next hundred years or so, saw about 450,000 Indian indentured workers arrive in Mauritius.

Amidst the cafés and tourists shopping for kitschy knick-knacks on the Caudan Waterfront is a statue of Seewoosagur Ramgoolam. On a high pedestal, the first prime minister of independent Mauritius, bespectacled, in a buttoned-up shirt, tie and jacket, holds up a book. Biographical accounts of Ramgoolam's early life tell an inspiring story of fortitude and perseverance. Born to an indentured worker-turned-overseer from Bihar and a young widow, Ramgoolam suffered the death of his father when he was seven and, at the age of twelve, lost the use of his left eye after an accident in a cowshed. Undaunted, he pursued his studies with earnestness, even enrolling himself in a Roman Catholic-aided school without his mother's knowledge and went on to earn a medical degree from the University of London.[9] He was knighted and groomed for leadership by the British (an association that seems to be commemorated by an alabaster-white marble statue of Queen Victoria fronting the stately Government House in a straight line 400 metres away). The father of the nation, framed by a cerulean blue sky, looks like he is sculpted in black stone hewn from the island's basalt hills, a reminder of the sun-scalded Indian indentured labourers from whom he is descended.

When they first arrived on the Mauritian shore, indentured workers, if they were not required to be quarantined, were received in depots in Port Louis. They were housed, medically treated and fed till their prospective employers arrived to take them away. Those few days made for a welcome hiatus to recover from a passage that was terribly harrowing for a great many of them who had never sailed so far and, in some cases, never seen the sea before. A ship doctor noted in his diary in 1883: '... coolies, after leaving India, are very homesick, they have entered another world and everything is new and strange to them.'[10]

One of these depots, restored by conservationists and declared a UNESCO World Heritage site, is at the far end of the waterfront, on the east side of the sheltered bay of Trou Fanfaron in Port Louis. The Aapravasi Ghat, as it is now called, a Hindi translation of the term 'Immigration Depot', was built in 1849 on the bones of a former shipyard. Its chalk-lined walls of grey basalt, spread over a 1,640-square-metre site, enclosing immigration sheds, a hospital block and service quarters from the 1860s, speak eloquently of the 'Great Experiment', which brought half a million workers to Mauritius, birthing a modern system of indenture that spread rapidly across the world.

Warehouses are an essential component of landside facilities developed alongside ports. Large, open or closed spaces are needed for storing goods before or after being transported by sea. What strikes one while walking about the Aapravasi Ghat is how starkly bare it is, an empty unencumbered space meant for accommodating as many numbers as possible. Except in this case, the numbers were human beings, people of flesh and blood, sensory perception and feelings. They would have felt the force of the sun, the prison-like greyness of stone and the constraining quality of the walls. A flat embankment at a lower level is the point where workers clambered off boats and stepped on land. Here is the centrepiece of the memorial, the entrance, a simple gate through which disembarking workers entered. And directly facing it, a single flight of stairs, charcoal-grey stone with lines of limestone, half in shadow, half in sunlight, leading up to a patch of blue sky.

When prospective employers came to take charge of their quota of indentured workers, they took them away to one of the 200-odd sugar estates spread over the island's nine districts, the largest number being concentrated in Plaines Wilhems in the centre of the island. In the early days, indentured workers were made to cut down forests, immensely laborious work for which large and extremely heavy volcanic boulders were removed, stacked in pyramids and carted away on barrows. The workers planted sugarcane on cleared land and built roads and sugar factories. Each camp housed an average of 300 labourers living in barracks made of local basalt stones joined with lime mortar and lime wash-coated interiors or straw huts plastered with mud and dung. A hut, a string bed, a pot and a good steel axe were the modest furnishings. As more and more workers arrived, small shops or dukkans emerged in the countryside. At first there were many more men than women, but over time more women arrived, customarily attired in saris or long skirts. Brokers or agwaa arranged marriages and soon there were children.

In England, there was a great thrust at the time on extending education to children of factory workers. Following the trend, the colonial administration expressed an interest in the education of children of indentured workers. But the attempt to provide education in English provoked a hostile reaction from the French. The Franco–Mauritian-dominated Legislative Council, backed by the Catholic Church, strongly opposed what they saw as British policies of anglicization and opened their own schools. An archbishop visiting the school at the Grand Bay Sugar Estate observed that several boys 'showed much intelligence and had a very pleasant manner' and the 'eldest girl of 14 read, wrote and ciphered well and led the singing of a beautiful French hymn'.[11]

As it happened, indentured workers wanted neither English nor the Creolized French patois of the region as a medium of instruction (in 1908, only 7,000 out of 60,000 Indo-Mauritian children were in French schools) and preferred to send their children to informal schools started by workers in their own languages. The proliferating numbers of workers drawn from various parts of India bred an amalgam of customs, dialects and rituals. Small Hindu shrines replicating French grottos appeared on pathways planted with red flags. Dark mountain paths hummed with sonorous readings of the Ramcharitamanas and Kabir. Clément Charoux's 1935 novel *Ameenah*[12] evokes the scene wonderfully through a pastiche of sensations: an aroma of masala, petrol, achar, pineapple, rum, ginger and November mangoes; the tinkling of temple bells; glimpses of minarets; freshly bathed women walking back from the fields, eyes chastely lowered to avoid the 'rodent gaze of men'. Scenes from other books evoke ghostly images of funeral processions and entire hillsides covered by graves of thousands of indentured workers felled by epidemics of malarial fever and cholera.

Having come to Mauritius with an idea of tracing Foolkore's identity, I am taken aback by the multiplicity of possibilities presented by a reading of the island's history. The best way to guess Foolkore's location and circumstances, it seems to me, is to take my cues from Mohanlal, to look at the few facts I have regarding my great-grandfather and try and match them to the various possibilities that exist. But since the preponderance of Indian indentured workers on the island makes indenture a natural starting point, I start from there.

For Foolkore to have been the daughter of an indentured worker in whose house Mohanlal was a tenant, the latter would have had to be living near the plantations in the interior where the only form of work available to him would have been to run a grocery shop or teach rural schoolchildren. I do not see a city-bred, English-literate man like Mohanlal running a dukkan in the wilderness of Flacq or Savanne. Nor is it likely that he knew Bhojpuri, Telugu or Creole, the languages and dialects which were commonly used by workers in Mauritius, and which could qualify him to teach their offspring.

Displayed on the walls of the museum attached to the Aapravasi Ghat are blow-ups of some of the 300,000 photographs of indentured workers taken by colonial authorities to make identity passes. Class and hard labour are clearly inscribed in them, the faces weather-beaten, stubble on chins, watery eyes, hair dust-matted and tousled. The style of a turban or an ornament hints at the history preceding the moment of photography. The migrants raise their heads obediently and gaze in three-quarter profile for the white man's records. I study their ebony-skinned faces for signs of emotion—sadness, joy, relief even—but I find no clue, nothing.

Though it does not seem likely that Foolkore came from a background of indenture, I feel like I need to explore the option more fully before discarding it. The Folk Museum of Indian Immigration is a permanent exhibition at the Mahatma Gandhi Institute in Moka showcasing, among other things, elements of indenture culture: musical instruments, jewellery and photographs of the brilliant flora amidst which they lived. Govinden Vishwanaden, head of the School of Mauritian and Area Studies, gives me the bad news that the registers of indenture arrivals are in the process of being digitized. It will be weeks before the process is complete.

I am deeply disappointed. I am aware that I have very little to go on: a smudged signature in a letter that may say 'Murli Murari' (I have learnt that 'Murari' is known to be a Brahmin name from the hilly Kumaon area in North India which, along with the first name, fits my uncle Vinod's hypothesis of Foolkore being a 'Brahmin lady'). But I have no other information, which means that I could be looking at records from the 1830s onwards since my great-grandmother's ancestors could have come to Mauritius at any time. But now, despite the impracticality of it, the news that I cannot look at the registers at all comes as a blow. Vishwanaden sees my downcast face and takes pity on me.

'What years do you want to look at?' he asks.

'The last decade of the 1800s,' I tell him, having decided to limit my search to a more practical range. He offers to make some registers available for me to look at under supervision in his office behind the museum.

Surrounded by filing cabinets and computers, I search the century-old pages, looking for three names and their variations to allow for the vagaries of colonial spellings—'Murli', 'Murari' and any name with 'Phool' (Ful, Fool, Phul or anything close). These are the entries I note down as I find them in the register of indentured arrivals:

- Phekuri Ahir, daughter of Sankaliya and Gujar (father), from Azamgarh (Bhadra)
- Phulasia Kakar from ... (unclear)
- Phulehai from Jainpur, Barsar
- Phulaiswari from Azamgarh
- Phulmaasi Ahir from Bikapur
- Phooljerea ...
- Durjani, a Jat from Salampur (Mathura)

- Murli, twenty, son of Heera and Pitani Ahir, from Fatehpur (scar on forehead, 5 feet 4 inches, came on the SS *Bancoora* from Calcutta, 6 August 1900), next of kin, Durga.[13]

◈

Manish's guest house in the central town of Quatre Bornes is close to the intersection of two roads, including one named after India's first prime minister, Jawaharlal Nehru. I picked it because it was centrally located and seemed to offer easy access to every other part of the island. There is a difference between looking at a location on a map of a place I have never visited sitting a few thousand miles away and finding myself in the place itself. Until I am in Mauritius, I do not know how proximate the urban and rural parts of the island are. What I have assumed rightly to be main arterial roads on a map pass through a rustic stretch that sits between the urban centre and the beachfront. Contrary to my expectations, I am not in a town but at its edge, amidst sugarcane fields—or what were formerly sugarcane fields—and the main road is a bleak, windy strip on the edge of undulating grass.

On a walk around the neighbourhood, I come across a small electronics shop and a grocery mall full of unsmiling shoppers lugging bags of grain and biscuits. Returning to the guest house I walk through a long, narrow lane that has the feel of a gaothan, the name given to a few protected pockets of old villages not yet swept up by urban transformation in Mumbai. In a yard, a big-hipped woman in a flower print dress is putting up her washing to dry and chatting with a friend seated in a chair behind the bushes. I pass a small shrine to Jesus, Mary and some deities I cannot identify. In the nineteenth century, French planters sold plots of land on the outskirts of their estates to indentured workers in a phenomenon known as the Grand Morcellement; many of those plots have been turned into vegetable farms and periodically I see a white Toyota van loaded with produce for the market, zipping over a thin path cutting through a sea of green.

Manish is a tireless host. I see him always with a cloud of anxiety hovering above him. It is off season, so there is only one other guest, but from the numerous recommendations tossing around online I can see that his place is popular and he is well-liked. He is keen on doing better. One evening he takes me to the market to fix a problem with my SIM card and asks if I would like to stop at a department store sale close by. I say yes, glad for an opportunity to see more of ordinary life on the island. Manish is deeply gratified, as if at last he has figured out what interests me. After that, he stops recommending conventional tourist spots for me to visit and does not bring up the possibility of my hiring him to drive me to them.

One morning, finding me at a loose end, he asks if I would like to look around his property and when I agree he takes me on a tour of the house and the yard, pointing out the improvements he has planned—a small pool, a garden, a makeshift gym. All the time he keeps up an anxious patter of questions, concerns that probably keep him up at night: 'How do I get more customers? Should I advertise? Should I use the internet? What should I do?'

We end up on the terrace. Manish points and following his finger I see a rainbow ... no, two rainbows! Two perfect, shimmering parabolas in front of us. It is a breathtaking sight: the grey sky, the bands of light, the smoky hills and the tall peak of the Corps de Garde. I have never seen anything like it. I am awestruck, mesmerized. Manish is unimpressed. It is probably a daily occurrence.

'You know, growing up I was poor, really poor,' he says. I am surprised by the sudden change of subject and the emotion in his gruff tone.

'So poor, you cannot imagine. I lifted loads as a porter, anything that required strength. Then I started growing vegetables. I bought a truck on loan and finally built a house. When I was poor, I never hoped for anything, but then I got married and my life changed!'

Manish's wife, Deepti (name changed), is tall and pretty with a gentle strength that fits well with Manish's account of a supportive partner. Her cheerful and energetic presence is a bright foil to Manish's persistent gloom. The only feature I find jarring about her is her speech. Like her husband, she talks to me in Hindi, but the melodramatic clichés peppering her speech are completely and bafflingly at variance with her personality. It is only after chatting with her for some time that I understand the cause: like many Indian Mauritians, she is a fan of Hindi television serials relayed from India on satellite antennae. In India, these long, contrived tales of vengeance and petty intrigue in families are popular but also widely panned for their regressive attitudes and unreal settings, and it is disconcerting to think that they could be taken for accurate representations of contemporary India or a model of emulation in the diaspora.

On Sunday evening I go down to the main house where my host family lives. I have decided to move to a more centrally located hotel. Manish's daughter who manages accounts agrees to let me settle my bill so that I can leave early the next day. I have phoned her to let her know I am coming down. I assume I am expected, but she has clearly not informed her parents because I find myself intruding on a scene of restful domesticity. Deepti is in the open kitchen, cooking and talking to her husband who is sprawled on an armchair in the drawing room. The grey cloud of anxiety that hovers about him has dissipated; he looks relaxed. A cricket match is playing on the television set, which nobody is watching. Through a half-open door to her room, I see the accountant daughter brushing her long hair.

Manish is surprised to see me. I wave and head to his daughter's room to settle accounts. When I emerge, I find him engaged in what appears to be a struggle between his relaxed avatar and the worried, service-oriented persona that he has always adopted around me. The two battle briefly and then the latter gives up. He waves me into a chair in front of the bright screen and offers me a glass of home-made wine.

11
Hits and Misses

Gold Nest is a no-frills business hotel, popular both with regular overseas guests and the local populace. Every day I see a large family or two celebrating a birthday or an anniversary in its Indian restaurant, which has faux wood panelling on the walls and white napkins flowering in goblets. I get a great deal on a top-floor corner room but because the hotel Wi-Fi does not reach it, I spend a lot of time in the lobby, which also gives me a view of the street. The St. Jean Road, running like an arrow through Quatre Bornes, is lined with shops on either side and there is an open-air market down the road on Sundays, where one can buy anything from slippers and fruit to brightly coloured woven baskets and sarongs. Quiet residential lanes lead off the commercial thoroughfare studded with banana trees and houses built in the Creole style, the loveliest of which, in my opinion, has powder-blue walls, gracefully curving railings in a darker shade of blue, white wooden shutters and sand-coloured trimmings. The hotel is a convenient place for people to drop in and many of my potential interviewees live close by. An academic called Shakuntala Boolell invites me to visit her in her flat on a parallel road. A sharp-featured middle-aged woman, Boolell is an associate professor in the Department of French Studies at the

University of Mauritius, but also writes on the Gujarati diaspora in the country.

She startles me with a question, 'Did you know that Gujarati-style ornaments were displayed in a shop window on Rue Deschartes in the nineteenth century?'

Rue Deschartes was the high street of the colonial era, a ritzy shopping enclave of the Mauritian haute monde where shopkeepers kept catalogues of the latest fashions and ordered them in large boxes from Paris. Mauritius may have been a backwater, but it was no laggard when it came to style, a certain European chic, of course, which I imagine did not have a place for ethnic Indian jewellery. The answer to Boolell's question, I discover, is a fascinating story of crime and enterprise on the high seas.

Historians of the age-old circuits of the Indian Ocean trade focus on the importance of Indian fabrics as a commodity of exchange. But underneath the billowing yards of cloth was another commodity, less fluid, less talked-about and crossing borders illegally: gold. Since the twelfth century, long, long before gold was discovered in the Transvaal, India's insatiable hunger for the yellow metal, a symbol of status and wealth at all levels, was fed by a well-organized, surreptitious network operating between Africa and India.

Shona-speaking miners extracted between 2 and 8 tonnes of gold each year, from around 4,000 diggings across the Zimbabwe plateau and in isolated deposits in present-day Limpopo and Mpumalanga. Semi-independent couriers marketed gold in the form of ore, dust, coins or ornaments to buyers at the coast, often in exchange for Indian cloth. Fairs, those appearing and disappearing ports of the littoral, served to tranship gold to various Indian Ocean ports, with the whole operation managed by vania merchant houses based in Mozambique.[1]

The actual function of transporting the gold, bypassing various colonial authorities that came to control the borders after the sixteenth century, was performed by couriers who criss-crossed the ocean carrying the contraband goods. One of these was Mayaram Soni whose surname 'Soni', means 'gold jeweller'. I ask a friend in Gujarat for help in tracing a biographical sketch of the smuggler. *Lejo Lahaavo Lok* by Harilal Godani[2] is a thin booklet in Gujarati and not very coherently written. But from it I learn that Mayaram Soni was born in Mahua, a small town close to the coastal town of Bhavnagar in the Kathiawar region of Gujarat, probably in the late 1700s.

After losing his father at an early age, he was sent to Bombay with a relative to be schooled in his community's traditional profession of jewellery making. At sixteen, he married a girl from Bhavnagar. By then, perhaps because of his vulnerability, his poverty and his semi-orphaned status, he was drafted into a gold-smuggling ring operating out of Bombay. Like other members of the ring, he travelled on steamers, carrying thin slivers of beaten gold between slices of potato in a fried snack called bhajia. His route touched upon Aden, Zanzibar and Madagascar and each trip earned him a princely profit of Rs 12,000. At some point, though, he ran out of luck and was arrested and sent from Madagascar to Mauritius.

No specific dates are mentioned in the skimpy account, but it seems to me that Mayaram was probably in a Mauritian jail in 1810 when the island changed hands between the French and the British. The ex-gold smuggler was put to work in Robert Farquhar's chain gangs of imported Indian convicts. It is hard to imagine a Gujarati jeweller, customarily of a small build and frail constitution, doing the back-breaking work of building bridges and roads. But long days of labour cemented a friendship between Mayaram and his co-workers. He was invited to live with them in their camp in the district of Pamplemousses near the botanical garden. Apparently, Mayaram had convinced the colonial authorities to let him stay on in the country after his release.

One day, Mayaram, a free man, was strolling in Port Louis and happened to pass a Genovese-owned jewellery shop. He entered it on an impulse and must have worked his charm, because the owner offered him a job. How long he worked at the shop is not known but Mayaram, with his knack for winning people's trust, became close to his employer, who died and left him the business. Mayaram Soni, proud owner of a shop in Rue Deschartes, put the traditional jewellery of western India on display in the window. He also brought his wife over to Mauritius and invited young men from his hometown to join him as well. Eighty Kathiawari families moved to Mauritius at his bidding. The Mayarams are a well-known family in present-day Mauritius.

The design for the Mauritius Commercial Bank in Ebene is an ellipse balanced on four travertine-clad pillars. It is a strange-looking building, like a landed spaceship, glossy with a steel-and-glass face and a million twinkling eyes. I pass it almost every day wherever I am headed and because the traffic moves slowly at this point up the slope, I invariably get a long, close look at its blinking façade. The design suits its location in the country's information technology hub, but it is a surprisingly rare example of a futuristic piece of architecture I come across in a country that is fairly wealthy.

An exporter of textiles and sugar, receiving over a million tourists every year and substantial foreign direct investment, Mauritius is one of Africa's leading economies and far ahead of India in GDP per capita rankings (at 75 to India's 137).[3] There is no visible poverty, no hollow-bellied children at the lights such as one sees in Indian cities. The only beggar I come across is a stout young man in worn clothes who boards a bus at the Mahatma Gandhi Institute in Moka to make an eloquent plea in polished English for financial help and exits with a hatful of notes and coins.

Yet, much of the urban built landscape in the interior of the island is dreary. Pizzazz and glamour are for the beachfront; the innards of the island, its small towns and commercial areas, pitted everywhere with its characteristic basalt hills, are sombre and do not reflect the colourful cultures from which most of its residents are drawn. The bits of India that I come across scattered everywhere have a dated feel, such as the shop display window opposite my hotel where mannequins in black and gold wigs strike a pose with silk saris draped over outstretched arms, like Indian air hostesses in advertisements from the 1960s.

I spend the first few days after my arrival at the National Archives Department of Mauritius. The archives are in an industrial zone in Coromandel, halfway between Quatre Bornes and Port Louis. It is hard to imagine a more incongruous setting for historical records. An opening in the wide main road leads to a maze of warehouses. A man in a DHL jacket turning a corner is the only sign of life apparent amidst massive buildings with corrugated-sheet doorways, wire fences and signboards. No eateries, no tea shops or hawker's carts; I passed the last one 3 kilometres ago. 'Pack some food tomorrow,' the receptionist says kindly on my first visit. I make a habit of carrying oranges in my bag. The archives are spread over two floors. The ground floor has the feel of a proper archive while on the first floor I am the only researcher in what appears to be an administrative office, with a forlorn lady called Neelam (name changed) to fetch files for me. The Z6A Series, containing logs of arrivals of non-indentured visitors, are hardbound registers, each the size of a legal ledger. They are heavy and since I do not have a precise date for Mohanlal's arrival, I need to go through many in a day. Neelam's flagging enthusiasm for fetching them is a source of concern. I feel guilty watching her haltingly and reluctantly get up from her chair to cart the heavy files back to the shelves and return with more. Then one day we chat and when she discovers that I have visited the ashram of her revered guru in South India, a bearded, smiling man in white, I see her spirits revive and the files seem to arrive at my table on wings.

But none of them contain what I am looking for. I go through piles and piles of ledgers, turning the glazed green-tinted pages with their scrawled contents—passenger names, ages, birthplaces, ship names and dates of their arrival—mechanically without result. It is tedious work and the hardest part is justifying its worth. My inner critic, ever ready to rebuke me for self-indulgence, begins to stir; I feel it counting hours spent with no visible result. Is there material for a book or not? Am I wasting my time? I feel my morale beginning to plummet when suddenly, suddenly, without any preamble or warning, I see it! I see my great-grandfather Mohanlal's name in a register of arrivals into Mauritius. It is so unexpected and at the same time so routinely placed among hundreds of others that it is at once unique and ordinary.

I look at it for a long, long time. The feeling is indescribable: relief, excitement, exultation … I want to whoop, wave my arms and break into a jig. None of which I can do in an office where people, strangers to me, are bent over their tables as if at a bank and where the plain warehouse walls are visible through the windows. Even Neelam is not at her seat. My phone is in my bag, which is in a locker downstairs. There is nobody with whom I can share this moment of discovery.

I take photographs with my small digital camera and make notes. The entry says: 'Mohan lall Permanandas'. The letters are clear; the writer, prone to flourish, has added curls to the first letters. There is an insertion between and above the two names, 'Killavale', it says. I imagine this young man, my ancestor, instructing the clerk to add a middle name—spelling it out and the clerk still getting it wrong.

Mohanlal arrived in Mauritius on 5 November 1904. His place of birth is given as Bombay, and he was twenty-four years old. The entry number is 21. The edges of the page are crumbly and inky marks have penetrated from the other side of the thinning paper. A couple of words here and there are in pink. The ship he travelled on was the SS *Secunder*. Among his co-passengers were Hafiz Mohamad, born Bombay, age forty-eight; Moonshi Porrukhan, born Bombay, age twenty-five; Boomfoo Hosan, born Bombay, age thirty-two. An internet search tells me that the SS *Secunder* was a three-masted, 260-feet-long, 1,662-ton steel cargo steamer originally with the Ardan Steam Ship Co. and owned by the Mauritius-based Hadji S. Seedick & Co. from 1901. It eventually passed into the hands of the colonial government of Mauritius and carried the mail between Mauritius and Rodrigues till 1928 or 1932 when it was finally broken up.[4] I take several photographs of the ink-stained page and note down the reference number for the register, 'Z2D 162',[5] with trembling fingers.

I like to think that what happens next is an outcome of my volatile mood, that my uncontainable excitement actually induces a siren to go off. But of course, it has nothing to do with me and is probably a frequent occurrence to do with the warehouses. Nobody around me seems at all surprised or affected by it. I sit with my fingers over my ears, waiting for it to stop. But it does not. It rises and falls and rises again, persistent, a long, yowling, ear-splitting sound: *Eeeyeeeeeeeeeeeeeee.*

Delirious over my find and groggy with hunger, I find it hard to sit still, so I cap my pen and head out to a long, broad veranda that runs along the length of the office. I have not ventured out into the veranda before, having always entered the office through a small anteroom at the head of the stairs. So I had no idea that there are large photographs displayed on the wall. They are prints or perhaps daguerreotypes taken of various aspects of early Mauritius and I walk past them slowly, savouring each view. Shadowy hills, heavy stone buildings, long beaches and luxuriant foliage, a few people, horses, the docks. At the end of the line is a visual of a long, handsome steamer in a gentle sea, framed by a Mauritian plateau. The caption says 'Debarquement de Boeufs (1900)' which means 'The Landing of the Oxen'. The steamer is also named. It is the SS *Secunder*.

◆

I take a break from poring over old newspapers at the National Library on Edith Cavell Street. A queue is forming at the street corner stall where a man is frying spiced split-pea balls known as gateaux piments. In a few minutes the lunchtime crowd will be pouring out of Mauritius Telecom, the State Insurance Company and other offices in the tall buildings around the park. Crowds will collect around the stalls on the other side of the square where vendors sell dhall puri, the Bihari dish recreated by homesick indentured workers. Les Jardins de la Compagnie is an oasis in the financial district. Two stone lions guard the gate of the rectangular garden, their great stone heads resting on large stone paws, suggesting calmness and permanence, a state of restfulness one would expect from a tropical paradise.

But the Mauritius I have encountered in historical accounts is erratic and combustible and has the tone of a rambunctious comedy of errors. Mahé de La Bourdonnais's colonists, for instance, were reputedly a rum lot recruited from the dregs of Breton and Bourbon society and inclined towards sloth, anarchy and drunkenness. Slow-travelling news from the metropole found a comical echo on the island. During the French Revolution, for instance, self-styled insurgents ran around displaying posters and threatening rebellion. They almost brought down a church, firing salvos for the slain Jacobin icon Jean-Paul Marat and set up a guillotine in the public square, in which the only head they managed to sever was reportedly of an unlucky goat.[6] The tone of farce matched the subversive use the island was put to after becoming a French Crown Colony, both to harass the British and to receive pirated goods poured into the island, attracting American traders.

Sun dapples the pathways, piercing through immensely high walls of creepers flooding down from ancient banyan trees. The clamour of people is absorbed by trees and sunlight, which lies over everything, including the tops of office buildings, setting their windows agleam. A man walks by, a transistor in his hand playing a song from a 1974 Bollywood film, *Ishk, Ishk, Ishk* (Love, Love, Love): '*Chal saathi chal—kab tak pukaare, aa mere pyaare, peeche ne reh ... aagey nikal* (Walk my friend, walk/How long I call, let's go my loved one/don't get left behind, get ahead).' It is peaceful and yet my mind is full of the moody past. I recall an account of a cyclone hitting the town on a March evening in 1868 and blowing the leaves off all the trees, lifting whole churches and bridges off the ground and setting every ship in the harbour adrift, some in the air on revolving columns of water. And I remember epidemics, pollution and storms that killed the social life of Port Louis in the nineteenth century, sending its elite residents to other parts of the island.

Something of that past lingers in the park that was once a cemetery for victims of a smallpox epidemic. And amidst the office workers and loiterers are statues of celebrated Mauritians scattered around the mighty banyans. There is a bronze Adrien d'Épinay striking an impressively argumentative pose in the central square of the garden. D'Épinay, who held famously regressive views on slavery, also secured some progressively democratic wins, such as the right of colonists to serve on the Legislative Council and the lifting of press censorship. There is Rémy Ollier, a mixed-origin journalist who successfully petitioned Queen Victoria for the entry of coloureds into the council of government. I don't find Adolphe de Plevitz, a German who made himself the unofficial protector of suffering indentured workers, but there is Charles Édouard Brown-Séquard, a full-bearded physiologist and neurologist who discovered a medical condition caused by damage to the spinal cord.

A recent and rare addition to this firmament dominated by nineteenth-century Frenchmen is a statue of Manilal Doctor. Manilal was a lawyer sent by Gandhi to help Indians fight for their rights. Gandhi visited Mauritius in November 1901 when the ship in which he was travelling to Bombay docked there for a considerably long time. He was not then as widely known as he would be, but news of his political activism in South Africa had spread to the diaspora and his visit was written about in the local Mauritian newspapers *Le Radical* and *Les Petites Affiches*. Though a plague epidemic restricted the Mahatma's movements, a banquet was held in the Anjuman Building on 13 November, attended by the Indian elite who heard Gandhi talk about the importance of education. Six years later, he sent Manilal, who provided legal advice to Indians in need and edited a local paper, *The Hindustani*. Manilal became a beloved presence on the island and there is fittingly a touch of the everyman in the way the sculptor has chosen to represent him in a short coat, his feet splayed, the tips of his hand touching.

I, CAVENDISH BOYLE, Knight Commander of the Most Distinguished—Order of Saint Michael and Saint George, Governor and Commander-in-Chief, in and over the Colony of Mauritius and its Dependencies &c., &c., &c.,

REQUEST IN THE NAME OF His Britannic Majesty, all those whom it may concern to allow MOHANLAL PARMANANDAS KILLAVALA ... (British Subject) travelling in Natal and South Africa to PASS FREELY and afford ... every assistance and protection of which ... may stand in need.

The document was stamped and certified as 'Given at Government House, Port Louis, in the Colony of Mauritius 16th Day of November 1905'.

I have come across this letter in the documentation I retrieved from the archives in South Africa. Sir Charles Cavendish Boyle was a kindly looking man in a captain's cap whose significant contribution to Empire was writing the anthem of Newfoundland. The letter reads like a passport at a time when there were no formal passports and suggests a measure of privilege for Mohanlal, which makes me wonder if he was in government service of some kind. The Colonial Office, based in London, required governors of British dependencies to send an annual account of administration in the form of 'Blue Books'. I find these, each Blue Book about 5 by 8 inches in size, with a spine thickness of an inch and a half and bound in hard blue covers, on which the year and the title is embossed in silver that has now faded. Some have a new label or the date written in chalk.

In the Blue Book of 1902, I find that Indians worked for the government mainly in minor but occasionally higher positions. Mamode Cassim was a cook in the customs department, Kootbarkhan a foreman on Flat Island, J. Dooknah a cemetery keeper, Prayag Balgobine a deputy postmaster, and M. Murat a master in the education department. A fifth-class clerk in the receiver-general's office earned Rs 1,200 annually in 1906 and teachers were paid Rs 960. Mohanlal does not figure in the Blue Books. [7]

◈

'How can I help you?' the director at the National Library asks me. She is a petite woman with coiffed jet-black hair. I have been told by a friend in Mauritius to look her up, so one afternoon I climb the stairs from the Reference Room and send in my card. A few minutes later I am seated across from her, separated by a table. Her office is neat and formal, yet filled with small personal touches, poised but not unfriendly.

'Have they been good to you downstairs?'

'Oh yes, the staff is wonderfully efficient.'

'Is there anything I can help you with?'

I hesitate. I have not planned to ask for anything, but it occurs to me that I could do with some help on a certain matter.

'Yes, actually …'

She nods—encouragingly, I think.

'I was wondering if you could advise me on where to look for a marriage certificate from a hundred years ago?'

She inclines her head, draws a breath and picks up her phone. Seconds later, her assistant, a tall, thin woman with a notebook, appears at the door. She introduces us and the two women confer in French.

The assistant looks at me and says, 'You have to try at the National Civil Office in the Emmanuel Anquetil building. Do you know it?'

I shake my head.

'I will send someone with you.'

We have been walking for a few minutes on Edith Cavell Street. Vishnoo (name changed), the wiry, shaven-headed young man who has been assigned to be my guide, is a familiar fixture downstairs in the Reference Room. I have seen him sorting out old newspapers with gloved hands and a mask to keep out the dust. Apart from a quick glance in the director's office, he has not looked at me. He leads the way, keeping a few feet between us. He walks fast and I follow briskly on the sunlit street.

Suddenly he turns around. 'I am inspired by Amitabh Bachchan. Do you like him?'

Startled, I mumble something about him being a 'wonderful actor'.

He is beside me now, but walking in a staccato manner, slightly in front then slightly behind and talking.

'I am also inspired by John Travolta.' He swipes a hand across his face. 'I am so lucky they both are alive! I feel they are guiding me.'

He falls silent. Then he speaks again. 'I want to go to India ... I do yoga, surya namaskar, meditation ...'

A few days ago, I met a doleful, large-bellied constable at the police barracks who said his most ardent wish was to visit India. It seems to be a widespread preoccupation. We turn off Edith Cavell Street and enter the Jardins de la Campagnie. My guide dodges a man with an umbrella.

'Where is your husband?' he asks abruptly.

'Arriving tomorrow,' I lie glibly.

He cocks his head, considering my answer. Then he asks: 'Can I sing for you? I want to sing a song for you.'

He does not wait for an answer but begins to sing '*Main pal do pal ka shayar hoon* (I am a poet for a few moments)', a song from the 1976 Amitabh Bachchan starrer, *Kabhi Kabhie*. He sings with the self-consciousness of a schoolboy and his heavily accented Hindi with its hard 'd' imbues his rendition with an unintentionally comical air. I hide my smile and let him lead me singing past the solemn statues and tramps of the Jardins de la Campagnie.

The Emmanuel Anquetil Building is a mini township. Thousands of people stream past me in the vast gleaming concourse, headed to one of the many municipal and government offices it houses. A hundred years ago most Indians married according to their religious rites and did not get their unions registered. But in 1905 there were 507 official Indian marriages in Mauritius and 95 in Port Louis the following year. If my great-grandparents did marry and register the marriage, there would be a copy of the marriage certificate. It could give me a name for Foolkore's family. The place to check is the Civil Status Enquiry Office, which is in a glass booth on the ground floor. People are seated on plastic chairs. Every time someone finishes his or her turn at the counter, the whole seated assembly gets up and moves one chair forward, like a game of musical chairs. Everyone is carrying important-looking files and plastic bags filled with papers. I hear murmurs about property, school admissions and post-death formalities. My inquiry for a hundred-year-old marriage certificate seems suddenly like a mirage. Vishnoo brings me a form to fill.

I am stumped by a question about 'Relationship with the deceased'. I can write 'Great-granddaughter' but how do I prove it?

I am directed to the seventh floor. The lift is out of order, so I huff and puff up the staircase, Vishnoo bounding ahead of me like a mountain goat.

The woman behind the counter is young, plump and unsmiling. I tell her what I am looking for. She listens to me without batting an eyelid. When I finish, she asks, 'Proof of relationship?'

I shrug and smile. 'I do not have anything to prove my relationship with my maternal great-grandparents.'

She shakes her head.

'Please!'

She shakes her head again.

'I am a writer from India. I only want information.'

She shakes her head again.

'Please! I do not want anything, just to look at the records.'

She shakes her head, impatiently this time, and firmly dismissive.

'Can I speak to someone? A senior officer?' She gives me a name on a floor below.

The deputy registrar of civil status, V. Saurty, is a middle-aged man in thick spectacles that give him a slightly owlish look. He patiently hears me out, writing down the names I give him and confirming the spelling. Then, without saying anything else, he picks up the phone. A few minutes later there is a knock on the door and the adamant woman from upstairs enters.

I feel a flutter of hope. Now, I assume, the deputy registrar will use his superior position to throw some weight behind my request. He will ask her to overlook my lack of proof of relationship and help me out.

Instead, the very opposite happens. The woman looks at me contemptuously. Then she looks at the man, who is presumably her boss or at least her senior, and unleashes an angry torrent of words. It is all in French and I cannot follow what she is saying, but there is no doubt that it is not helping my case.

The deputy registrar says nothing at all, letting the storm rage in his small cabin. I am shaken.

When she finally stops talking, he murmurs, 'Ça va ... ça va, tres bien.'

The door closes on her and on my sinking hopes. Trying to keep my disappointment from showing, I pick up my handbag, steeling myself for the inevitable brush-off. In my head I already hear the words 'sorry' and 'rules' and try to fix a polite smile on my face. But nothing like what I expect happens. Instead, I see Saurty pick up the phone and say, 'M-O-H-A-N-L-A-L K-I-L-L-A-V-A-L-A' into the mouthpiece. I hear him spell it out once with a 'w', another time with a 'v' and two 'ls'. He looks at me and asks what years I am looking at. I tell him 1904, 1905. 'Can you look right now?' I hear him ask. He puts down the phone and grins.

'They are digitizing the data in another office. My friend will call back.'

I am overwhelmed, afraid that I might begin to cry with relief. Saurty, quite unruffled by the waves of female hysteria tossing around in his small office, begins to tell me about a forthcoming trip to India. He shows me his itinerary. It is a dizzying whirl of cities spread across the country. I feel exhausted just looking at it.

'So many places? So far from each other?'

He shrugs. 'It's okay, no? Who knows when I will get the opportunity again.'

The phone buzzes. Saurty picks up the receiver and listens. I see him look at the piece of paper where he has written the alternative spellings I offered and hear him ask if they have been checked as well. He listens again. 'Merci,' he says and puts down the phone. 'No, sorry.' He shakes his head and I sense a note of genuine regret. 'There is no record.'

I am disappointed but relieved to have checked out the possibility.

12

Port Louis

In 1908, George Hawes, a captain and adjutant in the Third Battalion of the Royal Fusiliers, wrote to a fellow officer:

> We have now moved on to this comic little island ... Mauritius is an absurd place ... a wretched place to spend one's adjutancy in. We play golf and tennis every single day with exactly the same people in the rain, which is a kind of thick Scotch mist, except in November and December and January when it is fine, and February and March, which is the cyclone season and is quite past description. It is impossible to go out because it is impossible to stand up against the gale, and it is hot and damp, and we have to burn charcoal in braziers all the time to keep our clothes dry. And then the electric light goes out. What a life![1]

In 1910 he wrote:

> This second year is much the worst. We have all seen too much of each other, and these incessant tennis parties in the rain, the same dreary people, the same girls fishing for military alliances, the same bougainvillias and oleanders are enough to drive one

mad. There is something strangely unhealthy about this place. It is not that there is much illness ... but there seems to be something downright decadent in the atmosphere of this hot, over-fertile island. The smallness of it, too, and its remoteness—it is some 9,000 miles from England—add to this impression. Our mails arrive alternately at fortnightly and six-weekly intervals, and the local French papers, of which there are quantities, are beneath contempt and only, Frenchwise, concerned with the miserable local politics.[2]

In the early 1900s, there were only about 600 Britishers in Mauritius, all in a military camp in the centre of the island. Most of the French, 10,000 in total, had abandoned Port Louis, now a decaying town with open drains and frequent epidemics, and retreated to gracious mansions in the highlands. Those who had work in the capital, like heads of government departments and commercial concerns, brokers and professional men, would travel by train for 25 kilometres through stunning views of mountains and waterfalls to emerge at Port Louis, filling the streets with black (the colour preferred by French Mauritians who, it is said, would don a silk hat and a coat even if it was 90 degrees in the shade) and return in the evenings. Frenchwomen rarely went to Port Louis after it had lost its metropolitan sheen.

'It is essentially a city of men,' Allister Macmillan writes, 'a bustling emporium of trade, dominated by sugar and its potentialities', referring to thousands of tons of sugar stocked in great warehouses surrounded by wasps and bees seeking the 'delectable crystals'. It was also a town dominated by Asians.

The streets of the commercial section (are) choked ... with produce-laden carts drawn by great-horned oxen and driven by scantily clad Indians. Cross-legged on mats and cushions on the window-ledges of their stores, sit Mahommedan merchants, who close their establishments at mid-day on Fridays to worship Allah in the mosque, situated in the heart of the Asiatic quarter that pulsates with all the characteristics of the mysterious East: Indian women, clanking with jewellery on their arms and ankles and toes, and in their noses and ears, the vivid hues of the clothing of both them and their menfolk giving to the streets a kaleidoscope of colour; sombrely-clad Chinese, minus pig-tails now; itinerant vendors of cakes, drinks and concoctions 'wonderfully and fearfully made'; beggars in all stages of decrepitude; fowls and pigeons fattening on the droppings of grain from the carts and around the doors of the warehouses; and everywhere in the city are ownerless dogs of all kinds, suffering from the most loathsome forms of canine disease.[3]

In the twenty-first century, a hundred years later, I find the old Central Market in Port Louis surrounded by moneychangers and shops selling woven baskets from Madagascar and mobile accessories. Behind it is Chinatown. The island's small Chinese population is mainly descended from traders who came to Mauritius after the 1820s. They opened shops all over the island and often cohabited with Creole and Indian women. Kin Sen, age twenty-six, on the SS *Prorito* and Fok Suily, age twenty-two, and Cheong Law, age twenty-eight, on the SS *Taifu* were some of the names of travellers who came to Mauritius around the same time as Mohanlal. On a walking tour with Sadhna Ramlallah, who grew up in the old town, I enter shady pathways reminiscent of a time when the capital abounded with tamarind, date and banana trees, caladiums and magnificent yellow-flowered acacias, and come upon a few Creole-style houses in candy-bright colours with delicate grilles and individual motifs, like a star-shaped flower I see on a gate arch.

In and around these lanes the mercantile community had their offices. British firms like Blythe, Green, Jourdain & Co. and the French Pipon, Bell & Co. had set up shop alongside South Indian merchants. The growing influence of Gujarati and Chettiar firms in the Indian Ocean trade and the impossibility of negotiating loans, effecting mortgages or cashing bills without Indian agency was widely acknowledged. The British civil servant Bartle Frere wrote in 1873:

> Everywhere wherever there is any foreign trade, it passes through the hands of some Indian trader; no produce can be collected for the European, American or Indian market or imports distributed to the natives of the country but through him ... It is difficult to convey to those at a distance an adequate idea of the extent or completeness of the monopoly.[4]

The energetic Ratanji Bickaji had acquired a protégé, Pestonji Manekji, who imported mules from Muscat and Arabia and rice, wheat and coriander from India, and was an agent for various ships, including the square-rigged, 320-ton *City of Palaces*.[5] By the mid-nineteenth century Mauritius was importing thousands of bags and boxes of rice, tamarind, gram dhall, ghee, mustard oil, coriander and miscellaneous items such as turbans, in a year to meet the needs of indentured labourers, and the trade was mostly in the hands of merchants newly arrived from Gujarat. They brought food supplies and 'coolies' from India and exported sugar to Britain and then, when Britain moved to beet sugar from cane, diverted supplies to Bombay in such quantities that sugar came to be known among Bombay halwais or sweetmeat makers as 'miritz' after Mauritius.

Two streams of traders came from Gujarat. One was of the Memons, a mercantile community originating in Sind, believed to be Hindu Lohanas who converted to Islam under the influence of a Sufi saint in the fifteenth century (a less common hypothesis is that they were descended from Arab soldiers) and moved south to Gujarat, most of them settling in the Kathiawar peninsula. The other more prolific stream was of the Sunni Bohras from Surat district and which included the Turawas, the Boatawalas and also another leading merchant from Rander, Ajam Goolam Hoosen. The Memons had a bazaar in Rue des Limites and Queen Streets and dealt in groceries and building materials. The Sunni Bohras from Surat specialized in textiles and occupied a quadrangle formed by Royal, Bourbon, Farquhar and La Corderie streets.

Sadhna and I wander into the front office of a godown where a board on the wall lists the brands stocked (Complan, Crest Liquid, Flash, Glenrick, Kraft, Happy Mom, Signal) in the back or in a basement. A corner of the large space with a high ceiling serves as an office and is furnished with an eclectic collection of objects, such as a small antique chair with a carved backrest and green cushioning, an old-fashioned wall clock, a helmet, a computer and a big box of Dodo matches. A metal wire serves as a holder for paper bills, a crude, effective arrangement that I remember seeing in shops all over Bombay in the past. The proprietors are Memons. Dawood Abdulla Ibrahim, a fair, brown-eyed man with close-cropped hair tells us that his grandfather came to Mauritius at the turn of the twentieth century; his father, Aziz, who is sitting opposite him, has memories of a later time, of rationing during the Second World War when instead of rice-curry and salted fish they had to make do with 'mariok' (cassava); of large families and women curtained off from men in cinemas and cars, and of Sunday evening excursions to the sea, the races and a police band.

Along the pavement with its broad, square, sooty stones are more warehouses with stained walls and high metal doors. Heavy iron claws on open doors offering a view of sacks and cardboard boxes are drawn together at closing time. Creole women in printed skirts pass us carrying striped nylon bags on their shoulders and heads. The warehouses give way to shops, some of which display the name 'Desai' on their signboards. I have heard of the Desais, reputedly the first Gujarati Hindu family to join the rush of Gujarati Muslim traders in the wake of indentured labourers in the mid-nineteenth century. The first Desai who migrated came as an accountant but went on to enter business. We meet Girish Desai in a shop selling steel and silver kitchenware. He is slightly built and fair with delicate features and a moustache. When I introduce myself, he says excitedly, 'But I just read about you!' It appears that a local newspaper, *L'Express,* has carried a report on a talk I gave the previous day to a group of local public-minded professionals calling itself the 'Parlement Populaire' and Girish is struck by the serendipity that has caused me to appear in his shop literally a few minutes after he has seen my name. For my part, I tell him that I have been circling his surname on my list of leads to follow up on for many days and am happy to finally speak to a Mauritian Desai.

He laughs and tells me that it is true that his great-grandfather Ratanjee Desai came to the island to do chopda lakhvanu (keep accounts) in Gujarati for traders. He was from Sangalpur village next to Dandi, 30 kilometres north of Surat. The family was steeped in debt so after he had established himself, Ratanjee invited his brothers to join him and together they started a textile business which made a great profit during the First World War. In 1998 the family celebrated the completion of a hundred years in Mauritius, so the year of entry would be 1898, he reckons. Over the years the family expanded, the girls getting married to boys in Gujarat and staying on there with their husbands, while the boys returned to Mauritius with Gujarati brides.

A few paces from the Desai shop is the Jumma Masjid, built in 1853. In 1805, the government had given the Muslim seafaring lascars from India permission to build a mosque in Pagoda Street (now Dr Hassen Sakir Street) but over time, with the arrival of Gujarati Muslim traders, the space proved too small and the need for a new mosque was felt in Port Louis. A few years after it came up, this mosque too needed to be expanded, for which traders donated both cash, at the rate of 2 cents per rupee on every bag of grain traded, and free berths for artisans from India on their ships. They created a beautiful complex with wide arches and delicate grilles communicating the airiness of Creole design, heightened by the colour pairing of white and cerulean blue. Walking on the terrace around chalk-white domes and spires, we see the tops of fruiting mango trees. Houses on the street have verandas and triangular roofs that evoke the shape of a short man in a Chinese peasant hat. The walls are of basalt, neatly cut in a brick shape, and the windows are boarded up with blue planks. On the ground floor of a building across the street is a white wall with a shuttered window, also painted white. It is built in the old style, perhaps with a godown below and space for a shop and homes above.

Is this where my great-grandfather came to stay: in a trader's or a shopkeeper's household? He could have found work as an accountant, since all Gujarati firms were supervised by a chief clerk or Mehtaji.[6] He could even have been a teacher for traders' children. The Memons traced their origins to Sind and it could be one more possibility for Foolkore's identity. Is this the street where she lived? Amidst the warm vapour rising off lentils, whole spices and chilli nestling in their jute packing and the shouts of men as they loaded and unloaded their wares, pigeons scuttling between their legs as they pecked for grain on the basalt pavements?

13

Love Island

'Your great-grandmother could have been a Creole woman.' Dr Abdool Cader Kalla, grey-haired, in a stern pair of glasses, is a retired associate professor and deputy director of the Mauritius Institute of Education and a leading authority on Gujarati Muslims in Mauritius. We are in his study in his airy home in Beau-Bassin Rose Hill, a town I have passed through often on my way to Port Louis, even changed buses there. Stepping out of the familiar bus terminus, I find myself at a busy traffic intersection, almost getting knocked down by the crowd rushing past a train station and small Chinese eateries festooned with gaudy pictures of the dishes on offer. In a quiet residential street that connects the town centre with my destination, I find the name 'Atchia' on a signboard above a paint shop. The Atchias, a well-known Rosehill family, figure prominently in Dr Kalla's work. Ibrahim Atchia came to Mauritius from Barbodhan, a village in Surat district, on the SS *Kirkland* in 1861 and opened a dukkan alongside a straw hut house at the junction of Avenue Belle Rose and the main road to Mahebourg in the southeast. His family went on to grow sugarcane and sisal (used in making gunny bags) and run cinemas, though it was best known for its pioneering role in bringing hydroelectric lighting to Mauritius.

The Atchias established the Mauritius Hydroelectric Company in 1900 and set up a power-generating plant in Reduit that provided electricity to the towns of Beau-Bassin Rose Hill, Quatre Bornes and Moka.[1] Kalla's ancestors also came from Barbodhan though, unlike the redoubtable Atchias, they came without any capital. 'We were just poor farmers,' he says. 'Most of the Barbodhians were; some worked as carriers with a mule cart or as peddlers.'

Sitting across from Dr Kalla in a room stocked with books and papers, I consider his proposition that Foolkore could have been a Creole, a person of African, Malagasy or mixed descent. What comes to mind is a vivid description from a traveller's account, which I noted down but forgot where I had taken it from. The writer and his friends went on a picnic to the beach and watched Creole men catch a giant turtle. The turtles in this part of the world can be over a metre in length and over 400 kilograms in weight, so one imagines this was an operation requiring considerable strength. The fishermen pulled the animal by its scaly flippers and turned it on its back. Holding a flipper each, they dragged it ashore and hoisted it on a wooden barrel to take it to the market to sell. In a hut close by, an old black-skinned man, a former slave, prepared green bananas for his supper. After dinner, the writer and his friends lay on the grass to rest while the men did a dance for them. I imagine Foolkore as a Creole girl, watching this scene of revelry on the sand, crunching shells under her bare feet and brushing curly, salt-thickened hair from her blazing eyes.

'It was quite common for rich Gujarati men to marry Creole women,' Kalla says. 'It was a measure of status.' He lists examples: Ratanji Bickaji's papers acknowledged a son born in June 1812 from a Creole woman from Réunion Island; Manilal Doctor left Mauritius for Fiji with a Creole wife by his side;[2] a prominent contemporary Mauritius businessman, Dawood Rawat, had a coloured grandmother. 'Many men had two wives,' Kalla continues. 'My ancestor took his Creole wife to India. She took a pot of thyme with her, which still grows in our village. In Barbodhan, they call her the pardosan (foreigner).'

◆

'Situated on the eastern side of the mountain which rises above Port Louis, in the Mauritius, upon a piece of land bearing the marks of former cultivation, are seen the ruins of two small cottages ...'

So begins the celebrated French novel *Paul Et Virginie* by Jacques-Henri Bernardin de Saint-Pierre. A friend of Jean-Jacques Rousseau, Bernardin made Mauritius the centrepiece of his 1788 book, presenting it as an unspoilt natural paradise where two Frenchwomen, cast out by a judgmental society, seek shelter. The two women have children, a son, Paul, and a daughter, Virginie, respectively. The children grow up side by side on a tropical Eden, fall in love and expect to marry.

Fate intervenes in the form of an aristocratic aunt who summons Virginie to France, hoping to marry her to a wealthy man there. Virginie travels to France but refuses to marry her aunt's chosen groom. She is summarily dispatched, put on a ship to return to Mauritius in the dangerous hurricane season. A storm rages as her ship approaches the island and while her pining lover waits for her onshore, the ship is tossed and wrecked and Virginie succumbs to her fate, hands crossed upon her breast, eyes raised, like 'an angel prepared to take her flight to Heaven'.[3]

The innocent love story of two island children cut short by brutal civilization was an early celebration of cultural primitivism, which became one of the central ideas of the Romantic movement. Appearing on the eve of the French Revolution, the novel became a runaway hit and has spawned several theatrical and cinematic productions over the years. It also introduced Mauritius to the world and numerous *Paul Et Virginie* memorials scattered around the island attract tourists two hundred years after its publication.

The book has many references to India and Indians. Virginie's trip to France is accompanied by much fanfare. The great Monsieur de La Bourdonnais himself pays a visit to ensure that the girl is put on a ship to France in accordance with the wishes of her influential aunt. Before she can leave, though, she has to be suitably equipped. Vendors arrive at the humble huts bearing goods: '... the richest stuffs of India; the fine dimity of Gondelore; the handkerchiefs of Pellicate and Masulipatan; the plain, striped, and embroidered muslins of Dacca, so beautifully transparent: the delicately white cottons of Surat, and linens of all colours ...'.

At Virginie's funeral, after 'negresses of Madagascar and Caffres of Mozambique' have placed baskets of fruit around the corpse, and hung 'pieces of stuff' on trees, some 'Indian women from Bengal also, and from the coast of Malabar' bring cages full of small birds, which they release over her coffin. 'Thus deeply did the loss of this amiable being affect the natives of different countries, and thus was the ritual of various religions performed over the tomb of unfortunate virtue.'[4]

Paul Et Virginie in book, comic and DVD form is displayed next to sarongs and Ray-Bans in the shops along the beach. A large Indo-Mauritian family drives up in a Toyota van and sits in a circle on foldable chairs, eating noodles as clouds bank up like snowy mountains over an azure-blue sea. Occasionally I see a Creole boy and girl walk by hand in hand. But mostly it is outsiders like me who populate the beach: bodies glistening with suntan lotion on a deck chair, a tanned hand reaching for a cocktail under a thatched umbrella.

One also sees bridal couples, for Mauritius is a popular location for destination weddings. Its numerous hotels provide ample facilities for guests and its natural beauties provide a perfect photogenic backdrop. I come across a Southeast Asian couple taking photographs dressed in their wedding finery, the groom in a grey suit, the bride in lipstick and white lace holding a bouquet, outside the elegant seaside church of Notre Dame at Cap Malheureux. They look like they have been at it for some time. The groom is perspiring, the bride's smile is wilting and the photographer is a trifle tetchy as he marshals them into a frame with the distinctive long rump of Gunner's Quoin behind them.

Kushroo Aubeelack, a Mauritian of Indo-Sri Lankan descent, met film producer Maitreyee Dasgupta when he was studying medicine in Mumbai. Recently married when I arrive in Mauritius, the couple and their friend Bob, a Mauritian of Chinese descent, show me the sights on the island. We go scuba diving. We see giant lumbering tortoises and walk around aloes as tall as people amidst porous grey rock. We drive through fields of whistling grass watered by long metal sprays. We eat in pastel-coloured cafés and noodle shops and hear the pulsing beat of Sega nightclubs in Flic en Flac.

Where would a young courting couple have gone for entertainment in Mauritius a hundred years ago? The annual horse races sponsored by the governor and occurring over three days in July were intended to build a bridge between the British and the French, but they became the most well-attended and inclusive event on the Mauritian calendar. Nicolas Pike, a naturalist and the US consul to Mauritius in the late-nineteenth century, wrote an evocative account in his *Sub-Tropical Rambles in the Land of the Aphanapteryx*: 'From daylight every street is crowded with loads of chairs, tables, benches, and stands. Private carriages are driven up and left horseless within the cordon near the logos. Tents rise on the surrounding eminences as by magic, flags fly, tomtoms beat, the whole city is in a ferment.'

There are French and English ladies dressed exquisitely but 'only to a Northerner's eye, a leeile too rich for out-of-door costume'. And 'the grave, stout Arab, generally in a carriage drawn by a good pair of horses, with his little boys, in beautifully gold-embroidered robes and caps', the Parsi 'in long white dress and singular tall cap, hollow at the top ... and thousands of Indians of different races ...' *Toute l'île Maurice* is there, drinking, cavorting, gambling, shopping and feasting ... 'a sight almost unique in the civilised world'.[5]

◈

My last day in Mauritius happens to be my birthday and Kushroo takes us to his favourite spot on the island. We head to the southwestern coast and at some point he stops.

'Here?' we ask, looking incredulously at the faceless stretch of sand and scrub where he has parked.

He nods. We get out. He pockets the car keys and begins to walk, letting us follow, grumbling and muttering, for about a couple of hundred metres to a clump of trees with pointy needle leaves. We round a curve and let out a collective gasp. In Mauritius, where every turn of the coastal road offers a breathtakingly stunning view, this is possibly the loveliest I have yet encountered. Flat white sands caressed by a ripple of blue, completely hidden from the road but jutting out into the sea so as to provide a panoramic view of sand, sea, distant grey hills and, closer at hand, a creek bordered by a verdant green slope. Our heads swing back to our guide, insouciantly slouching, hands in his shorts' pockets, relishing our astonishment.

We stand contemplatively, drift about, throwing a pebble or two, sitting, musing. Conversation dwindles as the vista seeps into us, filling us with its serenity. In the prolonged silence, we become aware of a rustling behind us. It sounds like a wild beast nosing its way through the trees. We turn around in anticipation tinged with alarm. Now we hear a soft hum, a tinkle of bells and wheels. A crowd emerges through the gap in the trees, a procession of about fifty men and women following a man carrying a small Ganesh idol. They are brilliantly attired in silk kurtas and saris in turquoise, brown and orange. They surge to the other side of the cove where the water is shallow and the hillside is a bright green. A priest raises a lantern. People crowd around him, a phalanx dressed in the style of Indian television soap actors, in outfits so new that the whole scene has the look of an advertisement. A girl breaks off from the group to answer a cell phone. A young Creole woman, clearly a nanny wheeling a pram but dressed in a blue sari for the occasion, stands a little apart from the group. The idol is lifted by five men, each holding an edge of a tall red stool. In India there would be a jangling of musical instruments and wild dancing but here there is no music, no drums or bugles, just a soft clinking of a bell and a gentle immersion of the idol as clouds billow over mossy mountains. The procession disperses as swiftly as it arrived, leaving us alone to watch the sunset, a bright red light dissolving into blue.

I have come to this island with a question about who my great-grandmother was and I have been shown a polyglot society and a land of incredible beauty. It is answer enough.

PART FOUR

NATAL

14

Arriving

The ship by which Mohanlal and Foolkore travelled to South Africa from Mauritius was the SS *Afghan*, 312 feet long, built in 1877 by the well-known ship-building firm of Aitken & Mansel in Whiteinch and owned variously by Gellatly, Hankey, Sewell & Co., Glasgow, by the Mogul Steamship Co. and finally by Hajee Cassum Joosub of Bombay.[1] The ship was scrapped in March 1907, so this would have been one of its last few ocean crossings.

As a child, I had harboured a vision of Mohanlal on the boat as he approached his destination. I imagined him like Napoleon or Nelson, in a naval uniform, deep blue with ribboned medals and gold braids and a tricorne rising stiffly on his head. Like in those old portraits which I must have seen in some encyclopaedia or the other, he would gaze dreamily into the distance, his stance a three-quarter profile, suggesting that despite his weighty and important preoccupations he was aware of me looking at him and concerned about my future, which lay clearly on his broad, padded shoulders.

It was startling to have to reconcile this fanciful image with reality, to relocate the figure I envisaged standing on the prow of a boat, heroic and alone amidst a throng of sweaty bodies on a deck strewn with a paraphernalia of bedrolls, cloth bundles, metal tiffin boxes and water jugs. In my revised vision, Mohanlal, surrounded by passengers, mostly brown Indians like himself, wore a weather-battered suit and trilby and periodically dabbed at his reddening face and neck with a handkerchief. He was twenty-five or thereabouts and presumably changed in appearance by the time he had spent away from home ... gained a few pounds, perhaps grown a moustache. The callow Gujarati boy had acquired a worldly air, a preening touch of cosmopolitanism that might have made him look away from the deck, from the faces of his co-passengers and the occasional uniformed sailor leaning on a gleaming ship rail, and consider the glittering sea with a bored, knowing air.

Next to him, Foolkore studied the dirty deck floor—or so I expect from a teenage girl, a married woman of her time, who would not raise her gaze like a man. Perhaps there were tears in her eyes, recalling the parents, playmates and pets she had left behind. Not long ago she was a kid, playing on the sand or scrambling up a hill, and now she was pregnant and on board a ship heading into the horizon. Did her hand stray to her belly, feeling for the new life taking shape within? Did her eyelids flutter, just enough to give her a peek at the bright blue sea? Did the nearness of the man with whom her fate was tied evoke a frisson of excitement?

I imagine the young couple preoccupied with private thoughts in a gentle sea breeze, but in all likelihood, they were in the centre of a maelstrom. All around them, on the deck, in the galleys and even in the cabins and salons, anxious, whispered conversations were probably taking place about one and only one thing: the difficulty of entering Natal or any other port in South Africa. The passengers on the SS *Afghan* would be aware that stringent new laws had been passed to curb fresh immigration. The news had spread across the littoral, transmitted in official notifications and by word of mouth. They would have heard something of it in Bombay, Lamu, Port

Louis, Mombasa, Zanzibar or whichever port they came from. They would have consulted travel agents, procured documents and presented them to the shipping authorities, for the latter too, were liable and could be arrested for transporting 'prohibited immigrants' or passengers without the right qualifications or documents for legal entry.

Having crossed the first hurdle and in the excitement of setting off, the travellers might have felt emboldened. Whatever trial lay at the other end of the journey would be faced with equanimity and luck, or so they might have said to themselves. And they would have repeated it every time they remembered to worry till the unvarying sight of the sea and the steady movement of the ship lulled them into forgetfulness. But the anxiety never really went away. The new laws had reduced immigration by sea to a trickle. The authorities had the power to quarantine ships and send them back without allowing passengers to disembark. The grounds on which they could do this was the outbreak of epidemics at ports en route, but everyone knew that it was also a way of protecting the colonies from a flood of potentially undesirable migrants travelling on a particular ship.

It was not only the new migrants who were in danger of being turned away; even long-time residents of Natal had to produce all sorts of documentation, including domicile certificates, and even then they could be refused entry. As the last stop slipped away and the final leg of the journey commenced, passengers on the SS *Afghan* could no longer pretend it was nothing or ignore the sacrifices made, the rupees borrowed to pay for travel, all of which would go to waste if they were refused entry at their destination. Some openly wept.[2]

Was Mohanlal untouched by the anxiety bubbling around him? Did he have no cause for concern? One can wonder why he left Mauritius where he had clearly established a strong connection, at least with Foolkore's family. Illness and plague and the devastation caused by storms had driven away many from the island at the beginning of the twentieth century, but it was still open to Indians while South Africa, where they were headed, was most decidedly not.

Mohanlal did have an advantage over the bulk of the passengers, though, because of his education. Natal laws allowed educated men to enter if they could write a few sentences in English and Mohanlal could have been confident of passing such a test. Perhaps he had an offer of employment in Natal or was aware of some employment or business opportunity, which enticed him to leave Mauritius for Natal and risk the authorities at the gate. Or perhaps he was just foolhardy.

The passengers on board the SS *Afghan* would have seen a long, low, wooded hill jutting out into the sea. The 90-metre-high dune of silt and sand called isiBubulungu (the bulky thing) by the Zulus, also known as the Bluff, protected the harbour from southeasterly winds. At right angles, reaching towards it in the water like an index finger curving towards the tip of a thumb, was a low spit of land called the Point. Portuguese navigators thought that the natural harbour of Natal, on whose shores the city of Durban stands, was a lagoon at the mouth of a river flowing from the interior. They called the harbour Rio de Natal because Vasco da Gama passed the coast on Christmas Day in 1497. 'Natal' also means birth, fittingly, for it was where my grandmother was born.

The harbour was notorious for a treacherous sand bar which lay at its entrance and wrecked ships that ventured into its shallow waters. Large steamers had to park at the outer anchorage and lower passengers in large cane baskets onto tugs and lighters, which brought them safely ashore. A harbour board set up to find an engineering solution succeeded in dredging the sandbar. On 26 June 1904, in an event of immense significance for Durban's future, the 12,975-ton *Armadale Castle* entered the harbour and tied up at the jetty; an artist's rendering of the occasion shows women in long dresses and men in hats swarming alongside the looming steamer in wonder.

The ship carrying my great-grandparents, arriving more than a year after this signal event, would have sailed all the way into the pear-shaped lagoon and moored at the quayside, allowing them to disembark on a gangway. The Bluff would have risen to their left like a giant recumbent seal, a three million candle-power light blazing on its 195-feet high summit if it was dark. If their arrival was during daytime, they would have seen the piers and jetties and a railway line going all the way to the quay. They would have also seen a Boer-era stone building, which served as a customs house, and a new set of refreshment rooms advertising themselves as the 'JETTY TEA ROOM', the logo painted in capital letters on its neat awning. There were no bustling crowds as there were in Bombay and no smouldering backdrop of basalt hills that Port Louis offered but a wide curve of beach, spreading trees and gentle slopes. Documents inform me that the journey occurred at the end of the year. It was summer then for the southern hemisphere, a season of warm days, cool evening breezes and occasional thunderstorms.

This is how it might have been: an Indian man and a woman of unclear origin dressed (as described by a cousin who heard it from my grandmother) in a long skirt, a waist-length blouse and an odhni or a scarf, bangles and earrings, emerged from the harbour with their petis or trunks. Small boats with white sails floated near the shore where men in suits and women in long dresses and smart hats slumped on deck chairs, gazing at the sea. A long embankment ran along the beach and across the road was the broad stone façade of the Marine Hotel and the elegant arched entrance to the Durban Club, glimpsed through low trees spreading like wide umbrellas. Mohanlal and Foolkore walked or rode on a horse buggy through the quiet streets of Beach Grove past genteel two-storeyed houses and gardens. Another broad road, which they crossed, and they found the white city slip away. Several people appeared, brown skinned, dark-eyed. A cart loaded with goods clattered ahead to a warehouse. Oil lamps flickered in shop windows for electricity was not yet widely used and the minaret-topped white flank of the Jami Mosque announced the neighbourhood that would be their home for the next few years.

◆

I feel someone calling out to me on Dr Yusuf Dadoo Street, the erstwhile Grey Street in downtown Durban, an odd sensation on my first-ever visit to the Indian Central Business District (CBD). The Jami Mosque flares up on my left, lit by a noonday sun like a great white eagle. In its shadow, a stocky man lays out tomatoes and okra in bowls on a table. I am on edge from numerous warnings about the perils of the neighbourhood I am visiting. 'Very dangerous place,' people say when I tell them I am headed for the old Indian CBD, and stories of armed burglaries on the internet seem to back up their words. I carry a light wallet, stuff a hundred rand in my right sock and a cell phone in the pocket of my jeans to call a taxi when I am done. Snatches of tunes float from passing cars like an aural fragrance and there it is again, the feeling of being followed. It is nothing, I tell myself, just the breeze blowing in from the sea.

The streets are alive. Nighties flap on a mobile rack like agile chorus girls. A shopkeeper dresses a marionette. Shop boards carry visuals of schoolbags, shoes, T-shirts, dresses, sandals and towels. Handwritten signboards advertise 'Pure Vegetable Ghee', 'Continental Basmati Rice', Disprin and airtime. Boxes of Kleenex and toilet paper share space with sacks of grain, Hanuman figurines and ethnic Indian brands that one might find in the bazaars of small-town India: Mysore Sugandhi, Chandan Dhoop, Laxmi Dhoop, Chandni Nail Henna, Raaj Chunna and bottles of Sunlux perfumed hair oil at 12 rand apiece, with a picture of a white girl tossing her glossy mane. Across the road wide, squat buildings with flaky walls and shops on the ground floor sporting names like Khan, Essop and Hoosenjee.

I step into the Famous Bassa, an Indian-owned store that lives up to its name by spamming the tabloids with advertisements of its perennial sales. Lace and satin bedcovers are piled in heaps in the large, gloomy shop with a high ceiling, and long rolls of fabric are arranged on slanting shelves along the wall, reminding me of a time now long past when one bought fabric and took it to the tailors. As I emerge into the busy street I hear it again, a vague hissing sound that could be for anybody, but which I know is calling out to me. I feel something crawling up my elbow and turning, with a start I find it is incense smoke curling in my direction from a brazier. The man carrying it has bulging, kohl-lined eyes in an emaciated, bearded face.

'Bibi!' His voice is a whispered croak. 'Why you no cover your head?' A proselytizer from the Islam Propagation Centre, a wide, glass-fronted building opposite the Jami Mosque? Or maybe just a freelance man of God? He stares at me in horrified fascination. He is a fakir, small, hunched, harmless, and yet I feel afraid. The manager from the Famous Bassa store comes out of his shop, drops money into the brazier and makes a gently dismissive gesture, which the man obeys, retreating, fading into the crowd, then re-emerging into the noon brightness, walking slowly, black robes flapping around his emaciated frame.

15

The First Trader

For hundreds of years, Gujarat and East Africa had been knitted together by the comings and goings of traders. Small groups of Gujarati merchants had even settled overseas, scattering themselves along the coast, from the Persian Gulf to Kilwa in modern Tanzania and on small islands such as Socotra and Pate. Ships did not venture beyond Sofala, the point up to which monsoon wind patterns could be predicted, but merchants ventured inland, developing links with local traders in the African interior, exchanging cloth for ivory and gold.

Political shifts in the region brought an increased flow of Gujarati merchants to Africa. Many followed the Sultan of Oman when he moved to Zanzibar in 1840 and came to occupy high positions of power in his administration. Long before that, the establishment of the Portuguese Estado da Índia and the emergence of its East African colony as a vital way station from the colonial capital of Goa to the metropolitan capital of Lisbon saw many Gujarati vanias move there from the Portuguese enclave of Diu in Kathiawar.[1] A few of them trickled southwards from Sofala to Lourenço Marques. Located on an estuary where more than four major rivers meet, Lourenço Marques was named after a sixteenth-century merchant-trader who had explored the upper reaches of the estuaries. They led him to a bay, which he named 'Baía da Lagoa', Portuguese for 'Bay of the Lagoon', 'Delagoa Bay' in English. In the mid-nineteenth century Lourenço Marques was little more than a trading point with two streets and fifty-six stone houses protected by a small Portuguese fort.[2] Among its 1,100 inhabitants was an adolescent shopkeeper, a small-built Gujarati Memon boy, called Abdullah Haji Adam Jhaveri or 'Dada' Abdullah.

Dada Abdullah was a native of Porbandar, a pretty coastal town enclosed by white limestone walls in the peninsular region of Gujarat known as Kathiawar, 300 kilometres north of Surat. Many of the town's 15,000 people made a living from the sea, fishing in the estuaries, ferrying pilgrims to and from the religious centres of Dwarka and Somnath and trading in cotton, indigo, agate and ivory with West Asia and East Africa. It was common for men from the town to apprentice themselves at a very young age to merchant-traders in larger towns, where they would learn the ropes of the business before setting up on their own. Ten- to nineteen-year-old boys comprised 20 per cent of the local Indian population in Lourenço Marques.[3] How and when Dada Abdullah went there is not recorded, but he was a teenager running a store in this remote Portuguese town in 1870 or thereabouts when he was visited by his cousin, Aboobaker Amod Jhaveri.

Like Dada Abdullah, Aboobaker Amod had left Porbandar as a boy. He was fourteen when he headed for the big city of Calcutta and from there, he went to Mauritius as an employee of the reputed Port Louis-based Indian trading firm of Ajam Goolam Hoosen & Co. Setting out on his own or sent by the firm, he came on a steamer from Mauritius to explore opportunities on the African mainland. He disembarked at Delagoa Bay and probably sought out Dada Abdullah who may have put him in touch with patamares, as African agents were called, or in some other way helped the seventeen-year-old boy, the first passenger Indian in South Africa to reach the Transvaal, 100 kilometres inland from Lourenço Marques. For several months, he knocked about in Boer towns before making his way to the more promising Indian-populated territory of Natal where he opened two stores in 1872, in Verulam, close to the sugarcane plantations.

The city of Durban, emerging from the dense coastal forest around the bay, was then in a nascent state. Rutted roads and open drains ran past houses made of wattle, from a fragrant spring-blossoming tree from Tasmania, and daub or brick with the occasional corrugated iron roof visible on public buildings. It was not unusual for a rhinoceros or a dazzle of zebras to wander into town and blue-winged starlings alighted by the thousands on the long, outspread branches of a fig tree at the corner of Russell Street and what would become the Victoria embankment.

On Field Street, which ran at a right angle to the future embankment, a former indentured worker or free Indian called Baboo Naidu had opened a condiments store. Aboobaker Amod opened a store, his third in Natal and his first in downtown Durban, on an adjacent street. Not long after he had established himself, Dada Abdullah arrived from Delagoa Bay and opened a store close to his. Another relative, Moosa Hajee Cassim, tall and lean and older than both, came with his brothers Joosub and Suleman and set up stores in Natal and also in the Transvaal and the Orange Free State.[4] They brought bagfuls of gold coins with them, says the sparse literature on these early migrants.

News of business opportunities in South Africa spread to Mauritius, attracting Memon and Bohra traders there. It also filtered to India, triggering off an exodus from the villages on either side of the Tapi. From the green fields and hillocks that stretched for miles around the small white Kinara Mosque the young men arrived, clutching their tin trunks and battered by their long journeys. They came, a stream of Sunni Bohras with names like Badat, Bhabha, Bobat, Dockrat, Goga, Jeena, Mayat, Timol, Vanker and Vawda.

Passenger Indians gravitated to a vacant plot just west of the emerging commercial heart of the city. Here, where the Eastern Vlei straggled towards Cato Creek, the sandy expanse was covered with low scrub and reedy patches which sucked in wagon wheels, bringing them to a sticky halt. Grey Street ran through it all the way to the bay and streets running off it were named after the British royal family: Victoria, Queen, Albert, Leopold, Alice and Prince. In 1881, Aboobaker Amod and his fellow Memon Hajee Mahomed Dada purchased a site at the corner of Grey and Queen Streets from a free Indian, K. Moonsamy, for £150 and built the Friday mosque, the Jami Mosque. As they put down roots, the traders sent for young men from their villages, close and distant relatives they could trust and who were willing to put in long hours for low pay and sleep in poorly ventilated storage rooms behind the shops. Soon, streets bearing the names of British princes and princesses swarmed with bearded Indian men in long, loose black shirts and pyjamas.

The emerging community of traders was supplied by well-established networks with staples from Bombay, Calcutta, Madras and Port Louis and luxury goods from London. Some passenger Indians became distributors for white wholesalers. Warehouses with sloping roofs came up to store the vast quantities of lentils, pulses, oil, salt and grain arriving at the harbour. From twelve in 1885–56, the total number of traders increased to nineteen the following year and to seventy-four six years later in 1893. As in Mauritius, here too Memons and Surtis formed the main trading communities, augmented by Parsis, a handful of curio dealers from Sind and Muslims from the Konkan coast, south of the Bombay Presidency, the last being found mostly in the Cape.

Some Durban traders had shops not only in the Indian business district but also outside it in the exclusively white shopping area of West Street where, amidst banks, department stores and the city's oldest jewellery store, Caney's, were thirty-nine Indian establishments. Hoodamal, a Multani silk merchant, stocked Indian curios and fancy goods such as cashmere shawls and Chinese and Maltese silks at 476, West Street; M.C. Camroodeen & Co. dealt in hats, boots, underskirts and other imported clothing; and S.P. Mahomed & Co., tobacconists, sold cigars, cheroots and perfumes.[5]

By the late 1880s, the mostly uneducated pioneer-traders had a turnover of thousands of pounds from Natal alone and they soon opened branches in every borough and town in South Africa, advertising in trade journals like the *United Transvaal Directory* and *Longland's Transvaal*. Brothers, cousins and neighbours arriving on ships were employed in their shops or provided loans and goods to hawk in the countryside. These small traders trundled from kraal to kraal in a wagon, speaking Fanagalo, a hybrid of English, Zulu and Indian languages. They set up dukkans where Africans came to make purchases, sometimes arriving in groups on a weekend and sleeping behind the store before heading home with their stocks of mealies, cloth, beans, paraffin, corn and sweet potatoes, which they had bartered for skins, hides, chickens and eggs.[6]

It was a lonely life for the dukkawallahs out in the hilly, river-gouged midlands, beyond the reach of the railway, which as yet ran only up to Pinetown from Durban, pitted with visits from wild animals and burglars. They applied for firearms, complaining of lost livestock and horses. 'I was asleep and suddenly heard a bang,' recounts one applicant. 'A second bang caused my door to open. My room was in darkness. A candle was lit … I called out, "Who is there?" in Zulu. As soon as my voice was heard the light was put off, and one of (them) struck me with a stick on my head.'[7] Another Indian escaped a break-in at his shop near a colliery in Ladysmith in 1904 in the following manner: 'He ran out of the window, swam across a lake, hung from a tree, slept in the jungle, next day went to the police.'[8]

The big Durban traders diversified into new forms of business. E.M. Paruk, a Surti Bohra, bought the Glendale Sugar Mill and the Inanda Tea Estate. Aboobaker Amod acquired property in the lanes around the Jami Mosque and rented out rooms to newly arrived passenger Indians at 10 shillings a month. Some traders opened eating houses for young Zulu men who had begun to trickle into Durban from their villages in the highlands to earn money to pay new taxes levied by the colonial administration. Many Hindus had also joined the stream of migrants. Sonis, Khatris, Dhobis, Kanbis and other castes arrived from Gujarat and elsewhere to work as hawkers, artisans, shoemakers, goldsmiths, tailors, laundry workers and accountants, the last being so much in demand that they worked part-time for many clients simultaneously.

The British Natal Direct Line (so called because it bypassed the Cape of Good Hope) had a fleet of white steamers, each with a trademark buff, black-topped funnel and a central encircling chocolate band, and ran a monthly mail-and-passenger service between Bombay and Natal through Delagoa Bay and Beira. The German East African Line, owner of the SS *Kanzler* and SS *Reichstag*, operated the same route fortnightly with a stopover at Mahe. Dada Abdullah became an agent for the Bombay and Persia Steam Navigation Company, owner of the *Naderi*, long associated with the pilgrim trade to Mecca and managed by Turner Morrison & Co. Ltd. He also bought ships, a barquentine for local runs around the coast and the SS *Courland*, which he acquired from Donald Currie's African Boating Company for £16,000. Moosa Hajee Cassim bought a two-funnelled 1,500-ton steamer and called it the *Crescent*.[9] They soon became dominant players in the transportation of Indians: three-fourths of the approximately 2,000 passengers arriving in Natal over six months in 1896–97 travelled on board the *Courland*, the *Naderi* or the *Crescent*.

Even as they grew their businesses physically and across various streams, the Indian traders encountered risks and downturns. As many as eighty free Indians and twenty-two passenger Indians declared themselves insolvent in the depressed 1880s.[10] Their way of doing business, involving multiple contractual relationships and loans, also made Gujarati traders excessively prone to litigation. The sheths were often in court and had the best lawyers handle their cases. At the beginning of the last decade of the nineteenth century, Dada Abdullah was involved in one such case. He was suing his cousin and former business partner, Tayob Haji Khan Mahomed, for recovering outstanding dues of £25,000 for a purchase of some shops. He had a team of white lawyers arguing the case, but the records of the transaction were in Gujarati and he was in need of a bilingual person. His brother was visiting India at the time and sent word of a boy from their own native town of Porbandar who had recently returned to India after successfully clearing the barrister's examinations in London. Dada Abdullah offered a year's contract at a fee of £105 with first-class return fare, board and lodging to the boy whose name was Mohandas Karamchand Gandhi.

16

The Lawyer Gandhi

Gandhi arrived in Durban by ship on 23 May 1893. Slightly built, in his early twenties with curious bright eyes, he provided no hint of his approaching greatness; yet there was enough in his appearance to suggest that the Indian lawyer Dada Abdullah had engaged was no commonplace individual.

Mohandas Karamchand Gandhi was born in Dada Abdullah's hometown, Porbandar. Like most people in the coastal town, Gandhi was ever-mindful of its fluid edge. The sea was 'almost within a stone's throw' from the city's walls, he told a future biographer. 'It swept around the city so closely that at times it made almost an island of Porbandar.'[1] The breeze lifted off it and wafted inland, through temple streets and bazaars, to find the boy on the terrace of his three-storeyed house. The Gandhis were not Muslim Memons like Dada Adbullah but Hindus of the merchant vania caste and with a long record of state service. One of Gandhi's ancestors, Uttamchand Gandhi aka Ota Bapa, had been a legendary customs collector and his father was the chief administrator for the local ruler.

With the rise of the East India Company, Kathiawar, one of India's numerous princely states, became a British protectorate; that is, it continued to be in the hands of its erstwhile feudal lords but was supervised by a British political agent stationed in the capital, Rajkot, 150 kilometres inland. Gandhi's family moved to Rajkot and he attended Kathiawar's first English school, the Rajkot High School.

Just as in Bombay and Surat, a wave of reform was sweeping over Rajkot at the time, urging Indians to change their traditional mores to align with the superior understanding of the West. Young men, for instance, were convinced that Englishmen derived their enviable strength and ability to rule over India through the consumption of meat. A doggerel then in vogue among the boys at Gandhi's school went: 'Behold the mighty Englishman/ He rules the Indian small/ Because being a meat-eater / He is five cubits tall.'[2]

The promise of physical and moral strength tempted Gandhi to try the forbidden food, but the strong Vaishnava ethos of his upbringing did not allow him to swallow it and he vomited it out. The failed experiment did not diminish his fascination for the British, however, and when some years later, after his father's death, a family friend mentioned the possibility of travelling to England for higher studies, Gandhi jumped at the suggestion.

Nobody in the backwater of Kathiawar, where no more than a couple of boys matriculated every year, had ever travelled abroad to study. In pursuing this course Gandhi had to incur debt and also risk a potential caste boycott for breaking the taboo against crossing the dreaded kaala paani. Explaining his uncommon resolve, Gandhi later attributed it to ambition:

> I had a secret design in my mind to come here to satisfy my curiosity of knowing what London was like … I thought to myself that if I go to England, not only shall I become a barrister but I shall be able to see England, the land of philosophers and poets, the very centre of civilization.[3]

In London, the gawky Kathiawari boy took lessons in ballroom dancing and the violin, went to the theatre and was known to frequent Piccadilly Circus in a high silk top hat, fine striped silk shirt, double-breasted vest and patent leather boots, with gloved hands wrapped around a silver mounted stick.[4] He was overwhelmed by the elevator and bright lights of the Victoria Hotel and felt he 'could pass a lifetime'[5] in its rooms.

The return to India was a rude shock. Lacking connections, he could not find work in Bombay where he expected to start a practice. And when he did land a case, he botched it. 'I stood up but my heart sank into my boots. My head was reeling and I felt the whole court was doing likewise.'[6] He fled in shame to Rajkot where he focused on drafting petitions. But there, too, an incident occurred which put paid even to his greatly diminished aspirations. Persuaded by his elder brother, to whom he owed a great deal, and against his better judgement, he approached the British political agent for a personal favour. The furious agent had him removed, leaving Gandhi feeling humiliated and conscious of having further destroyed his prospects of professional success. The feudal politics of the town, familial obligations and the arrogance of the white agent crowded upon the sensitive young man, suffocating him. At this point, more than anything, Gandhi desperately 'wanted somehow to leave India'.[7]

And here he was, on tossing waves and a nippy wind that may have reminded him of his first big adventure, the one that took him to 'dear old London'. Memories may have flooded back, of the foppish youth aspiring to play the violin and twirl in a ballroom. After the initial enthusiasm had worn out, Gandhi found his affectations dropping away naturally one by one. Frivolous fancies did not hold his attention. In the city with its 'teaching institutions, public galleries, museums, theatres, vast commerce, public parks',[8] a space of a myriad options, he had discovered his true self in more sober passions such as vegetarianism and religious philosophy.

The brief period he had spent back in India had been deeply disappointing. But despite his recent setbacks, there was again a sense of possibility. Despite the fact that this new job was temporary and not quite commensurate with his qualifications, it was an escape from the privations of home and a second chance at proving his professional competence. The incident with the agent had disturbed him (a 'shock' that led him to change his life, as he puts it) and his appearance suggested the nature of his response. It was a combination that conveyed pride in his Indianness as well as in his English legal training. He wore a European frock coat, pressed trousers, shiny shoes and a turban ('Being a barrister-at-law, I was well dressed according to my lights and landed at Durban with a due sense of my importance'[9]). It also conveyed how little he knew about the society he was entering.

When he arrived in Natal, Gandhi 'had no idea of the previous history of the Indian emigrants'.[10] The large Indian presence in South Africa stemmed from the need for agricultural labour in Natal. Imported in 1860 after considerable debate, Indian indentured workers had proved greatly reliable and been engaged by the Natal Government Railway as well as the municipality. But the first contingent of indentured workers had gone back to India in 1871 after completing their contracts with complaints of such a serious nature against plantation owners that their export was suspended for a few years. It was only resumed in 1874 after new guarantees regarding medical care and abstinence from corporal punishment were put in place and the office of a Protector of Indian Immigrants was established.

The protector's authority was limited in practice by the influence of plantation owners who also enjoyed the favour of the courts. The proprietors of Reynolds Bros., owners of the Umzinto Plantation and Trading Company, one of the largest employers of Indians, were repeatedly given a free pass by the authorities despite a stream of horror stories involving intolerable living conditions, bestial assault of workers and suicide by overworked labourers emerging from their farms.[11] Even small white employers were high-handed in their behaviour, leaving the indentured Indian in a state of extreme vulnerability as the following case demonstrates.

A merchant named Hay found his servant, an indentured Indian called Isaac, with some playing cards in his hand. Annoyed by his apparent idling, he ordered him to get to work and open some wine cases, which Isaac proceeded to do with more noise than the task warranted, according to Hay who reported him to the authorities. A second criminal magistrate of London convicted Isaac for breaching Section 36 of the Immigration Law and being 'insolent to his master'. The *Natal Witness* reported in February 1906 that their lordships of the Supreme Court considered Isaac's appeal against the ruling and upheld the magistrate's findings.[12]

These instances of white misbehaviour and arrogance fitted into a fundamentally racist outlook, which perceived the indentured Indian in purely instrumental terms. The absence of recreation, of cultural nourishment and a severely distorted gender ratio led to a high prevalence of drunkenness and brawls among the workers. So strong was the stigma attached to indentured workers that it even repelled their own countrymen. Muslim passenger Indians— mistaken for 'Arabs' in their loose garb and Turkish caps—embraced the nomenclature, hoping it would distinguish them from the wretched indentured worker. Parsis called themselves 'Persians'. The former took pains to stress their religious taboos against alcohol and campaigned for facilities such as a graveyard and a maulvi to solemnize marriages, to demonstrate how much more culturally evolved they were than the indentured labourers who followed no proper marriage or burial rituals. Their efforts won them occasional commendations from the police and other authorities for their sobriety and good behaviour but did not alter their negative perception in the public mind. Indian traders found it hard to get credit from banks. There were separate spaces reserved for Indians in public spaces; they were kicked off footpaths and even a trader as reputable as Aboobaker Amod was arrested in November 1876 for contravening curfew regulations.

A few days after his arrival, Gandhi boarded a train in Durban on his way to Pretoria where the case for which he had been engaged was underway. His host Dada Abdullah had received him in Durban and introduced him to the Indian community's local notables. Gandhi met prominent merchants such as Adamji Miyakhan, and the stout Parsi Rustomjee and a few leading Christian Indians such as Subhan Godfrey from Mauritius, headmaster of a Protestant mission school, and Henry Louis Paul, a Tamilian Roman Catholic who had come to Natal from Madras and was an interpreter in the Natal Civil Service. Letters of introduction had been sent ahead to Dada Abdullah's lawyers and merchants in Pretoria. Gandhi had reason to feel cautiously at home.

It was late evening and he was alone in the first-class compartment. Contemplating the long ride ahead, he might have stretched out a little, loosened the buttons of his frock coat, peered at the passing countryside. The train reached the Natal capital, Pietermaritzburg, at 9 p.m. In Gandhi's own words:

> A passenger came next, and looked me up and down. He saw that I was a 'coloured' man. This disturbed him. Out he went and came in again with one or two officials. They all kept quiet, when another official came to me and said, 'Come along, you must go to the van compartment.'

'But I have a first class ticket,' said I.

'That doesn't matter,' rejoined the other. 'I tell you, you must go to the van compartment.'

'I tell you, I was permitted to travel in this compartment at Durban, and I insist on going on in it.'

'No, you won't,' said the official. 'You must leave this compartment, or else I shall have to call a police constable to push you out.'

'Yes, you may. I refuse to get out voluntarily.'

The constable came. He took me by the hand and pushed me out. My luggage was also taken out. I refused to go to the other compartment and the train steamed away. I went and sat in the waiting room, keeping my handbag with me, and leaving the other luggage where it was. The railway authorities had taken charge of it.

It was winter, and winter in the higher regions of South Africa is severely cold. Maritzburg being at a high altitude, the cold was extremely bitter. My overcoat was in my luggage, but I did not dare to ask for it lest I should be insulted again, so I sat and shivered. There was no light in the room. A passenger came in at about midnight and possibly wanted to talk to me. But I was in no mood to talk.[13]

Many thoughts went through Gandhi's mind as he sat shivering on the railway platform in Pietermaritzburg. He felt let down by the lack of warning; he had not known about the hostile environment for Indians in South Africa. But he also realized that others living there for pecuniary reasons and inured to the local conditions might not have regarded it in the same light as he did. The dilemma that faced him was his alone to resolve. 'Should I fight for my rights or go back to India, or should I go on to Pretoria without minding the insults, and return to India after finishing the case?' Late at night, he came to the conclusion that: 'It would be cowardice to run back to India without fulfilling my obligation. The hardship to which I was subjected was superficial—only a symptom of the deep disease of colour prejudice. I should try, if possible, to root out the disease and suffer hardships in the process'.[14] He decided to take the next available train.

More indignities awaited him the next day when he resumed his journey. He was punched by a coachman, made to travel on the footboard of a carriage and turned away from a whites-only hotel. By the time he reached Pretoria, Gandhi had been given a visceral experience of what it was to be a person of colour in South Africa. But he did not alter his decision and spent the following year in the pretty Boer town, working assiduously on Dada Abdullah's case.

He also put into practice another resolution he had made on that dark night in Pietermaritzburg, which was to take some steps, if that was possible, side by side with his work. These steps involved: public service, enlightening himself on the religions of the world and, lastly, preparing himself for his return to India and the law courts by following the advice given to him by a British Indologist, Frederic Pincott, to improve his general reading since, a knowledge of the world was 'a *sine qua non* for a vakil (lawyer)'.[15]

The young lawyer met with Pretoria's Indians and gave what he calls his 'first public speech'. He wrote to the railway authorities about the difficulties faced by Indian travellers and applied his mind to the political situation of Indians in South Africa. He learnt about an early piece of anti-Asian legislation, Transvaal's Law 3 of 1885, which barred 'persons belonging to any of the native races of Asia, including so-called Coolies, Arabs, Malays, and Mohammedan subjects of the Turkish Empire' from citizenship, from owning fixed property except in government-assigned locations and being required to register themselves with the authorities. A similar law passed by the Boer-ruled Orange Free State had virtually erased the Indian presence from its bounds; soon, it would be impossible for Indians to enter the Orange Free State even as staff on trains. The Transvaal government's act breached an agreement with Britain securing the trading and property rights of non-natives, so Johannesburg's Indians went in a delegation to call on President Kruger. The homey leader received them on his porch and dismissed their complaint with a Biblical reference, telling them that as 'descendants of Ishmael', they were 'bound to slave for the descendants of Esau'.[16]

Gandhi filled the long, lonely days in Pretoria with reading. Christian friends gave him Joseph Parker's *The People's Bible* and Joseph Butler's *The Anatomy of Religion, Natural and Revealed, to the Constitution and Course of Nature*. A Jain thinker in Bombay sent him Haribhadra Suri's *Shaddarshana Samucchaya* and Yoga Vasistha's *Mumukshu Prakaran*. Edward Maitland, with whom he had initiated a correspondence, sent him his co-authored book, *The Perfect Way: Or, the Finding of Christ*. He also read Max Müller's *India: What Can It Teach Us?* and was overwhelmed by Leo Tolstoy's *The Kingdom of God is Within You*.

In his autobiography he writes that a friend sent him *Dharma Vichar* by the Surti writer Narmad, published in 1885, which he read in Pretoria or later in Durban. 'I had heard about the Bohemian way in which the poet had lived, and a description in the preface of the revolution effected in his life by his religious studies captivated me. I came to like the book, and read it from cover to cover with attention.'[17]

17

Storm Gathering

In the mid-nineteenth century, the UK began to allow its settler colonies, including those in Canada, Australia, New Zealand and South Africa, a greater degree of autonomy in governing themselves. Natal was granted responsible government based on the system of parliamentary democracy in 1893, a few weeks after Gandhi arrived in South Africa.

By this time a great change had taken place in how South Africa was perceived in the Western world. For long a laggard in attracting settlers, South Africa's booming mineral economy had seen the number of new arrivals leap from 10,000 to 750,000 in a single generation.[1] As men, women and children streamed off the boats, breathing the crisp air with happy anticipation, South African towns doubled and even tripled in size. Durban, the city in which the Indian lawyer disembarked, had a sprawling green racecourse alongside a town hall, a theatre, a museum and a club, the rudiments of colonial life, housed in fine stone buildings. The fast-growing Natal government railway line had reached the Transvaal frontier and mining barons who had made a fortune fitting out bullock wagon expeditions to the goldfields moved from Pietermaritzburg to set up elegant offices overlooking the Durban harbour.

Indians were a strongly visible presence in the colony.[2] In the mid-1890s, 35,411 Indians and 45,707 whites comprised 6 and 8 per cent respectively of Natal's 584,326-strong population. By 1904, the Indian population had almost tripled to 100,918 and was less confined to the rural areas. Spilling out of their earlier confines, Indians were seen working as domestic servants for Europeans, as waiters in clubs, fixing streetlamps and cleaning refuse off thoroughfares for the municipality. The prospect of settler rule was disquieting for Indian merchants who had been grievously hurt by the anti-Asiatic laws passed by Boer governments in the Orange Free State and the Transvaal, and they opposed the granting of self-government to Natal, expressing their wish for continued direct rule 'by our beloved Sovereign'. Their concerns appeared to be more than justified, for the earliest piece of business taken up by the new legislature was the introduction of a bill, the Franchise Law Amendment Bill, to disenfranchise Indians in Natal.

The move affected only about 250 Indians who were entitled by the stiff qualifications (voters had to own property worth £50 or pay rent at £10 or more per annum) and enrolled to vote. Those who had enrolled had mostly done so at the request of their lawyer-friend Harry Escombe, who needed political support for his plans to develop the Durban wharf. Indian merchants had no interest in involving themselves in the politics of the colony, which was perhaps the reason why they did not initially react to the threat of disenfranchisement. In fact, they seemed unaware of the existence of the bill when they gathered at Dada Abdullah's farm in Sydenham in May 1894 to bid farewell to Gandhi who was leaving for India.

Sydenham was a fashionable spot for vacation homes on the forested ridge where elephants still occasionally roamed. It was just a few kilometres west of the Indian business quarter on Grey Street, though in those days of horse-drawn transport it must have seemed remote. The plan was to spend a day there. All the prominent traders were in attendance, men mostly in the age group of thirty to fifty and elaborately dressed in silken waistcoats, long shirts, caps and robes, mostly Muslim, with perhaps a few Hindu Tamilians and a Parsi.

Browsing a newspaper, Gandhi chanced upon a report about the second reading of the bill in the House and brought it to the attention of his fellow guests. The traders pleaded ignorance. Gandhi was also unaware of the bill. But the previous year, in September 1893, he had written a letter to the editor of a newspaper, the *Natal Advertiser*, responding to the arguments of a nascent anti-Asiatic league that had emerged in the colony to push for the disenfranchisement of Indians, and he had some thoughts on the subject. He explained to the traders how the Franchise Law Amendment Bill was a direct attack on the status of Indians in the colony, one that sought to demote them from a position of having rights equal or even comparable to those of the whites and to fix the community forever in a position of subservience.

The traders knew about subservience. They knew what it was like to walk in town well-attired, carrying their enamelled canes and umbrellas, and to be suddenly pushed off a footpath by an ill-mannered young white man. They knew what it was like to be squeezed into a reserved corner on a tram like caged animals and to hurry home after dark to avoid being mistaken for indentured workers out without a pass and thrown into jail. They knew helplessness when the colonial authorities barred mixed schooling but offered no alternative schools for Indian children. They knew bafflement when white authorities called their traditional ways of doing accounts deceitful.

At the same time, they were unsure about how to proceed. Their limited education had not prepared them to read and write in English. Christian Indians educated in missionary schools, who could write in English, were too close to white clergymen. The Indian interpreter Henry Louis Paul had the right instincts for a fight. In his previous job he had made allegations about his supervisor's theft of railway overcoats and rations meant for Indians; he had even campaigned successfully for the establishment of a higher-grade Indian school.[3] However now, as a civil servant, he could not be involved in political activism. He had to be counted out.

But suddenly, the traders were aware of another educated professional Indian amidst them. Gandhi was an outsider and yet sufficiently engaged with their problems. Listening to this young man's voice carrying over the chirping of crickets in the long grass, they might have felt the beginning of hope. They asked and Gandhi agreed to postpone his return, at first by a few weeks, and then indefinitely for the purpose of opposing the discriminatory bill.

◆

Gandhi applied for a licence to practise in the Natal Supreme Court. Dada Abdullah set him up in a double-storeyed building with an iron front gate facing the Durban Bay. In his early days, Gandhi was concerned with appearing 'civilized' by matching his dress and manners to 'the European standard'.[4] He even attired his family, which joined him later, in a similar fashion: his wife in a long-sleeved blouse and sari in the style of the anglicized Parsi, buttoned coats and leather shoes for his sons. Living in the upscale neighbourhood of Beach Grove was also a strategic move, putting him on par with professional white peers such as the attorney-general and future Prime Minister Harry Escombe who lived a stone's throw away from him and to whom he would be addressing his community's demands. The following entries in his diary for 1894 show how swiftly he had moved to communicate with Natal's politicians on the matter of the Franchise Law Amendment Bill.

JUNE 27, WEDNESDAY Telegraphed to the Speaker asking whether the (petition was) received ...

JUNE 28, THURSDAY Attended the 3rd reading which was postponed. There were many Indians in the gallery.

JUNE 29, FRIDAY Escombe said the debate in the second reading (was) the real reason for passing the Bill. The object was to prevent Indians from coming any more. Saw Robinson (Natal's first prime minister) before leaving ...[5]

The frail, soft-spoken young man who was faint with anxiety in a Bombay courtroom turned out to be astonishingly self-assured in his new role as a political organizer in Natal.

Nothing demonstrated his natural aptitude for this more than the enthusiasm he stirred up among the Indian business community. Durban's Indian traders formed the Natal Indian Congress on 22 August 1894 with a manager in Dada Abdullah's firm as president and Gandhi as honorary secretary, and over twenty vice-presidents who sat together self-importantly to be photographed as if on the verge of a significant new joint enterprise. The contagion spread outwards from the narrow confines of Grey Street, with Natal Indian Congress branches springing up in Pietermaritzburg, Newcastle and Charlestown where there were communities of Indian traders. Gandhi toured Natal's plantations and towns such as Verulam, cajoling funds from free Indians by placing his turban on the floor in an age-old gesture of supplication.

Whenever he could, Gandhi slipped in lectures exhorting his fellow men to improve themselves, particularly in the matter of cleanliness and temperance. His diary entry for Sunday, 1 July reads: 'About 100 Indians met. Spoke to them for 45 (minutes). Exhorted them to talk less & work more, to have (unanimity).' And again on Sunday, 8 July, he spoke for hours 'on political activity, drunkenness and self-respect'.⁶ He also found time in his busy schedule to volunteer as a nurse at a clinic for Indians run by Dr Lancelot Parker Booth, a light-eyed, bearded English surgeon who was the diocesan superintendent of the Natal operations of Saint Aidan's Mission and well-known as the pioneer of many 'Booth's Mission schools' in Durban. Nursing allowed Gandhi to be of service and indulge his interest in dietary experiments and health, and brought him into contact with Christian free Indians. Henry Louis Paul, moustachioed and with a smooth, high forehead, who he interacted with professionally and socially, became a friend.

Gandhi whipped up a storm of petitions, memoranda and letters to Natal legislators, the Colonial Office in London, to the press in Natal and in India, to the governor and to Dadabhai Naoroji, the educationist from Bombay who had co-founded a nationalist movement in India and gone on to become the first Indian in the British Parliament, representing Finsbury in north London as a Liberal in June 1892. Gandhi's aim was to draw attention to the plight of Natal's Indians and the discriminatory spirit of the Franchise Law Amendment Bill. And he brought the full weight of his training, his erudition and his passion for India to bear on the matter. His petition, with 9,000 signatures of the colony's Indians, to Lord Ripon, principal secretary of state for the colonies, who was responsible for overseeing Natal from London, read as follows:

> It is little comfort to those who are already on the List to know that they may vote, while their children never can, no matter how well educated and well qualified they may be. Indian parents who settle in the Colony ... would hardly like to see their sons pariahs of society ... wealth becomes useless if it gives a man no place in society ... The measure is so sweeping and so drastic that, Your Lordship's Petitioners humbly submit, it is an insult to the whole Indian nation, inasmuch as, if the

most distinguished son of India came to Natal and settled, he would not be able to have the right to vote because, presumably, according to the Colonial view, he is unfit for the privilege.⁷

When the Natal Legislative Assembly claimed that Indians did not deserve the vote because they lacked representative institutions in India, Gandhi responded acerbically and at length:

> ... your Petitioners beg to draw the attention of your Honourable Assembly to Sir Henry Sumner Maine's *Village Communities*, where he has most clearly pointed out that the Indian races have been familiar with representative institutions almost from time immemorial ...
>
> Professor Max Müller ... thus speaks of the much abused and more misunderstood Indian: 'If I were asked under what sky the human mind has most fully developed some of its choicest gifts, has most deeply pondered on the greatest problem of life, and has found solutions of some of them which well deserve the attention even of those who have studied Plato and Kant, I should point to India.'⁸

Gandhi's appeal was amplified by influential public figures such as Naoroji and the widely circulated *The Times of India*, which published a long leader about the 'gratuitous oppression and persecution' of Indians based on his petitions. The petitions themselves, in polished English, using lawyerly reasoning and highbrow references to Max Müller, Schopenhauer and the Upanishads, harping on the English reputation for fair play and appealing to Christian morality, emanating from a migrant community of dependent labourers and a few semi-literate traders at the southeastern tip of the African continent, caused bafflement and consternation among colonial administrators in London. And one imagines they led to some bemused confabulations in the high, narrow corridors of the Colonial Office and the majolica-ornamented courtyard of the India Office. The possible impact of these developments in India, where the first stirrings of a national movement were being heard, as well as in England, where property owners of colour had the right to vote and even enter Parliament, was a critical concern. It was uppermost in the minds of the two men who occupied the office of colonial secretary consecutively at the time of the debate over the Natal Legislature's Franchise Law Amendment Bill: the lavishly bearded George Robinson, first marquess of Ripon who was a viceroy in India in the early 1880s, and Joseph Chamberlain, a clean-shaven, short-haired, monocle-wearing businessman from Birmingham. A bill which 'involves in a common disability all natives of India without any exception' and which 'provides no machinery by which an Indian can free himself from this disability, whatever his intelligence, his education, or his stake in the country … would be an affront upon the people of India such as no British Government could be a party to,'[9] Chamberlain claimed and in April 1895, the Colonial Office withheld assent to the bill, which had become an act after its passing by the Natal Legislature in the first week of July 1894.

Natal's white colonists were outraged. Having expected to encounter no opposition from the customarily docile Indians, they heaped the blame on 'a young Parsee (sic) lawyer, a Mr Gandhi, who arrived here a few months ago'. Overnight, the twenty-five-year-old lawyer became the best-known and most controversial Indian in the colony. *The Star* of Johannesburg admired his lucid style but suggested that he should work for the 'just and humane treatment' of Indians throughout Africa rather than seek to 'achieve the impossible', namely, equal political rights. Gandhi was accused by other whites of being 'lawyer-like' and presenting only the 'pretty' side of Indian life while leaving out the 'pathetic' side, which was that the Indian was a creature of 'bestial habits, given to malingering and dishonest practices'.[10] Derisory rhymes were written about him; 'Goosie, Goosie, Gandhi, Oh!' was the title of one mocking poem which started: 'Oh, I am a man of high degree / And seek a proud position / For I must become, what seems to me / A proud politician.'[11]

Agitated rumours flew about, fuelled by the press. A reported plan by the Tongaat Sugar Company to import thirty bricklayers, carpenters, fitters and blacksmiths from India in August 1896 prompted an angry protest from European artisans. When two ships, Dada Abdullah's SS *Courland* and another Memon-owned ship, the SS *Naderi*, arrived in late December 1896 with a combined load of about 600 Indians, it seemed like the floodgates had opened 'for the entrance to the Colony of these dark and dismal people'.[12] Gandhi, who was returning from a visit to India on one of the ships, was said to be 'at the head of the advanced guard of the Indian army of invasion—the army that is to dispossess us of our country and our homes'.[13] A crowd of white protestors—sailors, carpenters, printers, shop assistants, tailors and bricklayers—accompanied by 500 native Africans brandishing sticks and singing war songs streamed to the Point and attacked him with kicks, cuffs, mud, stones and stale fish on landing.

18

Seeking Fairness

The M.K. Gandhi Library is a large, pleasant room in the old Indian quarter on Denis Hurley Street. Two-toned walls, white and pale yellow divided by a wooden trim, are broken by small half-glass doors, offering a view of the staircase landing with its enormous fire-hose reel. More square windows, high up on the wall above clothes pegs and hangars, probably for winter jackets, alternate with sepia-toned portraits in black frames of short-haired, bare-headed or turbaned men, most of whom I do not recognize. Long-handled fans and tube lights are fixed in the ceiling, which has slim round pillars supporting it. I see a few scattered titles, *Mathematics 8* and *MSDOS*, Deepak Chopra's *The Seven Spiritual Laws of Success*, plastic chairs and an African teenager reading from a notebook, all of which clearly belong to the present, but they do not counter the strong whiff of nostalgia evoked by the surroundings.

Much of it comes from the books ranged on the shelves of wooden cupboards—hardbound, embossed, covers faded and spotted with age and sporting the heavy bold fonts of the early twentieth century. *Yoga Lessons for Children, Phrase & Fable, Radha Soami Satsang Beas, The Laws of Nature: Infallible Justice, Ministry of Heaven, Romeo and Juliet, The Importance of Being Earnest, Bhowani*

Junction, Queen Kunti, Encyclopedia Britannica, Universal History of the World, New Popular Education, My Utmost for His Highest, Guesses at Truths, Hindu Scriptures, Ramayana, Gita. These were the sort of collections frequently encountered at one time in second-hand Indian bookshops, a mix of the English literary and popular with ruminations on Indian spiritualism, a revelation of what it meant to be culturally sophisticated in the modern era.

Parsi Rustomjee opened the library in 1921, a few years after Gandhi had returned to India, a fitting tribute to his pedagogical inclinations. Gandhi's belief in the beneficial effects of education made him wish for more professional and public service-minded men like himself in Natal to work for the migrant community. He made efforts to identify suitable young men in India, writing to them about the colony's prospects and trying to persuade them to make a move. The Natal Indian Congress also had a wing, the Natal Indian Education Association, to provide scholarships, conduct debating competitions and run a reading room for the local youth.[1]

For Gandhi, who admired the British, the fight against the Franchise Law Amendment Bill was not for political power but to 'resist degradation'. This was a founding principle of the Natal Indian Congress along with promoting 'concord and harmony among Indians and Europeans residing in the colony'.[2] His repeated references to civilization and degradation suggest a faith in the liberal promise held out by colonial thinkers like Cecil Rhodes who maintained that 'every civilised man' south of the Zambesi should be given a vote[3] and Macaulay who expressed hope that the 'public mind of India may expand under our system ... that by good government we may educate our subjects into a capacity for better government.'[4]

Gandhi believed that colour prejudice was contrary to British traditions and only temporary and local, and that British settlers could be made to see the error of their ways ('Is this Christian-like, is this fair play, is this justice, is this civilization?' he wrote in his 1893 letter to the *Natal Advertiser*[5]). His bitter experiences in South Africa had not yet shaken his faith in England as 'the land of philosophers and poets, the very centre of civilization'. The Indian community shared Gandhi's early zeal for the British Empire. 'God Save the Queen' was sung at every meeting in Natal. On the occasion of the sixtieth anniversary of Queen Victoria's reign, the Diamond Jubilee, celebrated throughout the Commonwealth on 22 June 1897, Natal Indians sent a silver shield inscribed with an address expressing a 'sentiment of loyalty and devotion' towards the British Empire and bearing twenty-one signatures, including Gandhi's. On the Queen's eightieth birthday on 19 May 1899, they sent a cable: 'NATAL INDIANS TENDER HUMBLE AND LOYAL CONGRATULATIONS TO HER MAJESTY ON HER EIGHTIETH BIRTHDAY. FERVENTLY PRAYING ALMIGHTY MAY SHOWER CHOICEST BLESSINGS ON HER.'[6] A few weeks later, Gandhi presented a souvenir and an address to G.M. Rudolph, the retiring magistrate of Ladysmith, by the Indians of the town.

The Anglo-Boer War came to Natal unexpectedly when the Boers, made jittery by British war rhetoric, launched a pre-emptive attack on the borders of the British colony in October 1899. Sensing an opportunity to raise Indians in British esteem by proving that they were not 'money grubbers' and 'deadweight' or 'useless for the defence of the country in which he has elected to live' as white settlers claimed, Gandhi called a meeting of the Indian community. The community agreed with his appeal to Indians to join the war on the side of the British and it offered its services 'unreservedly and unconditionally ... to the Government or the Imperial authorities'. In his letter to the colonial secretary in Pietermaritzburg, Gandhi wrote: 'We do not know how to handle arms. It may be that, if in no other direction, we might render some service in connection with the field hospitals or the commissariat.'⁷

Gandhi's friend Dr Parker Booth was approached and he agreed to train men as nurses and orderlies. Three hundred free Indians, mostly Indian Christians and working-class Tamilian Hindus, volunteered, along with 800 indentured labourers, who were given leave for the purpose by their employers. Many of the educated Indian elite, including Henry Louis Paul, also volunteered for the Ambulance Corps led by Gandhi. A photograph of the corps shows a group of about thirty Indian men arranged around a fifty-year-old Parker Booth, dressed in fatigues, their hats variously angled and askew. Despite their inexperience, the members of the Indian Ambulance Corps served creditably for six weeks, marching 40 kilometres a day, removing the wounded from the battlefield, dismantling Boer telegraph lines and so on, till the end of February 1900 when the British pushed the Boers back and the war moved elsewhere.

The corps was disbanded and its leaders received war medals. Indians gathered at the Natal Indian Congress Hall on Grey Street at 8 p.m. on Wednesday, 14 March 1900, to 'adopt congratulatory resolutions with reference to the recent brilliant successes of the British arms and the consequent relief of the beleaguered towns of Ladysmith and Kimberley'.⁸ In a conciliatory gesture they invited Sir John Robinson, the prime mover of the infamous Franchise Law Amendment Bill and now a former prime minister, to preside. Robinson, sixty years old and in ill health, a prophet-like figure, white-bearded and with a distant gaze, was inclined to be generous, praising Indians for their 'excellent work' and adding, 'I cannot too warmly compliment your able countrymen Mr Gandhi.' A Natal newspaper observed that this was 'the first occasion upon which Europeans and Indians in this Colony have met on a common platform for a common purpose'.⁹

But the warmth and bonhomie of the evening was a veneer. In truth, Indians had lost the battle for their rights against the Natal government and were more politically emasculated than they had ever been. Gandhi's crusade had taken white colonists by surprise but had not forced them to retreat. Advised by the Colonial Office to 'avoid the naked exclusion in terms of race', a new Franchise Bill, which effectively disqualified Asiatics from voting (on the grounds that they lacked a tradition of elective representation), was passed.

And, as it turned out, the Franchise Act was just one of a range of measures rolled out by the Natal government to curb the Indian 'menace' in the colony. The others were even more radical. A hefty punitive annual tax (as much as a year's earnings) was to be levied on indentured workers who wished to stay on in South Africa after their contracts ended which, in the words of a sympathetic white Natal farmer, amounted to a 'Shylock-like taking the pound of flesh'.[10] Local authorities were to be given sweeping and unchallengeable powers to reject applications for shop licences, a move clearly aimed at reducing competition from the Asian traders.

More to the point, Indian numbers were to be diminished by placing obstacles at the entry point itself. The Immigration Restriction Bill passed by the Natal government in 1897 and its subsequent amendments, called for specific conditions to regulate and monitor free immigration. It set the age of majority at twenty-one years for children seeking to join their parents and two years of residence in Natal for acquiring domicile status. Women issued with passports were identified by their marital name. Those likely to be a public charge (defined as possessing less than £5, and later £20, in cash), 'idiots', criminals, pimps, prostitutes and, finally, sufferers of leprosy, syphilis, smallpox and plague, were to be denied entry. Shipowners transporting illegal immigrants as well as other aiders and abettors were likely to be penalized. The condition for admitting non-domiciled persons was a literacy test. Applicants had to write an application to the colonial secretary in a European language.

Few Indians could meet such a requirement, certainly not the young, poorly schooled boys who came to work for Indian traders. Nor, as Gandhi argued, could Indians highly educated in Indian languages, a priest, for instance, or an accomplished teacher of vernacular learning. His petitions to the Colonial Office urging the inclusion of Indian languages in the entry test produced no result. His assertion that new Indians were not arriving in large enough numbers to justify 'any Act so drastic in its tendency, and so wide in its scope'[11] went unheard. Natal's restrictive Immigration Act came into force and became a template for other colonies.

The Natal government did not stop at legislation. Convinced of a pressing need to secure the colony against unauthorized entry by undesirable populations (namely, or at least chiefly, Indians), it designed an elaborate infrastructure of border control. The Natal Immigration Restriction Department was set up in 1897. It was staffed by two men from the Harbour and Fisheries Department, Harry Smith and Godfrey Dick. The former, Portsmouth-born, was thin-lipped and thickly bespectacled while the latter wore his hair slicked back from a broad forehead, imbuing his boyish good looks with a fitting touch of sternness. On their shoulders fell the task of organizing the mundane defence of the colony. They could draw on the help of the Water Police, ju-jitsu-trained men in smart white uniforms with striped arm bands whose job it was to chase smugglers and frog-march drunk sailors to their ships. Now, they also patrolled the 11 kilometres of wharves for prohibited migrants. Suspicious characters were detained on a derelict ship anchored in the middle of the bay. The Immigration Restriction Department also secured Natal's internal land borders. Checkpoints manned by the police came up near border crossings at Charlestown, Volksrust,

Van Reenen and De Jagers Drift, and travelling border police were posted on trains.[12]

As the Natal government went about determinedly putting in place its measures to minimize the Indian presence and influence in the colony, the Indian immigrant community's campaign floundered. The Anglo-Boer War ended on 31 May 1902 and the hectic post-war rebuilding in the Transvaal presented challenges for Indians there that laid a greater claim on Gandhi's attention. In 1903 he moved his base to Johannesburg. Two years later, my great-grandfather Mohanlal and my pregnant great-grandmother arrived in Durban on the SS *Afghan*.

19
Indian CBD

In the bright-yellowy sunlight, just beyond the railing, cars are waiting for the lights to change. Tall buildings, brown and peach, loom on the horizon, interspersed with signage. 'METRO LODGE' it says clearly on one shopfront. The ordinary street scene has the quality of a painted backdrop for me at this moment, walking amidst marble slabs and headstones. The graves are well-spaced-out in lines radiating from a small stone chapel. The progenitors of the colony lie here, including the plump-cheeked English traveller and trader Henry Francis Fynn. In 1823, he was among the group of traders led by Lieutenant F.G. Farewell, who reportedly cured the great Zulu Chief Shaka of a war wound and received a gift of 9,000 square kilometres of land around Port Natal in return. Pioneers, soldiers, aldermen ... I spot George Christopher Cato, the first mayor of Durban whose name graces public squares, creeks and hotels, in repose. And harbour master William Bell, department store owner William Greenacre and others whose careers were inextricably tied to the growth of the modern city.

Next door, a small white mausoleum stands over the grave of Sheik Ahmed, a Telugu-speaking Muslim who came to Natal on the SS *Truro* in 1860 and was discovered posthumously by Soofie

Saheb, a respected Islamic scholar of the Chisti order, who arrived in Durban from the Konkan-Ratnagiri coast a few decades later, to have been a Badsha Pir or 'king of the guides'. Beside the shrine, much visited by people of all faiths, on a patch of uneven ground, are the graves of Muslim traders. The pioneering Aboobaker Amod died of cholera in August 1887 at the age of thirty-five while visiting India,[1] but the redoubtable Dada Abdullah, who died in 1912 at the age of fifty-eight, is here.

Across the road is the entrance to the Early Morning Market. Back in time, free Indians owned or rented thousands of acres of land, which they cleared and planted with a variety of fruits and vegetables, including experimental strains (an archived letter I come across refers to a private agreement between an Indian and a landowner, Dr D'Emmereyde Charmoy, to lease 7 ½ acres of land at Cato Manor for planting fruit trees).[2] They hawked their produce in panniers slung across their shoulders all over Natal. A few free Indians settled on a mangrove-covered sandbank in the bay called Salisbury Island and took to fishing, catching Cape salmon, garrick, mullet and shad, which they dried and sold at £12 a ton. Free Indians were the main source of fresh produce in the colony at the beginning of the twentieth century.

Their descendants dominate the fresh produce stalls at the Early Morning Market. In an airy shed echoing with Bollywood songs playing on small CD players, one finds wire-mesh cages stuffed with plump white chickens, asters soaking in buckets and hillocks of aubergines, tomatoes, apples, oranges and thick-veined greens interspersed with packets of a fiery red masala and photos of Satya Sai Baba. Beyond, in an open enclosure where goods are unloaded, are the porters, strong, stocky black men, Ama-Mpondo from the Eastern Cape. Mambhedeni Malana, or Mr Longa-one as he is introduced to me as, was a sugarcane cutter in the Transkei homeland before he came to work as a porter at the market. He is darker and taller than his colleagues, dressed in rough working clothes and has powerful hands, the nails long and deeply set in thick fingers. His father transported goods in a rickshaw for bulk buyers at the market at a time when to haul goods without a work permit invited fines, jail and deportation. Africans preferred to rent barrows from Indians and unload their goods because they were willing to overlook the absence of permits, but they were no different from the whites, he says, and 'treated us like kaffirs, slaves'.

Under apartheid, Indian- and African-owned buses were not allowed access to the inner city, and the Warwick Triangle area became an important transportation hub, a role it continues to play with a taxi rank, a bus rank and railway stations linking it to the city's different nodes. Across the railway tracks, shoppers with baskets looped on their wrists look for cheap cotton wraps and household goods under a snarl of concrete flyovers, and rugged men in work-soiled shirts and beanies collect for a late breakfast. The stalls are out on the street, a few rough benches, tables hammered together from hoardings and wood fires supervised by women in frill-edged caps. Aluminium platters on the counter are filled with a variety of meat, a mound of round objects that look like cabbages, a pile of something that looks like seaweed and fossils dredged from the sea and some more regular-looking chopped bits that could be mutton or beef but which are, in fact, parts of bovine heads. The women come early in the morning to buy the heads whole from butchers and chop them into smaller pieces with an axe. This makeshift stall with its sooty clapboard walls and hungry diners is what I imagine native eating stalls in the Grey Street precinct looked like a hundred-odd years ago.

Two African men, sitting on the pavement in grimy shirts, hair unkempt, sharing a cigarette outside the West Street cemetery, stare suspiciously. This part of downtown Durban seems to me to have a temporary shifting quality, of markets setting up afresh everyday under sloping metal sheets without walls, of street corners that look like the edges have been sawed off as speed and commerce barrel through spaces meant for living. Perhaps I am recalling a diversion of the railway line from the docks in the late nineteenth century, which sent a whistling steam train right by the Indian neighbourhood at Alice Street where St. Aidan's Hospital stood. Parker Booth used to run a clinic from his home, 49, Cross Street, in a large iron-roofed bungalow with outbuildings, surrounded by a rusty corrugated iron wall before opening the St. Aidan's Mission Hospital, the first for Indian patients, in 1897 with funds from the Natal Indian Congress and Parsi Rustomjee.

Around here was also where Christian free Indians lived, most of them colonial-born and schooled in missionary institutions, of which there was a fair scattering in the city: Roman Catholic, Wesleyan Methodist or Anglican institutions including an orphanage for girls. In the Indian quarter there was a school run by Anglican nuns on Prince Alfred Street and a chapel on Queen Street. Durban's Christian free Indians sported Biblical names like Abraham, David, Gabriel, Lazarus and Paul and were Westernized in appearance and lifestyle, inclined towards sports and music, maintaining clubs for cricket, football and cycling and performing as minstrel bands in clown outfits and blackface. They worked mainly in the service or entertainment industry as waiters, cooks, nurses, photographers and musicians, though some among them were teachers, clerks and interpreters.

A map in a booklet called *Gandhi Sites in Durban* by Paul Tichman[3] shows me where the hospital stood, at the corner of Leopold Street (David Webster Street) and Cross Street, near an old bridge that ran to Alice Street (Johannes Nkosi Street). The map also tells me that I am passing by the corner of Dr Yusuf Dadoo Street and Dr A.B. Xuma Street (Commercial Road) where the old Congress Hall, the meeting place of the Natal Indian Congress, used to be. By the beginning of the twentieth century, the Natal Indian Congress was moribund for a variety of reasons and the hall was used less for politics and more for social and cultural activities.

Normal life had been disrupted by the Anglo-Boer War with Durban overrun by refugees. About 100,000 Britons had fled the Boer republics and taken shelter with friends and sympathetic church societies in Natal and the Cape Colony. Transvaal's Indians had naturally looked towards Natal and its large Indian community for help, and at Gandhi's request and with some reluctance the authorities temporarily eased the new immigration law to give them entry. After the end of the war in 1902, the English and the Boers, victor and vanquished, went into a long huddle over a potential union of the four colonies and the laws by which it would be governed.

The months preceding the war had seen much grumbling by the British about discrimination by Boers in the Transvaal. Sympathy for their own, who the Boers called 'uitlanders' or outsiders, had been extended to non-white races ('The treatment of the natives [in the Transvaal] has been disgraceful,' Chamberlain told Parliament in October 1899[4]) and was even employed to drum up public support in England for the war. Natal's Indians may have drawn some hope of restitution from these pre-war pronouncements, which explained the air of cautious anticipation marking the Indian CBD. Durban's traders were happy to put aside the din of petitions and meetings and get back to their businesses; some may have even regretted their involvement in a cause that had failed to deliver any relief and even worsened their prospects. The departure of the ringleader, the young man who had whipped up their enthusiasm and fighting spirit, only deepened the appearance of a political lull and a resigned acceptance of what was to come.

The void created by Gandhi's absence was partially filled by a weekly bilingual newspaper called *Indian Opinion,* which he started in 1904 to supply news and commentary. It was printed by a former Bombay schoolteacher who had established the first Indian printing press in Durban. The paper bore Gandhi's unmistakeable stamp and carried much of his writing, but it was edited by M.H. Nazar, a Surti, son of an English-educated engineer and civil servant who had studied law and medicine in Bombay and entered business with his brothers in England before moving to South Africa, where he ran an agency which arranged permits for Indians. A man with a small, serious face and a full moustache, Nazar was a familiar figure in the Indian quarter, often seen walking home to Sydenham after putting the paper to bed.[5]

He had shared Gandhi's political ideals, even joined the Ambulance Corps and was appointed joint secretary of the Natal Indian Congress when Gandhi left for India in 1901. He split the responsibility with Rahim Karim Khan, a barrister from Lincoln's Inn who had come to South Africa at age twenty-five in 1899 and joined Gandhi's office for a while before establishing his own network of clients.[6]

M.H. Nazar and R.K. Khan were the kind of educated Westernized professionals Gandhi had hoped to bring to the colony to take his place. 'The outlines of the work before us were fairly fixed ... Shri Mansukhlal Nazar was there and so was Mr. Khan,' he wrote, describing his state of mind while planning what might have been a permanent return to India in 1901. Some Indian youths, born and bred in South Africa, were about to return from England as barristers. The Indian migrant community was in good hands and Gandhi believed 'that my work in South Africa was now over'.[7]

But the community would not let him go so easily. When Colonial Secretary Lord Chamberlain announced a visit to the colonies following the conclusion of the Anglo-Boer War, members of the Natal Indian Congress requested Gandhi to come back to South Africa and lead the Indian delegation.

In the early period of his return, Gandhi was less involved in fighting for Indian rights and more engaged in other forms of activism. The young lawyer's evolving political consciousness operated at multiple levels. One of those was a deep and sustained engagement with forging a lifestyle that promoted self-reliance and presented an alternative to what was considered the norm in Western societies. Underneath his formal business attire was a restless spirit relentlessly preoccupied with life's moral and spiritual dimensions. In 1895 Gandhi had visited and been much impressed by a Trappist monastery in Pinetown outside Durban. Almost a decade later, on a train journey, he happened to read John Ruskin's polemic against classical economics, *Unto This Last*, and a plan evolved in his mind, which he put into action by purchasing a piece of farmland 22 kilometres from Durban.

The plot was in a wilderness studded with guava, mango, orange and mulberry trees and no provisions available for miles. The 4-kilometre path leading to it was rough and tended to get flooded in the rains. Snakes, some poisonous, were plentiful—one came across at least four or five a day. Water was brought from a stream. Self-reliance, equality and a minimum use of machine technology were the guiding principles of the settlement scattered over eight homes of corrugated-iron-and-wooden supports. A printing press occupying pride of place was set up for producing *Indian Opinion*, which had been moved there to save costs. M.H. Nazar had died suddenly of a heart-related ailment in 1906 and the paper was mostly managed by Gandhi's nephew Chhaganlal, who had come from India to assist him and who lived in Phoenix with Gandhi's wife and sons and other volunteers, including a few white men and women who shared Gandhi's evolving sociopolitical vision.

Gandhi himself did not live in Phoenix but visited often for varying lengths of time. One of those visits was at the time of what the British called the Zulu uprising. In early 1906, a force led by Zulu Chief Bambatha carried out guerrilla attacks on the British in response to the colonial administration's new poll tax. The administration responded by opening machine gunfire on Zulus armed with spears and fighting sticks, killing 4,000 men and arresting and flogging hundreds more. Gandhi raised an Ambulance Corps like the one he had led at the time of the Anglo-Boer War: two dozen men led by three Gujaratis of 'fine physique'. The corps was asked to tend to the wounded Zulus, which the British would not do, though reportedly they stood around and jeered. Sergeant Major Gandhi of the volunteer corps felt later that 'This was no war but a manhunt'.⁸

Following Tichman's map, I walk past the old office of *Indian Opinion,* now a plain brick façade topped by a satellite dish, a clothesline strung across it, abutted by a photo-framing shop. I am on Dr Yusuf Dadoo Street now, with its familiar bustle and acrid fumes. Tall office buildings of the Durban Central Business District loom up in the distance, contrasting with the Indian quarter's low skyline. Profits in the years between the two World Wars brought about an architectural transformation of the city centre, remaking the staid colonial town in the exuberant shapes and colours of art deco. Jazz-age chutzpah even entered the Indian CBD, though the buildings here combined the Miami look with eastern influences.⁹ Aboobaker Mansions, named after the first passenger Indian and built in 1937 at the corner of Dr Yusuf Dadoo and Denis Hurley Streets, is a classic representative of this type, with a balcony resting on fluted columns shading the sidewalk below. Bubble-patterned grilles add a delicate touch, though the pale blue walls sweeping around the street corner are solid and substantial, like a steamer. Opposite it, the Jami Mosque, expanded over the years to enclose a floor area of 975 square metres and hold 4,500 worshippers, making it apparently the largest mosque in the southern hemisphere, spreads its pearly white arms.

The sloe-eyed young men at the entrance of a building on the former Queen Street look at me suspiciously as I ask them the way upstairs.

'I am looking for an address,' I say, waving my slip of paper.

There is no change in their expressions. A million and a half people of Indian origin live in South Africa, constituting 2.6 per cent of the total population. An estimated 70 per cent live in KwaZulu Natal. From their appearance and speech, these men seem to be not old but new migrants and not necessarily Indian, but South Asian or from another part of the South Asian diaspora. They are in their twenties or thirties, dark hair fashionably styled and dressed in brand knockoffs, probably produced in their own garment workshop, the one in which I find them. I try again, speaking in Bollywood Hindi, mentioning my great-grandfather and emphasizing that my attempt to ascend the stairs of the building is only concerned with family ties and nostalgia. 'My brothers …' I do not think they believe me but they relax and smile and accompany me to the head of the stairs.

I am not alone. With me is Rafique Mayet or 'Rafs', a South African documentary photographer of Indian origin whose late father, a grille manufacturer, made much of the metal latticework in the neighbourhood. With his tall, bulky presence by my side, I lose my earlier trepidation, moving through the surging crowd as thoughtlessly as I would on home ground and pausing at will. From time to time, Rafs raises his camera and I feel emboldened to take mine out as well and let it hang visibly around my neck, disregarding potential muggers. I have sought Rafs's help in looking for Mohanlal's address in Durban.

Mohanlal lived in the Indian precinct. All the addresses from which he wrote letters to the colonial authorities and which I retrieved from various archives are a stone's throw from the Jami Mosque. In a letter in 1905 his address is 183, Grey and Victoria Streets (now Dr Yusuf Dadoo and Bertha Mkhize Streets). The following year it is 156, Queen Street (now Denis Hurley Street). In 1907, there are two new addresses: 158, Queen Street in August and 147, Queen Street in October. And then in the last set of correspondence that I come across, spread over July–August 1908, the address is 198, Grey Street. I am puzzled by Mohanlal's numerous changes of address, but I have the multiple addresses written out on a piece of paper and tallied with new street names and I am trying to identify the location of each.

We walk down Dr Yusuf Dadoo Street and turn into Denis Hurley Street. I know that in the past at least, the ground floor consisted of commercial units and the residences were above them. So, counting off the numbers on the shops we turn into the entrance that leads to the rear and upper portions of the buildings where Mohanlal's Queen Street addresses might have been. Barred entrances offer a glimpse of littered alleyways and fluorescent-lit garment workshops.

Upstairs, having got past the suspicious young men, we are in a long, narrow veranda leading past several locked doors. One of them is open and a small well-dressed man appears silently, smiling and beckoning us in. We ask if we can look around and he waves a welcome. The room he is in is large and piled with fabric. Rolled fabric, scraps of fabric, bags filled with fabric, heaps of folded fabric. In one of the inner rooms, on a microwave balanced on plastic crates, are mugs, spoons and a big round box of sugar. Open doors show two bathrooms with shiny, new floral tiles. The man keeps his eyes on us, smiling all the time. He is an unusual-looking man. His dark hair, fair skin and bulbous nose suggest a mix of Indian and Middle Eastern blood. He is oddly shaped, as if his body has been wrenched and badly put together. He wants to talk to us, to narrate a story of torture at the hands of the apartheid police. It is a chilling narrative and I am concerned that he has mistaken us for reporters. But it seems he just wants to tell his story and once he is done, he releases us, shaken, back to the corridor.

More corridors, more steps. We pass dusty electric metres and a bright red fire hose. We see homes above us, curtains and a man washing a steel plate. Below us is an Indian shopping centre, the well-known 'arcades' crammed with tiny stalls selling hats, clothes and African beads. The domes of the Jami Mosque are directly in front of us. We take a turn and now there are asbestos roofs, the warm brown façade of a church tower and an advertisement for a car wash. In the parking lot below us, a few men in white dishdashas, kurta-pyjamas and skull caps are on their way somewhere, carrying plastic bags and an aluminium tea kettle. On the street an African woman slouched against a lamppost contemplates her basket of wares. A wan Chinese woman moves in the shadows of her curio shop. Two Indian women in flower-print shirts and pants march past a biryani stall and a garment store where a bare-bottomed marionette awaits costuming and disappear into a store stacked from floor to ceiling with sewing machines. A sudden wind gusting down Denis Hurley Street sets everything in motion: rubbish, pigeons and cars, their stereos tossing bits of music into the rustling blue air.

The sun is directly above us, spreading a bright white desert light. A couple of shaggy woebegone palm trees greet us from a small roundabout. The streets are as busy as before. The shoppers seem to have burgeoned, and the hawkers are as eager to woo them. But the sound of cheap commerce and seedy vagrancy is muted for me. I hardly see the loiterers and loud hoardings; my mind is full of the brief journey we have just taken. I think of the corridors, the stairwells and the back lots and how they connect with each other to form a parallel concourse. We were traversing streets and the block up there without stepping out. As this idea takes clear shape in my mind, another thought begins to form. What if … I put my hand out to stop Rafs. 'If we can get from Queen Street to Grey Street from inside and walk all around the block, it could be that the addresses are closer than if you approach them from the outside. What if the addresses were just different parts of a set of rooms, like in a boarding house?' Rafs thinks about it. We are at a robot, the local term for a traffic light, on Bertha Mkhize (Victoria) Street. The light is almost flush with the building and its barred entrance. Rafs nods. And with this thought in our heads, both of us look up at the same time speculatively. We are in front of a two-storeyed building that clearly predates the other post-colonial buildings in the precinct. This one is different also because it displays an overtly Hindu vernacular architectural style. The mouldings, pillars and modest proportions are similar to Hindu homes in older parts of Gujarati cities. Later, I will see it described in an architectural guide as an 'Indo-African style with a few art deco features' and having a 'symphony of arches, balustrades and Dutch gables'.[10] Right now, I see a symbol of the Hindu 'Om' and below it block letters which spell out: SURAT HINDOO ASSOCIATION BUILDING.

PART FIVE

SETTLING

20

Indian Quarter

Before the development of Durban, the Bay of Natal was a large estuary fed by many rivers. Its mangroves rustled with the arrows of the Nguni who once ruled the land. Ghostly hyenas shrieked on the Bluff, terrifying elephant hunters long in their graves. And the spirits of sunk ships heaved and clanked at the Point. Did the turbulent breeze blowing in from the sea to the Indian quarter half a mile away fill the twenty-six-year-old Mohanlal with foreboding? Or did he sleep well, secure in his hopes for the future?

The answer is possibly contained in a heavy carton labelled 'CSO', an acronym for 'Colonial Secretary's Office', in black felt at the Pietermaritzburg Archives Repository. In a squat brown building belonging to the Department of Arts and Culture, with a South African flag gracing the lobby, stout, efficient women in work jackets hand out requisition forms and tough, muscled men trundle carts bearing the boxes requested. I feel the ribbon between my fingers, the texture of age-roughened satin. It is a pinkish-beige, the same colour as the stiff cardboard box which it binds, sliding through slits and tied in a bow, a mild trace of femininity and pliancy in the stodgy bureaucratic space of the archive. I untie the ribbon and am taken back to a tender couple starting life in a new city.

I assume Mohanlal and Foolkore could not have left Port Louis before 16 November 1905, which is the date on Mohanlal's 'passport' from the Mauritian Governor Cavendish Boyle. A mere three weeks later he was writing to the Natal colonial secretary from 183, Grey & Victoria Streets, Durban, applying for an interpreter's position in the Supreme Court of Natal:

> 183 Grey & Victoria streets Durban
> 8th December 1905.
> To the Honourable
> The Colonial Secretary
> Natal
> Respected Sir,
> I beg to apply to be admitted as a sworn translator and interpreter of the Supreme Court of Natal in Hindustani and Guzerati languages.
> I beg to remain
> Respected Sir
> Your most obedient servant
> MP Killavala[1]

The letter was written with care, the handwriting cursive, letters slanting rightwards with flourishes; in the signature, the 'm' and 'p' are joined and three odd little slanting dashes like salutes appear above 'Killavala'. The extreme alacrity (for the letter would have been written almost as soon as he got off the boat) and care evident in it suggest preparation on Mohanlal's part. Had he advance knowledge of opportunities for interpreters in Natal? How far back did his information go? Did he leave Bombay with Durban as his eventual destination or did he make his plan on information gathered in Mauritius?

The first known Indian interpreter in Natal was an English-speaking woman, probably educated by missionaries, who could write her name in Tamil and who arrived with the first contingent of indentured workers on the SS *Truro* in 1860. A decade and a half later, in 1875, an enterprising gent, M. Doorasamy Pillay, placed an advertisement in the *Diamond Fields Advertiser* in Kimberley:

> ... The undersigned begs to inform the public that they may seek for legal advice free from the difficulty they have to undergo in explaining the elements or circumstances of their case or cases to any of the legal members unacquainted with their Indian dialects i.e. Madrasie, Telvogoo (sic), Hindustanie and Sanscrit (sic) as well as French through illiterate interpreters ... to avoid inconvenience, misunderstandings, confusion and risks that may naturally occur.
> Signed M. Doorasamy Pillay[2]

For the next few years, the number of interpreters in the Indian languages was low and the quality of interpretation so abysmal that misunderstandings and confusion reigned. Often, indentured workers landed up in jail merely because of their inability to communicate with local authorities. 'Everyone I have met with in the Colony has dwelt upon the untruthfulness of the Indians,' Gandhi noted, observing that

> interpreters are expected to perform the Herculean task of interpreting successfully in four languages, viz., Tamil, Telugu, Hindustani and Gujarati. The trading Indian invariably speaks Hindustani or Gujarati. Those who speak Hindustani, only speak high Hindustani. The interpreters, with one exception (Paul), speak the local Hindustani, which is a grotesque mixture

of Tamil, Gujarati, and other Indian languages, clothed in extremely bad Hindustani grammar ... In the case of the Gujarati speakers the matter is still more serious. There is not a single Gujarati interpreter in the Courts ... while the struggle is going on, the Judge makes up his mind not to believe a word of what the witness says, and puts him down for a liar.[3]

In the interests of litigious Gujarati traders, Gandhi applied to be an interpreter in 1896 and was listed in the Natal Civil Service List of 1908 as a court interpreter and translator (Gujerati) from 1896. In 1904, a Gujarati Hindu teacher, M.M. Joshi, came to stay with a family friend in the Transvaal and was appointed as an interpreter in the Pretoria Courts.[4]

Presumably there were still openings for more interpreters in Natal, for an assistant undersecretary in the Natal Colonial Secretary's Office responded promptly to Mohanlal on 9 December 1905, informing him that to be admitted as a sworn interpreter of the Supreme Court, 'you should make application, through your Solicitor, to the said Court in the usual way'.[5]

But Mohanlal did not follow up immediately. He took a whole month to send a second letter. Perhaps it took him time to find a solicitor and when he did, it was the very reputable firm of Shepstone Wylie and Binns Solicitors and Notaries Public. They wrote to the colonial secretary on Mohanlal's behalf on 9 January 1906 from their office in 334, Smith Street:

We have the honour to address you on behalf of Mr. N R Killavala who is desirous of qualifying as an Interpreter to the Supreme Court. We understand that he has made an informal application to you already. The languages in which our client wishes to be examined in are Hindustani and Gujarati. He wishes if possible, to have the examination take place in Durban. We shall be glad if arrangements may be made for the examination.⁶

Mohanlal's solicitors had not bothered to get his initials right. The assistant undersecretary did marginally better by referring to him as 'N.P. Killavala' in his response, which was: 'It is entirely a matter for the court to deal with.'

In the next letter, dated 24 March 1906, Mohanlal dropped the careless Shepstone Wylie and Binns and engaged Archibald Findlay as his solicitor. This was an important development because Archibald Findlay, or 'Arch' Findlay as he signed himself, was going to play an important role in Mohanlal's story, though at present all he did was to write to Harry Smith Esq., Principal Immigration Restriction (IR) Officer at the Point in Durban with further details regarding Mohanlal's application.⁷

At this point there is a gap of a few months in the correspondence, possibly due to a lacuna in the records. It is a good time for me to take a pause from the archival correspondence as well and take a look around the neighbourhood in which Mohanlal and Foolkore had set up home. It has been about four months since they landed in Durban. We know Mohanlal's address from his letters regarding an interpreter's position in the Pietermaritzburg archives. I have already mentioned that his address changed frequently but in minor ways, sending him shuttling between Grey, Victoria and Queen Streets. I have suggested that he might have lived in a boarding house spread over these adjoining streets. I find that the Surat Hindu Association came into existence in 1907, but there might have been an informal association preceding it.

Mohanlal's living space was likely to have been small: a room and a kitchen, both sparsely furnished. Hindu passenger homes typically contained a cupboard, a bed stacked with pillows, a steel peti or trunk with a name and a location painted on it in white or red and another bag stowed on top of the cupboard.[8] From their window, my great-grandparents would have looked out at the tops of warehouses, one-storeyed blocks and sloping tin roofs punctuated by a brown church tower. They would have heard the rumble of trains carrying coal to the quay and the frequent hooting of steamers setting out on voyages. Those distant sounds would have been overlaid by the cosier smells and sounds of the neighbourhood, the loudest of which would have been the azan issuing from the Jami Mosque around the corner.

The mosque had become an impressive edifice now, with a congregation space for 500 and new minarets that could be seen for miles around. Its canny Memon trustees had invested £300 to buy an adjoining site, which they converted in part into shops and apartments to generate a steady income for the Natal Porbandar Trust that funded charitable enterprises in their hometown.[9] The Memons still held themselves to be above everyone else, particularly the Surtis, who they thought to be coarse and conservative, unlike their own pious and culturally refined selves. The Surtis, who had built fortunes as large as the Memons and had their own Edwardian-style mosque on West Street, resented the Memons' sniffy ways but both groups also had common concerns, which muted the long strain of competitiveness.[10]

The confrontation with the colonial administration, the excitement of forming the Natal Indian Congress and the hubbub caused by the petitions penned by Gandhi probably seemed like a mirage. The spate of anti-Indian legislation, which the community had worked so hard to prevent, was a reality and its impact was becoming increasingly evident. Half the passengers arriving on ships and entering the lists of those 'restricted' or not allowed to enter the colony were Indian. Some passengers found ways to enter surreptitiously by disembarking at a port before Durban—Beira on the northern coast of Portuguese East Africa or Delagoa Bay—and travelling to Durban less conspicuously by sea or through the interior, which was far from safe.[11]

The 1897 Dealer's Licence Act also saw the ejection of Indian shopkeepers from the town's main streets. George Molyneux, a thirty-year-old British military officer of Irish origin appointed as licensing officer in 1903 by the Durban Town Council, divided the town into areas where Indians and Europeans could shop separately and reduced the number of Indian shopkeepers and hawkers in the town by rejecting applications for the renewal of licences often arbitrarily or with vaguely worded objections such as: 'inability to write English', 'dishonesty', 'books not properly kept', 'undesirable applicant', and so on.

Shopkeepers thus denied put up their goods for sale and left. A tailor disposed of his shop for a song and disappeared overnight to evade immigration authorities. Whispers suggested that a barber in a fez was actually a Hindu roof tiler from Navsari, a secretly returned deportee.[12] Meanwhile, local authorities, egged on by white traders, moved in to repossess public space and take advantage of business opportunities in the neighbourhood: the vegetable-and-fruit market was moved from its traditional location on Gardiner Street and the first municipal eating house opened on 116, Victoria Street, in May 1905.

When Indian community elders met in the compound of the Jami Mosque after Friday prayers, the future of the community must have weighed heavily on their minds. The possibility that London might influence the ongoing negotiations between the English and the Boers over a proposed Union of South Africa still held out a faint hope of a more liberal outcome. But portentous events were underway in the Transvaal and the news, faithfully reported by Gandhi's *Indian Opinion*, would have been discussed with some concern.

I wonder what Dada Abdullah made of the circumstances. With Aboobaker Amod's passing and the return of Moosa Hajee Cassim to Porbandar, he was the senior-most of the early pioneers left in Durban. Gandhi's former host and supporter was now in his early fifties and the absence of a male heir might have given him a more detached perspective on the matter. His astute mind would have probably observed that regardless of how the political future shaped up, the days of runaway business expansion were over and the kind of success that poorly learned men like himself had been able to achieve in South Africa was no longer possible. The next generation was educated and well-travelled, like O.H.A. Jhaveri who had been to the United States, Europe, England and Egypt.[13] The supply of cheap, illiterate village boys, which had enabled traders to expand their businesses, had been curtailed. Many of the new arrivals in Natal were Hindu clerks who could pass the education test set by the immigration authorities. Mohanlal had arrived at just the right time when his professional skills were in demand.

Was his arrival at this time a mere matter of chance? I ask because the next set of letters that I come upon in the folders at the Pietermaritzburg archives are not only from Mohanlal but include two other Indians who had also submitted applications in November 1906 to be examined in Gujarati for interpreters' positions.[14] The new applicants moved in the same social circles as Mohanlal and had similar backgrounds. They were Shapurji Jivanji Randeria, represented by Tatham, Wilkes & Shaw of 7, Timber Street, Pietermaritzburg and Umashankar Shelat, represented by Aurthur E. Carlisle of 4, Imperial Buildings, Smith Street, Durban.

Randeria was a Parsi born in 1880 (making him exactly the same age as Mohanlal) and originally from Rander and then Bombay. Like Mohanlal, he had passed the senior bookkeeping examinations of the London Chamber of Commerce in Bombay. He arrived in South Africa five years before Mohanlal, in 1900 via Zanzibar, and had a travel document exactly like the one Mohanlal had acquired in Mauritius, signed by the British consul of Zanzibar, entitling him to proceed to any British colony with all the rights of British citizenship. Wide-lipped with a broad forehead and a serious mien, he is referred to in many places as a 'bookkeeper' but he was also a man of wide-ranging preoccupations. He ran a shipping and forwarding agency with his brother Nasarwanji and his signature, appearing on resolutions of the Natal Indian Congress, suggests that he was an active member of the organization. He was also a teacher and I come across a note written by him to Gandhi on 26 August 1901 from 107, Field Street, Durban, in his characteristic turquoise-blue ink on a sheet of beige notepaper, requesting the use of the Natal Indian Congress Hall for two hours daily to conduct an 'Anglo-vernacular class of about six pupils'. A pencil notation by Gandhi says: 'From 5 to 7 pm.'[15]

Shelat was one of the three Gujaratis with a 'fine physique' who led Gandhi's Ambulance Corps in the military action against the Zulus in 1906. He was a light-eyed young man with a fair, boyish face, wearing a checked jacket over a waistcoat and a buttoned-up shirt in a file photograph. He was a Brahmin, a former government servant from Baroda and Ahmedabad in Gujarat, and like Mohanlal and Randeria, he had an interest in education. In 1907–08, he wrote several letters and petitions signed by leading members of the Indian community to the colonial education department, drawing attention to the deliberately shoddy approach of the authorities towards the education of children of passenger Indians.[16]

It seems quite a coincidence that three Gujarati men of the same age and with a similar professional profile should be applying simultaneously to be interpreters. Were they friends from before? And had they hatched a plan together to try their luck overseas, encouraging each other to come to the colony and apply together for interpreters' posts? It seems to me to be a possibility. There is no sign that Mohanlal had met Gandhi yet, but a letter from his solicitors to A.R. Dunning, the chairman of the Board of Examiners, Indian Languages, on 20 December 1906 asks if there is any difficulty in getting an examiner and suggesting Gandhi, 'Advocate and sworn translator, at present in Johannesburg, who is coming to Natal and will be in Durban on the 27th inst:' and adding that 'Mr. Gandhi's qualifications for the post will be well known to you'.[17]

The response, if any, to this letter is not on file. There was clearly a delay in the proceedings referred to by all the applicants: Mohanlal's solicitors speculated that the absence of information about a forthcoming exam either through a letter or a notification in the government gazette suggested a 'hitch somewhere in the proceeding'. The speculation was not unfounded. There was no full-fledged examination board at the time and the administration was then still in the process of framing a notice regarding the rules for the Examination of Candidates for Interpreterships and Translatorships in the English and Indian Languages. The principal undersecretary, in a letter to Randeria's solicitors on 24 December 1906, explained that the delay was because rules drawn up by the Indian Board of Examiners for the regulation of examinations were 'under consideration'.[18]

On Friday, 15 March 1907, as *Indian Opinion* reported, the Natal Indian Congress Hall on Grey Street was 'prettily decorated'. The occasion was an important one, a reception by the Durban Indian community to felicitate James Godfrey, the second colonial-born Indian to return from London as a barrister. The first colonial-born Indian barrister, Joseph Royeppen, son of indentured labourers, had overcome extreme racial barriers at home to study law at Cambridge.

The Durban reception of March 1907, a celebration by the migrant community of a noteworthy achievement by one of their sons, was also tinged with the politics of the moment then underway in the Transvaal, which we will presently come to. It was a significant event and the Indian professional elite of the town, including notables such as Suchit Maharaj, a journalist and president of the Hindoo Temple, lawyers and interpreters R.K. Khan, Abdul Kadir and Bernard Gabriel, and others were present. The *Indian Opinion* report on the occasion mentions that M. Killavala and U.M. Shelat were also present and 'said a few words appropriate to the occasion'.[19]

The fact that Mohanlal was referred to by name in the brief news item and that he made a speech at what was clearly a distinguished gathering for a landmark event in the community suggests that he had established himself as a member of the professional elite, which seemed to have now expanded well beyond the Anglo-Indian community. It appears that Gandhi was occasionally present at their gatherings when visiting from the Transvaal. His strong faith in the value of a modern education (as yet unquestioned) and in social service permeates reports of their activities in *Indian Opinion*, where Mohanlal is mentioned. There are two more such items in *Indian Opinion*. In its issue of 8 December 1906, the newspaper thanked twenty-odd people by name, including M. Killavala and U.M. Shelat, for contributing to the 'Durban Indian Public Library' which opened on 1 September 1906, with 'money, periodicals, papers or self-sacrifice'.[20]

The last item in the issue of 27 April 1907 is about a visit to Springfield at the request of the editor of the newspaper to provide succour to indentured and ex-indentured Indians suffering from a malaria outbreak. Suchit Maharaj, Dr Nanji, Dawad Mahomed, Shelat and Killavala were present and a committee was formed, which also included Gandhi, his nephew and R.K. Khan.[21]

So clearly, by late April 1907 if not before, Mohanlal had met Gandhi. Shelat was present on all the occasions where Mohanlal is mentioned. Gandhi's associate Khan, and Suchit Maharaj were also part of the circle.

More than a year had passed since our young couple arrived in Durban and while I have dwelt at considerable length on Mohanlal's efforts to establish himself as an interpreter in the colony and his success at insinuating himself into the influential professional circle on Grey Street, I have sadly neglected to mention Foolkore. It is not forgetfulness on my part but a lack of information. It was the fate of women of her times to be left out of official records and the only way I can try to imagine her life is through the limited sociocultural accounts of her immediate surroundings that I can access.

The Indian quarter in Durban was more crammed than the traders' enclave in Port Louis. Houses and stores existed cheek-by-jowl amidst warehouses and the streets throbbed with commercial energy. Stepping down from her apartment, Foolkore would have found herself surrounded by shops and small businesses owned mainly by Indians but also by Greeks, Chinese and English owners. Let me pick two streets that appear in the addresses affixed on Mohanlal's letters in the Pietermaritzburg archives and construct a picture using the Natal Almanacs of 1905–07. On Queen Street, my great-grandmother would have strolled past S.H. Kyriakidis, cigarette maker; Chongson & Co., grocers; M.K. Mangan, storekeeper; North G. & Sons, machinery merchants; Phenix R.W., furniture dealer; Amod Essack, storekeeper; Chowson & Co., grocers; Cassim Khamisa, butcher; Valeb Jina, fruiterer; and Dayal Bikhda, tailor. On the adjacent Victoria Street, she would have found: A. Glozer, tailor; A.C. Spargo, cycle dealer; Warren Bros., chemists; Butterworth J., outfitter; Stein & Co., butchers; Krowitz H., general dealer; and Cheonlong & Co., grocers.

For fresh produce she might have walked across to the market set up next to the Jami Mosque and while she was going through the motions of selecting and weighing her wares, she might have heard people gossiping about the falling-out between the Memon sheths who controlled the Jami Mosque and the charismatic preacher they had brought from Gujarat to serve as an imam. Uncharacteristically, the tightly knit Memons had also begun fighting among themselves over the workings of their charitable trust in Porbandar. Natal's prominent Memon families, all related to each other, were bickering over two continents, a remarkable feat in those days of long journeys and slow communication.[22] Ordinarily the Surtis would have rejoiced at the Memons' discomfiture. But they had troubles of their own. Colonial-born children of Hyderabadi indentured workers were swarming their mosque on West Street and challenging the Surtis' dominance and their conservative Wahabi form of Islam.[23]

Leaving the gossipers behind and carrying her bag of vegetables, Foolkore would have entered a colourful mise en scène of kiosks selling travel insurance, trips on Indian and European ocean liners, Persian rugs, Turkish caps and waistcoats. She might have lingered outside a jewellery shop—a great many gold jewellers had set up shop in the Indian precinct—and dropped a coin into the outstretched palm of the crippled beggar who dragged himself past the open doorways of shops. Looking up at a passing cloud, she would have seen a crescent and a star, emblem of the Ottoman Caliphate, head of the ummah or Islamic community, high up on a pediment shining in the renewed sunlight.

A more cosmopolitan tone had diluted the Islamic character of the Indian precinct. An alluring aroma of hot samosas and sugary tea wafted from the snack shop on 154, Grey Street, owned by Ganda, a Hindu Gujarati who had arrived in South Africa as an eleven-year-old by tricking the immigration authorities. He had slipped into Durban after arriving from India and applied for identity papers claiming to be the son of a Johannesburg-based uncle; the uncle had earlier filed a false report for a missing son to make the story stick.[24] Foolkore might have made a purchase and, clutching the hot snacks, walked home. From the docks the wind would have carried the lilting voices of men singing as they tossed coal into the holds.

Foolkore would have been one of many women in the Grey Street precinct. Even after the tightening of immigrations laws, an average of fifty women, mostly new or old wives of passenger Indians, and about 200 children arrived every year in the first decade of the 1900s.[25] The once-bleak streets around the Jami Mosque where once-poor Gujarati village boys in loose black robes roamed now resounded to the dulcet tones and eager cries of women and children. A 1911 story in *Indian Opinion* titled 'Dakshin Afrika Darshan ane Be Mitre-no Samvaad (Introducing South Africa and Dialogue of Two Friends)' had two Gujarati Hindu clerks, Manharram and Udayshankar, and the former's wife, Manorba, discussing the pros and cons of bringing a wife to the colony. The seeding of a more family-oriented community and the growing number of Hindus, many of them colonial-born, led to a tour by Bhai Parmanand, a Hindu preacher of the Arya Samaj, in 1905 and the formation of the Hindu Young Men's Society.[26] Another Hindu missionary, Swami Shankaranand, arriving on the *Carisbrook Castle* three years later in October 1908, was greeted by hundreds of Hindu, Muslim and Christian Indians and even a few Europeans at the Congress Hall.[27]

I try to place my great-grandmother in this society. Foolkore, in a frilly blouse, young at seventeen and heavy with child—how do I place her in Durban's Indian quarter? The fact that I know so little about her identity makes the exercise purely speculative.

I run through possibilities. Women in Memon and Surti Bohra households practised purdah and restricted themselves to zenanas, with houses being so designed that it was possible for women to get into a closed carriage in one courtyard and exit in another without encountering passers-by. Was this cloistered environment her world? Or was her world the earthy camaraderie of Kathiawari Hindu women, gathering with song and gossip, one imagines, as they ground masalas and prepared pickles? Did she worship at the shrine of Badsha Pir, that attracted people of all faiths, in Brook Street? Did she visit the Umgeni Road temple or attend the public discourses of visiting Hindu preachers? Or perhaps look in on the Sunday service conducted by Subhan Godfrey in a schoolroom on Field Street? Did she know Olga Rachel, the white woman married to an Indian trader, A.M. Paruk? Did she feel a kinship with Zulus and Zanzibaris? How did she navigate the tight groups of women bonded by memories of their native towns in India? Did she find friends amidst the wives of men arriving from Mauritius? And did she know and would she have associated with the cultured, literate women who formed a women's association in 1907 for the 'moral and intellectual education'[28] of the community? Where did Foolkore fit in? If she fit in at all? I have no answer. What is known is that she gave birth to a baby girl sometime in 1906 and both she and the baby appeared to have done well.

The successful delivery of his child must have been a relief to Mohanlal, though the business of his interpreter's examination was still hanging fire and appeared to be far from concluded, with letters continuing to go back and forth. The documents are yellowed and discoloured. Some are torn and the pieces have been joined by translucent tape. Some are typed and sent from solicitors' offices, others are handwritten; Randeria wrote with a blue-green pencil on small pieces of paper torn out of a small notepad. Both he and

Shelat sometimes wrote directly for information while Mohanlal communicated mostly through his solicitor. Examination fees were debated, charged and deposited: a candidate paid £3.3 for each language he wished to be examined in for a first-class certificate, which was a requirement for an appointment at the Supreme Court. Questions came up, clarifications were provided after much discussion and outstanding shillings remitted. A process was being set up and the aspiring interpreters had to wait till it was elaborated. Weeks stretched into months.

21

The Sea, a Town

Sometime before November 1906, Mohanlal started working for his solicitor, Archibald Findlay, as a clerk-cum-accountant. The arrangement may not have been unusual, given the high incidence of litigation involving Indians. Gujarati traders, with their frequently evolving family partnerships and their high reliance on credit-based arrangements, required a variety of legal services. Agreements had to be drawn up, amended and abrogated (the *Natal Provincial Gazette* was filled with notices of dissolved partnerships and insolvency). Natal's largest rice importer, B. Ebrahim Ismail & Co., piled up debts of £98,000. Typically contested amounts were smaller, in the modest range of a thousand-odd pounds and sometimes even less: Hassen Maiter engaged a lawyer to compel his relative Amod Maiter of Verulam to honour two promissory notes of £25 each.[1] Then there were criminal cases involving indentured workers.

The tightening of the immigration law had opened up a new line of business for lawyers at the beginning of the twentieth century. In their haste to curb the entry of Indians into Natal, the authorities had not thought through the implications of the law on various types of travellers, which resulted in the creation of peculiar difficulties. What was to be done about an eighteen-year-old boy arriving after the age of majority for minor children was abruptly reduced from twenty-one to sixteen, for instance? Or the wife of a man domiciled in Natal bringing in a son by her first husband? Or about people arriving home from holidays abroad or returning after the Anglo-Boer War? Immigration authorities had to make ad hoc provisions to deal with these and other legitimate applicants.

These provisions took the form of 'embarkation permits' for short-term commercial visitors, 'transit passes' to meet the refugee crisis during the war, 'temporary permits' for 'deserving cases' and 'certificates of exemption' for priests, teachers, bookmakers and those 'well-known' to Europeans. Travellers, merchants and Muslim pilgrims setting out for Haj were issued with documents confirming their identity and their right of protection by the British Crown. Resident Indians also won the right through a legal challenge to apply for 'Certificates of Domicile' or 'Registration Certificates'.[2]

A domicile certificate I come across is a piece of regular paper, approximately 6 by 4 inches, crinkled, stained and yellow with age, stating: 'Issued by the NATAL HARBOUR DEPARTMENT ... In accordance with Immigration Restriction Act No. 1, 1897 *To certify that the person hereinafter described has produced evidence to my satisfaction that he has been domiciled in Natal*'[3] at a cost of 2 shillings, 6 pence, and certified with a red-and-blue stamp on the bottom right. Another has a scrawl confirming it was surrendered for a new certificate and a third is rubberstamped 'PASSED' by a 'Protector of Emigrants' at the India end. The changes of rules, requirements for witness affidavits, and thumbprints and signatures from appropriate authorities for procuring domicile certificates, created great anxiety among passenger Indians and generated brisk business for those involved in such procedures.

Archibald Findlay's office was at 339, West Street. His grandson, a practising lawyer in Durban, describes it as having a very large entrance hall leading into a waiting area with seats on the left. Beyond the waiting area was a strong room for important documents and then a long hall, at the end of which was a general office with a desk for a lady bookkeeper. The general office led to the partners' offices with desks for two clerks behind them. Findlay's letterhead read 'ATTORNEYS, CONVENYENCERS AND NOTARIES PUBLIC' and at the time he was serving as Mohanlal's solicitor he had just parted ways from a partner called 'Carlisle', whose name is crossed out on the stationery, and was soon to enter into a partnership with a Bernard Cowley. A short while later these two also parted ways and Bernard joined his brother Cecil to form Cowley & Cowley. Shifts in partnerships seem to have been commonplace and not necessarily acrimonious: the Findlays and Cowleys were in fact family friends and the latter part of the correspondence regarding Mohanlal's application for an interpreter's position was handled not by Findlay, but by Cowley & Cowley.[4]

Every morning, presumably, Mohanlal left the noisy Indian quarter and headed for West Street. As a qualified accountant he could have easily found work with one or more Indian trading firm but the fact that he chose to work for Findlay (while it may have been preferred for any number of reasons) tallies with what one of his granddaughters told me about his reported fascination for white people and his love of the English language and lifestyle. A man of his temperament would have enjoyed leaving his colourful residential neighbourhood with its resonances of home and venturing into a qualitatively different environment.

Like lawyers' clerks, he probably wore a grey suit to work. Woollen fabric for suits was imported from England through local wholesalers, the fabric for a two-piece suit costing a pound or less at the beginning of the twentieth century. Wide-bottomed trousers, a white cotton shirt, a jacket, a waistcoat, a watch with a chain and a metal guard above the elbow to hold up a sleeve was the style of the times.[5] Pushottam Valabh was the best-known tailor on Grey Street and collars and cuffs were washed by numerous dhobis or Indian laundrymen in the neighbourhood. Appropriately attired, perhaps twirling an umbrella, Mohanlal would have set out for work, covering the short distance in less than a quarter of an hour at a leisurely pace, his route taking him east on Queen Street towards Grey Street, then left on West Street.

Named after Sir Martin West who had been in Bombay with the British East India Company before becoming the lieutenant-governor of Natal in 1845, West Street was an important arterial road, broad enough for a full span of draught-oxen and wagons to make a turn on it with ease. A tram line ran down the centre towards the old town hall with its pretty façade of Corinthian columns and pilasters, not far from which were the law courts on Aliwal Street.[6] Mohanlal might have felt like a fine gentleman striding along the graceful boulevard abutted by trees, raised pavements and fine shops protected from inclement weather by awnings. Let me leave him, smart in his grey suit and hat, flushed from his exertions, approaching 339, West Street as I approach the city from the opposite end.

◆

It is not yet 1908 when a whaling station was established by Norwegians, leaders in the whaling industry, at the foot of Durban's south pier, emitting an overpowering stench of butchered whale carcasses over the seafront. But the Durban coast hummed with other kinds of activity. Ships arrived, filling up all the berths from Congella to the Bluff, spilling passengers like confetti. The wharf heaved with people, then miraculously emptied out until the next shipload appeared. Against the continuous swelling and abating of crowds, the heavy work of the docks went on alongside. The luffing cranes and shunting trains conducted their duet of clanks and sighs, the graving and floating docks prepared ships for overhaul and dredgers sucked and spat sand. The comings and goings of ships bookended time: the mid-week departure of the four-funnelled mail ship, the *Arundel Castle,* for instance, was a marked event in the city's calendar. A sizeable crowd collected to watch the ship leave amidst a great flurry of sirens and shouting and the playing of 'Auld Lang Syne' by the ship's orchestra. Once it was out of the breakwater, spectators watched, jaws agape, to know the fate of the Durban-based pilot: whether the swell would allow him to cross from the ship to the rowboat and head back safely to shore or carry him off to East London from where he would have to make his way back by train.[7]

Such were the simple pleasures in this port town. The war was over and refugees from Boer towns had gone home. White families from Natal's interior towns, having arrived for the day by train, spread out on the beach and frolicked in the frothing waters. On Sunday mornings, carriage drivers and grocers; drivers of fire engines that hurtled down the road, brass bells ringing and firemen shouting, 'Hi-hi-hi!'; and owners of wooden-tip rubbish carts pulled by Shire horses led their animals for a bathe and a romp in the warm sea, and good Christian townsfolk on their way to church were treated to the sight of horses in long lines heading towards the Umhlanga Rocks.[8]

Opposite the windswept Victoria Embankment, facing the harbour, was a small, stolid grey building housing the Durban Club, flanking offices of mining barons. The town centre was on a parallel street behind it where a new neo-baroque town hall was being built. Other public buildings were in the popular Renaissance Revival style with elements of 'free' classical late Victorian forms: stone façades with alternating horizontal bands of red brick and plaster, cupolas, clocktowers, bell towers and verandas. In Durban, unlike Bombay, colonial authorities did not seem to wish to impose themselves upon a native population with monumental architecture but instead to recreate a comforting, cosy dream of home.

Up in the Berea amidst blossoming mimosa and lilac trees were the burghers' homes—single-storeyed brick houses where canaries sang in latticed verandas and front rooms sported ornamental mahogany dining tables with fringed green chenille covers and curio-stuffed whatnots. The burghers' wives kept their households running and the silver gleaming with help from African helpers and an Indian or coloured nanny and gardener. Indian hawkers brought vegetables to their doors and one often saw a bare-footed Zulu rickshaw-puller hiking up the steep slope, porcupine quills on his head and bells clinking on his ankles.[9]

One of the houses in the Berea belonged to the Findlays. A family of sailmakers and shippers from the harbour town of Arbroath in Scotland, they had moved to Manchester and then to London, from where an asthmatic Archibald Findlay migrated to Durban following a mass movement from the highlands of Scotland to the colonies beginning in the middle of the eighteenth century. Through their wanderings, the family retained a sense of roots by naming all first-born sons 'Archibald' and passing down to each, in turn, the 'Archibald Findlay Chair', a 1683 ceremonial oak chair with a Scottish crest.[10] The émigré Archibald was a merchant. His son, born in 1880, studied at the Durban High School and went to Gonville and Caius College, Cambridge. An entry in the *Biographical History of Gonville and Caius College, 1349–1897*[11] confirms that Archibald Findlay was admitted in 1898 to study law, where one of his proud achievements was making it to the prestigious rowing team after a member fell ill and scoring a 'Blue' (blazer) of which, according to his grandson, 'he was very proud'.

Archibald Findlay was tall and thin. The shortness of breath that had afflicted his father had bypassed him and he was an energetic man with a zestful air who sang in the church choir and liked to go for long walks with his Irish terrier. Presumably, he was part of Durban's social whirl. The *Natal Witness* and *The Mosquito and African Sketch*, a magazine for the white settler community in 1906 and 1907, has photographs of tennis and polo matches, automobile clubs and bonneted women framed by bougainvillea. In the last week of June 1906, Hall Caine's play, *The Prodigal Son*, and *A Royal Divorce* starring Leonard Payne as Napoleon were staged at Scott's theatre. The Durban Turf Club held its winter meeting on 15 July, a day of cold wind and brilliant sunshine. If he attended any of these events, Archibald would have dressed for them in a light-coloured Assam silk suit. For work, he wore a black lightweight jacket of Alpaca wool, the uniform that made him part of the fraternity heading through the palm tree-lined garden fronting the stately law courts.

It was a picture-perfect world dipped in the pastel hues of acacia and hollyhock and emitting the subtle fragrance of vanilla and musk. Signs of trouble (the murder of a forty-five-year-old 'storeowner and well-known freemason' by a knife-wielding Chinese gang in Krugersdorp, for instance, or the killing of an inspector and a trooper, Armstrong N.P., in a showdown with armed members of a tribe living on the Zwaartop location) were few and far between, and dissipated like dull streaks in the summer sky. R.D. Furse of Eton College, author of the prize-winning essay for the Lord Meath Empire Day Challenge Cup between secondary schools of the British Empire in 1906, claimed that the colonies were like 'branches' replenishing the tree trunk.[12]

Let me return to Mohanlal waiting on West Street. Like his employer, he too had ventured to a colony. Yet, as he knew, many of the pleasures of the town—its gardens and esplanades, its pastry shops and malls, its libraries and beaches and pleasure halls where ladies in lace-trimmed crinolines danced to fiddles and concertina—were out of bounds for him. There were rules, spoken and unspoken, about where he could go, where he could sit or how he could travel. The colour of his skin was the factor that set the bar for his ambitions, not the fineness of his speech. But did he mind?

22

The Interpreters

In the last week of November 1906, Mohanlal sat opposite a white detective, C. Waller from the Criminal Investigation Department, in his home. Since I have no physical description of Detective Waller, I will picture him as the movie archetype—big-footed, broad-shouldered, square-jawed. On an evening in late spring, he would have wended his way through Grey Street past a blur of dark unfamiliar faces, foreign tongues and an acrid-sour miasma of dry chillies and sorghum. He would have read the signboards and counted off houses till he came upon the right house number and climbed the steps to Mohanlal's lodgings on Queen Street. I suppose Mohanlal greeted him warmly, offered him the high bed as a seat, which the detective probably declined, then the chair. The detective would have looked out of place in the small apartment with its sparse furniture. And the sounds of Grey Street floating in through the open window and the clatter from the shops below coming through the floorboards must have added to the awkwardness of the situation. I imagine much of this, of course, because I only know for certain what is recorded in the archives.

'Applicant is an Indian Clerk,' Detective Waller wrote in a logbook of the department on 1 December 1906 ('Indian Clerk' underlined heavily in blue pencil by him or someone else), 'working at Mr. Findlay's the solicitors West St:- He is a married man, 26 years of age.'

It is thanks to Detective Waller's report that I know about Mohanlal's employment with Archibald Findlay. Waller also claimed that Mohanlal was a married man, which suggests Foolkore's presence even though she is not mentioned. And the reason why the detective had paid him a visit was because my great-grandfather had applied for permission to keep a sporting rifle.

> 156 Queen St.
> Durban 23rd November 1906
> The Controller of Arms
> P'M'Burg
> Sir,
> I want to keep a rifle for sporting purposes and will be obliged if you will kindly give the necessary permission to keep it.
> I beg to remain,
> Sir,
> Your most obedient servant,
> (Signature) M.P. Killavala[1]

This letter is on a plain sheet of paper, typed at Findlay's office perhaps? Mohanlal's signature has changed, become large and confident, a swirling initial, the surname clear and a long line running below like a plinth. There is a stamp of the controller of arms, certifying that it was received on 24 November, and file numbers. The clip attaching the correspondence has left a rust mark on the top left. The controller's office appears to have acknowledged Mohanlal's application because there is another letter from him written on 29 November where he acknowledges receipt of 'your letter' and says: 'I shall be glad to receive the further communication mentioned in your letter.' On 30 December the controller of arms forwarded Mohanlal's letter to the chief magistrate, Durban. And some time over the next two days, the detective visited Mohanlal.

Continuing his departmental log entry of 1 December, Detective Waller wrote: 'He (Mohanlal) states that he wishes to have a sporting rifle for the purposes of shooting Buck etc. on the veldt. He has no farm or land. The gun will be kept in Durban except when taken out for use.'

On 7 December 1906, Mohanlal received a letter from the assistant undersecretary of native affairs.

> M. Killavala
> 156 Queen Street,
> DURBAN.
> In reply to your letter of the 23rd ultimo to the Controller of Arms applying for permission to possess a rifle, I have to inform you by direction of the Secretary of Native Affairs, that permission to possess a firearm cannot be granted to you.
> Signed
> Asst. Under Secretary for Native Affairs

I am not surprised by the rejection. Why did Mohanlal want permission for a sporting rifle? The request is so incongruous with his circumstances that I cannot hazard any guess as to his motives. I look for information. Records at the Pietermaritzburg archives show that on 22 January 1907, a month after the rejection of Mohanlal's application, a letter went out from the firm of Findlay and Cowley to the undersecretary for native affairs for information as to the necessary steps to be taken before the granting of permits for Indians to carry firearms.[2] The connection between the rejection of Mohanlal's application and this request for information is too strong to ignore.

The only explanation for Findlay's initiative in this matter is if Mohanlal's keenness on a sporting rifle was a matter of common concern. I ask Findlay's grandson if his grandfather was fond of hunting.

'Oh yes!' he says. Like many of his peers who took pride in their firearms, Archibald was the proud possessor of a couple of rifles and a shotgun which were kept not in his house in the Berea, but on the family farm 140 kilometres from Durban.

I look for information about the Cowleys in the archives and find that they had numerous Indian clients. Bernard Cowley is an indistinct figure, leaving no trace in the records, but Cecil cuts quite a controversial one. On 5 October 1907, he had an altercation with an assistant magistrate in Durban, about which he complained to the colonial undersecretary, claiming that the assistant magistrate made him wait for obtaining an interdict because he was engaged in 'personal business'. The assistant magistrate denied the charge and maintained instead that he had been listening to a case when Cecil Cowley ('beardless youth'), without being robed, had 'poked this interdict under my nose'.[3]

I am struck by the phrase 'beardless youth'. It reminds me with sudden force that these men, Archibald, Cecil Cowley and Mohanlal, were about the same age, in their mid-twenties, and by the looks of it, blessed with a similar youthful brashness. I wonder if the puzzling matter of Mohanlal's sporting rifle is an invitation to see beyond relationships of employer and employee, lawyer and client, white and Indian, and instead to think of them as young men, possibly friends? Gandhi had many white friends and even shared a home with a young white couple, Henry and Millie Polak, and with a Jewish architect, Hermann Kallenbach, their bonds developed over shared political, spiritual and dietary interests. Mohanlal did not have Gandhi's erudition or his wide philosophical approach, which enabled him to make friends easily with fellow seekers. But from the limited insight provided by archival papers, Mohanlal comes across as someone with not inconsiderable social skills and an ability to make his way in the world. Travel and the time he spent in Mauritius, where Indians were not discriminated against as they were in South Africa, may have given him a measure of self-confidence. South Africa's racial hierarchy did not allow for social mingling, but it was not impossible that an impetuous Cecil Cowley, a liberal-minded ('perhaps too liberal' according to his grandson) Archibald Findlay and Mohanlal, an adventurer in a foreign land, should have proposed to go hunting on the veldt together.

That is one hypothesis. Three men—two white, one Indian—making plans to go hunting. I have a second hypothesis, which I admit is weak and with no evidence at all to give it substance, but I will suggest it all the same in the interest of providing a wider and fuller range of possibilities. It links Mohanlal's interest in acquiring a sporting rifle to the sports clubs run by educated Indians. There were at the time in Durban, clubs for cycling, cricket and football for Indians, and it is not unreasonable to speculate that there may have been a club for hunting as well. An ambitious young man like Mohanlal, who had already eased himself into the social elite, would have seen merit in taking up an activity that provided opportunities for networking with the influential community of Indian teachers and interpreters. Henry Louis Paul, for instance, was the founder and president of the Natal Indian Football Association, the United XI Cricket Club, the Greyville Sporting Association and the United Sports Association.[4]

This possibility, highly speculative though it is, provides a close-up view of a significant component of the community of professional interpreters in Natal that Mohanlal was aspiring to join. The community itself was small with only twenty-six Indian interpreters scattered all over the colony. They served at the Supreme Court, at various magistrates' courts and at the Protector of Immigrants

Office, and earned as much as £250 a year. Their relatively high income and official positions gave them a prominence and status within the Indian community that had to be earned through certain attributes. Official government regulations required interpreters to be cultured (speak good English, not a 'broken patois', and be familiar with the literature of their language), to have a 'thoroughly good' personal character and to be married men with wives by their side in Natal.[5]

Natal's best-known interpreter and civil servant, Henry Louis Paul, appeared to possess all these qualities. Besides his linguistic abilities and his community engagement, he was a family man, as one can see from a sepia-toned photograph of a family wedding in which middle-aged Paul, small, balding, in a pale-coloured three-piece suit and bow tie, poses with his wife, Ellen Elizabeth Paul, and their numerous children, all attired in European style. In truth, Paul had been accused of committing adultery in 1886 and of planning to escape the consequences by 'hastefully' leaving the colony. His colleague David Vinden, postmaster, clerk and Indian interpreter attached to the Klip River Magistrate, was similarly charged by an enraged husband of taking his wife to Mauritius and fathering her baby.[6]

These revelations are from Prinisha Badassy's paper *Turbans and Top Hats: Indian Interpreters in the Colony of Natal, 1880-1910*, which studies a few well-known interpreters in the colony and paints a world of colourful, morally dubious characters accused not only of promiscuity but also of corruption and cut-throat competition. Frank ('rollicking') Ward was dismissed from the Umzinto Resident's Magistracy, where he was a clerk and interpreter, for drunkenness and preparing 'spurious petitions'. Chelivum Stephen, an interpreter in the Supreme Court, was accused of demanding bribes of 'fowels and eggs' from clients.

'If you do not give your tongue a rest by speaking ill of others. I will in time stop you by smashing your head and limbs,' wrote

A.H. Peters, an interpreter with the Pietermaritzburg magistrate, to a colleague. Stephens and Ward plotted to get Henry Louis Paul 'out of the Service' because: 'He is becoming too proud and would not associate with us and he thinks he is a European now.' The case studies here are of Anglo-Indian interpreters, but I find evidence of rivalry also in other Indian communities. In the published *Letters of M.H. Nazar*, for instance, Nazar refers to a case between the Indian lawyer and interpreter R.K. Khan and an educated businessman M.C. Anglia to come up in court on 1 April 1903, maintaining that: 'There seems to be no love lost between K(han) and Anglia and Osman (another interpreter). And the latter mix up private with public matters.'[7]

Mohanlal's motive in applying for a licence to acquire a sporting rifle remains unclear and I leave it unexplained against the pretention, competition and preening that were characteristic of the liminal space between the Indian and the white communities occupied by a very small group of men, which he aspired to be more fully a part of.

23

The Examination

The Boers established Pietermaritzburg as the capital of their republic, founding it in a fertile hollow at the foot of a tree-covered escarpment where the midlands of Natal rose 400 metres above the surrounding landscape. In 1843, the British took over and made it the seat of their administration in Natal. On a chilly June day in 1907, Mohanlal, Shapurji Jivanji Randeria and Umashankar Shelat traversed the 80-odd kilometres from Durban to Pietermaritzburg. It is likely that they had visited the city, a short train ride away, before. They might have seen its sights, its handsome assembly building and the massive red-brick city hall and been familiar with its pathways, now flush with camellias, hellebores and budding azaleas. Seven and a half thousand Indians lived in Natal's capital and comprised one-fourth of the population. Among them were rich traders who might have offered the three young men accommodation.

The long-expected government notice had finally appeared, announcing that examinations for interpreters in six Indian languages—Gujarati, Hindustani (including Urdu and Hindi), Tamil, Telugu, Malayalam and Caranese—were to be held twice a year in June and December on dates notified through the *Natal*

Government Gazette, giving potential candidates a fortnight to write to the colonial secretary of their intention to appear, with a non-refundable examination fee.[1]

Letters were sent and received:

30th May 1907
Gentlemen,

In continuation of my letter of the 24th December last, regarding S.J. Randeria's application to be examined in the Gujerati language, I have the honour to inform you that the next Indian examination will be held on the 21st and 22nd proximo – vide Govt. Notice No. 298/7, copy of which I enclose.

I also enclose for your information, a copy of the Rules.

If it is still Mr Randeria's wish to be regarded as a candidate for this examination, please advise me as soon as possible, at the same time forwarding the necessary fee.

I have the honour to be,
Gentlemen,
Your obedient Servant,
Assistant Under Secretary
Messrs. Tatham, Wilkes & Shaw,
Solicitors,
7, Timber Street,
Maritzburg.

On 11 June, a letter went out from the assistant undersecretary to Findlay and Cowley saying that: 'I have the honour to inform you that Mr. M.P. Killavala is hereby authorised to present himself at the forthcoming examination as a candidate for first class certificates in the Gujerati and Hindustani languages.'

A similar letter went out to U.M. Shelat at PO Box 520, Durban, authorizing him to present himself for examination in Gujarati.

The young men confirmed their wish to appear for the examination. The examiners were informed. One of them, Suchit Maharaj, sent a telegram to A.R. Dunning, chairman, Indian Board of Examiners, Pietermaritzburg: 'Yes I Will Come leaving here tonight.'

R.K. Khan, another examiner, also sent a telegram to Dunning: 'Your wire received shall attend two days ...'

At 10 a.m. on 21 June, the three candidates presented themselves at the Criminal Investigation Office on 251, PM Street, Pietermaritzburg.

The Indian Board of Examiners had selected a passage in Gujarati for them to translate into English, an incident from the saga of the thirteenth-century Gujarati king Karan Vaghela. This story of the last Rajput ruler of Gujarat whose abduction of a woman resulted in the loss of his kingdom and his family to the Delhi Sultan Allauddin Khilji is a staple of Gujarat's bardic repertoire, sung for hundreds of years. In the 1860s, as part of its project to 'recreate versions of English narratives and stories in Gujarati' the education board of the Bombay Presidency had commissioned Nandshankar Mehta to turn the tale into a novel, *Karan Ghelo,* the first novel in Gujarati.[2]

The passage was from Mehta's novel. It described Vaghela's daughter Devaldevli being taken to Devagiri to escape capture by Khilji's soldiers. On the way, in a forest Devaldevli and her guards encountered a woman in obvious distress, but so strange in appearance that she could well have been a witch.[3]

I am immediately reminded of the urban legend that gripped Surat in the aftermath of the Great Fire of 1837, of pregnant women's spirits waylaying young men. The Surti poet Narmad expressed his fear of the forested paths around his childhood home in his autobiography, *Mari Hakikat.* Narmad and Nandshankar

Mehta were contemporaries at the Irish Presbytarian Mission School in Surat. In fact, a biography of Nandshankar, written by his son, opens with a description of the myth of the ghostly woman and an unsuspecting young man.[4] For Mohanlal and his two friends, sitting for the interpreters' examination on that winter morning, the passage they were to translate might have evoked some nostalgia for books read in their childhood and a touch of chilliness that had nothing to do with their surroundings.

The translations turned in by Randeria, Shelat and Mohanlal are in the files at the Pietermaritzburg archives.[5] Mohanlal's is the first that I see, written on blue-lined sheets, an untidy sloping script, the ink falling unevenly, the letters not fully formed but left in a rushing sprawl over five pages with words added here and there as afterthoughts. At the end is his signature, rising up like a sail with a line running under. Here are the first few lines:

(P.M.Burg
21st June 1907)
Slowly the day went on passing and when it was right mid-day all heard a sound from a distance as if someone were crying. As such a horrible sound reached their ear in the noon all were rather terrified. Devaldevli thought that some one was in great trouble and that it was necessary to render assistance ... and when they had gone a certain distance they saw a woman sitting under a tree. She was crying loudly. The whole of the woman's body came to sight through the torn rags ... and the rags were so dirty that it was impossible to say of what colour they should be originally and lice and vermin had their abode there.

Umashankar Shelat's translation is next. His close, rounded handwriting fits into three pages. A frequent use of bracketed options suggests a tendency towards prevarication. At the end is his underlined signature, 'umshelat', with the date and place. His translation goes as follows:

> Day began to rise up by and by and at the time when it happened to be real afternoon all heard a voice from some distant as if someone is crying. All startled on hearing such a word (voice) at the time of afternoon. Devaldevli knows (thought) that someone has happened to be in great difficulty and it is required to help … after walking over to some distant they saw a woman sitting under a tree. She was crying with loud voice (loudly). Through the torn (illegible) which were put up on this woman (with which the body of this woman was covered) …

Randeria the bookkeeper used a thin nib and squeezed his ornate, well-formed letters into two unnumbered pages marked with the date (21 June 07) and his name (S.J. Randeria) on top and with many cancelled lines and words added as afterthoughts to the text.

> The day began to rise gradually, and when it was entire noon they heard from far distance the voice of someone crying. They all frightened when they heard such a terrible cry at the noontime.
> Devaldevli thought that somebody is in awful trouble, and as it was important to help she desired to stop the procession … after reaching to some more distance, they saw a woman sitting under a tree. She was weeping loudly. Through the torn rags which covered the body of this woman, the whole of her body was visible, and the rags were so dirty that it was impossible to find out the originality of the colour.

So, after months of correspondence, waiting and preparation, the much-anticipated examination had taken place. It was not over, for there was an oral test the next day for which the two examiners had been summoned. And after that the young men were free to do whatever they wished to—walk around Pietermaritzburg, observing the stark beauty of bare trees against Victorian buildings and the aloe and wild dagga flowering in gardens splashing orange all over town, or make their way back to Durban.

After the applicants had left, the examiners got to work. The markings on the papers allow me to read the examiners' minds. Whoever corrected Mohanlal's paper suggested that the word 'forced' should be replaced with the word 'obliged', objected to a 'they' being inserted when it was not in the text, opined that 'a certain distance' should be 'some', 'when' should be 'after' and 'went' should be 'turned'. Where Mohanlal had written 'came to sight' the examiner noted: 'construction materially altered'. He found a spelling mistake, a verb and a 'those' missing. He felt that the adjective 'deformed' should be 'ugly' and 'run' should be 'ran'.

The objections seem trifling in light of the reported paucity of interpreters in the colony, but apparently the standards for a first-class certificate were high and interpreters needed to have a thorough knowledge of the grammar and construction of the languages, as well as the particular terms and expressions used in legal and court documents. The government notice also maintained that a candidate could be disqualified for improper behaviour during the course of the examination. The latitude given to examiners was wide and clearly the three candidates did not impress them.

On 22 July 1907, the assistant undersecretary wrote to Shelat informing him: 'With reference to your recent examination in Gujerati, I have to inform you that the Chairman of the Indian Examination Board reports that you failed to reach the standard required for a certificate required as a translator in this language.'

Shelat, in fact, was considered the best of the candidates in Gujarati and English and did well in the oral test, but was let down by his translation. Mohanlal was found 'not competent to be a translator of these languages (Hindi and English)' by Suchit Maharaj in his letter to the chairman of the board of examiners on 28 June. R.K. Khan informed Dunning on 8 July that he found Mohanlal's translations of Gujarati into English 'somewhat weak'. Other comments from both examiners found his composition in English 'indifferent' and his knowledge of Hindi 'limited'. Mohanlal, who had appeared for two languages, Gujarati and Hindi, failed in both and Randeria also failed in Gujarati, for which he had appeared.

One would imagine that once the decision had been arrived at and communicated to the hopeful applicants the matter would end, regardless of its nature. But this is not what happened. When the results were communicated, a curious dance ensued in which all the figures named in the examination process seemed to be involved in a negotiation. There was a discussion among examining officials in the first place, which concluded that all three candidates could reappear for an examination after three months. The candidates themselves fired off letters to the Supreme Court, asking to be appointed as interpreters even though, as the court pointed out, they lacked the necessary qualification of a first-class certificate. They then tried a different tack. A second-class certificate was less demanding and made the holder eligible to undertake ordinary interpretations and record depositions in a magistrate's court. The candidates now wrote to the assistant undersecretary and to Dunning asking if they could be given second-class certificates. After some discussion, the examiners assented to the awarding of second-class certificates to the three.

As soon as they received the intimation, on 18 September 1907, Mohanlal's new solicitors, Cowley & Cowley, wrote to the colonial secretary:

> We are given to understand that interpreters to the Magistrate's Court may be admitted by the Colonial Office and we should be glad if you would do so in this case as our client wishes to

have any benefit that he is entitled to under the second class certificate granted to him.[6]

The colonial secretary's response was discouraging: all interpreters in the magistrate's court were government servants and there was no vacancy at present that could be offered to Mohanlal. Four days later, another letter from Cowley clarified that 'our client is not an applicant for a government job' but wants to be enrolled and sworn in as an interpreter so that 'he can give services if called on by a litigant'.

It went on in this way for a while, the protracted conversation demonstrating both a lack of clarity on the side of the authorities about a process that they were clearly still putting into place and a determined effort on the part of the candidates to claim as much ground as they could in the prevailing ambivalence.

I do not know what concessions Mohanlal and his co-applicants managed to wrangle. He had failed the interpreter's examination but he could try again and make use of his second-class certificate to take on assignments for individual clients. He also had his job with Archibald Findlay, so it is likely that he was not necessarily unsettled by his failure and still had opportunities to look forward to.

And when Diwali came around a few months later, in the first week of November 1907, I can assume that the mood in the Killavala residence was hopeful, not despondent. The community's Hindus had arranged a Diwali celebration at the premises of a Muslim trader, Abdool Latif, and the merchant elite, including non-Hindus like Parsi Rustomjee and Dada Osman, were there. The streets of the Indian quarter wore a festive look, most likely with tinsel banners, lanterns hanging from shop awnings and diyas arranged on windowsills. Firecrackers probably sizzled and burst in the evening sky. In a window above Queen Street, my great-grandmother may have laughed and clapped and pointed them out to her infant daughter.

PART SIX

CAPE TOWN

24

Moving

I left Mohanlal in late 1907 in a settled state, or so I thought. The last piece of documentation in the Pietermaritzburg archives regarding his efforts to become an interpreter in Natal's courts suggested that he could probably pick up individual assignments on the basis of his second-class certificate and reappear for the government examination. He had income from a steady job with Archibald Findlay, substantial enough, presumably, to support his family. He had a home, or a revolving set of homes, in the heart of the Indian precinct, a stone's throw from the stores and walking distance from his workplace. He had friends in the neighbourhood and a place in society, indicated by the mention of his name in the columns of *Indian Opinion*. One would assume that for a young man in his twenties, he had reason to be fairly satisfied with the life he had established in the space of a couple of years in Durban.

I am astonished to find then that far from putting down roots in Durban, Mohanlal, Foolkore and the baby were on their way to Cape Town in March 1908. The 1,300-kilometre journey from Durban, five days by steamer (the SS *Cowrie Castle*, third class), had not been undertaken on an impulse. Indeed, Mohanlal had been in correspondence with authorities in Cape Town for several months preceding his trip. On 18 October 1907 he wrote a letter to the chief immigration officer, Cape Town:

> Sir,
> I enclose herewith application re. my landing at Cape Town. I should be glad to receive an authority to land at Cape Town.
> I cannot manage to spend a sovereign for Permit or to furnish photographs....

I find this letter and his 'Application for Permit' filed in the Western Cape Archives and Records Service. The form indicates, among other things, that Mohanlal was not on a joyride with his family but intended to move location, for in answer to the question, 'In what country do you intend to make your permanent home?' he had written 'Cape Town'.[1]

Surprising as it is that Mohanlal would upend his comfortable life in Durban for a new, unfamiliar terrain, the timing is even more baffling. As previously when he left Mauritius for Durban, his journey to Cape Town came at a time when the Cape Colony, following Natal's example, had introduced new legislation to curtail fresh immigration. The legislation emerged amidst concerns that the colony was bursting at the seams with a flood of new migrants attracted by a post-war boom. The tipping point, however, was the news in September 1901 that a ship, the SS *Nowshera*, had left Bombay with an excessively large load of 800 passengers. The concern was that with Natal having made itself impregnable by means of its 1897 law, the SS *Nowshera* would empty its multitudes in the ports of the Cape Colony. The prospect evoked panic in Port Elizabeth, East London and Cape Town. The editor of the *Cape Times* whipped the anxiety into hysteria by writing about a 'horde of coolies' heading for the Cape ports, now 'a dumping ground' for 'the scum of the Far East'. Urgent legislation was needed to protect the colony 'from the undesirable elements from the East and European ports' he urged.[2] In 1902, the Cape Colony hastily pushed through an Immigration Act almost identical to Natal's anti-immigration law and tightened it in 1906.

When the SS *Cowrie Castle* surged towards its destination with the Killavalas on board in March 1908, the Cape Colony was well barricaded with appropriate laws and the machinery for their implementation. Mohanlal would have been aware of this fact because, prior to applying for a permit to enter the Cape Colony, he had asked for and received a copy of the Immigration Act and the latest amendments from the immigration officer in Cape Town. An acting chief immigration officer had even written to him (25 October 1907) in response to his letter applying for a permit, rejecting his request on the grounds that he had not provided a sovereign or photographs but also mentioning that:

> ... no restrictions will be placed on your landing, if you are in a position to satisfy the requirements of the Immigration Act, the principal of which are the ability to write out an application to the satisfaction of the Minister in the characters of a European language and the possession of £20 ... If the letter above quoted is in your hand writing it would appear that you are able to satisfy the requirements of the Immigration Act, so far as the writing test is concerned.[3]

Despite this mixed but encouraging response, Mohanlal's entry was by no means certain. A few months later when he and his family set out on their journey, an internal telegram between immigration authorities in Cape Town recorded that he, a (provisionally) 'prohibited' person, was approaching on the *Cowrie Castle*. Would he be allowed to land at his destination?

The suspense indicates the significance of the human factor in interpreting and applying laws. In this case, the person of greatest influence was the chief immigration officer of the Cape Colony, Clarence Wilfred Cousins. Who was Cousins? Ordinarily, information on middle-level bureaucrats is hard to come by but Cousins was a prolific writer who also kept a diary. And thanks to an extensive study drawing on his personal and official papers by Cape Town-based historian Uma Dhupelia-Mesthrie, we have insights and material to build a picture from.[4]

Let us begin then by observing the officer waiting in the harbour in the pale pre-dawn light.

'Immigration officers at a port may not lie abed of mornings like other more fortunate folk,' Wilfred (his preferred name) wrote in his diary[5], noting that at 4 a.m. in summer and a half hour later in winter, he was up and heading to work, presumably before the first seagull came flapping over the waves. Behind him, the familiar tableau of Devil's Peak, Table Mountain, Lion's Head and Signal Hill, spire, flat mesa and dome, would have hung eerily in mid-air, its base yet to catch the light. Ahead were the large forms of ships that had anchored in the bay during the night.

Since 1904, the administration of the Immigration Act of 1902, originally under the medical officer, had been handed to a designated officer in charge of immigration and labour. Wilfred, formerly deputy inspector of prisons and a superintendent of the East London Convict Station, was the second incumbent. The previous year, the official title of chief immigration officer of the Cape Colony under the 1906 Immigration Act had been conferred upon him. It put him in charge of all the Cape Colony ports with 500 ship arrivals every year. Seventeen staffers worked for Wilfred in a double-storeyed office on Parliament Street and a smaller office on the wharves. Berthed ships were guarded by constables and detainees were held in a fenced-in hut on an isolated part of the harbour.⁶ Wilfred also arranged for immigration controls along the internal land border.

The brightening sky would have revealed the tall, broad-shouldered man more clearly. He was in his early thirties, with brownish hair, a thick moustache and a small earnest face. He stood on a bobbing rowboat alongside the elegant white bulk of a Union-Castle liner, unmistakeable with its lavender hull and red-and-black funnels. A rope ladder dangled between the two and Wilfred braced himself for a lunge. A small misstep and he would be flung into the bilious green water. One imagines he would take such a mishap, were it to occur, laughingly in his stride, for life had taught him to be resilient and prepare for the unexpected.

Born in Madagascar, a missionary's youngest son, Wilfred had been imbued very early with a sense of purpose. In his childhood he had had a Malagasy nanny and rode donkeys with local boys, but these interactions merely lent an exotic touch to a strictly Christian English upbringing. The Cousins frowned upon naughtiness; their children attended Bible studies and socialized with English families at tea parties. Wilfred went to school in England and then did a BA in Modern History at Oxford. But life took an unpredictable turn when his mother fell ill and financial difficulties cut short his studies, forcing him to find work. He came to Cape Town, he said, because he was dissatisfied 'with one's prospects in England', because South Africa aroused his interest and he had 'a readiness for adventure'.⁷

In 1904 he sent a photograph of the colonial office staff to his family with the comment that 'in 8 years I have worked myself from the back row to the front'. It should not be assumed from this comment that Wilfred was easily satisfied; far from it. Nobody was as relentless as he in the pursuit of betterment, both economic and otherwise. He taught a Bible class, played organ for the choir at the Sea Point Congregational Church and in 1912, would be found marking papers for the History Department at the University of the

Cape of Good Hope for extra cash ('I have just got through a very hard day not only of office work but of six hours' correcting of exam papers—the most exhaustive of mental effort I know. Still it has to be done & so I must keep at it'). He also found time somehow for simple pleasures and a family life: '3 August 1909: Docks—a lovely moonlight morning, went down on cycle ... 9 August 1909: Alan's birthday.'[8]

Similarly, he gave his all to his job as an immigration officer, turning up for work at an unearthly hour in all weathers without complaint ('27 July 1909: To docks as usual—a frightfully rough morning with mail boat anchored 3 miles off B'water. Complexion—green. 9 August 1909: ... Frightful weather & got very wet going to docks.'[9]) and keeping an eagle eye on the coast. What did he think about when he stood there alone, in the eerie moments between night and day, with only the sea unfurling for miles in every direction? Did he think of his peers at Oxford and where they might be? Some might have become dons as he had hoped to be, passing on the mantle of learning to young minds. Some might at that very moment be confabulating beside warm fireplaces in dark, mahogany-panelled rooms at the Colonial Office in London. Well may they pride themselves on their influence and work on behalf of the empire but in the end it all came down to the man in the field, someone like him, and his rare competence to be a bastion between the open sea and the rocky land, the gatekeeper of the coast.

What was Wilfred protecting the Cape Colony from? Ships calling at Cape Town sailed along the Atlantic coastline of Africa and the Indian Ocean. The Union Castle Mail Steamship Company bore passengers from Southampton, England, via Madeira, and the Deutsch Ost-Afrika Line sailing from Hamburg brought passengers from Bombay, with stops at the eastern and southeastern African ports. The majority of migrants to Cape Town in the post-war boom era were white, travelling from Europe and Australia, and some Boers crossing domestic borders. White migrants and the prospect they evoked of white unemployment and white poverty created a worrisome problem for a society based on racial hierarchy. As a local publication, *The Owl,* explained in 1904: 'If the coloured races see that their work of any grade, is paid for at a higher rate than the same class of work performed by white men, they are not likely to entertain any strong conviction as to the superiority of white races.'[10]

Wilfred's purpose then was to keep out undesirable categories of both white and non-white races, a task he approached with zeal and Messianic conviction best comprehended in his own words. In his diary, Wilfred observed Russian and Polish Jews in their hundreds, smelled what he apprehended as their 'disgusting odour' and barred entry to 'the more miserable specimens … at the present time I have held up a consumptive Jew—and anyone who knows of their unsanitary domestic habits will not wonder—and a filthy young reptile whose hair is all falling out as the result of some scalp disease'.[11] He was also hostile to Madeirans, who were 'scarcely Europeans', and believed 'it has always been a mistake to admit the Madeira natives, as they have invariably drifted into the Town and there collected themselves with the lowest type of coloured people, and followed occupations which frequently brought them into the conflict with the Police'. Indians provoked his deepest indignation.

> Today we have had another boat with Indians, & Parliament St. has been so infested with them all day that our work must be exceedingly well advertised to members of parliament. I was thoroughly tired out by 6 o'clock. It is a dreadful exertion trying to keep level with the torturous ways of the wily oriental.[12]

On 14 March 1908 when the SS *Cowrie Castle* drew up at the harbour, I assume Mohanlal lined up with other passengers on the deck to be interviewed by an officer in the smoking room while a portly detective kept watch at the door. On most days, Wilfred would have been hovering about, a steaming mug of coffee in his hand, but on this particular day he might have been called away for some purpose when Mohanlal's turn came up, because the decision on his entry was conveyed to Wilfred by a letter from the officer on duty (whose signature is illegible) which is also in the files.[13]

When his turn came, Mohanlal would probably have already filled in or answered the queries in the extensive Declaration by Passenger Form. It is to this form, designed by the assiduous Wilfred himself, that I owe the discovery of my great-grandmother's name and other assorted bits of information. It is not clear who the handwriting on Mohanlal's form belongs to, but the name of the accompanying wife is entered as 'Foolkore'. The entry for accompanying children is illegibly recorded, but the single name looks like 'Manlee', which was perhaps an affectionate diminutive for my grandmother Damayanti who was about two years old at the time.[14] Mohanlal had £19 in cash and jewellery 'value more than £20. Gold chain n bangles etc'. In answer to a question about his property and business he wrote: 'I have immovable property at Surat-India. I have accounts in the Natal Government Savings Bank, Bank of Bombay and Government Savings Bank Bombay.' His response about his educational qualifications is only party visible and includes a claim that he passed an accountant's examination for the civil service.[15]

The form has scribbles and procedural markings all over it, but some writing in ink on the top right corner of the form appears to be Mohanlal's writing test. The writing test was meant to confirm literacy in a European language, but Wilfred also seemed to add his own arbitrary impressions in deciding the fate of the applicant. Harry Frangopaulos, a Greek general dealer arriving from Madagascar, who wrote 'I am a taket in Englis', was considered unwelcome because, as Wilfred noted on his passenger form, he was 'undesirable in appearance', with only £10.14s on him.[16] About a coloured American David Hawkins, Wilfred wrote: '(h)is writing is hopeless, and I take it that the minister would not favour the introduction of a coloured person of this type'.[17]

Mohanlal should have been nervous. He was a pound short of the required £20. Besides mentioning his property in India and his wife's jewellery, he threw in a cashable deposit receipt from the Bombay-based Goolam Baba Spinning and Weaving Co. Ltd. (for an amount equivalent to £34.13.4) which, fortunately for him, the officer on duty found credible. The officer was also impressed with Mohanlal's language skills. 'He writes extremely well,'[18] he wrote to Wilfred, informing him that after taking a returnable deposit, the officer had allowed Mohanlal and his family to enter.

25

Mohanlal in Cape Town

Historic photographs of Cape Town show me a sharply ascending, wide dirt road abutted by squat buildings, a few wagons on one side facing a pillared shopping arcade. Many of the photographs are of the coast: a pile of small Dutch-style houses overlooking a beach, fishermen in floppy hats dragging boats from shallow water, a lonely wagon trundling over an embankment. The pictures are permeated by the pervasiveness of sea and mountains and I am reminded of Mauritius with its cloud-tossed seascape and gloomy hills.

From the sea, as they approached the coast on the SS *Cowrie Castle*, Foolkore would have observed the sandstone mountain range that dramatically framed the city. She would have felt the massive looming presence of Table Mountain and its companion peaks at every step. According to the approximate information provided in the permit application, she was eighteen or possibly nineteen years old, a girl yet, and it was over two years since she had left home. I imagine the sight of these immense shapes and the turquoise waters triggering memories of Mauritius in her and filling her with a yearning homesickness; I see my French Creole-speaking teenage great-grandmother in her wide skirts, backed by the mountains.

However, it was not nostalgia for a mountainous landscape that had brought Mohanlal to Cape Town, I assume, but the prospect of work. In his application for a permit he had entered 'Accountant' as his occupation and written that he was employed by Messrs Cowley & Cowley Solicitors (presumably Findlay was somewhere in the picture), Durban. He claimed that he had never been to 'C.C.' (Cape Colony) before and in the cramped column space he or an official added that he was 'going to work clerk with Mr Jackard (illegible) Solicitor'. In the permit application, Mohanlal added another Cape Town solicitor, 'Mr. C. E. Price-Hughes', as a reference and claimed: 'I am in correspondence with the Registrar of the Supreme Court of the Colony of the Cape of Good Hope re. my admission as a Translator to the Supreme Court of Cape C.'[1]

There is much to chew on in these details. Surprising as it is that Mohanlal was choosing to start all over again, it is noteworthy that he had lined up a job with another white lawyer. As for his expectation of 'admission as a Translator to the Supreme Court of Cape C.' it is, to say the least, suspect, an empty boast, perhaps, or a ruse to impress the immigration authorities, for qualifications required of interpreters in the magistrates' courts and the Supreme Court in the Cape Colony were apparently even more demanding than they were in Natal. Indians acting as interpreters in the Cape Colony were expected to be proficient in and able to translate in two or more Indian languages and English and Dutch, unlike Natal, where they had to be able to read and write in a single Indian language and English. The most prominent and distinguished interpreters in Cape Town were the 'Booly Brothers', Essack and Tooraben Booly, who travelled all over the colony if an Indian was giving evidence in a case.[2]

Mohanlal, with his weak showing at the Natal interpreter's examination, does not appear to be a strong candidate for the Cape Colony Supreme Court. Yet, one cannot say what was on his mind, so I will assume that there was a game plan that is not fully discernible from the information provided in his application. And regardless of the chances of his success, there was much to delight his senses on his first visit to the colony. I imagine him walking about town and soaking in the urbanity of his new surroundings, the central Adderley Street, for instance, with mountains in the background and a row of fine buildings in the foreground. I believe he would have enjoyed the eclecticism of the colony once known as the 'tavern of the seas'[3] for the sustenance it offered long-distance voyagers. On the streets were descendants of slaves from West Africa and Madagascar and grandchildren of captives from India's eastern coast and from Southeast Asia, including Chinese prisoners, usually debtors exiled from Batavia and brought by the Dutch East India Company to toil as slaves.

As a British subject, Mohanlal would have relished the imperial spirit lingering after the Anglo-Boer War which had seen parading troops, cheered by thousands, streaming to the upper end of St. George's Street singing 'Rule Britannia'. He would have admired the city's fine architecture, particularly the newly built Italian Renaissance-style city hall in golden Bath stone and the Volunteer Drill Hall with its elaborate cast-iron fanlights and stairways. And the Parade, which they bordered, a public space where rich and poor mingled and the public gathered to express their grievances.

My great-grandparents would have come across Indians, of whom there were as many as 8,000 in the city, drawn from various parts of India. Konkani, Punjabi, Gujarati, Bengali and Tamilian passenger Indians sold trinkets and fruit on the quay, built houses and worked as domestic servants. Many were in blue-collar jobs in one or other of the city's numerous factories. A Gujarati, Bhana Poonja, was a bottle sorter at Ohlssons Breweries; Ebrahim Bassa, from Kolaba District, was a donkeyman with the Union Castle Mail Steamship Company; Bareyam Singh, a Sikh from Punjab, was a groom and stableman with custom and delivery agents A.R. Mackenzie & Company. The Hout Bay Canning Company and the Castle Wine & Brandy Company also had Indians on their rolls, as did the Cape Government Railways and the Public Works Department. Poohoomull Brothers, the Sindhi curio dealers from Durban, had a silk and curios store on Longmarket Street. Other prominent Indian businessmen included Ebrahim Norodien, a successful grocer and provisions merchant with many stores,[4] and Abdul Cador or Cadir, described in some accounts as a cigar maker from Mauritius, who was a general importer.

It was not a good time for the colony. The post-war boom had petered out by the middle of the decade and was followed by a depression. Rising living costs and high white unemployment had led to a revision of the liberal attitudes Cape Town was once known for and sharpened social divides. The passing of a General Dealers Act in 1906, similar to the one in Natal, had hurt Indian retailers and hawkers. Sir John Jackson Ltd.'s request for bringing 500 labourers from Punjab to develop the harbour in Simonstown was turned down by the authorities. Poohoomull Brothers was denied permission to bring even two men as domestic help from India. A group of native Africans were moved to Uitvlugt (N'dabeni), the city's first segregated suburb established in May 1901, 8 kilometres east of the city centre and, in 1906, a massive demonstration of the unemployed took a violent turn that left many Indian shops damaged. Mohanlal and Foolkore would have felt the tension in the air.

Most Indians lived in the city's sixth municipal district. Commonly referred to as District Six,[5] this was a mixed-race neighbourhood in the city bowl. Many Cape Malays, Muslims descended from

Indonesian exiles, and enslaved people from Asia and Africa lived there. The neighbourhood, with its buzzing markets, baths, Malay mosques and houses with their characteristically plain, unadorned walls, was also home to many Indians, prominently Konkanis who owned shops in District Six and who were called 'Babbies' by locals and relied on for credit or 'tick'. Malays and Indians mingled freely and often intermarried.

If Mohanlal was intending to set up home in Cape Town it was possibly here, in the district's lively, narrow streets. His declaration form under the Immigration Act, however, suggests that he had made other arrangements. To the question 'Address at Destination in full', Mohanlal had put down 'c/o Mr Gool'. The fact that Mohanlal did not need to add anything to this terse response, and that it passed muster, says something about the reputation of Mr Gool.

Joosub Mohammed Hamid Gool's family hailed from the mountainous regions of Central Asia but was settled in Rander where Joosub was born. He came to the Cape via Mauritius, starting out as a smous or an itinerant trader and becoming a prominent Indian entrepreneur with a wholesale and retail business in general provisions at 25, Church Street, best known as a supplier of a popular dried fish snack called Cape Snoek. His company, J.M.H. Gool & Co., traded as far as the Witwatersrand and secured a lucrative contract supplying the Indian troops of the British army stationed in South Africa (possibly through his brother who was in the army) with dried snoek and spices. Joosub was a leading Indian of Cape Town, a patron of the Hanafi Quwwat-ul-Islam Mosque in downtown Loop Street. He was also a friend and supporter of Gandhi. I come across many instances of their closeness while going through Gandhi's papers: Joosub taking on the responsibility of distributing *Indian Opinion* in the Cape Colony, for instance, and his son, who was studying medicine abroad, seeking a meeting with Gandhi while he was visiting London in 1906. Gandhi stayed with the Gools on his rare trips to Cape Town, as did many Indian visitors, for Joosub and his Malay wife, Wagheida, kept an open house. It is possible that Mohanlal knew Joosub personally either from Surat or Mauritius. But it is equally likely that he had been referred to the latter by someone in his Durban circle.[6]

According to a family memoir by Selim Yusuf Gool, the Gools lived in a large house with many rooms and stables at the back at 7, Buitensingel Street. It was at the top of Long Street near the Turkish baths and pools, opposite the German Lutheran Church in a white area bordering District Six.

A good friend of Joosub was Abdullah Abdurahman who lived in Albert Lodge, 7, Mount Street, a fine mansion on the edge of District Six. Abdullah, the grandson of manumitted Malay slaves, had overcome many handicaps to study medicine in Glasgow where he met and married a Scottish woman, Nellie Potter. He had returned home in 1895 and thrown himself into politics, becoming Cape Town's first coloured city councillor and, in 1905, president of the newly formed African Political (People's) Organization, representing the political and social interests of the coloured community. Abdullah's charisma made him a popular leader and his liberalism—like the early Gandhi he reposed great faith in the British Constitution and British democracy—resonated with the modernizing elite of the coloured working class.

Patricia Van der Spuy describes the Abdurahman home as a hub of avid discussion and a magnet for Cape Town's influential and intellectual figures, including South African politicians J.X. Merriman and J.H. Hofmeyr, and academics like Eric Walker, a historian at the University of Cape Town.[7] Nellie shared her husband's idealism, supported his demand for wider male enfranchisement and was a member, along with the celebrated South African writer and suffragette Olive Schreiner, of the Women's Enfranchisement League.

Alongside the vote, the Abdurahmans felt strongly about education. Nellie's father, a solicitor, had been active in the cause of securing free and compulsory education for Scottish children and Nellie was shocked by the state of affairs in South Africa. In 1905, Abdullah spearheaded a campaign against the School Board Bill, which gave resources to white education while leaving black and coloured education to the voluntary efforts of mission schools and then only up to standard IV. The struggle for education had a personal dimension, for the Abdurahmans' children were of school-going age, as were the Gools', and when Nellie's efforts to obtain admission for her children to the Good Hope Seminary School failed, the only option was homeschooling till Abdullah and others managed to set up the first second-class public school in Cape Town some years later.

Remarkably, the Abdurahmans had only two girls. Waradea, also called 'Rosie', famously became the first 'black' woman doctor in South Africa and her younger sister, Zainunnissa or 'Cissie' as she was known, went on to study law and came to be an important political figure. As young girls, the two had an extremely unconventional upbringing. The smallness of their family, very unusual for the times, gave them a greater share of parental attention than most of their peers. The fervid political talk swirling around them encouraged them to speak their own minds, even in large gatherings. Cissie, Rosie, their cousin Rukea and their friends, the daughters of the Gools, had a childhood that was unusually privileged and free of the conservative norms commonly applied to women.

Abdullah often went to 7, Buitensingel Street on his horse-drawn buggy for tea and a game of cards and he too was an equally warm host and welcomed guests to his home. Now let me imagine my great-grandparents, a young, relatively simple couple with a two-year-old child, in these settings. The Gool house was sprawling and tastefully appointed. The furniture was made of solid oak and the cold floors were covered with soft Persian carpets. Silverware and porcelain glimmered in the corners. The breakfast table heaved with meat and vegetarian dishes, buns, jam and beverages. The Abdurahmans' residence reflected an Edwardian gentility with a pianoforte and a well-stocked study. Amidst all this splendour and cultural refinement were people seriously discussing political issues of the day, including the education of young girls.

Rosie and Cissie Abdurahman were eleven and ten in 1908. They were confident young ladies who sang, played the piano and wrote poetry. And it was their future that was being argued about and fought for. I imagine my great-grandparents listening as the Gools and the Abdurahmans railed against the discriminatory colonial education policy and the importance of educating their daughters. I imagine Mohanlal, a teacher himself, stirred by their zeal. I imagine Foolkore observing the Abdurahman girls in frocks with bows in their frizzy hair and thinking how much she would like her own baby girl to grow up like them.

These are hypotheses, of course, but ancestry is a complicated business. People who plant seeds and start movements begin processes the scale and direction of which they cannot fully envisage. I feel I have found the key to one of the mysteries that triggered my pursuit of this ancestral trail. Perhaps this exposure to the Gool household led to the strange fact of my grandmother being sent to a convent school and that, in turn, shaped my mother's dreams for me, leading to an education that made me a writer in English and provoked questions that sent me on a search across an ocean. I do not know if my speculation is correct and if my great-grandparents ever set eyes on Rosie and Cissie Gool but in finding them as part of my journey, I feel I have closed a circle.

26
Taking Umbrage

The Cape Town venture did not stick, I assume, because a short while later, Mohanlal was back in Durban. I cannot say I am surprised, given how impractical it appeared to be. To try and start a new life in a city reeling from an economic downturn seemed short-sighted, to say the least. Did he seriously expect to be appointed as an interpreter at the Supreme Court? And did he even have a job with a Cape Town lawyer as he claimed? I find myself doubting his words. At the same time, I am conscious of the fact that I have access only to limited data and there may be more to the story than I can tell. What I can confirm at this point is that about five weeks after he had set out for Cape Town, Mohanlal, Foolkore and the baby were back in Durban's Indian quarter, having arrived by the SS *Norman* on 19 April 1908. Their address this time was Grey Street, which meant that they had a view of the busy street, the Jami Mosque and its minarets pointing to the cloudy skies.

All this I know because Mohanlal had embarked on a round of official correspondence with the customs authorities a few weeks after his return, which I find filed in the Pietermaritzburg archives. It began with this letter:

198 (Grey St.)
Durban 10th July 1908
The Collector of Customs.
Durban,

Sir,

re <u>Baggage Examination</u>

I arrived in Durban from Capetown on Sunday 19th APRIL last by the S.S. 'Norman', I noticed that an Official of the Customs Department had boarded the Ship from East London and the passengers were notified to be in readiness for baggage examination by a certain hour in morning of the 19th April last. I was with my family and it was with considerable trouble and inconvenience that we got ready for examination. When the said official came to my cabin (3rd class) he declined to examine my baggage and said that I should wait till the ship was in the harbour and the immigration officer had passed me. He asked if there were any more European passengers.

2. Now, Sir, I wonder if the Customs Department is to afford special convenience to Europeans and not to extend the same to Asiatics although the latter pay their passage money and Customs duties just as well as any one else.

3. Considerable delay and inconvenience has occurred in consequence of this action of the said—Official as appears from the fact that the following day (20th April) was also a holiday. It was on Tuesday 21st April that I (illegible) clear baggage … that it is not a little inconvenience for a man and his family to wait for their baggage for 2 days. The Immigration Restriction Act applies to all other passengers as well as to me. I fully explained this to the said Official and also said that I was exempted from the Act, yet he

did not examine my baggage. I shall be obliged if you will kindly let me know why such a course is adopted?
Yours obediently
(Signed) M.P. Killavala[1]

The letter, stamped as received with a rubber seal of the collector of customs, is followed by two handwritten notes exchanged internally within the department, both saying pretty much the same thing, so I quote the second, signed by 'C.B. Jones, Supervisor':

> In consideration of the fact that a period of three months has elapsed since the occurrence complained of I do not consider that applicant has much cause for complaint, the statement that he was unable to pass his baggage until the Tuesday is a pure fabrication as all baggage landed is passed on the Sunday unless for some reason the operation cannot be performed such as the passenger going straight to town without attending to his baggage.
>
> I expect the Immigration Official placed obstacles in the way of the clearance of the baggage as most of the baggage of Indians is fumigated on arrival.

On the basis of the notes, the following response was sent to Mohanlal:

Durban,
15th July 1908
Mr. P. Killavala,
198, Grey St,
Durban.
Re <u>Baggage Examination</u>

Sir,

In reply to your letter of the 10th inst., I have to inform you that so long a time has elapsed since the date on which the transaction appears to have occurred that I am unable to obtain any information sufficient to enable me to form any conclusion.
I have the honour to be,
Sir,
Yours obediently,
Collector of Customs

Not satisfied with the collector's letter, Mohanlal wrote again:

198, Grey St.
Durban, 20th July, 1908
The Collector of Customs.
Point, Natal
Sir,

re <u>Baggage Examination</u>

I have the honour to acknowledge the receipt of your letter No. K/C 47/08 dated 15th inst: I should be glad if you would kindly favour me with the information about the following:

1. Are any Orders issued, to the Search Officers of the Customs, not to examine the baggage of Asiatics coming to Durban from the Cape Colony, during the voyage but to do so after they are allowed to land?

    ... If so, from which Department such Orders originated?

2. What necessitated such racial and differential Orders?

    Yours obediently
    (Signed) M.P. Killavala

The collector replied on 23 July 1908:

> Mr. P. Killavala,
> 198, Grey St,
> Durban.
> <u>Baggage Examination</u>
> Sir,
> I have to acknowledge receipt of your letter of the 20th inst., and to inform you that no instructions have been issued that the baggage of Asiatics is to be examined after being landed but that it has always been the custom to defer the examination by this department until it has been passed by the Immigration Department.
> I have the honour to be,
> Sir,
> Yours obediently,
> Collector of Customs

Mohanlal wrote:

> Durban, 24th July 1908
> The Collector of Customs.
> Point.
> Sir,
> re <u>Baggage Examination</u>
> I have to acknowledge the receipt of your letter dated 23rd instant. In view of the fact that no one can land without a Pass from the Immigration Department, will you kindly alter the custom to defer the — examination of baggage by your Department until the examination by the Immigration Officer has been passed, at least in case of the Indian and other Asiatics coming from the Cape side.

2. The Alteration will prevent a lot of trouble and enable us to clear our baggage along with that of others thus stopping to a certain extent the ill-feeling arising from racial custom which has been applied to us and of which I was the prey. I hope that you will agree that an injustice has been done to me by the custom above mentioned.

I have the honour to be,
Sir,
Yours obediently,
(Signed) M.P. Killavala

Durban,
27th July 1908.
Mr. P. Killavala,
198, Grey St,
Durban.

<u>Baggage Examination</u>

Sir,

In reply to your letter of the 24th inst., I have to inform you that I am unable to alter the present methods of Baggage Examination. There is nothing to justify any change in the practice.

Please note that this correspondence is closed.

I have the honour to be,
Sir,
Yours obediently,
Collector of Customs

Undaunted, Mohanlal wrote a two-page letter to the colonial secretary in Pietermaritzburg on 28 July, reiterating his correspondence with the collector of customs and asking again for an alteration of the examination practice. The colonial secretary passed on his letter to the treasurer who was the minister in charge of customs and the under-treasurer sent a letter to Mohanlal on 4 August, ending with the paragraph: 'Enquiries have been made into the matter, and the Treasurer cannot find that there has been any ground for complaint and he does not consider that any change in the practice which at present obtains is called for.'

Reading this exchange, the first thought that comes to my mind is how much it resembles other exchanges between Westernized Indians and the authorities at the time. Interpreters in suits travelling by train for work in Natal often faced problems with contemptuous co-passengers and authorities as Gandhi did on his historic journey to Pretoria. Mohanlal's apprehension that Europeans received preferential treatment and that officials and rules showed a lack of consideration for Indian passengers is most likely justified. Indeed, the supervisor's suggestion that a delay in clearing baggage may have been introduced 'as most of the baggage of Indians is fumigated on arrival' appears to betray a common bias about race and hygiene. At the same time, Mohanlal's manner of commanding an alteration in official practice could appear overweening and the time lag of three months between the alleged offence and his complaint does make the customs official's scepticism seem not unreasonable.

This complaint, however, is the second of its kind made by Mohanlal. Eleven months earlier, he had written to the secretary for native affairs in Pietermaritzburg, expressing dissatisfaction about the manner in which his application for permission to possess a sporting rifle was rejected. It is not the rejection he was protesting but the wording of it:

158, Queen Street
Durban 29th August 1907
The Secretary for Native affairs
Maritzburg

Sir, <u>re permission to possess a rifle</u>

I beg to acknowledge the receipt of your letter of Dec 7th 1906, which I return herewith and **shall be glad if you will address same in a better way** (emphasis author's). I also enclose herewith for perusal and return a letter to me from the colonial office (capetown) of 10th May'07 to show how they address correspondence to me.

I have the honour to be,

Sir

Your obedient servant

M.P. Killavalla[2]

A few weeks later he followed up this letter with another on the same subject:

C/O 147, Queen St.

Durban, 18th October 1907.

The Private Secretary To His Excellency The Governor.

Maritzburg.

Sir,

I wrote a letter to the Secretary for Native Affairs on 19th August last. I wrote another letter to the Secretary to Government (Colonial Secretary) on the 12th ultimo on the same matter that is re. Arms. I regret to state that neither of the said letters has been answered or receipt thereof acknowledged. I should be glad if you could kindly inquire into this.

I have the honour to be,

Sir,

Your obedient servant,

M.P. Killavala

Mohanlal's indignation surprises me. The letter from the assistant undersecretary for native affairs rejecting his application for a sporting rifle licence was straightforward: 'permission to possess a firearm cannot be granted to you'. It is even more puzzling as a whole nine months had elapsed since the rejection and three months since the better-worded missives from the Cape Town colonial office that had opened his eyes to the respectful way he felt it should have been worded. Would a man suffering from a fit of self-righteousness wait so long to complain? Clearly the recipient thought little of his complaint because, a few days later, prodded by an initialled note from the governor's secretary asking the secretary for native affairs to 'address this', the undersecretary for native affairs wrote to Mohanlal, returning his enclosed letter from the Cape Town colonial office ('which called for no reply').

Why was Mohanlal picking up fights with the authorities? Why was he recalling slights and offences from months ago and demanding an official response to his grievances? This is the first time I have come across any hint of anger from Mohanlal about racial discrimination. Unlike his peers Shelat and Randeria, he had shown no radical inclinations. He had appeared to be content working for a white lawyer and his association with Gandhi and the professional Indian community in the Grey Street precinct had been on social and humanitarian grounds (donating books or time to a library, participating in an anti-malaria drive), rather than political. But in these letters are the first expressions of racial hurt that I have come across from him. The complaint about the rifle is handwritten, followed by a typed reminder, both executed in carelessness or agitation, untidy, illegible in places with gaps between letters, and the earlier confident slash under the whole name in the signature now a short line underlining his initials.

Was my great-grandfather, at the still-youthful age of twenty-seven, becoming conscious of racial injustice, of a kinship with his own race and of the need to act to preserve his dignity as well as that of his fellow Indians? And if so, was his change of approach caused by the external environment? Did circumstances prevailing at the time trigger a patriotic impulse, an affinity with his countrymen and a sense of seething injustice? It is highly likely because a great many things were happening at this time. To know more we have to catch up again with the original Mohan, Gandhi, and observe him on the verge of launching an extraordinary campaign in the Transvaal.

PART SEVEN

SATYAGRAHA

27

After the War

The coveted region of the Transvaal lay between the Limpopo River and the treeless Lowveld known as the Savannah. An ancient land, it was home to the Sotho, Venda and other Bantu-speaking peoples when the Boers decided to settle there. Underground lay seams of gold, deposited millions of years ago by raging storms and fires. Their discovery in 1886 set in motion a chain of events ending in a devastating war. Writer Henry M. Stanley, visiting the region before the outbreak of hostilities, stood on a ridge over the alluring gold-rich 62-kilometre-long Main Reef of Johannesburg and saw a panoramic view of 'mine after mine, each surrounded by its reservoirs, hills of tailings, lofty stores of ore, iron sheds, mills, offices and headgear structures'.[1] Paul Kruger was proved right in his prophecy about the misery that would ensue from digging up gold. The doughty Boer leader went to Europe when the war turned against his people and died in exile in 1904.

But it was his spirit, an earthy, orthodox personality, that the British sought to defeat in the aftermath of the Anglo-Boer War. The driver of this strategy was Alfred Milner. Appointed administrator and then governor of the Transvaal and the Orange River Colony (the former Orange Free State) in 1902, he moved his base from Cape

Town to the Transvaal, choosing to locate himself in Johannesburg rather than the capital, Pretoria. A lean, balding man of Anglo-German ancestry that showed in his narrow-eyed, unflinching gaze, Milner was an imperialist in the Cecil Rhodes mould with a consummate belief in British superiority. An Oxford alumnus, he was in Egypt before his appointment as high commissioner for South Africa and governor of the Cape Colony in 1897 and came to the Transvaal determined to convert it into a 'thoroughly British domain' where 'British interests, British ideas, British education' would prevail. His plan for bringing this about was to propose first, the large-scale immigration of people of British descent and second, to entrust the Transvaal with a measure of self-government only after a loyal majority was in place. He also instituted a new education system with English as the medium of instruction and promoted brisk development on the premise that 'every new railway, every new school, every new settlement' constituted 'a nail in the coffin of Boer nationalism'.[2]

To carry out his vision, he collected a group of young Oxford men, known as 'Milner's Kindergarten', to run the administration. One of them was Lionel Curtis, a tall, thin young man with handsome features and a thick shock of hair. Born in 1872, a rector's son, Curtis had enlisted to serve in the Anglo-Boer War and joined Milner after his discharge in 1900 as his secretary, moving to various administrative posts thereafter. As a student he had been interested in the Christian Socialist Movement, which believed that the Church should be involved in addressing social questions, and had worked as private secretary to the vice-chairman of the London County Council. In Johannesburg, he was appointed town clerk in 1901 to oversee the expansion and gentrification of the city. Two years later, the *Rand Daily Mail* reported that 'good solid houses'[3] of brick had replaced the timber-framed corrugated-iron houses of the past. Under Curtis's supervision, as much as £3.5 million was spent on capital works, sanitation, sewerage, roads and electric supply and the city's municipal area was expanded to become the world's largest, second only to Tokyo.⁴

When Gandhi moved to Johannesburg, a new city was being raised over the mining camp that existed in the past. The slapdash prospectors' town with its brothels, bars and tent settlements was being dressed in the sober accoutrements of commerce. The rat-a-tat of frenzied construction was heard everywhere, but despite the stone-faced commercial buildings and gaslights, Johannesburg was still 'raw and drab and dirty ... and a homely place in its fashion'.⁵ Gandhi, striding along the new, broad streets, would have seen managers, financiers and prospectors rubbing shoulders with diggers, transport operators, cooks and hawkers. He would have seen important-looking gentlemen hobnobbing with coloured Cape Town dandies and dark-haired Syrian women hawking goods in wicker baskets. His countrymen were scattered all over the Transvaal, sometimes only a few in one place (Lichtenburg and Bloemhof had six each), though in Johannesburg brown-skinned hawkers and Muslim shopkeepers in their snowy garments were an integral part of the city's tapestry.

The slightly built lawyer adapted easily to the hurried pace of the emerging metropolis, adding a beret-like cap to combat its seasonal chill. He had been enrolled as a practising attorney in the Supreme Court of the Transvaal in April 1903 and found office space and a room to live in at the corner of Rissik and Anderson Streets. He moved about on foot everywhere, even though he was busier as a lawyer than he had ever been before. In his limited spare time, he read books by John Ruskin, Henry David Thoreau and Leo Tolstoy. He was alone but had made friends among the Jews arriving in Johannesburg in considerable numbers, many from East Europe. Among them were a Lithuania-born architect, Hermann Kallenbach, a journalist from Britain, Henry Polak, and L.W.

Ritch, who was involved with the Theosophical Lodge established in Johannesburg in 1899, which Gandhi visited regularly.

In the run up to the Anglo-Boer War, the British had criticized the Boers for their treatment of non-Boers, raising hopes of a more progressive leadership; many black workers had gleefully burned their passes when the British arrived on the Witwatersrand in 1900, expecting them to be redundant under an enlightened British administration.[6] Gandhi had reason to be less optimistic, given his disappointing experience of campaigning against discriminatory laws in Natal. Yet even he was taken aback by the regressive tone of the new administration. Not only did the British not roll back discriminatory Boer-era laws but they threatened to apply them even more rigorously than the lax Boers.

Segregation, for instance, which the Boers had planned for but never got around to fully implementing, was taken up by the new administrators who sought to move African townsmen and Indians, including affluent Indians with shops downtown, to specified locations and markets outside the city centre. A plague scare came as a convenient excuse for the municipal administration to raze 1,600 buildings in the northwest part of the city and move their occupants, poor Africans and Indians, to a site next to a proposed sewage farm in Klipspruit, 16 kilometres southwest of downtown Johannesburg.

A similarly racially determined approach marked the manner in which entry into the Transvaal was being dealt with. The end of the war saw a rush at the borders. People of various ethnicities who had fled the province before the fighting commenced and many newcomers drawn by the lure of opportunity now massed at the margins, eager to enter. The rush seemed to catch the authorities unawares and a Peace Preservation Ordinance was hastily issued, barring entry to undesirable characters and limiting it to old residents with permits. There was no record of how many Indians had been in the Transvaal before the Anglo-Boer War (Indian leaders claimed the number to be about 13,000, a figure disputed by the local administration) since very few had complied with the unpopular 1885 Boer law requiring Asiatics to register themselves on payment of £3 each. While Europeans were allowed to enter freely, various tests were devised for Indians to prove their credentials and a newly set-up Department of Asiatic Affairs caused further confusion and delays.

The Transvaal had an organization, the British Indian Association, like the Natal Indian Congress, chaired by Abdul Gani of the firm Messrs Mahomed Cassim Camrooden. Gandhi took over much of its correspondence. I come across many typewritten letters on its behalf, corrected in ink on stationery with a letterhead: 'M. K. GANDHI Attorney' in a plain sans serif font enclosed by an ornamental motif and his tilted signature with a line underneath. The British Indian Association protested the forced removal of Indians from their homes and the procedural difficulties in immigration. In May 1903, Gandhi met Milner and told him that Indians 'needed rest from the constant changes of passes and permits'.[7]

In February 1903, Lionel Curtis was promoted as assistant colonial secretary of the Transvaal, which put him in charge of regulating the borders. At the age of thirty, it fell upon him to determine who constituted the idea of an undesirable immigrant in a utopian society of his making. Like for Cousins, the chief immigration officer we observed in Cape Town, the question opened up a range of prejudices, not the least those involving poor white immigrants. Portuguese Madeirans were largely considered undesirable because of their Catholicism and widespread illiteracy. Polish Russians were seen as illicit distillers, clannish and too friendly with Africans.[8] And Syrians were 'essentially an Asiatic ... the dirtiest kind of Asiatic' as Curtis wrote before he thought better of his observation and reached the ambivalent conclusion: 'we cannot say with any exactness where Asia begins and ends.'[9]

There was no ambivalence in Curtis's mind regarding Indians, however. It was his decided opinion that

> If the doors were thrown open to Asiatics we must look to a time, and that a time not very far distant, when the white population of this country would begin to assume to the Coloured population the same proportions which are to be seen in India. It would in fact become a country with a vast coloured population consisting of Asiatics and aboriginal natives, controlled by a very small aristocracy of whites who might or might not regard this country as their permanent home.[10]

Mauritius, with 9,000 whites and 264,000 Indians and a medley of Chinese, African and mixed-blood people making up the remainder of its 375,900-strong population,[11] was the spectre horrifying South Africa's colonial administrators. To which Curtis added a reminder that 'only the lowest class of Indians come to South Africa, and they are a most unwarlike class. Therefore, if the fate which I have described, is to befall this country, the Native population must, in the centuries to come, always be controlled by armies imported from Europe'.[12]

In 1897 Prime Minister Harry Escombe spoke of Natal being 'submerged under an Asiatic wave of immigration'.[13] Was it the sheer size of the country's population that sparked terror in the minds of white settlers, evoking images of mobs and waves? It could well have been, for the equally populous Chinese triggered similar fears among the white populace of the Transvaal. The uproar was about a plan floated by Milner after the war to import Chinese workers to meet a severe labour shortfall in the gold mines. Many Africans had decamped during the fighting and refused to come back to pathetically poor wages and hard labour. Acting on the recommendation of the Chamber of Mines, the Chamber of

28

The Asiatic Menace

Milner's policies made him enormously unpopular in the Transvaal. Boer hostility and resentment against the British predated the war and had taken the form of a cultural and political movement led by Boer intellectuals, calling themselves Afrikaners, in the Cape. Milner's heavy-handed approach provided a new impetus to this movement. Boer-run private schools sprang up in the Transvaal and the Orange River Colony using Dutch alongside English as the medium of instruction and promoting a sense of Afrikaner national consciousness among students. Leading Boer generals Louis Botha and Jan Smuts in the Transvaal and Barry Hertzog in the Orange River Colony emerged as trenchant critics of the Milner regime. They organized protest meetings about the decision to import Chinese labourers and wrote to the colonial secretary opposing the plan as a 'public calamity of the first magnitude'.[1] The colonial secretary refused to consider their petition as representing the opinion of the majority of the Boer populace, and Botha and his colleagues decided to form a party to demonstrate their strength. In January 1905 they announced the launch of Het Volk (The People) and demanded full self-government for both the Transvaal and the

Orange River Colony, an end to restrictions on the public use of the Dutch language and termination of the Chinese labour system.[2]

Jan Smuts, a Cape Town bred Afrikaner lawyer, journalist and politician, was a key figure in Het Volk. A 1905 photograph shows him to be a short-haired, smooth-complexioned man with a piercingly direct gaze, in an elaborate formal suit reflecting his Cambridge education and cosmopolitanism. Smuts was once an admirer of Cecil Rhodes but after getting offended by his bullying tactics against the Transvaal Boers, he left the Cape to ally with Paul Kruger and served as a general in the war. Before the war, as Kruger's state attorney, Jan Smuts had also been in consultation with the British representative in Pretoria on measures to regulate the economic activity and movement of the Indian populace. The new party he was part of took up the issue of the 'free influx of Asiatics', making what the white press deemed 'violent speeches' in the Transvaal countryside.[3]

Gandhi was aware of how Boers, with their religious conservatism, regarded Indians. He was also aware that a new organization calling itself the White League was vigorously campaigning against Indians being allowed into the Transvaal. He continued to write to various authorities and influential supporters in India and in London about Indian grievances in the Transvaal and other parts of South Africa. He also led Indian delegations to meet with colonial administrators. But his approach had undergone a qualitative change from his days in Natal. This time there were no stirring appeals to the public conscience, no references to Christian morality. He even advised his fellow Indians to be restrained and refrain from flamboyant celebrations of the occasional piece of good news, fearing a possible backlash. It would seem that he had reluctantly acknowledged the intransigence of white settlers and their unwillingness to share the spoils of Empire.

He may not have lost faith in the British yet, but it is likely that he had begun to perceive the wisdom of launching a battle for Indian rights in India itself. In his letters he indicated his expectation of returning to India when his work in South Africa was done. His keenness to involve himself in public life at home was apparent in the relationships he had initiated with influential Indian leaders, chiefly the founder of the Servants of India Society, G.K. Gokhale, whom he had adopted as his mentor.

Meanwhile, he devoted much of his time and a substantial part of his earnings as a lawyer to sustaining *Indian Opinion*. The paper was the medium through which Gandhi tried to widen the horizons of the South African Indian, to cultivate minds so far attuned to trade and survival. The newspaper profiled inspiring figures such as the founder of modern nursing, Florence Nightingale, the industrialist Jamsetji Nusserwanji Tata and the reformer Ishwar Chandra Vidyasagar. It carried news of the world and of Indian events such as the swadeshi movement in Bengal and reproduced Gandhi's talks on religion to the Theosophical Society.[4]

Henry Polak had become the paper's third editor, a role he performed from Johannesburg where he was simultaneously articling with Gandhi as a lawyer. He and his wife, Millie, lived with Gandhi who had moved to the suburb of Troyeville in East Johannesburg. As Ramachandra Guha points out in his book *Gandhi Before India*, it was the only Indian home in the white neighbourhood; Gandhi's wife and children had arrived from India, making it a full household.[5] The house was managed in keeping with Gandhi's idiosyncratic beliefs. His domestic duties included grinding flour for the day's meals, tutoring his children and applying home-made cures during illnesses. He walked 3 kilometres every day to his workplace, where he was kept busy all day with varied responsibilities. He had expanded his legal office and taken on juniors. Many of his clients were people who were seeking entry documents for themselves or for their family members.

In keeping with his more conciliatory approach, Gandhi came to accept and even agree with the colonial administration's determination to severely curtail the immigration of passenger Indians. 'Restrictions on immigration would be perfectly justified within reasonable limits,' he maintained in 1903.[6] This assertion marked a major shift from the Indian community's fervid opposition to the anti-immigration law in Natal a few years ago, when it had highlighted the law's adverse impact on Indian businesses and families and the unfairness of denying entry to Indians who were British subjects. The push now seemed to be for concessions such as an expansion of the literacy requirement to include Indian and not only European languages and so on, rather than a confrontation.

Transvaal Indians complied with the administration's vacillating demands regarding procedures for obtaining permits. Gandhi, however, made one specific request to the administration: to provide for the entry, by right, of a few educated Indians, including teachers and priests, for the cultural enrichment of the community.

> A free and healthy Asiatic community in the Transvaal would be impossible without, say, a few lawyers, a few doctors, a few teachers, and, it may be, a few preachers amongst them who are their own kith and kin. These should not come to the country on sufferance, but as a matter of right.[7]

On 10 May 1903, Gandhi wrote to his mentor Gokhale: 'It seems to be the settled policy of the Colonists that they would regulate immigration into their country. The real & effective stand we have therefore to take up is to fight legislation based on colour.'[8] This was in keeping with his view, often expressed in Natal and shared by his co-campaigners there, that the important thing was to 'resist degradation'.

Within the parameters of his diminished expectations, Gandhi was reasonably at peace. As he writes in his book *Satyagraha in South Africa*:

> The year 1906 was well under way … I had re-entered the Transvaal in 1903 and opened my office in Johannesburg about the middle of that year. Two years had thus passed in merely resisting the inroads of the Asiatic Department. We all expected now that re-registration would satisfy the Government and confidently looked forward to a period of comparative peace for the community.

He would have been less sanguine had he read the political wind better. By 1906, Milner had retired, shadowed by the failure of his anglicization experiment. Transvaal was granted responsible government with elections due the following year. Milner's replacement, Lord Selborne, was meant to smoothen the transition to self-government and encourage a rapprochement between the two rivals of the Anglo-Boer War. A new spirit of South Africanism was afoot and the unity between the British and the Boers was further cemented by their opposition to non-whites and Indians in particular.

In the early months of April 1906, meetings took place between key figures in the administration regarding the 'vexed refugee affair'. Assistant Colonial Secretary Lionel Curtis met with police chief Captain Fuge and Registrar of Permits Montfort Chamney. The latter was a light-haired, chubby-faced Irishman with a stylishly scruffy moustache in his forties who had been a tea planter in northeast India and joined Lumsden's Horse, a corps of 250 mounted infantrymen (mostly public-school boys who had failed to get into Sandhurst[9]), raised in 1899 by Dugald McTavish Lumsden of the Assam Valley Light Horse for the Anglo-Boer War. Though he stayed on and joined the civil service in South Africa after the war, India was still on his mind. He contributed an article on 'The India Rubber of Commerce (Caoutchouc)' to the April 1905 edition of the *Transvaal Agricultural Journal* and published a book, *The Story of the Tea Leaf*, almost three decades later, in 1933, with the New Indian Press of Calcutta. His familiarity with India and his ability to speak Hindustani had probably steered him to his present position. *Indian Opinion* complained in 1903, though, that he lacked independent power.

This was set to change. Curtis and Chamney discussed new staffing requirements for the registrar of Asiatics' office. Chamney, as the registrar of Asiatics, would draw an annual salary of £1,000 and Principal Clerk Mr Cody would be paid £380. Other staff would include two verification clerks, a lady inspector, a record clerk, a typist, a white boy messenger and, at £48, the lowest-paid staffer, an Asiatic orderly. Additional clerical assistance and travelling costs were budgeted at approximately £450 each. Finally, Mr Burgess was to be the coast officer with a salary of £500.[10] Like Chamney, Edwin John Burgess had joined Lumsden's Horse, leaving the Imperial Secretariat in the Government of India, and stayed on with the Transvaal Civil Service after the war. His job as coast agent required him to be stationed in Durban.

But Curtis had something more radical in mind than office reorganization. The concern that had put the three men in a huddle, that was articulated repeatedly by their superiors and widely echoed by ordinary white settlers, was that Indians were surreptitiously entering the Transvaal in great numbers. The Indians, they believed, had started an industry in fake permits and passes that was supported by agents in South Africa and as far away as Bombay. Indian leaders tried to counter these allegations by pointing to statistics put out by the administration itself to prove that the fears were exaggerated, but the authorities were unmoved. An impression grew that Indians by nature were deceitful and prone to corruption. Gandhi's complaint that the few Indians who did gain unauthorized entry into the colony were helped by white officials went unheard.

It was against this background that Curtis now proposed a discontinuation of 'our present futile attempts to block the ports of entry'. Neither he nor his colleagues openly admitted that the futility as he saw it was linked to poor planning. The process of gathering records from other parts of South Africa for the approaching unification of the region would have revealed to him that the machinery of surveillance and control in Natal and the Cape Colony, so impressive in appearance, was in actuality desperately flawed. As noted earlier, in their hurry to block immigration, legislators had not thought through some basic issues, such as the paperwork for non-migratory forms of travel, and had opted to fill the lacuna with ad hoc measures such as 'embarkation permits', 'transit passes', 'temporary permits', 'certificates of exemption', and so on.

The haphazard way these numerous documents came into being meant that they were inconsistent in their formatting and often issued as standalone documents without being recorded in any formal index. In Natal, the immigration head admitted 'great troubles' in keeping accurate records of the permits he gave out on a daily basis and in 1904, the man in charge of the Cape office estimated that he felt certain of the bona fides of only one in every dozen applications. At some point, Godfrey Dick in Durban admitted the 'extreme weakness of my office … thousands of residence certificates have been issued without written application or record'.[11]

The Transvaal had similarly messed up by issuing varied forms of documentation and frequently changing its guidelines, resulting in loopholes that Curtis believed were exploited by Asiatics, whom he described as having an aptitude 'for trickery and fraud' and 'a race to whom bribery is second nature'.[12] A communication from the police commissioner to the chief secretary of permits revealed a confused state of affairs:

> The system was that when any Asiatic came to Johannesburg on a regular permit which used to be granted on the recommendation of the British Indian Committee by the Superintendent of Asiatic Affairs, his name was registered and a residential pass granted. If any doubt existed as to the character of the new arrival the residential pass was withheld and a temporary pass given pending enquiry. After the withdrawal of Martial law anybody who came up on a permit was given a residential pass as before; those who came up without permits were given temporary passes pending such time as some settlement could be come to ... I am afraid the confusion has arisen owing to the want of definite instructions as to how Indians were to be dealt with.[13]

Having failed to devise an efficient and foolproof system of checking an allegedly high proportion of unlawful entry at the borders, Curtis did not envisage improving the system but rather thought of replacing it altogether. His solution was to replace gatekeeping with policing by creating a register of every Asiatic, male or female, young or old, in the Transvaal.

> Every Asiatic, male or female, whether born in the country or imported, shall be placed on a new register and furnished with a new permit. Each leaf in the new register will consist of three parts, two counterfoils and the permit. The two counterfoils will contain in duplicate the name description (-) a record of his 10 finger prints will also be taken ... These finger marks will be reduced by the finger print experts to their digit formula.

On the permit itself the right thumbmark alone will appear but the formula will be written in the opposite corner ... We could then discontinue our present futile attempts to block the ports of entry.

Each individual was expected to produce the permit when asked and allow the police entry into their homes for checking it. The project was suffused with the aura of science, technological progress and the glamour of Edward Henry, since the basis of its functionality was the recording of fingerprints. The infrastructure for fingerprinting was readily available as the Foreign Labour Department had finished fingerprinting Chinese workers, and Henry Burley and Cecil Harcourt Lees were free to apply their skills to other groups.

On a cool April day, Curtis, to be recalled in later years as a third-class scholar with pedantic inclinations he espoused with the zeal of a prophet,[14] committed these thoughts to paper. His confidential report on the 'Position of Asiatics in the Transvaal'[15] covers thirty pages. I imagine him dictating it to a stenographer in an office with high ceilings and leather upholstery. Did he lean back in a chair and look out of the window at a bed of daisies or did he pace the floor, glancing at polished mahogany and a picture of the king, a portly Edward VII in full military regalia, on a wall?

A sense of urgency and self-importance is communicated by the typescript, which has a few changes by hand and numerous typos, errors of punctuation and spelling left uncorrected. His signature is boxy, an initial and the surname 'L Curtis', looped, cursive and ascending to the right. Below it is his designation: 'Assistant Colonial Secretary. (Div. II)'. The report is addressed to the colonial secretary and dated 1 May 1906. In the archival folder where I read it, the report is accompanied by a covering letter to the lieutenant governor from the governor's office, a formal letter with the royal coat of arms in a red seal at the top. Curtis believed he had devised a system which would 'keep the Transvaal a white man's country' and for which 'a debt of gratitude, the fulness of which the people of this country will never know, is due to [my] office'.[16]

Somewhere in the report, though, is an acknowledgement that he was aware of the implications for the Indian community of what he was about to do and a note of remorse as well, for he writes:

> I must say without hesitation that the exclusion of Asiatics is the most odious duty which I have ever been asked to carry out. I would go even further than this and say that the duty of excluding British Subjects with a certain number of favoured exceptions, from a British country, is the most odious duty which a British Government could legitimately undertake. It can only be done by methods which have much more in common with Russian than with British ideas.[17]

29

Resisting Degradation

On the afternoon of Tuesday, 11 September 1906, Indians downed their shutters and left their duties. Traders, hawkers, waiters, helpers wended their way to the wide street that ran like an artery through the mining town. Some had not been on Commissioner Street for a while and would have been startled to find that the tacky 20-feet-high bamboo sheet, painted to resemble a brandy bottle, that used to be a familiar landmark, was no longer there. Instead, a massive steel-and-masonry structure occupied the entire block between Eloff, Commissioner, Market and Joubert Streets. It was the Carlton Hotel, a monument of plush modernity like Bombay's Taj, boasting the latest air-conditioning, waterborne sewerage, emergency power, a central plug-in vacuum-cleaning process, a Turkish bath and a marble swimming pool. The soaring edifice might have stopped the Indians momentarily and caused some among them to amble at a slower pace, gazing into the shops fronting the hotel at street level, particularly Sieradzki's with its flashy ostrich plumes.[1]

Then they picked up speed, hastening past the New Exchange and the Bank of Africa and joined others like them, collected under a canopy fronting the ornate façade of a theatre known as the Empire

Palace of Varieties.² The theatre, which had hosted famous British variety artists and screened the first film shown in South Africa, had closed weeks before because the owners were building a new theatre further up the street, and the vast hall where once the city's hoi polloi gathered in the luminescence of a brilliant chandelier now saw 3,000 brown-skinned Indians crowd in, filling up every available space. There were big Gujarati Muslim traders with branches all over the Transvaal and a combined asset base of £800,000. There were Tamilian free Indians, many in hawking or menial jobs, led by Thambi Naidoo who had left his home in Mauritius as a boy and done odd jobs in the Cape before coming to Johannesburg and establishing himself as a leading transporter.

The meeting to protest the Asiatic Law Amendment Ordinance drafted by Lionel Curtis and soon to be introduced in the Legislative Council was organized by the Hamidia Islamic Society, a Muslim merchants' organization, and the British Indian Association. The chairman of the latter, Abdul Gani, presided over the proceedings from a sofa covered with a yellow silk cloth.³ An invitation had been sent to Colonial Secretary Patrick Duncan who sent the Registrar of Asiatics Montfort Chamney to represent him. The former tea planter sat stiffly in the crowd, understanding enough Hindustani presumably to comprehend its rage.

Prominent figures in the Indian community rose up one after another to have their say. A Pretoria merchant, Sheth Haji Habib declared: 'We are not going to get justice at the hands of the British Government. It kills us with sweet words; we should not be deceived …'.

Nanalal Shah waved his old registration certificate. 'This register contains my name, my wife's name, my caste, my profession, my height, my age, it bears even my thumb impression. Is all this not enough? How can anyone else use this register? Does the Government want now to brand us on our foreheads?'⁴

Amidst the hubbub was Gandhi, thin, intense-eyed, delicate and visibly moved. Ever since he read the contents of the proposed ordinance in the *Transvaal Government Gazette Extraordinary* of 22 August 1906, he had been deeply disturbed. The degradation he had sought so valiantly to escape was thrust upon the community. Every Indian entitled to reside in the Transvaal was to apply for a certificate of registration with his or her name and fingerprints on it (like a criminal, for in colonial India it was criminals who were required to provide fingerprints) from the registrar of Asiatics. She or he was to produce the certificate before any police officer whenever and wherever required, even while walking on public thoroughfares, or face a fine and imprisonment. Police officers could enter private houses to inspect certificates. Indians had to show their certificates while entering the colony or for conducting business or while applying for licences.

'I have never known legislation of this nature being directed against free men in any part of the world,' he observed. Indentured Indians were subject to restrictions but, as he pointed out, 'these poor fellows can hardly be classed as free men' and the penalties imposed on them were 'a mere fleabite when compared with the penalties laid down in the Ordinance'. What shocked Gandhi profoundly was the realization that the implementation of the ordinance would criminalize the Indian community as a race ('It is not possible to describe in words the underlying spirit ... the condemnation of the whole community'). The ordinance, if passed, '... would spell absolute ruins for the Indians in South Africa ...'. In his mind it was

> a question of life and death ... Better die than submit to such a law. But how were we to die? What should we dare and do so that there would be nothing before us except a choice of victory or death? An impenetrable wall was before me, as it were, and I could not see my way through it.[5]

But as each speaker rose to have his say, he saw a path open up. Respected members of the community such as Nanalal Shah and Abdul Gani vowed to be jailed rather than register themselves under the proposed law. Haji Habib said, 'There is no disgrace in going to gaol; rather it is an honour.' The commitment was reiterated in a resolution adopted by the gathering:

> In the event of the Legislative Council, the local Government, and the Imperial Authorities rejecting the humble prayer of the British Indian community of the Transvaal in connection with the Draft Asiatic Law Amendment Ordinance, this mass meeting of British Indians here assembled solemnly and regretfully resolves that, rather than submit to the galling, tyrannous, and un-British requirements laid down in the above Draft Ordinance, every British Indian in the Transvaal shall submit himself to imprisonment and shall continue to do so until it shall please His Gracious Majesty the King-Emperor to grant relief.[6]

The die was cast. A promise had been made and there was no looking back. Following the mass gathering at the Empire Theatre, Gandhi and a Gujarati businessman H.O. Ally set out for England to try and stop the ordinance. They met Secretary of State for the Colonies Lord Elgin and his undersecretary Winston Churchill. Lord Elgin, a Liberal and a former viceroy of India, seemed sympathetic to the Indian cause and withheld royal assent from the ordinance. The overjoyed petitioners set out for home but realized they had merely been handed a reprieve. White settler societies everywhere were then in the process of curbing coloured immigration and with a representative government about to take over, Elgin had no intention of making a serious intervention on behalf of the Indians.

Elections were held for the Transvaal in March 1907 and Het Volk won by a majority. Smuts became deputy prime minister and colonial secretary under the prime ministership of Louis Botha. The elected assembly of fifty-eight members met and, on the very first working day, 23 March 1907, unanimously adopted the bill for the Asiatic Law Amendment Act (No 2 of 1907), the first real item of government business in the newly elected Parliament of the Transvaal Colony.

At the National Library of South Africa, opposite a tall grey building housing the Department of Home Affairs on Pretoria's Johannes Ramokhoase Street, I look at leatherbound gazettes of the Transvaal government for the year 1907 and find news of a raging East Coast fever and efforts to contain it through the branding of 'suffering and neighbouring cattle'. In the week ending 29 June 1907, the patent office received notices from Walter Benjamin Pickles for 'an improved method or process of recovering metallic tin from waste or scrap tin plate' and from Archibald Frank Stevenson for 'improvements relating to pneumatic hubs for vehicles'. Trademarks were registered for Old Scotch Whisky by John Dewar & Sons. Cross Road beginning at Silverwright Street in Luipaardsvlei Township and ending in Monument Street, Krugersdorp township was proclaimed a public road. Somewhere in the picture of quotidian life painted by the miscellanea of governance is this item: 'Government Notice No. 716 of 1907 Asiatic Law Amendment Act 1907 – Regulations – provided for registration of all Asians and children born (caste/sub sect – names of wives, where born etc).'[7]

30

Forward Ye

The imperial government approved the Asiatic Registration legislation and the act came into operation on 1 July 1907. A roving registration office was set up to implement Curtis's game plan. It was to visit all the towns of the Transvaal and every Indian male (the provision for women was dropped) had to register with a full set of fingerprints.

The Indian community declared a boycott of the 'Black Act', as they called it. The Hamidia Islamic Society and the British Indian Association toured the Transvaal with volunteers to picket the registration office wherever it halted. The picketing was mostly peaceful, but it would be a brave or foolhardy man who would enter the registration office in full view of his community and visiting notables. And few showed any inclination to do so. The meeting of Indians at the Empire Theatre had been punctuated with references to 'honour' and 'God', and the campaign was enveloped in a religious zeal. Gandhi exhorted the people to stay away from the registration office and court arrest if necessary. The boycott campaign was a milestone for Gandhi who had so far relied on the constitutional approach of appeals and petitions.

It was also the beginning of a new technique of political campaigning, which would come to be the hallmark of his style. Its inspiration then was thought to be the passive resistance movement in nineteenth-century Ireland where many rural communities refused to pay rent to British absentee landlords or work for their local land agents at harvest time (the word 'boycott' derives from Captain Charles Boycott, a land agent in County Mayo ostracized by his local community in 1880 during a non-cooperation campaign). Gandhi was at pains to point out a distinction between the two. As he wrote to Johannesburg's *Rand Daily Mail* on 1 July 1907: 'I call the passive resistance (to the Asiatic Registration Act) to be offered by the Indian community "so-called", because, in my opinion, it is really not resistance but a policy of communal suffering.'[1] Among other sources, he possibly drew upon traditions of self-punishment that were practised in India and in his native Kathiawar, where the performance of traga or infliction of wounds on oneself had a strong presence in practice and folklore.[2] The name he gave the political technique that he fashioned was Satyagraha and it comprised two parts: 'agraha' or a determined opposition which, when used 'in a right cause is sat', or truth.[3]

Indian Opinion played cheerleader. 'Forward ye all to battle, the bugles sound. Raise the cry and take the plunge, for victory's around,' it wrote, quoting the rebel-poet Narmad. In another issue it wrote: 'Why should you suffer taunts, my brother? To be cowardly is a disgrace. Suffer not insult; death is far better.' The course of action was clear: 'No one should have anything to do with the Permit Office. No one should enter (the Colony) with a new permit. Going to gaol is for us like receiving an honour.'[4]

Registration opened in Pretoria on 1 July 1907. Only a hundred Indians registered out of a population of 1,500. Every succeeding town saw a low turnout. The community kept the morale of the resisters high by sending congratulatory telegrams (from Johannesburg to Pretoria: 'The Indian community with one voice exhort them to persevere in this their first struggle to assert their rights as civilised men and not be trampled upon as beasts.') and exerting social pressure. On 17 August 1907, *Indian Opinion* wrote: 'Bravo Pietersburg ... Pietersburg has surpassed Pretoria, and a citadel that was supposed to fall at a mere touch has proved impregnable.'

All the action was in the Transvaal, but Indians across South Africa were watching closely. They were aware that the fate of the new law would determine how they would be treated as well in a future Union. In Durban, a group of Indians staged a play in which local actors mocked the registration office, talking about how its officers, Chamney and Cody, were left twiddling their thumbs because no Indian showed up for registration. The Indian precinct around Grey Street was abuzz. One imagines that people would have talked of nothing else and conversation in barbers' shops and tea stalls probably revolved around the latest reports in *Indian Opinion*. In this fervid, stormy and combative ambience, on 29 August 1907, Mohanlal wrote a letter to the secretary for native affairs in Pietermaritzburg asking for the rejection of his application for permission to keep a sporting rifle to be 'address(ed) ... in a better way'.

In the Transvaal, the registration process ended as scheduled on 31 October with only 551 Indians registering,[5] a fraction of the Indian population. Arrest warrants were issued against twenty-three resisters, including Gandhi and Leung Quinn, chairman of the Chinese Association, who had joined the campaign on behalf of Chinese migrants who were also affected by the controversial law.

After jailing dissenters, the government seemed to relent. A meeting was arranged between Gandhi and Smuts and the Indian leader was freed after spending twenty days in jail. But this is where matters get confusing. Gandhi believed that Smuts had agreed to his offer of voluntary registration by the Indian community in return for withdrawing the Asiatic Registration Act. The logic behind his offer was that volunteering cooperation made Indians partners in an exercise to prevent unlawful immigration, while the force of a law criminalized an entire race by holding all Indians guilty of wrongdoing, a charge they had to repeatedly disprove by proffering proof of registration. Believing that the administration had accepted his point of view, he suspended the campaign and registered himself, and most of his fellow Indians followed suit.

The reported concessions being contemplated by the colonial administration in the matter of Indian registration raised concern in the white community. Appeals poured in from all over the Transvaal. White residents of Machadodorp, Krugersdorp, Belfast, Barberton, Potchefstroom, Zeerust, Ermelo, Boksburg, Pietersburg, Bethal, Standerton, Benoni, Wakkerstroom and elsewhere held meetings and penned these missives. There was even a dispatch from the Natal governor enclosing a resolution from the inhabitants of Newcastle and Dundee and from the Dundee Agricultural Society. The content, with slight variations in the wording, supported the Transvaal government's policy of 'alarm' on the 'Asiatic question'.[6]

I get a sense of the fractious mood of the time in the 1906 Christmas number of *The Mosquito and African Sketch*, where a cartoon shows a tall Englishman reading a book and, with his free hand, shoving a turbaned black-faced man off a stool behind a door that says: 'Municipal Office'. An article in the *Natal Witness* in May 1908 says:

> Those who apologise for the Indian trader have never had their living filched from them by an Indian; they have never seen the trade on which they depend for food and clothing for themselves, their wives and children, pass across the road to a black man, who spends next to nothing on his household, has

no stake in the country and practically sends all his earnings across the sea.[7]

Was Smuts browbeaten by the agitated white response into reneging on his promise? Or had Gandhi been mistaken when he assumed that Smuts had agreed to withdraw the act? The question remains unanswered. Smuts denied making such a promise. The upshot was that the registrations voluntarily made by the community were validated and the Black Act also remained. The government went further and passed an immigration law on the lines of Natal and the Cape Colony, restricting entry to the Transvaal on grounds of prostitution, criminal history, lunacy, liability to become a public charge, danger to the public health (suffering from an infectious disease) and illiteracy in a European language. Educated men therefore could enter but would have to register themselves under the repugnant law.

The Indians resumed their agitation. Indian activists courted arrest by hawking on the streets without licences to protest the linking of registration with licences. Gandhi decided to highlight his demand for a few men of learning to be allowed in as 'a matter of right'. The person selected for this mission was Shapurji Sorabji, a cousin of the Durban businessman Parsi Rustomjee. Sorabji was born in the Adajan neighbourhood of Surat and had matriculated from the Surat High School. He spoke fluent English and worked as a bookkeeper and manager of a Muslim-owned shop in the Natal town of Charlestown, where he also occasionally acted as an interpreter at the local court. As arranged, he entered the Transvaal on 24 June 1908. When his grace period ended and he refused to apply for registration under the Asiatic Act, 'an un-British and disgraceful Act', he was ordered to leave the Transvaal. He defied the order and was sentenced to a month's imprisonment with hard labour. Released on 19 August, he was deported to the Natal border.[8]

With his photograph splashed in the local Indian press, Sorabji, with his broad shoulders and serious mien, became widely recognizable. Congratulatory messages poured in. *Indian Opinion* provided the names and addresses of his wife and family members where well-wishers could directly send their felicitations. And for the next few weeks, the focus of the struggle shifted momentarily from the hawkers and tradesmen who had filled the jails in the early part of the struggle to the educated, professional passenger Indian.

31

Educated Protesters

Durban's railway station, housed in a Victorian building of red brick, ran over with Indians on the evening of 13 August. Five hundred or more collected to cheer on some of their most distinguished representatives who were taking the plunge into political action. They were entering the fray in solidarity with the Indians of the Transvaal and on behalf of Indians all over South Africa. The send-off was reported by *Indian Opinion* as being 'most enthusiastic'. The paper carried a small, hurried report on one of the inside pages in its 15 August 1908 issue, inserted amidst other news of the ongoing struggle, under the headline 'Durban Leaders go to the Rand'. The report said: 'Messers Dawad Mahomed, Parsee Rustomjee, M C Anglia, S J Randeria, M P Killawala, Adam H G Mahomed of CapeTown and others left by the Johannesburg mail train on Thursday evening. Interesting developments may be expected.'

This is the first time I have seen Mohanlal's name associated with any form of political activity. He is in distinguished company and it is a cause that allies neatly with his identity as an educated professional, a person of a certain class and standing in the Indian community and hence also bearing with it a certain responsibility, which he appears to have finally shouldered. I wonder if there was a tipping point. What was it that pushed him towards action? Was it the example set by Sorabji? Was Mohanlal inspired by the way a young man, so much like himself, had thrown himself into the fray and taken a blow for the community? Or was it peer pressure? Shelat, Randeria and others who Mohanlal hobnobbed with socially in the Grey Street precinct were all participating in the campaign and it might have been awkward for him to stay away. Or it could be that he was primed for action, that the preceding months had seen his anger grow, and the petulant outbursts over the rifle rejection letter and the baggage examination matter were indications of his growing indignation and racial humiliation that were now given the possibility of an outlet, which he grabbed with both hands.

Prodded by some or all of these motivations, on that August evening in 1908, my great-grandfather—teacher, interpreter and accountant—must have donned his jacket, bid my great-grandmother and their baby daughter goodbye and proceeded to the station. He would have made his way through the crush, feted and cheered on. There may have been an anointment with vermillion, garlands and drumbeats. The group of twenty-one heading off 'with the object of assisting their Transvaal brethren in their struggle against the Registration Act'[1] included the top brass of the Natal Indian Congress: Dawad Mahomed, Parsi Rustomjee and M.C. Anglia. Anglia, a Surti Bohra, was a partner in a shipping agency representing the Natal Direct Line, advertised with a ribbon banner in commercial directories. He was an educated man, fluent in English and French. Adam H.G. Mahomed, son of Joosub Gool and president of the British Indian League, had come from Cape Town, so this was a strong show of support from the Indian community in South Africa. The others of the company included a number of educated men, government interpreters and former civil servants. From the chests of some volunteers hung medals marking their service in the Ambulance Corps for the Anglo-Boer War and the 1906 military action against the Zulus. A more detailed report on some of these individuals appeared in *Indian Opinion* a few weeks later, on the occasion of their court appearance where they were defended by Gandhi's associate Polak.[2]

U.M. Shelat, Mohanlal's companion at the interpreters' examination, described himself as an 'agent, interpreter and bookkeeper' who 'held an Interpreter's certificate from the Natal Government Board of Examiners in certain Indian languages and in English ... He had studied English for seven years in various Indian leading schools and at one time was a Government Servant under the Baroda Government'.

S.B. Medh described himself as a 'commercial broker, interpreter, book-keeper, teacher, and with several other qualifications ... He held a senior certificate in accountancy from the London Chamber of Commerce'.

H.I. Joshi had studied at the Ahmedabad High School and claimed to be a bookkeeper and an interpreter. All these men had served as sergeant-majors at the time of the Zulu uprising. And Randeria, a 'certified accountant', who held a 'passport issued to him by the British Consul at Zanzibar purporting him to proceed to any British colony with all rights of British citizenship there' had served in the Ambulance Corps during the Anglo-Boer War.

The others were M.N. Goshalia, a 'book-keeper and interpreter' and Mohanlal Killavala, 'interpreter and teacher who said that he had interpreted before the Natal Courts on many occasions. He had an official appointment as interpreter. He was a Government servant in India. Yesterday he had interpreted before that very court in an Indian case'.

A photograph in a booklet[3] published years later shows one of the crusaders, Harishankar Ishwarlal Joshi, middle aged, broad faced with a thick moustache and heavy-lidded eyes. He wears a stiff-collared white shirt, elegant, faintly striped coattails, leather shoes with socks and a small turban on his head. His fingers are laced at the knee and behind him is an arrangement of a painted screen, a small ornate writing table on which are some books and an inkwell. This carefully mounted image is probably representative of the type of man who boarded the train to the Transvaal that mid-August day in 1908, albeit an older version, for these men were still youngsters, mostly in their twenties, adventurous and spirited. They were all from western India, many from Surat, with strikingly similar biographies. I note that Shelat and Mohanlal were interpreting in the courts, which suggests that they had been allowed to do so despite their failure in the interpreters' examination.

According to the lunar calendar, it was the night after a full moon, so an eerie light would have lain over the landscape the train passed through, dotted occasionally with houses but mostly empty fields. The bleak surroundings may have mirrored Mohanlal's anxiety about the repercussions of his action on what lay ahead for himself and his family, a concern that might have dissipated amidst the gay atmosphere in the compartment filled with talk, laughter and a spirit of camaraderie, which made the journey seem little more than an escapade perhaps.

They would have reached Newcastle at the foothills of the northern Drakensberg Mountains. The coal-mining town had a large Indian community and many Indians came to the station with refreshments for the Satyagrahis. Charlestown, at the top of Laing's Nek Pass, was the last town on the Natal side of the border and when the train stopped, they found leaders of the Hamidia Islamic Society and the British Indian Association in their white tunics waiting there, having come to join them from the Transvaal. The train chugged on, carrying the 'invaders' to the historic town of Volksrust where the Boers had once rallied to drive the British off the Majuba Hill.

They were in the Transvaal! The police had advance warning of their arrival and were waiting for them in Volksrust. But it seems that they were not detained long, for soon after, they convened for a public meeting in Suliman Kajee's store in town. The leaders made rousing speeches and joyfully announced that Natal and Cape Indians were adding their 'expressions of sympathy and money, the active assistance of their leaders'[4] to the cause of getting the (Asiatic) act repealed.

The plan was to cross the border into the Transvaal, refuse to register, court deportation and cross the border again to court arrest. In the meantime, while they were in the Transvaal, they were to fan out and visit Indian homes in various towns to collect registration certificates and bring them to Johannesburg where the documents would be publicly burnt in a show of rebellion against an administration that the Indians believed had reneged on its promise to withdraw the offending law. At Volksrust, the large group divided itself into smaller groups. Dawad Mahomed, Parsi Rustomjee, M.C. Anglia and Randeria went to Krugersdorp, Potchefstroom and Klerksdorp; Shelat, Joshi, Medh and Mohanlal went to Pretoria. They would have knocked on doors, most likely accompanied by a local leader, and explained their purpose. Word would have spread and householders would have handed over their permits, registration certificates and trading licences for the much-anticipated protest.[5]

Gandhi sent a letter to General Smuts, informing him that the heads of the Natal Indian Congress and the British Indian League of Cape Town, 'each representing a different faith or clan of India', were at the Transvaal border; that the jails were swelling with Indian resisters and that registration certificates were 'pouring in' ('by Sunday, it is highly probable that we will have at least fifteen hundred'). He appealed to Smuts:

once more, therefore, to revert to the draft Immigrants' Restriction Bill that was shown to me, and to accept the amendments suggested by me, leaving the question of educated Indians open ... If you cannot ... I am afraid that the resolve to burn the certificates at the Mass Meeting on Sunday must be carried out ...[6]

The mass burning of registration certificates and trading licences was a key moment in the Satyagraha campaign of 1907–08. Its dramatic apogee was actually more than one event but the first took place on 16 August 1908. The weather was most likely pleasant but the sky, like most August skies, was probably cloudy and hinting at rain. An iconic picture of the event shows a sea of people, those visible in the forefront wearing hats, those afar just indistinct spots. Estimates of the number in news reports varied from 700 to 3,000. An iron cauldron requisitioned from an Indian trader's shop was set up on a stage on the right. The leaders from Natal, Cape Town and the Transvaal were at the scene, as was Mr Leung Quinn. Gandhi was there, of course, and Essop Ismail Mia, chairman of the British Indian Association, who presided over the proceedings.

Gandhi spoke at great length and, uncharacteristically for him who believed in being courteous even to his bitterest enemies, was trenchant in his observations on the registrar of Asiatics, Montfort Chamney. Writing in his autobiography many years later, he would note that despite their colour prejudice, local officials who were responsible to public opinion in South Africa 'had a certain courtesy of manner and humility about them' unlike officers who had previously served in India and carried the 'habits of the autocracy'[7] from there. Chamney was presumably one such individual and Gandhi alluded to him in his speech with phrases like '... hopeless incompetence and ignorance ... Mr. Chamney has been tried, and has been found wanting ... unless he is removed from this department, there will be no peace'. He said:

> I claim to be a colonist. I claim to have passed a fair measure of my life in this country, and if this country, the welfare of this country, demands that Asiatic immigration should not proceed unchecked, then I should be the first man to say, let that be so ... but having accepted that position, I should claim that this country is just as much mine as any other colonist's, and it is in that sense that I put forward that claim on behalf of my countrymen ... It cannot benefit the colonists to have British Indians in the Transvaal who are not men but who may be treated as cattle even though it may be show-cattle ...
>
> What is this fight that we are engaged upon? To my mind, its significance did not commence with a demand for the repeal of the Asiatic Act, nor does it end with the repeal of the Asiatic Act ... the lesson I would have my countrymen to learn from this struggle is this: that unenfranchised though we are, unrepresented though we are in the Transvaal, it is open to us to clothe ourselves with undying franchise, and this consists in recognizing our humanity, in recognizing that we are part and parcel of the great universal whole ...[8]

The critical moment arrived. The account provided in *Indian Opinion* is replete with emotive phrasing: 'determination and a bitter merriment', 'badge of slavery' and 'poured oil upon the flames'. The Johannesburg correspondent of London's *Daily Mail* compared the event to the Boston Tea Party.[9] The *Transvaal Leader* had a detailed description:

> A large three-legged pot was then filled with the registration certificates, about 1,300 in all, and about 500 trading licences.

Paraffin was then poured in, and the certificates set on fire, amid a scene of the wildest enthusiasm. The crowd hurrahed and shouted themselves hoarse; hats were thrown in the air, and whistles blown. One Indian, said to have been a leading blackleg, walked on to the platform, and, setting alight his certificate, held it aloft. The Chinese then mounted the platform, and put their certificates in with the others ...[10]

A week later, on 23 August, the ceremony of burning certificates was repeated with a fresh batch brought in by volunteers. These included the Natal men who had gone to Pretoria to collect certificates for burning. It is not clear if Mohanlal and his companions, Shelat, Ishwar Joshi and S.B. Medh were at the first burning ceremony, but they were present at the second as indicated by this *Indian Opinion* report of 29 August 1908:

> Amongst those present who gave encouragement to the people, were the Durban leaders, anxious only for the time when they should be summoned before the Court to pay the penalty of their patriotism ... It is only necessary to add that the meeting broke up when some 525 more certificates had been consigned to the flames amidst loud cheers, Mr. S. Haloo and Mr. U.M. Shelat assuming the role of stokers ...

Over the next few days, the Durban group stayed in the Transvaal, awaiting their inevitable arrest and deportation to Natal, which for Mohanlal and his companions seems to have occurred on 28 August or thereabouts.[11] Natal Indian Congress leaders Dawad Mahomed, Parsi Rustomjee and Anglia, accompanied by Randeria, were arrested in Pretoria a few days earlier. They were at the Anjuman-e-Islam Hall discussing arrangements for collecting certificates when a Superintendent Betts served the arrest and deportation order. It appears that the process of collecting registration certificates and burning them continued, for there is a reference to another mass meeting in Pretoria on 'Friday' (presumably 28 August) reported on by Gandhi in his 'Letter from Johannesburg' for *Indian Opinion*, which he wrote:

> was very well attended and great enthusiasm was evinced. Though a large number of certificates were burnt, I must say that the number received was not so large as it should have been. In Pretoria, only 60 certificates were received—this number is exclusive of those from the Madrasis—and this is not nearly enough …[12]

Soon after, twelve men, including Mohanlal, Shelat, Joshi and Medh, were ordered to be deported. As planned, the deportees re-crossed the border into the Transvaal without permits and were arrested and given prison terms; six weeks in Mohanlal's case. They were imprisoned in the town of Volksrust that lay on the Natal border, in the shadow of the Majuba Hill at an elevation of 5,429 feet. The jail was on the site of a former concentration camp for Boers during the war. It was in a forbidding stone building in the middle of a vast, empty, treeless expanse. Nights were intensely cold and days too when a breeze was blowing. A courtyard with a black stone floor was at its centre. After two Africans had escaped by breaking through the tin roof, it was covered with a strong iron ceiling and barbed-wire netting.[13] The large cells were punctured with two small windows at the top, which let in a weak glimmer of light barely augmented by a dim lamp. A bucket of water and a tin tumbler stood in each cell and a bucket in a tray filled with liquid disinfectant served as a makeshift toilet. A couple of planks fixed to 3-inch-high legs, two blankets, a limp pillow and matting was the bedding.

On 10 October 1908, *Indian Opinion* reported that like the Johannesburg prison previously, the Volksrust gaol 'overflowed with Indians'. There were thirty-seven Indians in Volksrust jail, nineteen of whom were awaiting trial. The jailers were apparently lenient, particularly in matters of religious observance, and allowed Muslims to receive special food for the holy month of Ramzan and Parsis to wear their sacred vest and thread. The officers, including the gaoler, apparently behaved 'well' and did not require more than a salute from prisoners as obeisance, which was presumably a contrast from elsewhere. The Indians made up their own duties. Muslims fasting for Ramzan were excused from strenuous work; the rest cleaned the cells or occupied themselves with other sundry jobs. Shelat and Medh prepared the food—'mealie pap in the morning, plenty of rice with a green vegetable (such as cabbage, etc.) for the midday meal, and rice in the same quantity with beans in the evening'.[14]

Gandhi, who was briefly at Volksrust, supplied most of these details, claiming that apart from the absence of ghee there was not much to complain about and that the Indians were 'so happy in gaol that one should think of it only as a palace'.[15] And from the descriptions of communal activity, the resisters' time at Volksrust does appear to have been a convivial experience. Mohanlal's six weeks was only half of the three-month term awarded to some others such as Rustomjee, Anglia and Randeria. But for a young man, newly engaged as he was in a crusade, with no previous experience of hardship, a cell on a bleak, cold hillside might have strained his endurance.

32

Hind Swaraj

In November 1909, first-class passengers on the SS *Kildonan Castle*, bound for Cape Town, saw an Indian man on the deck. He was slightly built and had a delicate face with protruding ears, a pointed chin and a thick moustache. His hair, while not short, was parted off-centre and lay smooth and flat on his scalp. His dress—a high collar, tie, jacket and shoes of an English gentleman—indicated that he had a modern education and status. Some may have recognized him from press reports and whispered to each other that this was the infamous 'Gandhi' who had created such a rumpus in South Africa, and that he was returning from London where he had gone to represent the Indian migrant community on the eve of the formation of a Union of South Africa.

What they would not have known was the turbulence that lay beneath the unremarkable exterior. A few months before this journey, Gandhi was in chains, breaking stones and sharing a prison cell with hardened criminals and murderers. The Satyagraha campaign, which had seen over 2,000 Indians suffer jail terms, had dwindled to stray cases of resistance. Many Indians had lost their livelihoods; almost 500 were deported. Parsi Rustomjee had spent fourteen months in jail. Gandhi's own sons had courted arrest. Had the sacrifices been worth it? The community had given up on the campaign and most Indians had re-registered themselves in the Transvaal. In England, political bigwigs had given Gandhi the cold shoulder. Borne steadily across an immense, heaving ocean, Gandhi had reason to feel defeated.

But on those long days, surrounded by an unvaried expanse of sea and a wide, open sky and time stretching ahead unbroken, some other impulse had taken hold of him—his calling as a thinker/writer. As the guiding force of and the chief contributor to *Indian Opinion*, Gandhi was used to putting his thoughts into publishable form. But on the *Kildonan* he wrote like never before, he wrote like a man possessed, writing so fast that his right hand ached and he had to use the other to write letters. 'I have written because I could not restrain myself.'[1]

He had no eyes for the glistening sea or for the gulls that floated alongside the ship, their white wings gleaming in the sunlight. He did not notice his co-passengers and barely registered what he ate, or so one presumes, for he covered 275 sheets of the ship's notepaper with 30,000 Gujarati words in ten days. His thinking and his articulation were clear, so clear that only three lines were scratched out and very few words corrected. The outcome was a book written in his mother tongue, Gujarati, called *Hind Swaraj* (Free India), his most controversial piece of writing, banned by the colonial government in India as a seditious text and little appreciated even by many of his ardent admirers. It was his creed, one which set out an idea that went beyond immediate struggles and strategies and expressed a way of looking at the world. *Hind Swaraj* outlined an argument against modernity and its concrete forms such as technological determinism and industrial capitalism. Rather than paint individuals and nations or even the West itself as an enemy, Gandhi described the hold of modernity in the extractive form it had been given as being responsible for the ills confronting humanity.

This book did not draw upon the vortex of legal reasoning, political manoeuvring and personality differences in which he had been caught up for fifteen years. His reasoning seemed to draw on a more visceral response to his myriad experiences. One sensed the impact on him of living in one of the world's most materialistic and thrusting urban spaces, the visual wallop of soaring bank façades, of roads effulgent with electric lights, fluttering banners on department stores and the shouting signs of the kinescope. One felt the effects of war, the panic of fleeing Boer women and children and the pain he had witnessed at first hand of Zulus under fire.

In a sense, *Hind Swaraj* was a repudiation of his own self, the part of him that had elevated British culture and manners to the heights of aspiration and to whom status and virility had been so important. In 1909, Gandhi still believed in the importance of appearances in conveying an equality with the colonial authorities, but in the years that followed he would drop his fine Western suits to adopt a rough peasant's dress and lead a campaign of mineworkers and indentured workers, a sharp contrast to his early campaigns which seemed to be preoccupied more with the interests of traders and other passenger Indians than the poor.

In his private life, Gandhi had been trying out a series of experiments that went side by side with this evolution. He had dabbled in alternative health cures and diminished his reliance on machinery. Phoenix, with its tin-roofed shacks and vegetable plots, was the test case for his evolving ideas, which he would replicate in Tolstoy Farm set up in 1910 outside Johannesburg. Gandhi's determined efforts to fashion spaces of opposition to the stranglehold of a materialistic modernity fed into *Hind Swaraj*.

Gandhi's metamorphosis bears a startling resemblance to another celebrated figure from his native Gujarat—the fiery writer, thinker and reformer Narmad, whom we met earlier in our passage through

Surat and intermittently elsewhere. The gifted radical tossing off verses and experimenting with new forms of writing may seem like an unlikely precursor to the leader of India's freedom movement, but the similarities are remarkable. Both were cosmopolitan individuals with eclectic influences. Both used Western literary forms, the essay and the autobiography, and ran weekly publications to spread their ideals. The most striking parallel, however, is in their political understanding of modernity.

When we left Narmad, he was emerging triumphant from a contentious battle with Hindu traditionalists. In the years that followed, he continued to make waves in his conservative milieu with his radicalism and his scandalous personal life. But underneath his stormy exterior an even more intense storm was brewing. He was writing *Rajyarang*, a history of the world published in 1874 when he was in his early forties. The process of writing this work made him reconsider his own past in a fresh light. He came to believe that his old ideals were the fancies of an inexperienced youth carried away by a foreign influence. The later Narmad claimed that the reform movement was misguided because it encouraged Indians to doubt themselves by denigrating their past. He said that Europeans pursued worldly desires, giving primacy to pravriti (materialism), rather than nivriti or selflessness.[2] Many of these ideas were echoed in *Hind Swaraj* where Gandhi wrote, among other things, about Western civilization making 'bodily welfare the object of life', taking note 'neither of morality nor of religion'. Both saw English education as a source of their enslavement to the materialistic ideas of the West, which they eventually shrugged off. The question-and-answer style of *Hind Swaraj* may have also borrowed from Narmad's *Dharmaji Jnasa*.

On those lonely November days on the ocean, I imagine Gandhi finding solace in the companionship of the brilliantly febrile poet from his homeland.

❖

After his time in jail in September–October 1908, Mohanlal disappears from the South African Archives. Later correspondence that I find in the archives at the Sabarmati Ashram in Ahmedabad suggests that he was in India by 1909–10. I cannot say what made him go back to India and if indeed his return was meant to be a visit or an abandonment of the overseas dream for a permanent return home. If it was a visit, then his return to South Africa would have been contingent on his ability to provide evidence of domicile, because the union-wide Immigrants Regulation Act of 1913 put an end to all new Indian immigration. Some like the British-born suffragist and journalist Mabel Palmer maintain that the freeze on immigration, though it seemed discriminatory, benefited the Indian migrant community: 'Had Natal remained open to unrestricted immigration from the congested populations of India who were living near the margins of subsistence, wages and standards of living in Natal would certainly have become depressed.'[3] Gandhi too had long given up the demand for unrestricted immigration and focused his efforts on raising the status of Indians already present in the eyes of colonial settlers.

If Mohanlal's return was a more permanent decision, then I do not know its cause. It could be homesickness, a family issue, his responsibilities towards his wife back home, an intolerance for racial discrimination, or a mix of all these. The lack of schooling facilities for Indian children in South Africa was also a serious problem. In 1909, only 324 of the 3,284 Indian children in school in all of Natal were girls, most of them very young; overcrowding and a shortage of teachers still kept many children out of school. My grandmother would have been four years old in 1910 and her future and that of any future offspring might have been a consideration in planning a return. Whatever be the reason, by 1910 it seems that Mohanlal, Foolkore and their child were in Bombay.

With the family's return to home ground, my journey also comes to an end. I had set out to retrace my great-grandfather's trail, to discover something of my great-grandmother and know more about Mohanlal's doings and see if they connected with that other ancestor I share with a billion other Indians—Gandhi, Father of the Nation. I have succeeded beyond my expectations. I have found out my great-grandmother's name, age and her likely birthplace. And I have found my great-grandfather leaving home as a young man and maturing into a campaigner for the rights and dignity of his countrymen. My story is ready for the telling.

But there are those papers that I have not looked at in the National Archives in Pretoria ...

PART EIGHT

PRETORIA

33

Archive, Pretoria

156, Queen St.
Durban, Natal.
27th June 1906.
To
The Honourable
The Colonial Secretary
Pretoria.
Sir,
I beg to apply for a Permit to enter and reside in the Transvaal.
I enclose herewith a copy of a document which I possess.
Thanking you in anticipation.
I beg to remain,
Sir,
Your most obedient servant,
Sg M.P. Killavala
Encl:
(The enclosure is a copy of Mohanlal's 'passport' from the Mauritius governor, Cavendish Boyle.)

This letter is in a set of documents titled 'TEMPORARY Authorisation to Visit Transvaal'.[1] I am back in South Africa nine months after my first visit. A chance sighting of a travel grant from the Indian Council of Historical Research, which I successfully applied for, has made a second visit possible in October 2013 and I am pleased for the opportunity to tie up loose ends. I am even more delighted to arrive in spring, when the jacaranda is in full bloom, carpeting the streets with wet, mauve petals; the bus ride from Hatfield station in Pretoria is a cruise through lavender clouds and the Union Buildings a fairy-tale vision in a lilac haze. In such a season, to be shut indoors is a shame. The surroundings of the National Archives are particularly bleak: dreary administrative government blocks, a lonely gas station offering pie and a soda across the road and a freeway heading out of town. But the unexamined cache of documents in Pretoria has niggled at me. I do not expect them to tell me anything substantially different from what I already know, but it will be good to have explored the possibility and, once I am done, I look forward to wrapping up my story.

But right away, the documents surprise me. The letter shows that in June 1906, almost two years before he joined the Satyagraha campaign and crossed the border into the Transvaal, Mohanlal wanted to leave Natal and settle in the Transvaal.

I am surprised because I have seen nothing to suggest any such interest before and baffled because it does not make any sense for him, so well-settled in Natal, to be uprooting himself to go live in other colonies in South Africa. I have been surprised already that he tried to make a move to Cape Town and assumed it was a plan he had not thought through. But now, faced with this application to settle in the Transvaal, I am not so sure of my hypothesis. Perhaps there is another explanation, a restlessness for instance, that does not allow him to stay for long in one place? And if that is the case, then why does he choose destinations that present the greatest difficulty? Post-war Transvaal on the eve of tightened immigration restrictions, including the proposed Asiatic Registration Act, was the hardest place in the region to enter. Mohanlal found out just how unlikely it was for him to be allowed to enter the Transvaal from the response he received. His application was sent by the colonial secretary to Registrar of Asiatics M. Chamney, who wrote a brief letter of rejection:

> July 7, 1906
> Sir,
> With reference to your Application for a Permit to reside in the Transvaal, I have the honour to inform you that it is regretted that Authorisation cannot be issued in your favour.
> Sd/ M. Chamney
> Registrar of Asiatics.

I take a deep breath. This is the largest and most formal reading room I have been in. It has the look of a conference room, with its long rows of stations and a reception desk miles away. Occasionally a porter comes by with a stack of boxes on a trolley. There is only a handful of users besides me this morning. An elderly white couple who entered the premises at the same time as me and whom I saw in the locker room, pulling out pencils, erasers, Post-Its and magnifying glasses from their rucksacks with the sureness of experienced mountaineers, are seated side by side, their foreheads almost touching. From overheard conversations at other archives, I suspect their mission involves a wayward relative or an ancestor who served overseas. I marvel at their enthusiasm. My gaze wanders to another typical denizen of the archives, a reedy-thin, pimply student in a white T-shirt with some lettering on it. He has an impressive array of equipment arranged on the table, including a camera mounted face-down on a tripod around which he moves restlessly, peering through the lens, then fiddling with a setting or an angle, standing back and forwards and back, shaking his head in a dissatisfied way. I return to my great-grandfather.

Mohanlal did not follow up on his application immediately. One would think he had given up the idea of visiting the Transvaal. But four months later, on 24 October 1906, Mohanlal wrote to the registrar of Asiatics reiterating his request:

M.P. Killavala U.S.F.
ACCOUNTANT. Translator etc.
To the Registrar of Asiatics
Colonial Secretary's Office, PRETORIA.
Sir,
Referring to my Application dated 27th June last to enter the Transvaal, I beg the favour of further consideration on the following grounds:-

1 ... That I have a Passport (copy herewith) to travel in South Africa wherein Sir Cavendish Boyle – the Governor of Mauritius – REQUESTS, IN THE NAME OF HIS BRITANNIC MAJESTY, to allow me and my wife travelling in South Africa to PASS FREELY and afford every assistance etc. Now Sir, I believe, you will give effect to the Request in His Majesty's name by H.E. The Governor of Mauritius.

2 ... That I am an educated man – a British Indian Subject by Birth – and have passed the Bombay University Final Examination and London – Accountancy – Examination and that I was for some time a Government Servant.

3 ... That I am not a merchant or anything of the kind, but I am an Accountant, Translator and Interpreter, practising in this Colony.

I beg to remain
Your most obedient servant
Sd M.P. Killavala

This renewed application has the weight of detail and self-importance. Mohanlal appears to be appealing to the authorities as an educated Westernized man, a bureaucrat and someone who had the backing of an English governor. It had the desired effect. Chamney replied more favourably on 27 October 1906:

Sir,
With reference to your letter of the 24th instant—I should be obliged if you will be good enough to call on the Coast Agent for Asiatic Affairs No. 7 Mandelsloh's Buildings, Durban, in respect to your application for a temporary authorisation to visit the Transvaal.
Sd M Chamney

Ten days after his more hopeful response, on 7 November 1906, however, Chamney wrote abruptly to Mohanlal to reiterate his original rejection:

… regret that the decision conveyed by my communication of the 7th July last cannot be altered.
Sd M Chamney
Registrar of Asiatics

Far from dampening Mohanlal's spirits, this second rejection (elided in his letter to Chamney which followed), was met with an upbeat response:

156 Queen St.
12th November 1906.
To
The Registrar of Asiatics.
PRETORIA
Sir,
Re <u>Temporary Authorisation</u>
I beg to acknowledge the receipt of your letter of the 7th inst.

2 ... Your letter of the 27th ultimo gave me some satisfaction and hopes which I can still entertain. As desired in your letter of the 27th ultimo I called on the Mr. Burgess – The Coast Agent in Durban, who called me to his office on the 1st inst: for a second time. When I went for the second time my thumb impression was taken. I think that the Coast Agent reported favourably both times.

3 ... However to avoid any future misunderstanding ... I am prepared to give every information which you want to enable me to obtain your permission to live in the Transvaal for a short time.

4 ... I herewith enclose a reference and will give you some more if necessary.

5 ... I have visited several Colonies and during my travels I have never yet been refused entrance in any of them and consequently if there should be a final refusal to my request it means wasting passage money and disappointment after considerable trouble of the voyage. And what bitter feelings might be roused in the minds of the Indian Public, should I describe my experience before them?

6. The laws have exceptions too, and the Officers are vested certain discretion which I request you to exercise in my case.

I beg to remain, etc.,
Sd M.P. Killavala

A testimonial enclosed is from 'Louis Paul, Chief Interpreter Magistrate's Court, Durban', dated 12 May 1906:

> This is to certify that I have known Mr. Mohanlal KILLAVALA for about six months, I come into contact almost daily with him. He is a respectable man and as I am aware he is straightforward and honest.

This is an interesting testimonial and indicates again how quickly Mohanlal had inveigled himself into the professional Indian community in Durban. A recommendation from a senior civil servant like Henry Louis Paul should have carried weight, but Chamney was unmoved and wrote back the same day: 'It is my honour to inform you that the decision conveyed by my communication of the 7th instant cannot be altered.'

I would think that having met with such resistance, Mohanlal would have given up on his wish to head to the Transvaal, more so given how invested he appeared to be in Durban at this point, for this was the period in which he was preparing to appear for his interpreter's examination for a position in the Natal courts and applying for permission to keep a sporting rifle to shoot game on the veldt. But he was not thwarted. Between 20 November 1906 and 23 October 1907, he continued to send applications for permission to enter the Transvaal. Disregarding rejections, he escalated his request to a higher and higher authority, starting with the colonial secretary, then the Transvaal Governor Lord Selborne and finally His Majesty's Principal Secretary of State for the Colonies in London the Right Honourable Earl of Elgin. In between he wrote again to Chamney asking for reasons for his rejection (6 December 1906: 'With reference to your last letter to me refusing to grant Temporary Authorisation, I shall be obliged if you will furnish me with your reasons'). He mentioned airily to Chamney that he was not 'particular about the period for visit' and that he could provide names of people known to him in the Transvaal, ('furnish some more Europeans if you like'). In a long missive to the colonial secretary on 8 January 1907, he begged to submit respectfully 'facts', which he hoped would persuade the recipient that his case was one of 'urgency'.

The facts he drew attention to were:

> ... that I am a British Indian Citizen by birth and as such I have certain rights and that a pass to visit your Colony is one of them. That it is improper to include His Majesty, the King Emperor's subjects and especially an educated man like me with Asiatics which term includes illiterate—non-British people too ... That my father and grandfather served the British a very long time. And that I am a Bombay Government servant on leave ... That I have passed the Bombay University School Final Examination and the London National Union of Teachers Examination ... That there are restrictive Rules in Natal too but they do not affect the educated man. Further that I have travelled in many parts of India, have been to Ceylon, Singapore and the Far East, to Mauritius and finally am in Natal but never have I yet been refused travelling. I have finished my stay in Natal long since and it is now some months since I am in communication for a simple thing like the visiting pass. It is very inconvenient, expensive for me to prolong my stay in Natal ...That I am the Vice President of a Theosophical Society and therefore I have some religious mission also in my trip to the Transvaal.

Even at a distance of a hundred years, the reasons tumbling pell-mell from Mohanlal's pen seem somewhat insubstantial. He cajoles, he wheedles, he threatens; he throws around claims but so loosely and like afterthoughts that they seem like untruths ('Vice President of *a* Theosophical Society'). Some, like his claim of being a 'Bombay Government servant on leave' and extensive foreign travel make me leery only because of the offhand way he throws them in. My suspicions are apparently not unfounded: in an internal communication on 25 March 1907, Chamney wrote to His Excellency the Governor, High Commissioner's Office, Johannesburg:

> I have ascertained from the Coast Agent for Asiatic Affairs at Durban that the statement made by Indian Killavala that he is in service of the Indian Government is false. He may have done clerical work in one of the government offices at Bombay but if he did he discontinued such work long since and I have been unable to ascertain for what reasons he left.

Why was Mohanlal so desperate to go to the Transvaal in 1906–07? The question remains. Meanwhile, what I find to be of note is that surprisingly, despite Mohanlal's patent dissembling, exaggerations and dogged refusal to accept no for an answer, the colonial authorities were not unkindly disposed towards him. Though the response at each level was a firm rejection, the papers discussing his case present in the folder along with the correspondence reveal that his case was given due consideration and responses were even worded with tact. The colonial secretary writing to Mohanlal on 4 January 1907, for instance, couched his rejection in terms of policy, maintaining that 'the issue of temporary authorisations in favour of Asiatics to visit the Transvaal has been suspended except in cases of extreme urgency'.

When Mohanlal wrote to the governor, the governor's office wrote to Chamney to ascertain the facts. It asked the registrar of Asiatics how it should respond to Mohanlal and the Colonial Office in London in turn asked the governor's office. Even Lord Elgin in Downing Street signed a letter on 27 November 1907 sent to the governor's office in Pretoria asking: '... as Mr. Killavala appears to be an educated man, and describes himself as a servant of the Bombay Government I should be glad to learn whether your Ministers will be prepared to grant him a permit under section 17 (1) of the Asiatic Law Amendment Act.'

The reason why Mohanlal's application was firmly turned down despite his strenuous efforts and success in making himself heard in the corridors of power is contained in a formal set of documents addressed from the governor, Lord Selborne, to The Right Honourable The Earl of Elgin and Kincardine, K.G., G.C.S.I. etc., Colonial Office, London. It contains the decision emanating from a source no less than the office of Louis Botha, prime minister of the Transvaal. I quote it in part:

MINUTE 25.
14 January 1908
MINISTERS have the honour to forward to His Excellency the Governor an extract from the Registrar of Asiatics ... regarding the character of Mr M.P. Killavala, and regret they are unable to recommend the issue of a temporary permit to visit the Transvaal in favour of this applicant
Louis Botha

The signature is of the prime minister of the Transvaal—a lush, decorative 'L' and a little band below the scrawled name.

As mentioned in the letter, this conclusive decision to reject Mohanlal's application rests on a report from Chamney, which in turn is based on a background check provided by E.J. Burgess, coast officer for Asiatic affairs in Durban. I quote the operative paragraph:

E/2308 7th May 1907
Indian Mohanlal Parmanandas Killavala.
This Indian applied in June last for a permit to enable him to reside permanently in the Transvaal, and as he had no claims in support of his application the issue of a permit was refused. On the 24th October'06 he asked for re-consideration of his application and on the 29th of the same month the Coast Agent for Asiatic Affairs at Durban wrote that he could not recommend the issue of authorisation to enable Killavala to enter the Transvaal. He stated that he was a dangerous man and that his object in desiring to proceed to this Colony was to start a Permit Agency.

'Permit agent' is a term I have come across occasionally in the course of my research. I have found it used loosely to describe legitimate and illegitimate activity related to immigration. General or permit agents were licensed to help prospective immigrants with paperwork. Lawyers and interpreters also performed this role. Archibald Findlay, Cowley & Cowley and other white legal firms were on a list[2] compiled by the principal immigration restriction officer in Natal, as were R.K. Khan and Gandhi, (who was also often scoffingly called a 'permit agent' by colonial authorities, alleging a pecuniary motive in his public work). Mr Solomon, the most successful attorney in the business of getting declarations for Indians seeking domicile certificates, made an estimated £4,000 off 1,700 clients annually. Fixers or agents hung around immigration offices and enjoyed a semi-formal status with officers, often playing a useful role in helping to smooth over difficulties caused by cultural and linguistic differences. And then there were brokers who worked more clearly outside the pale of the law, faking documents, smuggling people over borders and so on. Many agents would probably have committed the occasional trespass for a client, which gave the term an ambiguous quality. What made the colonial authorities believe that Mohanlal might start a permit agency? I quote, more extensively, Chamney's report on Mohanlal, which is referred to in Botha's letter as being an extract from the registrar's 'Notes on the Illicit Ingress of Asiatics to the Transvaal':

E/2308 7th May 1907.
Indian Mohanlal Parmanandas Killavala.

This Indian applied in June last for a permit to enable him to reside permanently in the Transvaal, and as he had no claims in support of his application the issue of a permit was refused. On the 24th October '06 he asked for re-consideration of his application and on the 29th of the same month the Coast Agent for Asiatic Affairs at Durban wrote that he could not recommend the issue of authorisation to enable Killavala to enter the Transvaal. He stated that he was a dangerous man and that his object in desiring to proceed to this Colony was to start a Permit Agency.

Mr Burgess further informed me that on the arrival of the S.S. "General" on the 15th October the applicant boarded the steamer and addressed him on the subject of an Indian named Mahomed Moosa, who was attempting to land with the object of proceeding to the Transvaal, although he was not a legally authorised resident. Killavala, who has lived some time in Mauritius, asked Mr Burgess if he could address him in French, and appeared to be about to offer him a bribe. The reason he desired to communicate his intentions in French was probably due to the fact that the Natal Immigration Restriction Officer, who was also present, cannot speak that language. This officer refused to allow Mahomed Moosa to land, but Killavala through some means or other managed to get him ashore, probably during the night. He then went to a Durban Solicitor named Findlay and procured from him a personal letter to Mr Burgess offering him a bribe if he could procure a permit for Mahomed Moosa. This letter was handed to Mr Burgess by Killavala himself, and in due course forwarded to me. I consulted Mr Duncan, who was then Acting Lieutenant-Governor, and on his instructions addressed the Law Department with the object of bringing Solicitor Findlay to justice. The matter was referred by the Law Department to the Natal Authorities but I am advised that no action has been possible because Findlay has disappeared.

34

Twist

The chilly calm of the Pretoria archives is pervaded by the humid, pungent air of the Durban Harbour. Somewhere behind me an invisible projector whirrs and I see a figure appear on my mind's screen, a tall, lanky white man in a suit of alpaca wool. Then a second man appears, an Indian in a suit of a different, less expensive material, and with him is another Indian, unshaven and dishevelled by travel but quick on his feet. The figures race lightly through moonlight and shadow and melt into the dark town.

The film runs out with a sputter. Oh no, the sputterer is me, trying to find words to convey my consternation at what I have just discovered. 'Mohanlal … you …!' Adjectives come to mind, none of them particularly respectful, and I refrain from saying them out loud. I am in shock, astounded, unable to take my eyes off the page. Every detail is resonant. The Durban Harbour where Mohanlal arrived from Mauritius. Mohanlal attempting to bribe an officer in French—an interesting application of his linguistic skills! Mohanlal and Findlay plotting to get an unauthorized migrant off the ship. Mohanlal appealing to governors and bureaucrats with his fine words and cosmopolitan air; a bit like Gandhi writing eloquent petitions to parliamentarians and newspaper editors. Of course, my great-grandfather's eye was on private gain and Gandhi would surely have disapproved. On the other hand, here were two Indian men in their twenties at different times, seducing and discomfiting the empire's servants with their eloquence in the colonizer's language. I begin to laugh. In the sepulchral gloom of the reading room, I shake with silent laughter.

It had always seemed suspicious to me that a young man from a genteel family would take off in the manner that my great-grandfather did and return as suddenly without explanation. The lack of information, of details and anecdotes surrounding his uncommon foray across the ocean; the silence behind a journey with a great impact on my near and dear ones, seemed curious and gave me a sense that there might be something to uncover. I had a hunch, a writer's intuition that there was a story to be found. But never did I envisage an explanation as full of intrigue as it has turned out to be. I am stunned but also filled with that peculiar quality of delight that comes at the end of a spectacular whodunnit. Nothing I ever imagined could match the revelations lying in these old, discoloured papers. My great-grandfather has surprised me in a way that I had never expected.

In the last section, when I left Mohanlal gravitating towards the Satyagraha movement, I assumed that the adventurous interpreter had been affected by a recent sensitivity to racial injustice. His letters to colonial authorities complaining of mistreatment as an Indian followed by his actual participation in the protest campaign suggested that he had been moved by Gandhi, whose ability to inspire people was legendary: he made people feel 'augmented in his presence beyond personal desert and native capacity', wrote Erik Erikson.[1] That is what I believed had happened. Mohanlal's experience of racial discrimination had coalesced with Gandhi's vision. The two Mohans had become one.

I suppose it was inevitable that my mind should follow what can be described as a familiar plotline. The trajectory of the Satyagraha campaign dominates accounts of the time and place. And understandably so, because the Gandhi biography and the evolution of his brand of non-violent resistance has important lessons for the world. Fate placed a young, idealistic Indian lawyer amidst a constellation of influential white leaders, from the poster boy of imperialism, Cecil Rhodes, to Jan Smuts, future prime minister of South Africa and a progenitor of the League of Nations (with Alfred Milner, Lionel Curtis, later proponent of imperial federation, and a young Winston Churchill reporting on the Anglo-Boer War in the mix). That Gandhi threw a gauntlet to these doughty representatives of an invincible empire makes for a true David-and-Goliath story, the stuff of riveting drama.

But now looking at the new evidence before me I wonder: what if this epic contest was undergirded by another story, one that had been obscured in the noise and din of battle? A story where the narrative was not about a confrontation between great men but about a collaboration between ordinary, undistinguished men? A blurry tale hovering below stairs, preoccupied not with ideals and utopias but with mundane considerations of survival and profit? As we know, the monumental face-off between Gandhi and the empire's leaders had its foundations, at least partly, in the lowly business of illegal immigration. Lionel Curtis designed the racially discriminatory Black Act to prevent what he foresaw as a tidal wave of Indians entering illegally into the Transvaal. The Indian community claimed that the cases of unauthorized entry were small in number and enabled by unscrupulous white officials. In the outcry of a community protesting about being criminalized by a blatantly racist law, the issue at the heart of it was all but forgotten. And this is where it appears my slippery ancestor is leading me and whom I must follow.

I meet Andrew MacDonald at the Centre for Indian Studies in Africa, a research centre at the University of Witwatersrand. Andrew is a historian who has recently been awarded a PhD from St. John's College, Cambridge University, for his 2012 thesis entitled 'Colonial Trespassers in the Making of South Africa's International Borders 1900 to c. 1950'. He writes about smuggling syndicates from Madeira, Assyrian bogus priests, peripatetic nightclub dancers, travelling farmhands and other migrants including Indians. His chapter, 'The Identity Thieves of the Indian Ocean: Encounters in South Africa's Immigration Record Rooms' is a fascinating survey of unauthorized immigration by Indians in the early twentieth century in all of South Africa. An affable young man, he demonstrates a fondness for his shady subjects, seeing them not as criminals but as resourceful 'subaltern migrants (who) developed their own vernacular responses to colonial power' and negotiated 'long-distance mobility within certain structural constraints and opportunities'.[2]

I go back to my stock of books and papers and find that there are references to unauthorized entries in Surendra Bhana and Joy B. Brain's *Setting Down Roots: Indian Migrants in South Africa, 1860–1911*, which I had overlooked. I also find frequent references to permit fraud in *Indian Opinion*. I come across references to illegal immigration in a 1908 enquiry in Zohra Dawood's 1993 MA thesis, 'Making a Community: Indians in Cape Town, circa 1900–1980s'. Lastly, I look at recent work by Uma Dhupelia-Mesthrie, including her 2011 paper called: 'The Form, the Permit and the Photograph: An Archive of Mobility between South Africa and India'.

The question uppermost in my mind as I go through these materials concerns the scale of illegal Indian immigration. Gandhi and Indian community leaders insisted that white politicians greatly exaggerated the scale of illicit entry and pointed to estimates put out by officials to validate their claim. At a glance, these scholarly papers do not contain any startling revelations regarding numbers. Indeed, the figures then quoted by authorities and repeated by Indian leaders appear to match Andrew MacDonald's estimate of an annual influx of 500 to 1,000 illegal Indian immigrants.[3] This is not a negligible addition to an Indian population estimated to be 150,000-strong in the 1911 census, but it could not really be said to constitute the 'flood' feared by white settlers.

What I am startled by, and what none of the many books I have read about the dramatic face-off between Gandhi and the representatives of the British Empire in South Africa have prepared me for, is how substantial and widespread a phenomenon illegal immigration was. Indians evolved myriad schemes of subversion in response to anti-immigration laws. The phenomenon was pervasive, involving a whole range of people from the tout, the forger and the white officials whose complicity was critical to the scheme's success, to social workers and members of the Indian professional elite. Descendants of illegal migrants and agents told Dhupelia-Mesthrie that there was no shame associated with these practices. One said 'that economics required a certain action, and you would act according to the need of the time, whether it was legal or illegal'.[4] For merchant houses permits, legal or illegal, were just one of the 'paper forms necessary for business'.[5]

Gandhi's struggle in South Africa was about the treatment of people on land. But Mohanlal's story appears to mix the terrestrial with the waters of the Indian Ocean. The mighty concourse, an ancient highway, was altered by the advent of European imperialism, by 'technology, industry and capitalism', which according to Michael Pearson, leading scholar of the Indian Ocean, marked a 'systemic or qualitative change' in the region.[6] Traders accustomed to freely moving on the waters and providing employment to their kin clearly found ways around prickly borders. They were helped by a range of eclectic characters who we are about to meet. Our story has taken a turn with the thunder of protest against oppression mingling with the pliant currents of opportunism.

Thoughts of spring and the glorious lavender-strewn streets are forgotten. Armed with a list of references from scholarly papers, I return to the archives in Pretoria and Pietermaritzburg, fill in requisition slips and watch boxes stack up around me, leading me into the murky world of what Andrew MacDonald calls 'illicit border crossers' and 'identity thieves'.

◆

The evidence for illegal immigration is in the form of letters, going back and forth between officials and departments and between members of the public and the administration. They contain warnings (an anonymous letter dated 29 August 1905 warns of a Chinaman from Mauritius soon to land in Durban: 'Very bad man who you will recognise by mark on the temple of the head'), notices of arrests and deportations, and descriptions of modus operandi. The most significant source of information are reports of an internal inquiry conducted in 1915 into the operations of the immigration office in Cape Town and Pretoria with regard to Indian immigration in the Cape Colony and the Transvaal. It occurred some months after Gandhi had left South Africa, but the reports offer a vivid and little-known insight into the world he occupied. Let us begin with one of them.

Cape Town: April signals the arrival of autumn, a time of fair days and clear skies. On one such possibly lovely day in 1915, an investigation was underway in Carlton Buildings into reported irregularities in the functioning of the Immigration Department by the Immigration (Departmental) Commission. The official reporter, F.W. Spencer, noted down the proceedings, his notes typed up and filed away in a government folder where I find them a hundred years later.⁷

Case No. 21 was about an Indian, Cassim Jaffer, who applied in person for an entry permit and was granted one on 8 May 1912. A routine matter till it was revealed that Jaffer was not in Cape Town at the time but in India. The person who actually visited the office and put his thumbprint on the application was an Indian permit agent by the name of Abdullah Dawood, apparently a regular fixture on the premises of the immigration office and well-known to all the officers there.

Richard Walsh, the fingerprint expert attached to the Criminal Investigation Department (and an Edward Henry acolyte, no doubt), confirmed irregularities in the application (instead of a right and left thumbprint, only one had been applied twice) and that the thumbprints belonged not to Jaffer but to Abdullah: 'There cannot be any doubt about that. One mark is quite enough for me to swear the identity of any man!'

Senior Clerk William van Reede van Oudtshoorn, who had been taking a particular interest in Asiatic Permits since 1905 and under whose supervision the breach occurred, admitted to knowing Abdullah ('The man called Abdullah Dawood is well-known to me if it is the man they call "Fatty" …') and asserted that 'it would not be possible for him to have signed this declaration in front of me and put his thumb prints there without my knowledge'.

Not true, Abdullah Dawood claimed. 'I came to this office and saw Mr. van Oudtshoorn. Mr. van Oudtshoorn knows me well. I am often at the office. Mr. van Oudtshoorn wrote out the application … the thumbprints are mine, they were taken at the same time.' And of the £11 which he collected for delivering the permit to Jaffer: 'I did not keep anything for myself. I paid the whole amount over to Mr. van Oudtshoorn.'

More depositions were made. They produced revelations of sovereigns being surreptitiously put in the hands of Mr van Oudtshoorn and another official, a Mr Bamberger. Suspicions were aired against two white lawyers, a Mr Van Ryneveld and Mr Biuhmont, who frequented the office. Ebrahim Norodien, president of the British Indian Union and previously of the South African Indian Association and the Konkani Muslim League, alleged that Indian agents handling potential immigrants sought permits for £5–50 'putting people in country at hardship'; and that immigration authorities worked with these agents: 'If you go with an agent, you get a permit in an hour, without can take three months.' Advisers from the Konkani Muslim League claimed that one agent alone had brought in 200 immigrants at a profit of £1,500 and another that 'not one quarter of the fraud had come to light'.

More circumstances were disclosed, such as the rivalry between Ebrahim Norodien and Abdul Cadir, the cigar maker from Mauritius. There was talk of how money and information circulated in the Asian enclaves of the city. About European and Indian merchants, fruit sellers, bootmakers, butchers, hawkers and office clerks who provided false testimonials to permit seekers. About clerks at the United Tobacco Company and Salt River Railway Station and market agents Fock, Bell & Co., who had collectively issued over 500 dodgy letters of recommendation.[8]

The proceedings of the 1915 inquiry in Cape Town provide a window into the elaborate and well-synchronized processes that had evolved as a reaction to harsh anti-immigration policies. A critical need, as we see in Case No. 21, was for an entry permit. This was just one of the many documents that had suddenly become essential. Documents of identity, domicile certificates, licences to prove domicile and permits to leave the domicile were some others. Sometimes documents were lost or stolen or permits expired. Or prospective immigrants without the necessary qualifications under the laws sought papers to enable entry. An industry in fake documents sprang up to meet these various needs. As we have seen, the applicant could be impersonated by someone else for a fee. At other times documents were created by a local person, applying multiple times. These documents were sometimes sent directly to potential immigrants. But as the market became more complex, they were sent to 'clearing houses' in stores, hotels, cafés and brothels in Lourenço Marques, Beira, Zanzibar, Mombasa, Mauritius, Bombay, Madras and Calcutta. According to Andrew MacDonald, skilled brokers facilitated the collection and distribution of residence certificates, even making door-to-door visits in Indian villages and calling on individuals who were known to be considering a move.[9]

To understand other ways of illegal entry, let us move to Portuguese Mozambique on the east African coast. This was a popular transit point because of its proximity to the Transvaal, its large Indian community and the existence of gold syndicates doing business with jewellers on the western Indian coast.[10] Migrants headed for South Africa arriving at Beira or Delagoa Bay could hole up here unobserved till the time was right. Suliman Makda and Allibhai, suspected agents, ran the Islamick Hotel in Lourenço Marques (now Maputo).[11] Lourenço Marques was also the base of a man named in reports as 'Naudeer' or 'Nahzir', son of a Karachi-born policeman in Mauritius who had been jailed for fraud in Mozambique and ran a brothel with Mauritian girls in Avenida Central. The British in South Africa knew him as the 'foremost dealer in Indian permits' and warnings such as this one, issued on 12 October 1905 from the British consulate-general in 'Laurence Marques' to the Transvaal police, were routine:

> Dear Captain Fowle,
> I enclose a copy of a report which has been handed to me by our Agent here. Naudeer is a Mauritian who is continually in trouble

with the Portuguese authorities for getting Indians ashore on the strength of permits to enter the Transvaal which he alleges belong to the Indians but which I have reason to believe are lent to the Indians in their paying anything from £2 to £5 ...
Yours sincerely,
(Sgd) M.D. Neel[12]

From Lourenço Marques, immigrants were taken across the South African border in a couple of ways. An official communication between immigration authorities pointed to the involvement of a man in a suit. 'Quite a number of coolies, Banyans, etc.' were seen leaving every day by train at 7 a.m. in the charge of an Indian 'dressed in the European fashion' who returned to Lourenço Marques after dropping them off on the other side of the border.[13]

They were most likely taken to Komatipoort on the border between South Africa and Mozambique. A former crossing on the Komati River that metamorphosed first into a camp and then into a town when the Boers began building a railway to Delagoa Bay in 1886, Komatipoort was an important entry point for illegal migrants. Komati station, as I make out from a 1901 photograph, was a plain building with a pitched roof, narrow arched doorways and windows backed by gentle hills. A few people hung around the railway tracks. On the morning of 10 November 1906, Dahyabhai Shankarbhai, an Indian known locally as 'Patell', approached Lance-Sergeant McDougall, a constable at the Komatipoort station. He placed three silk handkerchiefs on the table and told him: 'I will give you £2 for every Indian you let through without permits ... You can make £100, £150. There is a Sergeant at Volksrust who makes plenty of money; a person at Newcastle gives the Indians small square tickets and they give the tickets to the Sergeant who is paid accordingly.'[14]

Lance-Sergeant McDougall reported the matter to higher authorities in Barberton. Nothing further was heard about the sergeant accepting bribes at Volksrust, but Dahyabhai and two of his clients were arrested and McDougall was promoted to the rank of second-class sergeant. After Dahyabhai, another Indian, A.P.D. 'Fram' Patel, an interpreter attached to the police at Komatipoort, was found guilty of a similar fraud and the authorities tightened controls on the town.[15] A 1917 photograph of migrants captured from Komatipoort shows fourteen Indians looking like travel-weary lawyers in their white shirts and dark jackets.[16] Now the illicit traffic found a new way across the border, which was to detrain at Roseanna Garcia on the Portuguese side or at some other station with weak security or corruptible officers and take a detour through the jungle using African guides and a chain of safehouses.[17] On 17 August 1912, a union agent in Lourenço Marques wrote to the immigration restriction officer, Durban, tipping him off about a party of seven Indians (all on the prohibited list) and a 'kafir' guide heading for Durban or Glencoe in Natal. Hormasjee Cawasji Variawa, a Parsi also known as 'Bali Dali', was accompanying them from the Portuguese Swaziland border, taking them south to the northern bank of the Pongola River by train to a station just before Vryheid where he had a house. Police claimed that another Parsi, Framji Soorabjee Koopa of Dundee, was also involved.[18]

Illegal migrants were given training to fake their way through a test of domicile. They were taught common words in English, Dutch and 'Kaffir', told names of railways stations and given a description of the town they were purportedly from, with the Indian neighbourhood, the post office and the magistrate's court mapped out. The authorities often received tip-offs: an Indian storekeeper, R.S. Devay of Fairbreeze Hotel Tongaat, Natal, wrote to the attorney general, Durban, and police superintendents of Durban and Pietermaritzburg, to complain about 'hundreds and hundreds of Indians' landing in Natal and entering on false pretences.[19] In November 1906, an untidy handwritten letter from a 'Suratwala' complained that Parbhoo Govind and Nana Narn had entered through Delagoa Bay in September on false papers: 'They do business in Bombay presidency making lots of money on human trafficking through Delagoa Bay'.[20] These tip-offs reflected rivalries between Indians and were of dubious credibility. But by 1912, 1,080 fraudulent certificates and another 1,665 'old certificates' (i.e. those without thumb impressions) still in use had been confiscated in Durban. Arthur P. Donnelly, an ex-constable, was discovered at home in 1910 with a fingerprint apparatus and a large batch of blank certificates bearing forged signatures.[21]

35

The Unravelling

The British Empire liked rules. And discipline. Milner wanted to modernize South Africa and thrust the old-fashioned, rustic Boers into an efficient new future. Curtis wanted to make a city with clear lines for different races. British rule was all about regulation and standardization. But in fact, disorder and an inordinately high degree of corruption reigned in the immigration system, as was evident from the state of affairs exposed in Cape Town and Durban.

Revelations from the Transvaal were even more disconcerting. The British Indian Association accused Chamney, one of the architects of the Black Act, of accepting bribes remitted to a London account.[1] No direct evidence was offered but the discovery of a thousand cases of forgery in his department in the preceding six months alone was damaging. After taking over 900 pages of complaints from more than 200 Transvaal Indians, the commissioner of a 1915 inquiry concluded that the Pretoria office had been 'entirely abandoned to the most ingenious and vicious frauds by perjury and deceit'.[2]

In March 1906, two detectives, O'Rorke and Savage, saw a blank Asiatic Permit Form (No. 13865) in the possession of an Indian who informed them that these forms were being sold for £15 each at the permit office in Pretoria by Mr Cody, principal clerk and second-in-command to Chamney. The matter somehow reached the lieutenant governor's ears and on enquiring of the governor, Lord Selborne, he was told:

31st March 1906
My Dear Sir Richard,
The enclosed memorandum from Fowle (ex-Chief Secretary of Permits in the Transvaal) shows that neither he nor Curtis is to blame for the theft of the Permit Forms, which appears to have been solely due to the carelessness of a clerk employed by Curtis ...[3]

Another prominent figure to be implicated was the fingerprint expert Henry Burley, who had been transferred to the Asiatics division of the Department of the Interior and had begun the process of fingerprinting Asian males in the Transvaal from 1907. Investigators found Burley's record cabinets consistently unlocked and insecure. Initial visits by the commissioner found Burley in 'an excitable and agitated state of mind'.[4] Acting on legal advice, Burley refused to give evidence and immediately resigned from his post. The commissioner urged a warrant of arrest and reported to the minister of the interior that 'a very vast field of crime has only been slightly exposed'. The department suffered from 'deeply hidden corruption' and had been under the 'mysterious control' of agents.[5]

Clearly, the impression of order and rectitude exuded by the administration was a façade. A closer look reveals that civil servants who appeared indomitable in their effort to restrict Indian immigration were not only weak and corruptible but also acutely fragile themselves, being vulnerable to all kinds of setbacks and frequently disappointed by their seniors.

In 1913, for instance, Wilfred Cousins, the formidable chief immigration officer in Cape Town, was stabbed with an 18-inch butcher's knife in a case of mistaken identity. The assailant was an Indian migrant who had been fleeced by an Indian agent and told that the exorbitant fee for processing his papers was a bribe for the 'white man'. Enraged and assuming that the white man referred to was Cousins, the Indian attacked him. The pertinacious officer, so dogged in his dutifulness, his piety and efforts to better his situation, apparently had had no inkling of the murky goings-on in his department and their revelation could not have sat easy on his broad shoulders. He never spoke much publicly about Indians thereafter and claimed that 'the career of a lifetime' had been damaged.[6]

I look up Henry Burley's partner, Cecil Harcourt Lees, and find that he was sent to France to fingerprint 100,000 Chinese recruited by the British to support the frontline troops as labourers on the western front during the First World War. The work of fingerprinting went on in large sheds with records maintained by a sizeable staff of army clerks and an extensive equipment of vertical filing apparatus. After the war, Lees went on to work for the Intelligence Service in Ireland and was shot in 1921 outside a hotel in Dublin by four young men belonging to an Irish Republican Army (IRA) unit.[7]

A less dramatic story but one that speaks eloquently of the potentially risky fate awaiting a civil servant is the one I piece together from various archival entries concerning E.J. Burgess, the coast agent for Asiatic affairs in Durban.[8] Burgess, whose adverse report resulted in the rejection of Mohanlal's application to travel to the Transvaal, was shuttled from position to position in the Transvaal civil service which he had joined in 1900. He was with the customs department, a supervisor of Asiatics; a replacement for a Mr Jackson at Johannesburg; seconded to the Rand Plague Committee; a chief clerk in the Foreign Labour Department where his services were again requisitioned, this time by the colonial secretary, to act as registrar of Asiatics for four months and, later, in May 1906, when the Asiatic Department was established, appointed the government coastal agent at Durban on a salary of £500, a position he had to abruptly vacate.

The merry-go-round damaged his financial prospects. In a letter, he wrote: 'My position is unique ... I have twice risen to a responsible position carrying a salary of £500: On both occasions the result of transfer in the interests of the State, in the end I have been retrenched. Those I have left behind, live and flourish.' His colleagues had security, leave and pension while he lost gratuity amounting to four and a half months of full pay. He had reason to be bitter.

In between he tried for employment at the colonial office in England and in Canada, which he did not get, despite Lord Selborne recommending him for employment to the governor-general in Ottawa. Blessed with a 'strong physique', Burgess even tried his hand at farming. Eventually, in his early thirties, and not surprisingly, given the way he had been treated, he left the service of the Transvaal government. The last bit of information I find about him is that he had started business as a general agent (which would ironically have included dealing in permits) at 8 & 9, Rand Provident Buildings, Jost Street.

◆

On 28 April 1906, an Indian, C.M. Pillay, a sworn translator in the Transvaal Supreme Court, wrote a long and detailed official letter complaining about the poor functioning of the Asiatic Office.[9] Instead of a serious and thoughtful response, his letter drew a swift rebuke from Chamney who wrote to the colonial secretary:

> This is another case of a disappointed Asiatic Permit Agent who has lost his lucrative business through the transfer of the Permit Office to this Department, and now desires to throw

all the discredit he can upon its administration ... There is ample evidence that the man (Pillay) is notoriously mixed up in illicit Permit dealing, and similar evidence is in my possession regarding another Permit dealer Dr. Pereira, who is also Indian and an interpreter at the Magistrate's Court, Johannesburg.[10]

What is one to make of this?

Interpreters were apparently in an extremely advantageous position when it came to opportunities for engaging in malpractices involving permit fraud. They could freely enter record rooms and access cabinets where documents were kept and alter them if they were so inclined. Like lawyers, they were also in frequent contact with agents and permit seekers. The fact that so much of the business of illegal immigration revolved around documentation implied a degree of literacy and an ability to comprehend the laws, latest amendments to rules, loopholes and the required documentation for immigration. Mission-educated men and interpreters were pivotal to the enterprise and among the names thrown up by the investigations were members of the Indian social and professional elite.[11]

Officials then had reason to suspect Indian interpreters. But mixed with their justifiable suspicion was racial bias, which sharpened into disdain when faced with educated Indians. 'Killavala is an Indian of the worst Baboo type'[12] is how he was described in the official exchange regarding his application to settle in the Transvaal, the emphasis on 'Baboo type' suggesting, perhaps, a mocking of Indians mimicking Westerners. And with the term 'permit agent' being freely bandied about, one cannot be certain, for instance, about whether the men named were guilty as alleged.

Was Mohanlal really a permit agent or merely the victim of white bias? Like many other lawyers, his employer, Findlay, handled cases of immigration and dealt with permits. In the letters of the Indian lawyer M.H. Nazar I come across a reference to permits lying in his office on 14, Mercury Lane.[13] Findlay and Mohanlal may have been guilty of a single indiscretion involving a client when they helped a prohibited immigrant disembark, or they could be habitual offenders, but apart from being barred from visiting the Transvaal, Mohanlal suffered no long-term repercussions for the incident on the SS *General* as reported by Burgess. Findlay, who was alleged to have 'disappeared', continued to practise and build a successful career as a lawyer in Durban and was even licensed as a commissioner of oaths, while Mohanlal went on to interpret in the courts.

But, on the other hand, if Mohanlal was fully involved in the business of enabling unauthorized entry by Indians, as the correspondence between colonial officials in the folders of the Pretoria archives alleges, then I have to revisit my story and construct a new speculative theory to fit my findings.

How did it all begin, for instance? Gandhi was noticed as a good fit for Dada Abdullah's legal case by his brother while on a visit to their hometown, Porbandar. Is this what happened here as well? Did someone spot Mohanlal, a young man with a resourceful mind and proficiency in English, and recruit him for a part in a border-crossing enterprise? Who could it be? Someone from the migrant merchant communities around the Tapi, come home for a visit? Someone in Bombay, one of the many Parsi agents who boarded steamers arriving from South Africa to solicit residence certificates belonging to returning or deceased migrants?[14] Or someone connected with the Punjabi-owned passenger[15] and shipping agency at the docks which offered forged permits, tutoring for admission tests and lodgings to clients before departure, the whole exercise costing Rs 80, almost as much as the fare to South Africa? Or an acquaintance who had settled overseas and who wrote to him of plentiful opportunities?

Perhaps he had had no inkling of the enterprise when he left Bombay, only a zest for adventure and new horizons and a yearning to try his luck as an interpreter in foreign lands. Perhaps it was in Mauritius, in the island in the middle of the ocean, that he came to be aware of other ways to turn a buck. Perhaps someone, an interpreter on holiday from Natal or Pretoria or a local street smart, brought him up to speed. All we know is that he left Mauritius in 1905 with an endorsement from the governor, Sir Cavendish Boyle, similar to the one Randeria had from Zanzibar. In light of what I now know, the 'passport' could well have been forged; such testimonials and official letters were easily obtainable.[16]

Over the next few years, Mohanlal travelled to or tried to travel to places where it had become hard for Indians to enter. Durban, Johannesburg, Cape Town. What I took to be restlessness could be a dedicated permit agent exploring new possibilities emerging from tightened immigration restrictions. His eagerness to be enrolled as an interpreter in the courts and his employment at a white-owned law firm, which I presumed to be aligned with his personality and qualifications, were also useful attributes if he were so inclined to participate in permit fraud.

As I gather from various sources, the permit fraud business bore no taint. Many who functioned as agents, translating between aspiring migrants and immigration officials and providing necessary documents by hook or by crook, saw themselves as essentially helping their communities. Abdul Cadir countered charges of corruption and scheming with the immigration department in Cape Town in 1908 by painting himself as a prominent social worker.[17] With a well-oiled system in place for repurposing old documents or churning out fraudulent ones and handlers routinely accompanying prohibited immigrants across borders, Mohanlal may not have been unusual, but just a cog in the wheel.

It is when I come to what I assumed to be his emerging political consciousness that things become confusing. Between August 1907 and August 1908, he wrote to two separate officials taking umbrage at offences such as the wording of a letter written to him and a delay in inspecting his baggage. Was he genuinely outraged? Or was he possibly attempting to paint himself a victim of racial prejudice for use in his application to visit the Transvaal? As he writes in one letter: 'And what bitter feelings might be roused in the minds of the Indian Public, should I describe my experience before them?'

And then I come to the act that made him a Satyagrahi, his participation in the protest against the Asiatic Registration Act, an act of defiance ending in imprisonment. Let me go back to that day when Mohanlal left home for the railway station where he joined the group of educated protesters travelling from Durban to the Transvaal. As he made his way to the station amidst cheering crowds of Indian supporters, as he settled in the compartment where his fellow agitators were gathered, as the train took off and he saw the countryside speed by, what was he really thinking?

Mohanlal and his fellow Satyagrahis were given the job of heading off into various Transvaal towns to collect registration certificates, permits and trade licences for burning. Identification papers were the stock-in-trade for fraudsters dealing in permits. Whether they were merely appropriated, altered or forged, they were the mainstay of the business. The introduction of fingerprinting and better filing reduced fraud considerably but did not stop it.

One would think that the documents Indian migrants were submitting for burning were the kind of papers permit dealers would have acutely coveted on behalf of Indians eager to enter the colonies. If Mohanlal was indeed a permit dealer, this would have been akin to a burglar getting the key to a treasury. Gandhi's 'Letter from Johannesburg' for *Indian Opinion* (31 August 1908) refers to a mass meeting in Pretoria (not the same one Mohanlal attended on 23 August but presumably one held a few days later, on 28 August), but expresses disappointment and surprise with the low collection of passes: 'I must say that the number received was not so large as it should have been. In Pretoria, only 60 certificates were received.'[18]

Let me revisit the scene of 23 August then, on the grounds of the Hamidia Mosque. There were crowds. There was a cauldron and a fire. S. Haloo and U.M. Shelat were stokers. Rectangles of paper fluttered in the pot. Pale folded sheets against sooty metal. The light weight of paper forms, precious markers of identity, tossed in a cauldron. Cheers from the crowds, heat from the fire and Mohanlal close at hand. What did he do?

PART NINE

THE SEA

36

View from Mumbai

'Albertopolis' is the nickname given to a cultural district in South Kensington built from the proceeds of the Great London exhibition of 1851, which dazzled the world with its display of the empire's exotic curiosities and technological superiority. The Great London Exhibition was the brainchild of Albert, prince consort of Empress Victoria. His gilded bronze statue, surrounded by figures symbolizing colonial expansion, art, science and commerce, is the centrepiece of this district around which are arranged the Science Museum, the Victoria & Albert Museum and the Natural History Museum.

Bombay's Albertopolis sprang up around a statue of Edward VII astride a black horse at the southern edge of the esplanade. It housed the Bombay University, the Royal Institute of Science and the Prince of Wales Museum. The last-mentioned was a grand stone-walled edifice topped by a bulbous white dome, a cross between a Moorish castle and the Golconda fort, named after Albert's grandson, the future George V. Opposite the museum was Bombay's premier college, also my alma mater, named after the Presidency's illustrious governor, Mountstuart Elphinstone.

Entering through the tall gates of Elphinstone College, I am thrown back in time. It is exam season and in the late afternoon there is nobody about to interrupt my daydreaming. My footsteps echo through the stone-flagged corridors. Memories wash over me. A life-sized painting of Mountstuart Elphinstone looming over the staff room. Pigeon droppings on desks. The rancid taste of cheap tea over which we argued, oh-so passionately, about the issues of our times: jailed dissidents in the USSR and the anti-apartheid movement in South Africa. The dull gleam of a banister, the strum of a guitar in the sunlit courtyard ... It all floods back.

The stone walls of the corridors at ground level are separated from the outer walls of the building. In the space between these walls are storage rooms of the Maharashtra State Archives containing records of the erstwhile Bombay Presidency. The inner walls are pitted with arched recesses under which we whiled away time between classes. These recesses had grilles and occasionally, if someone had moved a stack of boxes or a crack appeared between cupboards, one caught a glimpse of men with handkerchiefs tied around their faces to protect them from dust as they worked in the shadowy rooms. But mostly we were oblivious to the mountain of colonial paper, correspondence between departments, countries, civil servants, petitions, orders, bills and what not, history and its wisdom, slowly mouldering away around us.

I say so to the sari-clad woman sitting in the office of the Maharashtra State Archives on the first floor. She is brisk, friendly and amused by my revelation. 'So, what has finally brought you here?' she asks. I hesitate. I recall the classroom next door, in the corner, at the head of a flight of wide stone stairs. I recall Miss Jussawalla, a Parsi, over six feet tall, the most brilliant and intimidating teacher I have ever known. She taught us Edmund Spenser's late sixteenth-century epic poem, *The Faerie Queene,* aimed 'to fashion a gentleman or noble person in vertuous and gentle discipline'.[1] The corner classroom was divided into two with a wooden partition. On the other side of the makeshift wall, my boyfriend took a class in political economy: 'From Jevons to Keynes'. I want to tell this nice woman that so much that happened here was responsible for sending me across an ocean to find my ancestors. In a sense, this is where it all began: growing up and becoming curious about the world, and my place in it. And this is why I am here. But an archive is a place of cold records and clear categories, not inchoate sensations, so I mutter something about immigration and customs and presently a few long ledgers and a well-thumbed directory are placed before me.

Fans ruffle the warm, humid air. In Yann Martel's *The High Mountains of Portugal* the protagonist, prying open an old handstitched volume in an archive, hears the spine make a 'sound of small bones breaking'. A similar anxiety makes me spread my arms protectively around the documents crackling dangerously in the breeze. I have no idea at all what I am doing here and what I hope to find. But as I get accustomed to reading notes written by hand, familiar names, places and events float up from old, brown-stained pages. On 5 June 1902, eminent lawyers and members of the Bombay Presidency Association wrote to the secretary of state for India in council, seeking relief for Natal-based Indians from 'pinprick legislation'.[2] The Surat Anjume Islam wrote to the Bombay governor on 9 September 1908 expressing concern about 'the zoolum (oppression) and partiality with which the natives of India are treated in Transwal and other parts of Africa'.[3]

Amod Watly, a thirty-year-old hawker with a scar on his left hand living in Church Street, Pietermaritzburg, and Ameersee Purshottam, a twenty-four-year-old sweet-maker, also with a scar on his left hand, were two among 800 passengers on the *Nowshera* leaving Bombay on 7 September 1901 for Natal, East London, Port Elizabeth and Cape Town. The protector of emigrants examined domicile certificates of passengers and 'passports' signed by Lord

Milner and wrote that: 'I have no reason to believe that the people are being sent under any system of organisation to defeat the provisions of the Emigrations Act. They allege they are sent for by relatives already there …'[4]

But officials in Bombay were aware that the arrival of the ship with its unusually large contingent of passengers would send alarm bells about an Indian invasion ringing in Cape Town. Letters passing back and forth between departments discussed 'the existing political condition in South Africa' rendering the presence of Indians there 'in increased numbers undesirable as being liable to involve the Government of India in problems difficult to deal with' and the use of plague as a ruse to curtail immigration (in a communication on 11 March 1903, the Government of India Home Department [Sanitary-Plague] urged the dropping of 'the farce of plague restrictions' since the Natal Government had 'long since adopted legislation to protect itself from immigration …'[5]).

Though they knew the possible consequences of letting the *Nowshera* depart with its surging passenger load, Bombay officials did not stop it because it was owned by the British India Steam Navigation Company whose chairman, Sir William Mackinnon, was closely allied with British political interests in East Africa. Germany was a political contender in the region and competition between the two nations was waged on many grounds, including over shipping (a telegram from the Home Department, Government of India, on 8 September 1901, admitted: 'we just started line with view prevent Germans monopolising trade'[6]).

From the expanded perspective offered by the colonial office in Bombay, one can see how the needs of commerce and geopolitics clashed with the keenness of South African authorities to limit Indian immigration. The desire of some white colonists in South Africa for Indian labour also blurred the clear racial boundaries laid down by anti-immigration laws. Geo W. Hoare wrote to the protector of emigrants, Bombay, on 16 July 1902 to say: 'I have lately returned from South Africa with the express purpose of engaging and taking back to South Africa Indian servants for some of the principal clubs and hotels in Pretoria, Johannesburg, Blomfontein and Pietermaritzburg.' Undeterred by an unfavourable response, Hoare sought a personal interview with the chief secretary, Government of Bombay, pointing out that 'the Rand Club Johannesburg is the wealthiest Club in South Africa and counts amongst its members the most influential financial men in that country'. Anticipating further hurdles he advertised in Indian newspapers (*Advocate of India* and *The Times of India*) for applicants, proposing to take them, surreptitiously it seems, to South Africa via Delagoa Bay.[7]

I recall a similar plea in the Pretoria archives from a Mr Silverthorne, who was importing 110 camels in 1904 to 'complete an experiment' that required the animals to trek all over the country after entering from Delagoa Bay. When he was told to hire locally instead of bringing twenty Indians from Zanzibar to handle the animals, he insisted that he needed 'men who are thoroughly conversant with the habits of the camel'[8] and set out for Zanzibar anyway.

37

Mohan at Home

At the archives in the Sabarmati Ashram in Ahmedabad, which house an extensive collection of Gandhi's papers, I come across a letter written by Mohanlal to Gandhi. The letter dated 16 September 1913 was written from Poona, a city 150 kilometres from Bombay. From the internet I find his name on a list at an educational institution in the city, so I presume he had a job there after his return from overseas. He appeared to have found work in keeping with his pedagogical inclinations, a far cry from his purported adventures. He made no mention of those in his letter but did refer to his jail term as a Satyagrahi. By this time, it is likely that Foolkore had passed away and my grandmother was in the care of her stepmother.

This letter to Gandhi is handwritten in pencil, a scrawl filling up two small sheets of beige paper. Mohanlal spelt his surname differently and expressed a desire to return to Durban. I find no response from Gandhi.

Ravivar Peth
Poona 16/9/13
M.K. Gandhi Esq
My Dear Sir
I have a mind to return to Durban where I have lived for over 2 years. I shall be obliged if you will kindly let me know whether my claim to enter the Colony of Natal should be based on my previous stay in the Colony or the Immigration authorities will require me to pass the usual Test. The chief point is the statement in the application to enter, that the applicant has not been convicted etc. You know, I was one of the natal people who entered the Transvaal and I suffered six weeks. Does this conviction come in the way of the applicant - anyway should I inform the Immigration authorities about this verbally or in the application or whether I can write the application as usual and maybe no statement about the said affair.
Hope you and family are well.
Yours Sincerely
Mohanlal P. Killawalla[1]

38

Sea Tales

From 1888 to 1931, Gandhi made fifteen voyages. He was a good sailor, steady-footed on the swaying deck, enjoying the 'stormy surge and the splash of the waves' and captivated by the moon and stars dancing in the water. In *The Good Boatman: A Portrait of Gandhi*, his grandson Rajmohan Gandhi points out that while hospitals, law courts, railways and cars were attacked in Gandhi's critique of modern life, *Hind Swaraj*, ships were spared. In 1925 Gandhi said that 'the sea was an epitome of adventures' and that Indians 'needed the spirit of adventure in their national life'.[1]

Emigration folders in the Maharashtra State Archives show the spirit of adventure and a desire for marine excursions well and kicking among Indians of the time. Letters pour into the Bombay government asking for information. Murli Dhar Sharma writes on a sheet of onion paper from Jangi Chabutra Ajmer requesting: 'Will you kindly send "The Rules & Regulations" which a man desirous of going to serve as a clerk in His Majesty's dominions in Africa should be acquainted with.'[2] Hirji Fulji of Juna Bazar Brouch writes in a light, running hand about his plan to travel to Africa with 'one man named Dulpat Ram Bhaishanker' and asks about a passport ('I am given to understand by the Public that a pass-port is required for entrance to these places').³ The protector of emigrants and superintendent, preventive services, writes on 7 May 1900: 'The east coast of Africa from Natal to Suakin, and the adjacent islands of Zanzibar, Madagascar, Seychelles, the Mauritius and Réunion are full of Indians in almost every walk of life, and as they are not permanent settlers there is a continuous stream of Indians backward and forward.'⁴

The mobility was unstoppable, one finds. Towards the end of the nineteenth century, an outbreak of jigger (a skin infection from sand fleas) caused a temporary suspension of emigration from Bombay but, as a flurry of letters from health officials and political agents and their assistants reveals, steamers started stopping to pick up transoceanic travellers at smaller ports along the western coast. Passengers set out for Zanzibar and Madagascar from lesser-known ports such as Nawanagar, Junagadh, Bhavnagar, Porbandar and Mandvi in such profusion that the commissioner of customs felt concerned enough to write on 15 March 1900 that 'if matters continue thus, it is not improbable that there may very soon be little or no embarkation of such passengers at Bombay itself'.⁵

Telegrams and letters flowing between colonial offices around the ocean and Indian government departments point to the ebb and flow of employment opportunities and migrant traffic. A rumour that 'a great many Indians are leaving for Chinde hoping to be able to work for Central African Railways' invites a warning on 7 May 1903 from His Majesty's commissioner, British Central Africa: 'Please inform proper authorities there is no prospect of employment on Railways or elsewhere in Protectorate.'⁶ In April 1901, Messrs Killick Nixon & Co., agents of The Perim Coal Co. Ltd., seek clarifications on hiring labourers under the Indian Emigration Act 1883. There is movement from Jullundur and Hoshiarpur to Australia. And in November 1902, the Seychelles is being promoted: Passage with food for deck passengers is Rs 25 each; climate is 'hot but healthy';

sailing time from Madras to Seychelles for steamers during the northeast monsoon is ten days and during the southwest monsoon, fifteen days, while sailing vessels take five and six weeks respectively.[7]

The circulation of people across the ocean was not driven by hard labour alone. In 1897, Sir Sultan Muhammed Shah, Aga Khan III, the forty-eighth Imam of the Nizari Ismaili community (later, in 1906, one of the founders and the first president of the All-India Muslim League) married Shahzadi Begum, the daughter of his uncle Aga Jhangi Shah, in Poona. He married again, Mlle Theresa Maglioni in Cairo in 1908, and twice thereafter, but this wedding was his first and members of his peripatetic business community packed their finery and set out on steamers to attend.[8]

Then in 1900 a party of Indian jugglers and dancers prepared to set out for Trieste, having been engaged to perform at the exhibition in Paris for a payment of Rs 500–600 each, or so the Articles of Association of the 'Societe des Grande Attractions' to which the party was contracted said. Thomas Cook was the facilitator and the person making arrangements at the India end was a certain Motilal Nehru, whose son would become free India's first prime minister.[9]

◆

Bombay's Albertopolis is no more. Edward VII and his horse have long been toppled and reportedly lie in some overgrown corner of the local zoo. The Prince of Wales Museum has been renamed the Chhatrapati Shivaji Maharaj Vastu Sangrahalaya after the warrior king of the Deccan. The 'Royal' has been deleted from the Royal Institute of Science and, in any case, India's latest stories of scientific and technological prowess, particularly in space and software, are playing out elsewhere, in the southern city of Bengaluru. Bombay University, now the University of Mumbai, one of the world's largest universities, has moved to the suburbs, leaving behind ornate buildings like empty shells. Post-colonialism arrived like a tidal wave sometime towards the close of the twentieth century, putting African and Indian texts on the syllabus of the English department. Mine was one of the last to receive a more classical literary education, which included Shakespeare, the Romantics and Chaucer's colourful *Canterbury Tales*.

> *Thanne longen folk to goon on pilgrimages*
> *And palmeres for to seken straunge strondes*
> *To ferne halwes, kowthe in sondry londes;*
> *And specially from every shires ende*
> *Of Engelond to Caunterbury they wende,*

> (Then folk long to go on pilgrimages,
> And palmers to visit foreign shores,
> To distant shrines known in many lands;
> And specially from every shire's farthest end
> Of England, they travel to Canterbury)[10]

And now, here, in this book, I believe I have written some travelling tales of my own people.

Acknowledgements

It would be clear from reading this book and the citations, how much I owe to a great many scholars and writers whose work provided the foundation and the scaffolding within which I could make sense of my findings. I was fortunate also to be helped by the generosity of friends and acquaintances.

Many of these have been referred to in the text, and others I mention here.

I am grateful for advice and introductions to Gopal Gandhi, Prabhakara S. Motnahalli, Achal Prabhala, Debjani Banerjee, Ishani Duttagupta, Munish Gupta, Prashant Hedao, Rahul Vohra, Miriam Joseph, Geeta Rao and Ingrid Srinath.

In Mauritius, my thanks to Ouma Seebaluck, Babita Bahadoor, Amenah Jahangeer-Chojoo, Sada Reddi, Vijaya Teelock, Dolly and Parenivel Pillay Mauree and Rachna and Dr H. Gopal.

In South Africa, my thanks to Isabel Hofmeyr, Sharad Chari, Dilip Menon, Ashwin Desai, Thembisa Waetjen, Ruth and Goolam Aboobaker, Marcel Henry, Stan Joseph and Gegê Leme. To fellow travellers William Jackson and Pauline Conley; and a special mention for Marleen Roberts who I wish was still here for me to share the book with.

Acknowledgements

My thanks to the efficient and hard-working staffers at all the various archives and libraries I frequented and to the collectors and guides in the field. To Salim Mulla and Ahmed Randeria in Kholvad and Kathor respectively for sharing their collection of materials on Sunni Bohra émigrés. To Kiran Desai at the Centre for Social Studies in Surat and to Ramesh Sevak who facilitated my meetings in the villages outside Surat. To Urvish Kothari for helping me locate a biography of a nineteenth-century adventurer in Ahmedabad. To Tridip Suhrud and Kinnari Bhatt for facilitating my work at the Sabarmati Ashram Preservation and Memorial Trust.

This book could not have been accomplished without assistance from a number of institutions and fellowships.

Travel grants from the Homi Bhabha Fellowships Council (2012-13), the Indian Council of Historical Research (2013) and the Dorabjee Tata Trust (2015) partly covered my overseas travel expenses. My thanks to the late Shashi Chitre and the late A.N. Singh for their support.

The Centre for Contemporary Studies (CCS) at the Indian Institute of Science (IISC) was my home for the first half of the writing of this book. My heartfelt thanks to IISC, to the CCS chairman, Raghavendra Gadagkar and to my CCS family. In particular, to my colleague the eminent historian Rajan Gurukkal for encouraging and validating my instinctive approach.

I am grateful for a rewarding stint as a writing fellow at the Johannesburg Institute for Advanced Study (JIAS) in 2018. Thank you, Peter Vale and everyone who kept the wheels at JIAS turning. I am grateful also for a residency at the Institute for Advanced Study in Nantes in 2019. Thank you, Alain Supiot and Françoise Rubellin for the space and the opportunity. Thank you Pushkar and the trustees of the International Centre, Goa for the time and space in 2022 to complete the manuscript. I was lucky to engage with a community of erudite scholars and writers in each of these places

Acknowledgements

and the feedback I received on my presentations has fed into the book in numerous ways.

I also presented a part of this work at the 2021 Spring School in Family History for the Srishti Manipal Institute of Art, Design and Technology's Center for Public History. Thank you, Indira Chowdhury for inviting me and for our conversations over the years.

Thank you, Sonu Chinna, Hutokshi Doctor and Ashok Gopal for providing valuable feedback along the way. And my fellow Elphinstonian, Piyali Warner, for the translation from Middle English. Thank you Parikshit Dalal and Ramona Adhikari for the much-needed escape hatches in Bengaluru. Thank you Hemal Shah and Anju Venkat (my guardian angels), Nilofer Rustomji, Arup Mukherjee, Chitrita Majumdar, Navina Venkat, Sumita Hattangadi, Nandu Rao, Bishaka Datta and Kerman and Nitin Nadkarni for getting me through the last, unexpected hurdle.

To Bikram Grewal and Uday Balakrishnan, my thanks for your kind interventions.

Thanks to the wonderful team at HarperCollins India: To Udayan Mitra for his unstinted support and enthusiasm for the book. To Swati Chopra, ex-HCI, for our initial parleys. And to Amrita Mukerji and Gayatri Goswami for wrestling with the manuscript with care, thoughtfulness and precision (and much gratitude, Gayatri, for your meticulousness).

And thanks to my agent, the force that is Kanishka Gupta, for so assiduously and capably steering the book out into the world.

◆

My grandmother, who I call Damayanti in this account because I am told it was her given name at birth though nobody called her that, died in 1998. My mother died two years later. Their passing was a trigger for me to think seriously about pursuing the puzzle that had preoccupied me since I was a child. Partly, it was the realization that time was fleeting and partly it was the feeling that enough time had passed for the events of the past to have acquired an air of abstractedness. Some of us are given to asking questions that add to our understanding of the world. I was fortunate that aunts, uncles and cousins of my extended maternal clan agreed to further my inquiry by sharing with me their thoughts and memories and searching for photographs, letters and other possible remnants of the past. My deep gratitude to them. Some did not live to see the book, but I carried the idea of you and the story that ties us across the seas.

Notes

Scan this QR code to access the notes.

Index

Aapravasi Ghat, 115, 118
Abdullah, Dada, 165-66, 169-70, 176, 183, 197, 218
Abdurahman, Abdullah, 265–67
Abraham, 199
Adajan neighbourhood of Surat, 308
Aden, 4, 51, 126
Aeneid, 28
Africa, 3, 6, 9, 38, 52, 66, 70, 75, 125
African Boating Company, 169
African National Congress, 77
Afrikaners, 289
after the war, 281–88, 294
Aga Khan III, 374
agents of The Perim Coal Co. Ltd., 373
Age of Discovery, 8
agricultural labour in Natal, 174
Ahmedabad, 11, 219, 324, 370
Ahmed, Sheik, 196

Ajam Goolam Hoosen & Co., 165
Alaska, 66
Al-Bahr-Al-Hindi, 4, 6
Algoa Bay, 59
Allibhai, 350
Ally, H.O., 302
almanacs, 96
Ambulance Corps, 192, 201, 203, 219, 312
Ameenah (Charoux), 117
America, 9, 31, 33, 62
American Civil War, 1865, 36
American Revolutionary War, 16
Amod, Aboobaker, 165–67, 169, 218
  arrest, 176
  death, 197
Anassamy, Vellivahel, 113
ancillary jobs, 69
Andhra Pradesh, 21
Andrews Library, Surat, 28

383

Anglia, M.C., 240, 310-11, 314, 317
Anglo-Boer War, 42, 71, 106, 191, 195, 200–03, 262, 281-82, 284-85, 288, 294, 312, 344
Anglo-German ancestry, 282
Anglo-Indian community, 221
Anglo-Indian interpreters, 240
Anjuman-e-Islam Hall, 317
anti-apartheid, 77, 366
anti-Asian legislation, 178, 181
anti-Asiatic league, 182
anti-colonialism, 77
anti-immigration laws, 346, 368-69
   in Natal, 292
anti-Indian legislation, 216
Arabian Sea, 3, 45
Arabia/Arabs 6, 15, 17, 105, 143, 175, 178
Arbuthnot, E., 113
archipelago, 20, 109
Ardan Steam Ship Co., 130
A.R. Mackenzie & Company, 263
Armenians, 15
art deco façades, 40
Arundel Castle, 231
Arya Samaj, 224
Asiatic Act, 308, 316
Asiatic community in the Transvaal, 292
Asiatic immigration, 286, 316
Asiatic Law Amendment Act, 303, 338
Asiatic Law Amendment Ordinance, 300, 302
Asiatic Registration Act, 305, 307, 331, 361
Asiatic Registration legislation, 304
Assam Valley Light Horse, 294
Astrabad, 19
Atchia, Ibrahim, 147
Atchias, 147-148
Atlantic, 8, 12, 58, 256
Attenborough, Richard, 77
Aubeelack, Kushroo, 151
Aungier, Gerald, 24, 50
Australia, 3, 39, 51-52, 59, 66, 180, 256, 373
Avenue Belle Rose, 147

Badassy, Prinisha, 81–83, 239
Badat, 167
badge of slavery, 316
bafta, 10, 12, 14
bagla, 4, 6
Bahrain, 45
'Baía da Lagoa,' 165
Baker, Herbert, 72
Balaji Chakla, 13-14
Balgobine, Prayag, 134
'Bali Dali,' 352
Ballard Pier, 47-48, 53
Bangalore, 110
Bank of Bombay, 32, 35-36, 48, 258
Bank of Western India, 32

Bantu, 60-61
Banyans, 13, 15, 351
Barbodhan, 7, 39, 147–149
Basra, 6, 11
Bassa, Ebrahim, 262
Batembu, 65
batilas, 12
Bay of Natal, 61, 211
'Bay of the Lagoon,' 165
Beau-Bassin Rose Hill, 147-48
Begum, Shahzadi, 374
Beira, 52, 169, 350
Bell, William, 196
Bengal, 17, 21, 150, 291
Bengali juncos, 11
Benjamin, Walter, 303
Benson, A.C., 51
Berea, 85, 231-32, 237
Berlin Conference, 70
Bertillon, Alphonse, 287
Bhabha, 167
Bhaishanker, Dulpat Ram, 372-73
Bhana, Surendra, 345
Bhat Bazaar, 48
Bhavnagar, 126, 373
Bickaji, Ratanji, 112-13, 148
Big Hole, 65
Bihar, 21, 110, 114
Bikhda, Dayal, 222
Biographical History of Gonville and Caius College, 1349-1897, 232
birames, 11
Biuhmont, 349
Black Act, 76, 304, 308, 344, 354

Blue Book of 1902, 134
blue-collar jobs, 262
Boatawala, Haji Eesop, 38, 42
Boatawalas, 144
Bobat, 167
Boer-ruled Orange Free State, 178-79
Boers, 60-61, 64-65, 68, 71, 73, 191-92, 200, 217, 241, 257, 281, 284, 290, 293, 313, 318, 351, 354
  farmers, 66
  farms, 65
  hostility and resentment, 289
  nationalism, 282
Bombaim, 20
Bombay, 20–22, 24–27, 29, 31, 33, 36, 41-42, 44, 51, 90, 97, 101, 106-07, 112-13, 126, 130, 133, 143-44, 158-59
  city-building spree, 46
  as commercial city, 32
  large clock tower, 45–47
  neighbourhoods, 44
  old harbour, 50
  Taj Mahal Palace, 50
  university library, 45-46
Bombay Bank, 35
Bombay Chamber of Commerce, 33
Bombay Gazette, 52
Bombay Gazetteer, 35, 37
Bombay Green, 31, 33, 34
Bombay Marine, 20

Index

Bombay Native School, 26
Bombay port, 34, 38
Bombay Presidency, 26, 34, 167, 243, 353, 366-67
Bombay Supreme Court, 30
Bombay Town Hall, 31
Bombay University School Final Examination, 336
Bon Espoir estate, 113
Boolell, Shakuntala, 124
Booly Brothers, Essack and Tooraben, 261
Booth, Parker, 185, 192, 199
Bori Bunder station, 31-32
Botha, Louis, 289, 303, 338, 340
Botswana, 39
Boycott, Charles, 305
Boyle, Cavendish, 133-34, 212, 305, 329, 332, 360
Braamfontein, 81
Brahmins, 17, 22, 29, 47, 92, 119, 219
Breckenridge, Keith, 287
Briggs, Henry George, 40
Britain, 21, 24-25, 59, 66, 69, 71
British, 59, 64, 67, 73, 106, 112–14, 116, 126, 132, 134, 143, 151
   citizenship, 218-19
   colony, 59
   democracy, 265
   liberalism, 73
   metropolitanism, 48
British Central Africa, 373
British Constitution, 265
British consul of Zanzibar, 218-19, 312
British East India Company, 230
British Empire, 21, 71, 74, 113, 191, 233, 346, 354
British Guiana, 22, 51
British Indian Association, 285, 300, 304, 313, 315, 354
British Indian Citizen, 336
British Indian community of the Transvaal, 302
British Indian League of Cape Town, 311, 314
British Natal Direct Line, 169
Britishness, 108
British Parliament, 23, 185
British royal family, 167
British settlers, 59, 70, 190-91
British Slave Compensation Act 1837, 114
British superiority, 282
Brittany, 11
Brown-Séquard, Charles Édouard, 133
Bruce Fawcett & Co., 32
Bulfontein, 65
Burgess, Edwin John, 294, 334, 338, 340-41, 356-57
Burhanpur, 11
Burley, Henry, 288, 297, 355
Burma, 25, 51
Bushmen, 58, 60, 65
business opportunities in South Africa, 166
Butler, Joseph, 179

Byrne, Joseph Charles, 62, 85

Cabo da Boa Esperança, 58
Cabo das Tormentas, 58
Cadir, Abdul, 263, 349, 360
Calcutta, 16, 21, 26, 32, 120, 165, 167, 294, 350
calicoes, 12
California, 66
Cambay, 5-6, 9, 11
campaigning against discriminatory laws in Natal, 284
Campbell, Margaret Roach 'Killie,' 85-86
Campbell, Marshall, 85
Camp des Lascars, 112
Camp Malabar, 112
Canada, 51, 59, 180, 357
Candia, 70
Canterbury Tales, 375
Cape, 21, 58-59, 61, 64, 66
  diamond deposits, 64
  mineral wealth, 66
Cape Colony, 61, 71, 95, 200, 252–54, 256, 261, 264, 271, 282, 295, 308, 347
Cape Government Railways, 263
Cape Malays, 263-64
Cape of Good Hope, 58, 95, 169-70, 256, 261
Cape Snoek, 264
Cape Times, 252-53
Cape Town, 72, 92-93, 95, 100-01, 251-52, 255-56, 268, 276, 347-48, 355-56, 360, 368
  Mohanlal in, 260–67
Cape Town Archives Repository, 82, 94, 252
caravels, 11
Carisbrook Castle, 224
Carlisle, Aurthur E., 218, 229
Carlton Centre, 75
Cassim, Mamode, 134
Cassim, Moosa Hajee, 166, 169-70, 218
caste, 90
  -based social hierarchy, 49
  from Gujarat, 169
Castle Wine & Brandy Company, 263
Catholicism, 285
Cato Creek, 167
Cato, George Christopher, 196
Caudan Waterfront, 114
Central African Railways, 373
Central Market, Port Louis, 142
certificates of exemption, 228, 295
Ceylon, 21, 51
Chamberlain, Joseph, 187, 200-01, 287
Chamber of Mines, 67
Chamney, Montfort, 293-94, 300, 306, 315, 331, 333, 335–38, 340, 354-55, 357
Charlestown, 184, 194-95, 308, 313
Charmoy, D'Emmereyde, 197
Charoux, Clément, 117
Charter Act of 1813, 25

Chartered Mercantile Bank of
    India, 32
Chatsworth, 88
Cheonlong & Co., 222
Chettiar Hindu community, 113
Chhaganlal, 202
Chhatrapati Shivaji Maharaj Vastu
    Sangrahalaya, 374-75
China/Chinese, 15, 24-25, 31-32,
    69-70
    labourers, 287–289
    labour system, 290
    prisoners, 262
Chinai, Chimanlal Chabildas, 43
Chinese Association, 306
chintzes, 12
Chitta, Somji, 14
choksis (assayers of gold and
    silver), 13
cholera, 20, 117, 197
Chongson & Co., 222
Chopra, Deepak, 189
Chowson & Co., 222
Christians, 9, 15
    era, 27
    free Indians, 185, 199
    Indians, 176, 182, 224
    mission, Port Natal, 85
    morality, 186-87, 290
Christian Emigration and
    Colonisation Society, 62
Christian Socialist Movement, 282
Chronological Tables (Patel), 27
Churchill, Winston, 302, 344

Cities of Gujarashtra (Briggs), 40
City of Palaces, 143
civil servant, 201, 239, 287, 335,
    356
Civil Status Enquiry Office, 137
clandestine trade, 24-25
*Classification and Uses of Finger
    Prints*, 287-88
cleanliness and temperance, 184-
    85
Coast Agent for Asiatic Affairs at
    Durban, 337, 339-40, 356
coastal steamers, 47
Coast Guard service, 48
Colesberg Kopje, 65
Colombo, 107
colonial/colonialism, 70, 74
    authorities, 204-05, 231, 339
    capital of Goa, 164-65
Colonial Office in London, 134,
    185, 256, 338
Colonial Secretary's Office (CSO),
    211, 297
colonizer's language, 343
coloured immigration, 302
colour prejudice, 178, 190-91,
    315
Columbus, 9
Commercial Bank of India, 32
communal suffering, 305
community service, 41
Compagnie des Indes, 11
Confederate ports, 34
conflagration, 23

Congella, 67, 230
conversazione, 46
Cook, Thomas, 374
coolies, 22, 62, 115, 143, 178
Corps de Garde, 121
cosmopolitanism, 50, 158, 290
Cotton Green, 31
cotton mania, 31–43, 46
country boats, 11
Cousins, Clarence Wilfred, 254-55, 355-56
Cowley, Bernard, 229, 237
Cowley, Cecil, 237-38
Cowley & Cowley, 229, 339
Cowley, Messrs, 261
Cowrie Castle, 253, 257
Creole-style houses, 124, 142
Creole woman, 144, 147-48, 153
Crescent, 169-70
Criminal Investigation Department, 234, 288, 348
Crown Mines, 68
Crown rule, 31
cultural enrichment, 292
cultural nourishment, 175
cultural primitivism, 149
Currie, Donald, 169-70
Curtis, Lionel, 282, 285, 293–95, 297-98, 300, 344
custom houses, Tapi, 17

Da Gama, Vasco, 8-9, 58, 160
Dahyabhai, 351-52
Daily Mail, 316

'Dakshin Afrika Darshan ane Be Mitre-no Samvaad,' 224
Dalal Street, 49
Dalpatram, 28
Damayanti, 89, 258
Dasgupta, Maitreyee, 151
Dasha Porwad vania community, 43
da Silveira, Antonio, 9
Dave, Narmadashankar Lalshankar, 22–24
David, 199
Dawood, Abdullah, 348
Dealer's Licence Act, 1897, 217
De Beers Consolidated Mines Limited, 66
Deccan, 16, 32, 374
degradation, 299–303
De Jagers Drift, 194-95
de La Bourdonnais, Bertrand-François Mahé, 111, 113, 131, 150
Delagoa Bay, 52, 71, 165-66, 169, 217, 350–53, 369
Delhi, 105
Democratic Republic of Congo, 39
Department of Arts and Culture, 211
d'Épinay, Adrien, 114, 132
Derby Street, Greyville, 100
Desai, Girish, 145
Desai, Maganlal Prabhalal, 41
Desai, Ratanjee, 145

de Saint-Pierre, Jacques-Henri Bernardin, 149
descendants of Ishmael, 179
'Deshatan' (Mulji), 43
Deutsch Ost-Afrika Line, 255-56
Devaldevli, 243-45
dhandho (business), 49
Dharmaji Jnasa, 323
Dharma Vichar, 179
Dhobis, 169
Dholka, 10
Dhupelia-Mesthrie, Uma, 254, 345-46
diamond,
  deposits, 64
  diamond-processing industry, 39
  fields, 64-65
  production, 66
Diamond Fields Advertiser, 213
Dias, Bartolomeu, 58
diasporic population, 93
Dick, Godfrey, 194, 295
dingris, 12
dirāt al-matlaq, 4
Discourse of Western Planting (Hakluyt), 59
discovery of gold, 38, 68
discriminatory colonial education policy, 267
disenfranchisement, 181-82
distorted gender ratio, 175
District Six, 263–65
Diu, 11

Dockrat, 167
documentation, 134, 159, 251, 295, 358
documents for legal entry, 159
domicile certificate, 159, 228, 339, 349
Donnelly, Arthur P., 353
Dooknah, J., 134
Draft Ordinance, 302
Drakensberg, 61
Dryden, John, 28
Dr Yusuf Dadoo Street, 162, 199, 203
Duncan, Patrick, 300
Dundee Agricultural Society, 307
Dunning, A.R., 220, 243
Durban, 52, 61-62, 77-78, 80, 82, 84, 87–89, 92, 95-96, 98-99, 166, 180, 196, 216, 222, 230, 237, 251-52, 261, 352-53, 360
  harbour, 180, 342
  traders, 167-68
Durban Bay, 183
Durban Bus Terminal, 86
Durban City Hall, 95
Durban Club, 161-62, 231
D'Urban Elephant, 84–87, 98-99
Durban Harbour, 85, 180, 342
Durban Indian Public Library, 221
Durban–Pietermaritzburg transport, 86
Durban Town Council, 217
Durban Turf Club, 233
Dutch, 9, 11, 16, 59

convoy, 105
ships, 106
Dutch East India Company, 11, 59, 105, 262
Dutoitspan, 65
Dwarka, 44, 165

East Africa, 25, 52, 164-65, 368
East Asia, 11
eastern belt, India, 21
Eastern Cape, 99, 197-98
East India Company, 171-72
East London Convict Station, 254
Edith Cavell Street, 131, 135-36
educated protesters, 310–19
Edwardian gentility, 267
Edwardian-style mosque on West Street, 216
Edward VII, 51, 297, 365, 374
Egypt, 21, 218, 282
Eldo Travels, 86-87
Elgin, Lord, 302, 338
Elphinstone College, 26, 28, 33, 366
Elphinstone, Mountstuart, 26, 365-66
embarkation permits, 228, 295
Emmanuel Anquetil Building, 135-36
Empire Palace of Varieties, 299–303
employment, 29, 160, 235, 288
Empress of India, 38, 69
England, 33-34, 64, 69, 116, 141, 172, 191

Englandma Pravas (Mulji), 27
English, 9, 16, 20, 26
-educated engineer, 201
emigrants, 62
imperialism, 59
language and lifestyle, 229
staffer, 14
English Company, 14
English East India Company, 11, 106
Bengal, 17
control in India, 16-17
educating Indians, 23, 26-27
factory, 15
indentured workers, 21-22
modern banks, 32-33
monopoly of, 25
naval force base, 20
president, lifestyle of, 15-16
revenues, 16
in Surat, 17
entrepreneurs, 25-26, 61, 70, 112
epidemic, 117, 132-33, 141, 159,
Erikson, Erik, 343
Escombe, Harry, 181, 183, 286
escutcheon, 16
Essack, Amod, 222
Essenwood, 85
Ethekwini Municipality, 95
European companies
imports, 12
presence along the Indian coast, 16
proliferation of, 13-14

Europe/European, 8-9, 11–13, 25, 27, 29, 34, 45-46, 58-59, 106, 111, 181
  ducats, 12
  language, 194, 292, 308
  merchants, 8
'Europeans Only' policy, 50
examination, 241–48
ex-indentured Indians, 65, 221
ex-indentured worker, 97

fabrics, 15
Faerie Queene, The, 366-67
family-oriented community, 224
famine, 37
Famous Bassa, 163
Fanagalo, 168
Farewell, F.G., 196
Farquhar, Robert, 112, 126
Fiji, 22
A Financial Chapter in the History of Bombay City (Vachcha), 36
Findlay, Archibald, 227–29, 232-33, 237-38, 248, 251
fingerprinting, 287-88
  Chinese workers, 297
firangis, 19
first class certificates, 242
first trader, 164–70
Folk Museum of Indian Immigration, 118
Foolkore, 95–101, 117–20, 148, 157-58, 161-62, 212, 215, 222, 224, 251-52, 258, 260, 263, 268
Forbes, Alexander Kinloch, 27
Forbes & Co., 32
Foreign Labour Department, 288, 297, 356
Fort Custom House, 48
France, 16, 64, 149-50, 288, 356
Franchise Act, 193
Franchise Law Amendment Bill, 181–83, 185, 187, 190, 192
Franco-Mauritian-dominated Legislative Council, 116
Franco-Mauritian elite, 113
Frangopaulos, Harry, 258-59
free immigration, 193
free Indians, 65, 67, 170, 197
free migrants, 21
French, 9, 11, 106, 112, 126, 141
French Company, 12, 16
French Crown Colony, 132
French East India Company, 111
French Huguenots, 59
French Revolution, 131, 149
Frere, Bartle, 46, 143
Frith & Co., 112
Fryer, John, 13
Fulji, Hirji, Juna Bazar Brouch, 372-73
Fulpada, 22
Fynn, Henry Francis, 196

Gabriel, Bernard, 221
gaddas, 13

Galton, Francis, 287
Gandevi weavers, 10
Gandhi Before India (Guha), 291-92
Gandhi (film), 77
Gandhi-Luthuli Documentation Centre, 86
Gandhi, Mohandas Karamchand, 43, 73–75, 92, 133, 170, 285, 305–07, 315
   affectations, 173
   arrest, 76-77
   birth, 171
   colonial administration, 292
   dietary experiments and health, 185
   in Durban, 171, 176
   English legal training, 174
   life in South Africa, 78
   in London, 173
   memorials, Johannesburg, 78
   in Natal, 174
   in Pretoria, 179
   in Rajkot, 172
   religious conservatism, 290
   return to India, 173
   in South Africa, 180
   vegetarianism and religious philosophy, 173-74
Gandhi, Rajmohan, 372
Gandhi Sites in Durban, 199-200
Gandhi Square, 75–83
Gandhi, Uttamchand, 171
Gangadas, 17-18, 20, 40

Gani, Abdul, 285, 300, 302
Gardiner, Allen Francis, 85
General Committee of Public Instruction, 23
General Dealers Act, 263
German Chancellery, Berlin, 70
German East African Line, 169-70
German/Germany, 59, 64
   shipping companies, 67
Ghafur, Mulla Abdul, 11-12, 37
Ghorkhodu, Rustomjee Jiwanji, 42
ghurabs, 12
Gilbert, Humphrey, 59
Girgaum, 44
Glendale Sugar Mill, 169
global fortune hunters, 67
Global Organization of People of Indian Origin, 98
Goa, 11, 164
Godani, Harilal, 126
Godfrey, James, 220
Godfrey, Subhan, 176, 225
Goga, 167
Gokhale, G.K., 291–93
gold, 38
   discovery of, 38, 68-69
   fever, 66
   fields, Transvaal, 67
   finds, 67
   mine dumps, 68
   smuggling, 125–27
Gold Nest hotel, 124
Gold Reef City, 68
Gombroon, 11

Gone with the Wind, 85
Good Boatman: A Portrait of Gandhi, The, 372
Goolam Baba Spinning and Weaving Co. Ltd., Bombay, 48, 259
Gool, Joosub, 264–67, 311-12
Gool, Selim Yusuf, 265
Gopalpura, 22
Goshalia, M.N., 312
Government Savings Bank Bombay, 48, 258
Govind, Parbhoo, 353
Graham, Maria, 26
Grand Bay Sugar Estate, 116
Grand Morcellement, 121
Great Britain, 16, 20
Great Escarpment, 61
Great Fire of 1837, 44, 243–44
Great Indian Peninsular Railway, 46
Great London Exhibition of 1851, 365
Great Trek, 60
Greenacre, William, 196
Green, Henry, 28
Grey Street in downtown Durban, 162
Grey & Victoria Streets, 205, 212
Greyville, 100
Greyville Sporting Association, 238
Griqua, 65
Growing: Seven Years in Ceylon (Woolf), 107

Guangzhou, 4
guerrilla force, the Deccan, 16
Guha, Ramachandra, 291
Guinea cloth, 12
Gujarat/Gujarati, 5, 9-10, 20, 26, 34, 92, 126, 143–45
 calico, 10
 cities, 207
 coast, 11, 44
 diaspora, 125
 Hindu family, 145
 hinterland, 32
 houses, 44
 interpreter, 214
 merchants to Africa, 164-65
 middle class, 48
 naus, 11
 society, 41
 traders, 214, 227
  prone to litigation, 170
Gujarati Muslims, 6, 145–47, 300
Gujarat Mitra newspaper, 42
Gujarat Vernacular Society, 27
Gulf of Aden, 4
Gulf steamer, 108
Guru Nanak, 96

Habib, Sheth Haji, 300, 302
Hadeda, 84
Hadji S. Seedick & Co., 130
Haggard, H. Rider, 66
Hakluyt, Richard, 59
Halbe, Lakshman Moreshwar Shastri, 27

Index

Hamidia Islamic Society, 300, 304, 313
Hamidia Mosque, 77, 362
Hanafi Quwwat-ul-Islam Mosque, 264
haoris, 12
Harbour and Fisheries Department, 194
Harbour Board, 160-61
harbour Rio de Natal, 160
hatmen, 19–30
Hawes, George, 140
Hawkins, David, 259
Haynes, Douglas, 41
Heaton, Messrs, 46
Hejaz, 4
Henry, Edward, 287-88, 297
Hertfordshire, 64
Het Volk, 289-90, 303
High Mountains of Portugal, The, 367
Highveld, 61, 66
Hind Swaraj, 320–25, 372
Hindu Lohanas, 143
Hindus/Hinduism, 4, 22, 29–30, 43, 46-47, 96
   as migrants, 169
   missionary, 224
   traditionalists, 30, 323
   vania caste, 12
   Young Men's Society, 224
Hindustani, 133
Hindu Tamilians, 182
Hiralal, Kalpana, 86
HMS *Minden,* 20-21

Hoare, Geo W., 368-69
Hoerikwaggo, 58
Hofmeyr, J.H., 265
Hollanders, 15
Home News, 33
Homer, 46
Hong Kong, 49, 51
Hoodamal, 168
Hoosen, Ajam Goolam, 144, 165
Hosan, Boomfoo, 130
Hout Bay Canning Company, 263
humanity, 316, 321
human stampede, 67

Ibrahim, Dawood Abdulla, 144
illegal
   immigrants, 193-94
   Indian immigrants, 346
   migrants, 346, 351-52
illiteracy, 285, 287, 308
Illustrated London News, 26
Immigrants Regulation Act of 1913, 324
Immigrants' Restriction Bill, 314-15
immigration, 158-59, 295
   laws, 227-28
   systems, 354
Immigration Act of 1902, 194, 253-54
Immigration Act of the Colony of the Cape of Good Hope, 95
immigration authorities, 217-18, 223, 228, 253, 261, 349, 351, 371

Immigration Restriction Act, 193, 269-70
Immigration Restriction Department, 194-95
Immigration Restriction (IR) Officer, 215
Imperial Authorities, 191, 302
Imperial Opium Department, 48
Inanda Tea Estate, 169
indentured Indians, 175, 301
indentured workers, 21-22, 38, 62, 80, 114–18, 120, 133, 174-75, 182, 193, 213, 227, 288
Indian
  children in South Africa, 325
  Christians, 192
  community, 191, 217, 219, 276, 298, 301-02, 304–07, 313, 344-45
  diamond fields, 65
  dyes, 12
  emigrants, 174
  fabrics, 125
  freedom movement, 323
  immigration, 324, 345–47, 355, 368
  labour, 368-69
  languages, 168, 194, 213-14, 220, 241, 261, 312
  migrant community, 201, 320, 324
  migrants, 361
  quarter, 199, 211–26
  rights, 202, 291
  in South Africa, 177-78, 301
  spiritualism, 190
  trader, 143, 170, 176, 184, 194, 307
  in Volksrust jail, 318-19
Indian Central Business District (CBD), 162, 196–207
Indian Council of Historical Research, 330
Indian Mutiny in 1857, 106
Indian Ocean, 3, 5, 7–12, 17, 58, 105, 107, 125, 345-46
  trade, 44, 125, 143
Indian Opinion, 79, 83, 200–03, 217, 220-21, 224, 251, 264-65, 291, 294, 305-06, 309-10, 312, 316, 317–19, 321, 345, 361-62
Indian Public, 334
indigo, 6, 10, 15, 165
Indonesia, 59
Indonesian islands, 105
industrial capitalism, 321-22
inequality, 87
insurance companies, 35
Intelligence Service in Ireland, 356
interpreters, 234–40
  in Indian languages, 213, 218–21
Irish Presbytarian Mission School, 28-29, 244
Irish Republican Army (IRA) unit, 356
Irons, William Jonah, 62

isiBubulungu, 160
Islam, 4, 143
Islamic community, 223
Islamick Hotel in Lourenço Marques, 350
Islamic world, 9
Islam Propagation Centre, 163
Islands of Cyprus, 70
Isle de France, 106, 111
ivory and gold, cloth exchanged for, 164

Jackson, Ashley, 107
Jaffer, Cassim, 348
jagat nakas, 17
Jagat Seths, 17
Jain, Oswal, 33
jama (credit), 13
Jamaica, 22
Jami Mosque, 162, 167, 169, 203–06, 216-17, 222–24, 268
Japan, 70
Jardine, Matheson & Co., 25
Jardine, William, 25
Jardins de la Campagnie, 131, 136
Java, 21
Javanese square-rigged ships, 11
Jeejeebhoy, Jamsetjee, 25-26, 33, 50
Jehangir, Cowasjee, 35, 45
Jhaveri, Abdullah Haji Adam, 165
Jhaveri, Rao Bahadur Naginchand, 40
Jina, Valeb, 222

jingoism, 69
Jivanji, Maneckji, 25
J.M.H. Gool & Co., 264
Johannesburg, 68, 71, 75, 77-78, 80, 82, 87-88, 92, 220, 282–84, 291, 310, 316, 318, 322, 337, 360
Indians, 179
John Dewar & Sons., 303
joint-stock companies, 35
Jones, C.B., 270
Jones Street, 66
Joosub, Hajee Cassum, 157
Joshi, Harishankar Ishwarlal, 312-13
Joshi, Ishwar, 317
Joshi, M.M., 214
Jumma Masjid, 145

kaala paani, 172
Kadir, Abdul, 221
kaffirs, 65
kafilas, 15
Kajee, Suliman, 314
Kalkadevi temple, 23
Kalla, Abdool Cader, 147–49
Kallenbach, Hermann, 78, 237, 283–84
Kamathipura, 47
Kanbis, 169
Karan Ghelo (Mehta), 27, 243
Kathiawar, 47, 126-27, 144, 165, 171-72, 305
Kathiawari Hindu women, 225

Kathor, 7
Kemp, Sam, 67
khalasi, 4–8, 37-38
Khamisa, Cassim, 222
Khan, Farouk, 100
Khan, Nawab Mir Muzaffar Hussein, 42
Khan, Rahim Karim, 201, 221, 240, 243
Khatris, 169
Khetwadi, 44
Kholvad, 3, 7, 39, 67
Killarney, Johannesburg, 88
Killavala, M.P., 13, 24, 40, 41, 47, 49, 89, 134, 212, 221, 242, 253, 270–73, 275, 310, 312, 333, 335, 339-40
Killie Campbell Africana Library, Essenwood, 85
Kimberley, 64, 79, 192, 213
Kinara Mosque, 3, 7-8, 37, 166-67
King Charles II, 20
King James, 14
King John II, 58
King Solomon's Mines (Haggard), 66
Klip River Magistrate, 239
Kolaba district, 262-63
kombi (shared taxi), 87
Konkani Muslim League, 349
Konkan-Ratnagiri coast, 197
Korana, 65
Kothari, Rita, 92
kraals, 62

Kruger, Paul, 68-69, 179, 281, 290
Kufa, 6
Kung, 11
Kutchi, 47
KwaZulu Natal, 204
Kyriakidis, S.H., 222

Lajpur, 7, 39
Lakhpati Hospital, 40
Lala, Ratanchand, 33
La Mercy, 84
Lamu, 158-59
Lancashire, 31, 33
Lanyon baths, 66
lascars, 112, 145
Latif, Abdool, 248
Law, Cheong, 142
Law Department to the Natal Authorities, 341
lawlessness, 17
Lazarus and Paul, 199
Lees, Cecil Harcourt, 288, 297, 356
Legislative Council, 61, 116, 132, 300, 302
Legislative Council of South Africa, 287
Lejo Lahaavo Lok (Godani), 126
Le Pouce, 112
Le Radical, 133
Les Petites Affiches, 133
Letters of M.H. Nazar, 240
Lettres des Courses, 106

Index

L'Express, 145
licence renewal, 217
Limpopo river, 125, 281
lineage, 90
Lisbon, 58, 164
literacy test, 193
Liverpool cotton market, 33, 36
local Hindustani, 213-14
London, 11, 25, 32, 46, 51, 62, 72-73, 107, 114, 232
London Accountants' Examination, 49
London Chamber of Commerce, 218, 312
London County Council, 282
London National Union of Teachers Examination, 336
Longland's Transvaal, 168
Lord Carnarvon, 71
Lord Curzon, 52
Lord Kimberley, 64
Lord Meath Empire Day Challenge Cup, 233
Lord Ripon, 185
Lord Selborne, governor of Transvaal, 335, 338, 355, 357
L'Orient, 11
Louis XV, 112
Lourenço Marques, 164–66, 350–52
Lowji-Wadias, 26
Lumsden, Dugald McTavish, 294
Lusikisiki, 99
Luthuli, Albert, 77

Lutyens, Edwin, 72

Macaulay, Thomas Babington, 23, 27, 51, 190
MacDonald, Andrew, 345–47, 350
Macedonia, 85
Mackinnon, William, 368
Macmillan, Allister, 141
Madagascar, 105, 111, 126, 142, 150, 255-56, 258-59, 262, 373
Madras, 16, 21, 26, 167, 350, 374
Madressa Anjuman Islamia, 67
Maglioni, Mlle Theresa, 374
Maharaj, Suchit, 221-22, 243, 247
Maharashtra, 26
Maharashtra State Archives, 366, 372
Mahatma Gandhi Institute, Moka, 118, 127
Mahe, 108
Mahebourg, 147
Mahomed, Adam H.G., 311
Mahomed, Dawad, 221, 311, 314, 317
Mahomed, Memon Hajee, 167
Mahomed, Messers Dawad, 310
Mahomed, Tayob Haji Khan, 170
Mahua, 126
Main Reef of Johannesburg, 281
Maitland, Edward, 179
Majuba Hill, 313, 318
majurs, 15
Makda, Suliman, 350
Malabar, 4, 11, 20, 45

paraus, 11
teak, 45
Malacca, 21
Malay/Malaya, 51-52, 178
  archipelago, 11, 70
  mosques and houses, 264
  slaves, 59, 265
Maldives, 7
Malindi, 9
Manav Dharma Sabha, 28
Manchester, 232
Mandela, Nelson, 77
Mandvi, 44, 373
Manekji, Pestonji, 143
Mangan, M.K., 222
Manharram, 224
Manor, Cato, 197
Mansfield, William, 47
Marathas, 17, 47
Marat, Jean-Paul, 132
Mari Hakikat (Narmad), 243-44
Maritime Museum, Greenwich, 21
Markovits, Claude, 92, 96
Marseilles, 52
Martel, Yann, 367
Mascarene Islands, 109
Mascarenhas, Dom Pedro, 109
Masonic Temple, 78
Massawa, 5
Matabele, 65
matriculate examination, 49
Mauritius, 21-22, 38-39, 42-43, 62, 65-66, 100-01, 105–23, 125–31, 133–35, 137, 140–46, 157, 159-60, 165–67, 238, 260, 263–65, 286, 300, 340, 347, 349, 373
  Britain's naval machinery, 106-07
  Chinese population, 142
  Dutch in, 105
  Europe-bound traffic from India, 107
  French in, 106
  indentured workers, 114–17
  Indian migrants, 111–13
  Mayarams, 126-27
  mercantile community, 143
  migrants, 118
  plantation owners, 113-14
  traders, Gujarat, 143-44
Mauritius Commercial Bank, Ebene, 127
Mauritius Hydroelectric Company, 148
Mauritius Institute of Education, 147
Mauritius Telecom, 131
Mayet, Rafique, 204, 207
M.C. Camroodeen & Co., 168, 285
McDougall, Lance-Sergeant, 351-52
Mecca, 11
Medh, S.B., 312, 314, 317–19
medieval port town, 12
Mediterranean Sea, 8

Index

Mehta, Nandshankar Tuljashankar, 27, 243-44
Melbourne, 51
Memons, 143-44, 146, 165–67, 216, 223, 225
merchants, 10–18, 25, 33, 143, 176, 181
Merriman, J.X., 265
Messrs Killick Nixon & Co., 373
metropolitan capital of Lisbon, 164-65
Mexican dollar, 12
Mia, Essop Ismail, 315
migrants
   communities, South Africa, 79
   community, 186-87, 190, 195, 221
   workers, 39
Milner, Alfred, 73, 281-82
Milner's Kindergarten, 282
mines
   dumps, 68
   gold, 68-69, 286, 288
   shaft, 68
   workers, 69, 288
mining, 64
mission-educated men and interpreters, 358
Miyakhan, Adamji, 176
M.K. Gandhi Library, 189
mobility, 373
modern banks, 32-33
modis (stewards), 13
Mogadishu, 7

Moghuls, 10, 13-14, 16, 20, 38
Moghul style durbars, 41
Mogul Steamship Co., 157
Mohamad, Hafiz, 130
Mohammedan, 178
Mohanlal, 8-9, 13, 17, 20, 22, 41–43, 47–53, 77, 80, 88–91, 95–97, 101, 107-08, 117-18, 129-30, 134, 142, 157–62, 204-05, 212, 214-15, 218–22, 225–27, 229-30, 234–40, 241, 244, 246–48, 251–53, 258-59, 261–65, 267-68, 270–74, 276, 306, 312–14, 317–19, 324-25, 330–33, 335
   Archibald Findlay as his solicitor, 215
   Bombay to Durban, 52-53
   bribe an officer in French, 342
   in Cape Town, 260–67
   case, 318
   in Durban, 204-05, 268
   employment with Archibald Findlay, 235
   family, 47–52
   language skills, 259
   lodgings on Queen Street, 234
   official lists, 80–83
   Satyagrahis, 361
   travel document, 48-49
   on West Street, 229-30, 233
Moka, 118, 127, 148
Moluccas, 21
Mombasa, 52, 159, 350

moneylender, 18, 34
monopolistic trading, 11
monumental architecture, 231
monumental face-off, 344
Moonsamy, K., 167
Moosa, Mahomed, 340-41
moral and intellectual education, 225
Morris, Jan, 52, 72
Moses Mabhida Stadium, 84
Mosquito and African Sketch, The, 232-33, 307
Mossel Bay, 58
Mount Edgecombe, 84
Mozambique, 111, 125, 350-51
Mpumalanga, 125
Muglisara, 40
Muhammad, Mulla, 19
Mulji, Karsandas, 27, 29-30, 43
Müller, Max, 179, 186
Mumbai, 31, 120
Murat, M., 134
Murray's Guide, 47
Muscat, 11, 45, 112, 143
Museum Africa, Newtown, 78
Muslim
  fasting for Ramzan, 319
  sect, 37
Mzimkulu river, 61

naam (debit), 13
Naidoo, Thambi, 79, 300
Naidu, Baboo, 166
Nanavat, 13, 17, 41

Nanji, Dr, 221
Naoroji, Dadabhai, 185-86
Napoleon, 106, 157
Napoleonic wars, 16, 106
Narmad, 22–24, 28–30, 41, 44, 243-44, 322-23
Narn, Nana, 353
Nasarwanji, 219
Natal, 22, 39, 42-43, 61-62, 64, 67, 85, 134, 157–60, 166, 168–70, 174, 180-81, 193, 213
  anti-immigration law, 253, 292
  -based Indians, 367
Natal Advertiser, 182, 191
Natal Almanacs of 1905-07, 222
Natal Civil Service 176, 214
Natal Courts, 312, 335
Natal Direct Line, 169, 311
Natal Government Gazette, 241-42
Natal Government Railway, 174
Natal Government Savings Bank, 48, 258
Natal Immigration Restriction Department, 194
Natal Immigration Restriction Officer, 340-41
Natal Indian Congress, 184, 190, 199–202, 216, 285, 311, 314, 317
Natal Indian Congress Hall, 192, 219-20
Natal Indian Education Association, 190

Natal Indian Football Association, 238
Natal Legislative Assembly, 186-87
Natal Mercury, 62, 85
Natal Porbandar Trust, 216
Natal Provincial Gazette, 227
Natal Supreme Court, 97, 183, 212
Natal Witness, 175, 232-33, 307
Nathji, Trawadi Arjunji, 17
National Archives and Records Service, 82
National Archives Department of Mauritius, 128
National Archives in Pretoria, 329–41, 369
National Civil Office, Emmanuel Anquetil Building, 135
National Library, Edith Cavell Street, 131, 135
National Library of South Africa, 303
Native Share and Stock Brokers Association, 33
Natural History Museum, 365
Natural Science Museum, 95
Naudeer, 350-51
Navayats, 6, 9
Navsari, 10, 25, 39, 217
Nazar, Mansukhlal, 201
Nazar, M.H., 201-02, 358-59
Ndwedwe, 99
Nehru, Jawaharlal, 120
Nehru, Motilal, 374

Nelson, 157
neo-baroque town hall, 231
new education system, India, 23
New Indian Press of Calcutta, 294
New Main Street, 66
New Zealand, 51, 59, 180
Nizari Ismaili community, 374
Nokwe, Duma, 77
non-domiciled persons, 193
non-indentured migrants, 52, 128
non-labour immigrants, 52
non-violent
   protest, 73
   resistance, 344
Norodien, Ebrahim, 263, 349
North G. & Sons, 222
Notre Dame, Cap Malheureux, 151

Odisha, 21
Office of the Collector of Customs, 48
Ohlssons Breweries, 262
Old Customs House in Ballard Pier, 47-48
Old Fort Prison, 77
Ollier, Rémy, 133
Olpad, 25
opium, 24-25, 33, 35, 45, 48
   trade, 24-25, 35
opportunism, 12
Orange Free State, 61, 71, 73, 178-79, 181
Orange river, 61, 64

Orange River Colony, 281-82, 289-90
orthodoxy, 29
Osman, Dada, 248
Ota Bapa, 171
Ottoman Caliphate, 223
Ottomans, 11
Ottoman Turks, 8
Overland Mail, 33
Owl, The, 257
Oxford, 69, 255-56, 282

palkhi, 16
Palmer, Mabel, 324
Pamplemousses, 126
Pan Africanist Congress, 77
pandemonium, 15
Paper Currency Act, 32
Parakhs, 14, 17
parekhs (examiners of coins), 13
Paris, 92, 125, 374
Paris Exposition of 1878, 45
parish graveyard, 20
Parker, Joseph, 179
Parmanandas, 40, 47
Parsi carpenters, 20
Parsis, 26, 35, 40, 42, 46, 50, 79, 112, 152, 167, 175, 352, 359
Paruk, E.M., 169
passenger Indians, 39, 167, 169, 170, 219, 262
Patel, Cowasjee Sorabjee, 27
Paul, Ellen Elizabeth, 239
Paul Et Virginie (de Saint-Pierre), 149-50

Paul, Henry Louis, 176, 183, 185, 192, 238–40, 335
Pax Britannica (Morris), 52, 72
Payne, Leonard, 233
Peace Preservation Ordinance, 284-85
permit agent, 339, 357-58
Persia, 17, 26
Persian Gulf, 11
Persian Gulf to Kilwa, 164
Persians, 15, 175
Peters, A.H., 240
Phenix, R.W., 222
philanthropic work, 45
philanthropist, 35, 40, 46, 59
Phoenix, 322
Phoenix Settlement, 78
Pietermaritzburg, 61, 82-83, 86–88, 176–78, 180-81, 241, 243, 273-74, 347, 352-53
  archives, 215, 218, 222, 236, 244, 251, 268
  colonial secretary in, 191-92, 273
  magistrate, 240
Pietermaritzburg Archives Repository, 211
Pillay, C.M., 357
Pillay, M. Doorasamy, 213
Pillay, Sammy, 66
Pincott, Frederic, 178
Pinetown, 168, 202
pinprick legislation, 367
Place d'Armes, 111
plague scare, 284

Plaines Wilhems, 116
Point de Galle, 25
Polak, Henry, 283-84, 291
Polak, Millie, 237, 291
political instability, Indian Ocean region, 17
political manoeuvring, 322
political shifts, 164
Pondicherry, 112
Poohoomull Brothers, 96, 263
Porbandar, 44, 47, 165-66, 170-71, 218, 223
Porrukhan, Moonshi, 130
Port Elizabeth, 92, 252-53, 367
Portland, 49
Port Louis, 107, 111–13, 115, 127-28, 134, 137, 140–47, 149, 161, 212, 222
Port Natal, 85, 196
Portuguese, 8–11, 19-20, 44, 58, 71
    authorities, 351
    navigators, 160
    sailors, 105
    Swaziland border, 352
Portuguese East Africa, 217
Portuguese Estado da Índia, 164-65
Portuguese Mozambique, 350
post and telegraph services, 32
post-colonialism, 375
post-war boom, 252, 256, 263
post-war Transvaal, 331
Potter, Nellie, 265-66
poverty, 126-27

Presidency Chartered Bank of Bombay, 35
Prester John, 9
Pretoria, 72, 82-83, 176–79, 282, 305-06, 314, 317-18, 347, 354, 359–62
Pretoria Courts, 214
pre-war pronouncements, 200
Price-Hughes, C. E., 261
primary schools, western India, 26
Prince Maurice of Nassau, 106
Prince of Wales Museum, 365, 374-75
Princess Catherine of Braganza, 20
Pringle, Thomas, 60
Proclamation of 1858, 38
Prodigal Son, The, 233
prohibited immigrants, 97, 159, 360
Protector of Immigrants Office, 238-39
Protector of Indian Immigrants, 80, 174
public burning of identification documents, Indians, 77
putchuk, 15
Pydhoni, 44

Qaisar-i-Hind, 38
quarantine ships, 159
Quatre Bornes, 120, 124, 128, 148
Queen Elizabeth II, 89
Queen Street, 144, 167, 205, 215, 222, 230, 234, 236, 274

Queen Victoria, 31, 38, 69, 114, 133, 191
quicksilver, 12
Quinn, Leung, 306, 315

Rachel, Olga, 225
racial/racism, 73-74
    barriers, 220
    discrimination, 73, 276, 324, 343
    hierarchy, 238, 257
    humiliation, 311
    injustice, 276-77, 343
radicalism, 323
Rajkot, 172-73
Rajyarang (Narmad), 323
Raleigh, Walter, 59
Ramcharitamanas, 117
Ramgoolam, Seewoosagur, 114
Ramlallah, Sadhna, 142
Rampart Row, 33
Rand Club Johannesburg, 369
Rand Daily Mail, 282-83
Rander, 6, 9
Randeria, Shapurji Jivanji, 218-19, 225-26, 241, 244-45, 247, 276, 310–12, 314, 317, 319
Rand Plague Committee, 356
Ratna Prabha (Halbe), 27
Razai, 19
Readymoney family, 26, 35
Reddy, Enuga, 77, 83, 101
Red Sea, 6, 11, 14
Reduit, 148

Registration Act, 311
religious
    dominance, 8
    fanaticism, 29
Renaissance, 72, 231, 262
Republic of Mauritius, 105
Republic of Natalia, 61
Resident Indians, 228
resist degradation, 190, 293
Réunion Island, 109, 148, 373
Reynolds Bros., 175
Rhodes, Cecil, 64–74, 190, 282, 290, 344
right qualifications, 159
Ritchie Stuart and Co., 34
Ritch, L.W., 283-84
Robinson, George, 187
Robinson, John, 62, 192
Rodrigues, 109, 130
Roeland Street, 93
Roe, Thomas, 14
Roman Catholic, 176, 199
Rothschilds, 66
Royal Divorce, A, 233
Royal Institute of Science, 365, 374
Royal Navy, 20
Roychand, Premchand, 33–36, 45, 50
Royeppen, Joseph, 220
Rudolph, G.M., 191
Rue Deschartes, 125, 127
Rue des Limites, 144
'Rule Britannia,' 262

Ruparam, Mahipatram, 29
Ruskin, John, 69, 202, 283
Russia, 39
Russo-Japanese War, 52
Rustomjee, Parsi, 42, 176, 190, 199, 248, 308, 310-11 314, 317, 320-21
Ryneveld, Van, 349

Sabarmati Ashram in Ahmedabad, 370
Safavids, 11
Saheb, Soofie, 196-97
Saint Paul, 85
Salisbury Island, 197
Salt River Railway Station, 349
sandbanks, 22
Sandhurst Road, 47-48
Sandton, 88
Sangalpur, 145
Sankalias, 13-14, 17-18
sanyasis, 22
Sassoon, David, 24
Satyagraha campaign, 73, 305, 315, 320-21, 330, 343-44
Satyagraha in South Africa (Gandhi), 75, 92, 293
Satyaprakash, 29
Satya Sai Baba, 88, 197
Saurty, V., 138-39
savannah, 60, 281
School Board Bill, 266
School Book Society, 26
School of Mauritian and Area Studies, 118

Schopenhauer, 186-87
Schreiner, Olive, 265
Scott, Gilbert, 47
Scottish emigrants, 62
Sea Point Congregational Church, 255-56
second-class certificate, 247-48, 251
self-confidence, 238
self-identification, 18
self-punishment, 305
self-realization, 78
self-reliance, 202
semi-bondage, 21
Sen, Kin, 142
Seoul, 105
Seven Years' War, 1756, 16
Seychelles, 51-52, 109, 373-74
Shah, Aga Jhangi, 374
Shah, Nanalal, 300, 302
Shahpore, 42
Shah, Sultan Muhammed, 374
Shaka, king of the Amazulu, 61
Shakespeare, 46, 375
Shanghai, 49
Shankaranand, Swami, 224
Shankarbhai, Dahyabhai, 351
Sharma, Murli Dhar, 372
Sharpeville Massacre, 77
Shelat, Umashankar, 218-19, 221-22, 226, 241, 243–47, 276, 312–14, 317–19
short-term commercial visitors, 228
Siberia, 67

Index

Sindhis, 92, 96
Sindworkies, 92, 96
Singh, Bareyam, 262-63
Sir Seewoosagur Ramgoolam International Airport, 109
slavery/slaves, 12, 21, 27, 59-60, 62, 107, 111–14, 132, 148, 179, 198, 262, 264
smallpox epidemic, 132
Smith, Adam, 9
Smith, Harry, 194, 215
Smuts, Jan, 289, 290, 344
Sobukwe, Robert, 77
social mingling, 238
social reform, 29
Sofala, 164
Solicitors, Cowley, 261
Somnath, 165
Soni, Mayaram, 126-27
Sonis, 169
Sorabji, Shapurji, 308
South Africa, 22, 38-39, 42-43, 73-74, 77–80, 85, 87, 90-91, 93, 97, 100-01, 133-34, 158, 160, 354
    experiences in, 191
South African Civil Service, 288
South African Indian community, 100
South African Republic, 38
South America, 70
South China, 4
Southeast Asia, 11, 96, 262
southern Africa, 66

southern hemisphere, 161, 204
Spanish rials, 12
spice trade, 11
Springfield, 221
Sri Lankan praus, 11
SS *Afghan*, 157–60, 195
SS *Courland*, 169-70, 188
SS *Cowrie Castle*, 251, 253, 257-58, 260
SS *Dwarka*, 52
SS *General*, 359
SS *Kanzler*, 169-70
SS *Kildonan Castle*, 320-21
SS *Kirkland*, 147
SS *Naderi*, 169-70, 188
SS *Norman*, 268
SS *Nowshera*, 252, 367-68
SS *Prorito*, 142
SS *Reichstag*, 67, 169-70
SS *Secunder*, 130-31
SS *Taifu*, 142
SS *Truro*, 62, 196-97, 213
St. Albans, 62
Stanley, Henry M., 281
State of the Nation Address, 93–95
steamships, 51, 107
Stein & Co., 222
Stephen, Chelivum, 239
Stevenson, Archibald Frank, 303
St. Jean Road, 124
St. Pancras station, London, 46
Story of the Tea Leaf, The, 294
submarine cables, 51
Subramanian, Lakshmi, 17

Sub-Tropical Rambles in the Land of the Aphanapteryx, 151
sudhar (reform), 28
Suez Canal, 45, 66, 107
Sufi, 7, 144
Suily, Fok, 142
Sultan of Oman, 164
Sunni Bohras, 11, 37, 43, 144, 167
superstition, 27
Supreme Court of Natal, 212
Surat, 3, 9–11, 13, 20–22, 24–26, 28, 32-33, 37–44, 48, 144, 147, 165, 265
    elites, 41
    Maratha attacks, 16-17
    Parsi population, 42
    in the seventeenth century, 14–16
Surat Anjume Islam, 367
Surat Fort, 17–19
Surat High School, 308
Surat Hindu Association, 215
'Suratwala,' 53
Suri, Haribhadra, 179
Suvali, 10, 13, 14
Sydenham, 181

Table Mountain, 57–63, 72, 94, 254, 260
Taj Mahal Palace, 50
Tamil Nadu, 21
Tanzania, 164
Tapidas, 14
Tapi river, 3, 6, 8-9, 14, 17, 19, 22, 37, 39, 67, 166, 359
Tata, Jamsetji Nusserwanji, 50, 291
'tavern of the seas,' 262
teak-rich forests, 20
technological determinism, 321-22
Tejpal, Goculdas, 33
telegraphs, 51
Temple, Richard, 45
temporary authorisation, 330, 334–37
temporary permits, 228, 295
textile manufacturing regions, 16
Thane, 32
Theosophical Society, 291, 336-37
Thessalonica, 85
Third Battalion of the Royal Fusiliers, 140
Thoreau, Henry David, 283
Tichman, Paul, 199-200
Tigris, 6
Times of India, 30, 43, 186, 369
Timol, 167
Tindall, Gillian, 45
Tokyo, 49, 283
Tolstoy Farm, 78, 322
Tolstoy, Leo, 179, 283
tombs, 16
Tongaat, 84
Tongaat Sugar Company, 188
traders, 169
    emerging community of, 167
    Indian, 170, 176, 184, 194, 307-08

trading, 165
  houses, 11
  licences, 314–16
transit passes, 228, 295
Transvaal, 38-39, 61, 66–68, 71, 79, 125, 179–81, 214, 217, 221, 281–86, 288–90, 330, 340, 354
Transvaal Agricultural Journal, 294
Transvaal Civil Service, 294, 356
Transvaal Indians, 292, 354
Transvaal Leader, 316
Transvaal's Law 3 of 1885, 178
Travolta, John, 136
Treaty of Vereeniging, 71
Trinidad, 22
Trou Fanfaron, Port Louis, 115
Troyeville in East Johannesburg, 291
Tugela river, 61
Turawa, Ismail Ibrahim, 38, 144
Turawa Mosque, 42
'Turbans and Top Hats: Indian Interpreters in the Colony of Natal, 1880-1910,' 80, 239
Turkish Empire, 178
Turks, 15
Turner Morrison & Co. Ltd., 169-70

Udayshankar, 224
Umarkhadi, 44
Umhlanga Rocks, 231
Umtata, 67

Umzinto Plantation and Trading Company, 174-75
UNESCO World Heritage site, 115
Union Buildings, South Africa, 71-72
Union Castle Mail Steamship Company, 255-56, 262-63
Union of South Africa, 73, 217, 320
United Provinces, 21
United Sports Association, 238
United States of America, 52, 70
United Tobacco Company, 349
United Transvaal Directory, 168
United XI Cricket Club, 238
University of Bombay, 45, 49
University of KwaZulu-Natal, 86
University of London, 114
University of Mauritius, 125
University of Witwatersrand, 80-81, 345
unlawful immigration, 307
Unto This Last, 202
Upanishads, 186-87
Urbs Prima Indis, 44–53. *see also* Bombay

Vaal river, 61, 64
Vachcha, Dinsha E., 36
Vaghela, Karan, 243
Vahed, Goolam, 86
Vaishnava ethos, 172
Valabh, Pushottam, 229

Valley of Euphrates, 70
Van der Spuy, Patricia, 265
vanias, 6, 12-13, 29, 41, 49, 53, 125, 164
   poorer, 13-14
   Surat, 17-18
Vanker, 167
Van Reenen, 194-95
Variawa, Hormasjee Cawasji, 352
Vasistha, Yoga, 179
Vawda, 167
Vedas, 23, 28
Venetians, 8
Vereenigde Oost-Indische Compagnie, 11
Verulam, 62, 166, 184
Victoria & Albert Museum, 365
Victoria Embankment, 166, 231
Victory House, Harrison Street, 78
Vidyasagar, Ishwar Chandra, 291
Vincot, Sam, 66
Vinden, David, 239
Vishwanaden, Govinden, 118-19
Volksrust, 194-95, 313-14, 319, 351-52
Vora, Virji, 12
Vrededorp, 79

Wadia, Jamsetjee Bomanjee, 21
Wadia, Lowji Nasserwanjee, 20
Wagheida, 265
Walker, Eric, 265
Walsh, Richard, 348
waning of trade, 17
Waradea, 'Rosie,' 266-67

warehouses, 45, 115, 128–30, 141-42, 144-45, 167
Warwick Triangle area, 198
Water Police, 194-95
Waterval Boven, 79
Watly, Amod, 367-68
Watson's Hotel, 50
Wealth of Nations, The (Smith), 9
Wellington, 51
Wesleyan Methodist, 62, 199
West Africa, 12, 262
west coast, India, 22
Western Cape, 60
Western Cape Provincial Archives and Records Service, 93, 252
western Europe, 11
western India, 5, 8, 11, 16, 26, 28, 37, 48, 95, 127, 313, 350
Westernized Indians, 274
Western literary forms, 323
Western ports, 12
West Indian islands, 22
West Indies, 22
West Street, 168, 216, 223, 228–30, 233
   cemetery, 198-99
Westville, 86
white protestors, 188
white unemployment, 257, 263
white wholesalers, 167
wholesale bazaars, 45
widow remarriage, 27, 29
Wilhelmstrasse, 70
Witwatersrand, 66-67, 264, 284, 287,

Women's Enfranchisement League, 265
Woolf, Leonard, 107
working-class Tamilian Hindus, 192

Xhosa tribe, 60

Zainunnissa, 'Cissie,' 266-67
Zanzibar, 52, 126, 159, 164-65, 312, 369, 373
Zanzibaris, 225
Z6A Series, 128
Zheng He, 7
Zimbabwe plateau, 125
Zoroastrians, 26
Zuid-Afrikaansche Republiek, 61
Zulu, 99, 106, 168-69, 196, 202-03, 312
Zululand, 61, 85
Zulus, 160, 203, 219, 225, 312, 322
Zuma, Jacob, 94-95

About the Author

AMRITA SHAH is a former editor of *Elle* and *Debonair*, an ex-contributing editor with the *Indian Express*, and has worked for the US-based Time-Life News Service. She has been a fellow of the Centre for Contemporary Studies at the Indian Institute of Science, the Institute for Public Knowledge at New York University, the Johannesburg Institute for Advanced Study and the Research Institute Advanced De Nantes. She is the author of the award-winning *Ahmedabad: A City in the World* (2015), *Vikram Sarabhai: A Life* (2007) and *Telly-Guillotined: How Television Changed India* (2019). She is based in Mumbai.

HarperCollins *Publishers* India

At HarperCollins India, we believe in telling the best stories and finding the widest readership for our books in every format possible. We started publishing in 1992; a great deal has changed since then, but what has remained constant is the passion with which our authors write their books, the love with which readers receive them, and the sheer joy and excitement that we as publishers feel in being a part of the publishing process.

Over the years, we've had the pleasure of publishing some of the finest writing from the subcontinent and around the world, including several award-winning titles and some of the biggest bestsellers in India's publishing history. But nothing has meant more to us than the fact that millions of people have read the books we published, and that somewhere, a book of ours might have made a difference.

As we look to the future, we go back to that one word— a word which has been a driving force for us all these years.

Read.

    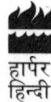